LA RESTAURANTS

Editor
Alain Gayot

Managing Editor
Sharon Boorstin

Contributing Editors
Erika Beck, T. Hart Monroe Brogna, Louis Charles, Margaret Clark, Roger J. Grody, Joan Gamberg, Max Jacobson, Cheryl Janecky, Catherine Jordan, Bobbie Katz, Steve Knight, Leslee Komaiko, Larry Lipson, Yvonne Mason, Neal Matthews, David Nelson, Andrea Rademan, Dennis Schaefer, Sherrie Strausfogel, William Tomicki

Directed By
André Gayot

GAULT MILLAU

Paris ▪ Los Angeles ▪ New York
London ▪ Munich ▪ San Francisco

GAYOT PUBLICATIONS

The Best of Beverly Hills
The Best of Chicago
The Best of Florida
The Best of France
The Best of Germany
The Best of Hawaii
The Best of Hong Kong
The Best of Italy
The Best of London
The Best of Los Angeles
The Best of New England
The Best of New Orleans
The Best of New York
The Best of Paris
Paris, Ile-de-France & The Loire Valley
Paris & Provence
The Best of San Francisco
The Best of Thailand
The Best of Toronto
The Best of Washington, D.C.
The Best Wineries of North America

LA Restaurants, NYC Restaurants, SF Restaurants
The Food Paper, Tastes Newsletter

http://www.gayot.com

Published by Gault Millau, Inc.
5900 Wilshire Blvd.
Los Angeles, CA 90036

Please address all comments regarding *LA Restaurants* to:
GaultMillau, Inc.
P.O. Box 361144
Los Angeles, CA 90036
E-mail: gayots@aol.com

Advertising Sales:
Debbie Eskew
5900 Wilshire Blvd.
Los Angeles, CA 90036
323-965-4841 Fax 323-936-2883

Production: Walter Mladina
Page Layout and Design: Mad Macs Communications
Illustrations: Jerry Mahoney

ISSN 1098-0296

Printed in the United States of America

Contents

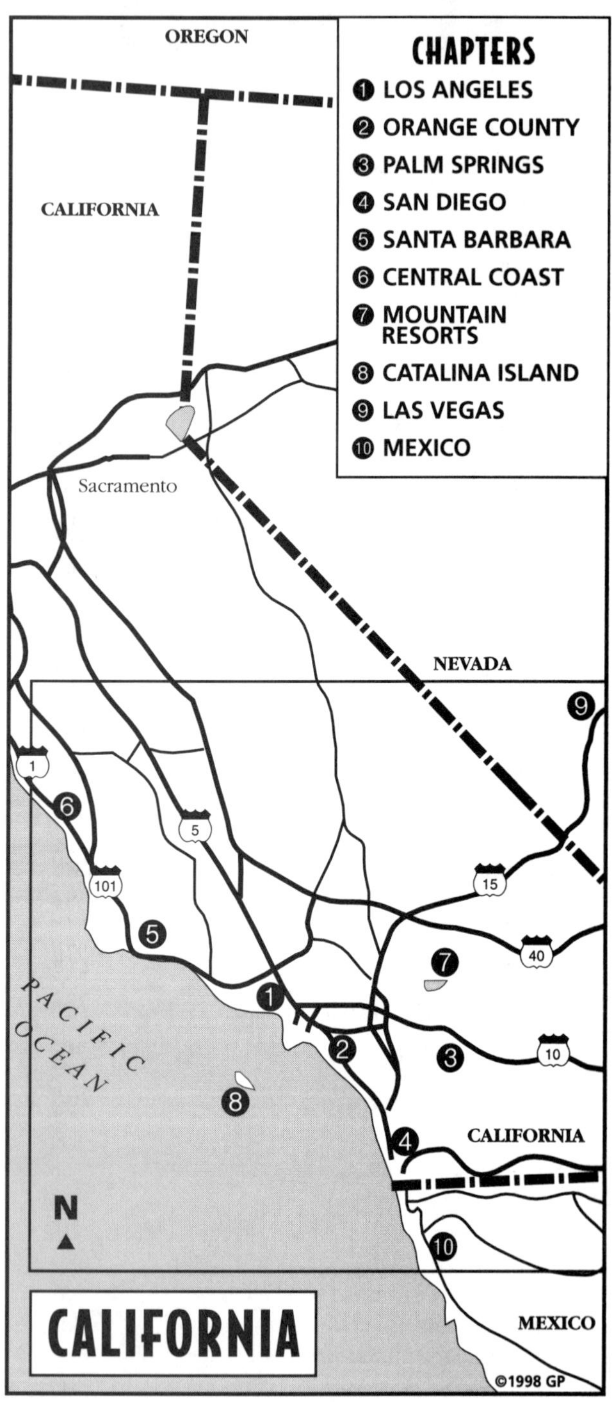
OREGON
CHAPTERS
1 LOS ANGELES
2 ORANGE COUNTY
3 PALM SPRINGS
4 SAN DIEGO
5 SANTA BARBARA
6 CENTRAL COAST
7 MOUNTAIN RESORTS
8 CATALINA ISLAND
9 LAS VEGAS
10 MEXICO
CALIFORNIA
Sacramento
NEVADA
1
5
101
15
40
10
PACIFIC OCEAN
CALIFORNIA
N
MEXICO
CALIFORNIA
©1998 GP

GLOBAL CUISINE 2000

At the end of the nineties, as we hurtle towards the millenium, we're happy to report that the Southern California dining scene is alive and well! After somewhat of a slump in the early part of the decade, restaurants, cafés—and even ethnic hole-in-the-walls—are opening wherever we look. Residents and tourists alike are discovering—or rediscovering—the joys of eating out. Why do we love it so? Dining in restaurants not only means time-out from cooking, but it allows us to have social interaction, to people-watch (humans are social animals, after all), to experience the myriad cuisines and cooking styles that are out there. And in Southern California, there are seemingly zillions. That's why this book is so useful. We'll guide you to the best eateries in every category. Then, with our Menu Savvy section in the Index, we'll help you take the mystery out of ordering. If you want news of restaurant openings after our publishing date, consult our website: **http://www.gayot.com**. And our companion guidebook, **The Best of Los Angeles & Southern California**, will fill you in on the hotels, attractions, sights, arts & culture of the Southland.

The unparalled diversity of Southern California's population means that right here in our midst, we can find restaurants serving cuisines such as Hunan, Cantonese, Oaxacan, El Salvadoran, Uzbekstan, Thai, Vietnamese, Peruvian, Ethiopian, Indian and Korean, not to mention French, Italian, Spanish and Middle Eastern. In additon, today, we're seeing the birth of a new cuisine in the Southland. Chefs are inventing dishes and labeling them "New American," "Fusion," "Pan-Asian," "Eclectic," "Contemporary," "International" or "Pacific Rim." Perhaps we should group them all together under the label "Global Cuisine," for the dishes all reflect a combination of the techniques, flavors and textures found in several ethnic cuisines at once. Whatever we call what our talented restaurant chefs are producing in their kitchens, we lift our glasses to them—their creativity and dedication is what keeps dining out exciting!

André Gayot

LA RESTAURANTS

RIGHTS

Although the publishers have made every effort to ensure that the information was correct at the time of going to the press, the publishers do not assume and hereby disclaim any liability to any party for any loss or damage caused by errors, omissions, or any potential travel disruption due to labor or financial difficulty, whether such errors or omissions result from negligence, accident, or any other cause.

SPECIAL SALES

Gayot Publications are available at discounts for bulk purchases, direct sales or premiums.

- Makes a great gift that will put your name in front of important clients over and over again—and at a small cost.
- Links your firm with internationally respected publications.
- Orders over 1,000 can be customized with your logo on the cover at no extra charge.

Call our toll-free number for information and orders:

1 (800) 532-3781

OR WRITE US:
Gayot Publications
5900 Wilshire Blvd.
Los Angeles, CA 90036

E-mail: Gayots@aol.com

DISCLAIMER

Readers are advised that prices and conditions change over the course of time. The restaurants, shops and other businesses reviewed in this book have been reviewed over a period of time, and the reviews reflect the personal experiences and opinions of the reviewers. The reviewers and publishers cannot be held responsible for the experiences of the reader related to the establishments reviewed. Readers are invited to write the publisher with ideas, comments and suggestions for future editions.

OUR RESTAURANT RATING SYSTEM

Clearly, a good many of our restaurants are well worth your hard-earned dollars, and our team of professional restaurant critics has canvassed Southern California to steer you right. Some words of advice: when you find a restaurant whose cooking, atmosphere and price range suit you, patronize it regularly instead of continually dashing off to the latest spot where Leonardo di Caprio was reputedly seen. Being a "regular" at a restaurant—so that you know at least some of the staff and they know you—is the best way to get a good table, good service and extra effort from the chef. Besides, supporting a restaurant you like is one way to help ensure that it'll still be there the next time you call for a reservation. And be as adventurous as the city and its chefs—for if it's true that we are what we eat, opt for being exciting, progressive and exotic.

Restaurant Categories

For each chapter—organized by geographic area—there are three restaurant sections:

DINING

Fine-dining palaces, trendy trattorias, steakhouses, French bistros and restaurants serving every imaginable ethnic cuisine. We have rated each of them (see rating system below) and pointed out details about the decor, look and ambience. They've also recommended some of their favorite dishes.

AND ALSO...

Restaurants that we have not rated, but we want you to know about anyway. Some of these places are new; many have been around so long, they're too often overlooked.

QUICK BITES

Spots where you can stop for an informal meal, and/or get a meal for a bargain. Here we categorize the burger joints, diners, trendy cafés, noodle shops, happening bars, pizza parlors and ethnic eateries galore—from taco stands to terrific Cuban, Russian, Yucatecan and even Mongolian dives—where you can eat for $15 per person and under. There are literally thousands of such places in Southern California, so we've included only the best. Forgive us if we've left out your favorite—for now, at least, your secret is safe!

Using Our Rating System

What decides the rating of a restaurant? What is on the plate is by far the most important factor. The quality of produce is among the most telling signs of a restaurant's culinary status. It requires a great deal of commitment and money to stock the finest grades and cuts of meat and the finest quality of fish. There is tuna, for example, and there's *tuna*. Ask any sushi chef. One extra-virgin olive oil is not the same, by far, as the next. Ditto for chocolates, pastas, spices and one thousand other ingredients. Quality restaurants also attune themselves to seasonal produce, whether it be local berries or truffles from Italy.

Freshness is all-important, too, and a telling indication of quality. This means not only using fresh rather than frozen fish, for example, but also preparing everything from scratch at the last possible moment, from appetizers through desserts.

What else do we look for? Details are telling: if all the sauces are the same, you know that the kitchen is taking shortcuts. The bread on the table is always a tip-off; similarly, the house wine can speak volumes about the culinary attitude and level of an establishment. Wine is food, and wine lists and offerings can be revealing. A list doesn't have to be long or expensive to show a commitment to quality.

Finally, among the very finest restaurants, creativity and innovation are often determining factors. These qualities, however, are relatively unimportant for simply good restaurants, where the quality and consistency of what appears on the plates is the central factor. A restaurant that serves grilled chicken well is to be admired more than a restaurant that attempts some failed marriage of chicken and exotic produce, or some complicated chicken preparation that requires a larger and more talented kitchen brigade than is on hand. Don't be taken in by attempted fireworks that are really feeble sideshows.

Our rating system works as follows: restaurants are ranked in the same manner that French students are graded, on a scale of one to twenty.

The rankings reflect only our opinion of the food. The decor, service, ambience and wine list are commented upon within each review.

Restaurants that are ranked 13/20 and above are distinguished with toques (chef's hats) according to the table below.

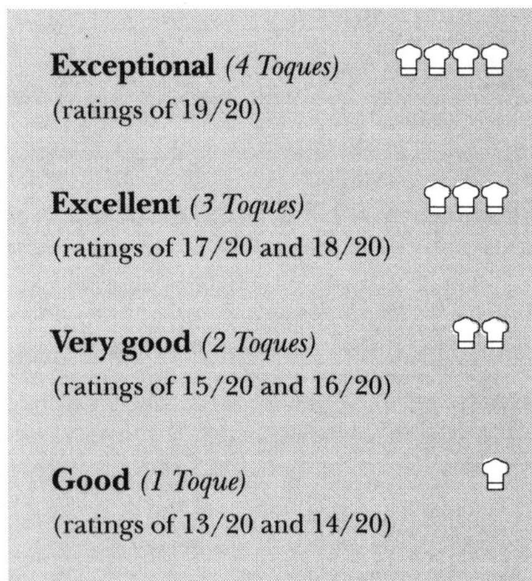

Exceptional *(4 Toques)*
(ratings of 19/20)

Excellent *(3 Toques)*
(ratings of 17/20 and 18/20)

Very good *(2 Toques)*
(ratings of 15/20 and 16/20)

Good *(1 Toque)*
(ratings of 13/20 and 14/20)

Keep in mind that we are comparing L.A.'s restaurants to the very best in the world. Also, these ranks are relative. A 13/20 (one toque) may not be a superlative ranking for a highly reputed (and very expensive) restaurant, but it is quite complimentary for a small place without much culinary pretension. We know that diners often choose a restaurant for reasons other than the quality of the food—because of its location, type of cuisine—or just because it's a fun place to spend an evening.

Our Pricing System

In our DINING and AND ALSO.. reviews, we code restaurant prices using one to four dollar signs. **Prices reflect the average cost of dinner for one person including appetizer, entrée, dessert, coffee, tax and tip. Not included is wine or other beverages, which vary greatly in price.** Restaurants often change their menus—and their menu prices. Forgive us if a restaurant is more expensive when you visit it.

$ = under $20

$$ = under $35

$$$ = under $50

$$$$ = $50 & up

Symbols

All credit cards taken .... A

Visa ....

MasterCard ....

American Express ....

Diners Club ....

Discover ....

Reservations suggested ....

Valet parking ....

Ties suggested

Romantic setting ....

Heart-healthy dishes ....

View ....

Outdoor dining ....

Advice & Comments

FUSION OR CONFUSION?

Before Nouvelle Cuisine was introduced to Los Angeles in the '70s, followed by California cuisine in the '80s and New American, Fusion, Pan-Asian, Mediterranean and Pacific Rim cuisine in the '90s, it was easy to classify restaurants by their cuisine—there was American, French, Italian, Continental, Chinese, Japanese, Greek etc. Period. Today, however, the lines between the cuisines have blurred, and chefs create their own style of cooking—which might combine elements of some—or all—of the above.

We find it hard to slap labels on the type of cuisine that a restaurant serves, yet we must for the sake of indexing—and so that readers will have some hint of what they'll be served when they dine there. In most cases, we have labeled a restaurant's cuisine according to what its owners and chefs call it. But that doesn't always make things easier. For we've found that though one restaurant may describe its cuisine as Californian, another as Contemporary and another as Eclectic, their dishes may be quite similar—innovative takes on new and old themes, concocted of fresh regional ingredients and using a combination of elements from various ethnic-cooking styles. But in the long run, who cares what we label a restaurant's cuisine? After all, it's not what type of cuisine you're eating that's important—it's how it tastes. And we hope it tastes great.

JUST HOW CASUAL IS CASUAL-CHIC?

In L.A., people don't usually dress up to go out, but they do dress with style. In a handful of the more conservative places, men still wear ties, and jackets are almost de rigueur. But in the trendy spots, anything goes—fur coats to leather pants, cowboy boots to Reeboks. One wouldn't want to overdress for Spago Hollywood or Mimosa, or underdress for Spago Beverly Hills or L'Orangerie.

CELEBRITIES IN THE KITCHEN

When you make reservations in a place with a famous chef, check to be sure he or she will be there and not traveling across the country demonstrating his or her cooking style. Also, all chefs have good days and bad, so don't be too put off if your experience is less stellar than was ours; with luck it will be better.

THE GRUNGE REPORT

In Los Angeles County, at least, the Department of Health and Environmental Safety is making it easy for restaurant-goers to know the truth about what goes on behind closed kitchen doors. As of 1998, all establishments handling and serving food are required to post current health and environmental inspection findings where everyone can see them. So if you don't see that Department of Health and Environmental Inspection card with an "A" or—at worst—a "B" in the window, ask the management for it. There may be a reason why they're hiding it.

THAT'S MY CAR!

Most restaurants in our car-dominated culture have parking valets, most with a mandatory cost of around $3. Be prepared to tip the valet $1 or $2 more. If you want your Ferrari handled with TLC, tip him *before* you hand over your keys.

SECOND-HAND SMOKE

As of January 1998, smoking is banned inside all L.A. County restaurants—and bars. However, you may find yourself in a bar, at least, where this new rule is not enforced. In any case, you can always smoke on a patio. In fact, you'll find many restaurants with sidewalk seating just for that purpose. Despite the smoking ban, cigar smoking is "in" at many spots (if only on their patio). Look for special designated "Cigar Nights" for the boys—and girls—who love a good stogie.

YOU'RE IN SUNNY CALIFORNIA

There are increasing numbers of outdoor cafés in this city (some, perhaps, in reaction to the no-smoking ban inside restaurants). Those spots that have a patio, a terrace or sidewalk tables are indexed in the back of the book under the heading "Outdoor Dining."

SO FRESH, IT'S STILL SWIMMING

Increasingly, it's easier to find superbly fresh seafood from around the world in restaurants—Atlantic farm-raised salmon and Hawaiian ahi tuna are undoubtedly the most popular. For the best fresh fish, go to any of the city's highest-rated sushi restaurants, or those Honk-Kong-style Chinese seafood restaurants where the fish swim happily in their tank until moments before they're cooked.

HOW MUCH IS ENOUGH?

Leaving a tip equivalent to fifteen percent of your pretax bill (including drinks) is customary. If you feel the service was above and beyond the call of duty, or you're with a large party, you may wish to leave eighteen to twenty percent. Only a few restaurants handle tipping European-style, by adding fifteen percent to the bill. Some restaurants automatically add a gratuity only for large groups (which tend to undertip).

Sample Review

The following key explains the information provided in our reviews.

Top Restaurants: Food Rating

TOQUE TALLY

Restaurants are in the Los Angeles, Pasadena, S.F.Valley, S.G.Valley or South Bay areas unless indicated: OC (*Orange County*), PS (*Palm Springs*), SD (*San Diego*), SB (*Santa Barbara*), CC (*Central Coast*), NB (*Northern Baja*), Cat (*Catalina*), Mts (*Mountains*), LV (*Las Vegas*).

18/20

Patina

17/20

L'Orangerie
Valentino

16/20

Ago
The Belvédère
Campanile
Chinois on Main
The Dining Room Ritz-Carlton Laguna Niguel (OC)
Drago
Four Oaks Restaurant
Gustav Anders (OC)
Jiraffe
Jozu
L'Arancino
Lavande
Mille Fleurs (SD)
Pascal (OC)
Spago Beverly Hills
Vincenti Ristorante
The Wine Cask (SB)
WineSellar & Brasserie (SD)
Yujean Kang's
Yujean Kang's Pasadena

THE TOQUE, CIRCA 1700

Have you ever wondered about the origin of that towering, billowy (and slightly ridiculous) white hat worn by chefs all over the world? Chefs have played an important role in society since the fifth century B.C., but the hats didn't begin to appear in kitchens until around the eighteenth century A.D. The toque is said to be of Greek origin; many famous Greek cooks, to escape persecution, sought refuge in monasteries and continued to practice their art. The chefs donned the tall hats traditionally worn by Orthodox priests, but to distinguish themselves from their fellows, they wore white hats instead of black. The custom eventually was adopted by chefs from Paris to Peking.

15/20

Azzura Point (SD)
Bistro K
Café Pinot
Chinois (LV)
Citronelle (SB)
Citrus
The Dining Room, Ritz-Carlton (PS)
Downey's (SB)
Gardens at the Four Seasons
Ginza Sushi-Ko
Golden Truffle (OC)
The Hotel Bel-Air Dining Room
Joe's
La Marina (SB)
Le Chardonnay
Locanda Veneta
Lunaria
The Mandarin
The Marine Room (SD)
Matsuhisa
Napa (LV)
Pangaea
Pinot Bistro
Porter's
The Regent Dining Room
Röckenwagner
Shiro
Spago Hollywood
Spago Las Vegas (LV)
Star of the Sea (SD)
The Stonehouse (SB)
Troquet (OC)
Zenzero

14/20

Alto Palato
Arigato Sushi (SB)
Arnie Morton's
Antonello (OC)
Asanebo
The Belgian Lion (SD)
Bernard's
Bistango (OC)
Bistro Laurent (CC)
Bombay Café
Border Grill
Boxer
Brothers (CC)
The Buffalo Club
Ca'Brea
Ca' del Sole
The Cellar (OC)
Chaya Brasserie
Chaya Venice
Checkers Restaurant
Coyote Café Dining Room (LV)
Crustacean
Cuistot (PS)
Diaghilev
Drai's (LV)
El Bizcocho (SD)
Emeril's (LV)
Empress Pavilion
Five Crowns (SD)
Fresco Ristorante
Gadsby's
Geoffrey's
George's at the Cove (SD)
Granita
The Grill on the Alley
Hal's Bar & Grill
Harbor Village
Harold & Belle's
Hoppe's at 901 (CC)
Il Pastaio
The Ivy
Jillian's (PS)
Joe Joe's
Joss
Katsu
La Cachette
La Serenata
La Serenata de Garibaldi
Lake Spring Cuisine
Le Dome
Louie's (SB)
Maple Drive
McCormick & Schmick's
Michael's
Mimosa (SB)
Mimosa (LA)
Morton's of Chicago (OC, SD, LV)
ObaChine
The Palm
Pane e Vino (SB)
Parkway Grill
Perroche
Pinot Restaurant & Martini Bar
Pizzicotto
Polo Lounge
Posto
Primi
Remi
The Ritz-Carlton Marina del Rey
Ruth's Chris Steak House

Scott's Seafood Grill (OC)
72 Market Street
Splash
Sushi Nozawa
Sushi Roku
Sushi Sasabune
Tahiti
Takao
Talesai
Terraza (LV)
Terraza of Bel Air
Tommy Tang's
Toscana
Trattoria Amici
21 Ocean Front (OC)
Typhoon
Vida
Woodside
Xiomara

13/20

A Thousand Cranes
Admiral Risty
All India Café
Allegria
Allegria (Long Beach)
Angeli Caffé
Arirang
Arroyo Chop House
Asakuma
Aunt Kizzy's Back Porch
Authentic Café
Baccio (SB)
Bamboo Inn
Barsac Brasserie
Bay Café & Fish Market (SB)
Beach City Grill
Bistro 45
Bistro by the Water (OA)
Bistro Garden at Coldwater, The
Bistro of Lunada Bay
Bistrot Provencal
Blue Shark Bistro (SB)
Brigitte's (SB)
Broadway Deli
Brophy Brothers (SB)
Brother's Sushi
Bucatini (SB)
Buccaneer Bay Club (LV)
Ca'Dario (SB)
Café Beaujolais
Café Bizou
Café Buenos Aires (SB)
Café del Rey
Café Pierre
Café Provencal (OA)
Café Rodeo
Café Roma (CC)
Carlitos Café (SB
Case de Sevilla
Cava
Cava (SB)
Celestino
Chad's (SB)
Chan Dara
Charming Garden
Chef Rick's (CC)
Chez Melange
Chianti
Chianti Cucina
China Star
Cicada
Cinnabar
Claes Seafood (OC)
Coco Pazzo
Cucina Paradiso
Da Pasquale
David's
Delmonico's Seafood Grille
Depot
Divino
Dragon Regency
Drai's(LA)
Dynasty Room
East India Grill
El Emperado Maya
El Encanto Dining Room (SB)
El Rey Sol (Baja)
Emilio's (SB)
Fin's
555 East
Gaylord
Gennaro's Ristorante
Gilliland's
Girasole
Granville's (OC)
Grill Ritz-Carlton Huntington, The
Hong Kong Paradise
Hu's Szechwan Restaurant
Hugo Molina Restaurant
Hugo's
Ian's (CC)
Il Grano
Il Moro
Indochine
Intermezzo (SB)
Isis (LV)
Ivy at the Shore, The
J.R. Seafood
James' Beach
Jitlada
JW's Steakhouse (OC)
Kappo Sui (OC)

Kass Bah
Katsu 3rd
King's Pine Ave. Fish House
Kitayama (OC)
L'Opera
La Bamba
La Bruschetta
La Loggia
La Luna Ristorante
La Parilla
La Parisienne
La Scala (LV)
La Vie en Rose (OC)
Lafayette (OC)
Laurel (SD)
Lawry's The Prime Rib
Le Colonial
Les Deux Cafes
Library, The
Limbo Restaurant
Little Door, The
Locanda del Lago
Ma Dolce Vita (SB)
Madeo
Mandalay
Mandarette
Manhattan Wonton
Company
Marouch
McCormick & Schmick's
(OC, SGV)
McCormick's & Schmick's
McPhee's Grill (CC)
Memphis (OC)
Meritage (SB)
Michi
Modo Mio
Mon Kee
Monroe's
Montecito Café (SB)
Morton's
Mr. Stox (OC)
Muse
Nicola
Nouveau Café Blanc
Ocean Avenue Seafood
Ocean Seafood
Off Vine
OnePico
Original Sonora Café, The
Orso
Otani Garden (PS)
Out Take Café
P.F. Chang's (LV)
Pacific Dining Car
Palace Café, The (SB)
Palace Court (LV)
Pamplemousse Grille (SD)
Pane e Vino (LA)
Paradise Café (SB)
Patio, The (SB)
Patricia at Cunard's (PS)
Piatti (SB)
Piero's
Pinot Hollywood
Prego
Prego (OC)
R-23
Rainwater's (SD)
Red
Restaurant Devon
Ritrovo
Ritz, The (OC)
Rix
Ruth's Chris
Steak House (LV, PS)
Saddle Peak Lodge
Schatzi
Seoul Jung
Shanghai Reds
Shenandoah Café
Sofi
Spumante
Stella Mare's (SB)
Stony Point
Sushi-Ko
Taiko
The Terrace
Thee White House (OC)
Tommy Tang's Pasadena
Top O' The Cove (SD)
Tosh Il Koo
Trattoria Farfalla
Trattoria Mollie's (SB)
Tutto Mare (OC)
Twin Palms
2087 An American
Bistro (OA)
2424 Pico
V.I.P. Harbor Seafood
Restaurant
Vintner's Bar & Grill (CC)
Warszawa
Water Grill
Wolfgang Puck
Café (LA, LV, OC, SD)
Yang Chow
Your Place (SB)
Zia Café, The (SB)
Zooma Sushi
Zov's Bistro

LOS ANGELES AREA MAP

Covering the Los Angeles Area,
San Fernando Valley,
Pasadena & The San Gabriel Valley,
and South Bay

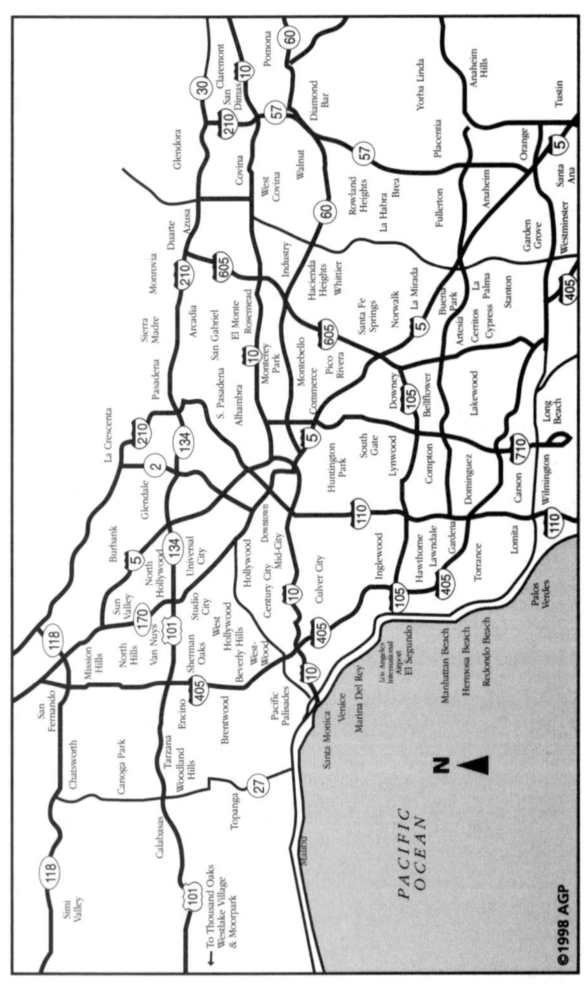

Los Angeles Area

LOS ANGELES AREA

Encompasses L.A. proper and all of the **Westside**, including **Bel Air, Beverly Hills, Brentwood, Century City, Culver City, Downtown, E. Hollywood, Hancock Park, Hollywood, Malibu, Marina del Rey, the Melrose-Fairfax area, the Melrose-La Brea area, the Mid-Wilshire area, Pacific Palisades, Santa Monica, Silverlake, South-Central, Venice, West Hollywood, Westwood and West L.A.**

DINING

A THOUSAND CRANES JAPANESE 13/20 

New Otani Hotel, 120 S. Los Angeles St., Downtown 90012
213-629-1200, *Breakfast & Dinner daily, Lunch Mon.-Fri., Brunch Sun., $$$*

Sophisticated Japanese dining in glorious surroundings. A Thousand Cranes embodies the Japanese aesthetic of blond-wood walls and Spartan tatami rooms looking out on a neatly sculpted garden, where rocks and stones are arranged harmoniously and water trickles gently into a pond. The menu offers a wide variety of classic Japanese dishes, including beef shabu-shabu and sukiyaki. Special features include a sushi bar, a tempura bar and on Sundays a Japanese brunch where East and West collide.

AGO ITALIAN 16/20 

8478 Melrose Ave., W. Hollywood 90069
323-655-6333, *Lunch Mon.-Fri., Dinner nightly, $$$*

A Hollywood mogul haunt in a spot that has seen others—e.g.Cicada and Silvio's—come and go. The backers include Robert De Niro and the Weinstein (Miramax) brothers, but the real news is that "Ago" is short for Agostino Sciandri, one of the best Italian chefs (also of Toscana) in L.A. In this swank setting, where the open kitchen is framed in marble and two levels of seating provide great sight lines, Sciandri delivers such dishes as silken tuna carpaccio, fettuccine showered with shaved white truffles, branzino with steamed spinach and a 20-ounce Florentine-style T-bone steak. The list of Italian and Californian wines is stellar.

AL AMIR LEBANESE 12/20

5750 Wilshire Blvd., Mid-Wilshire 90036
323-931-8740, *Lunch Mon.-Fri., Dinner Mon.-Sat., $$*

This opulent restaurant mixes classic Middle Eastern with moderne. You'll find many dishes you've never encountered, such as Lebanese salads made with lamb brains or lamb tongues and raw lamb "tartare." There are also all the popular Middle Eastern standards, from kabobs to shawarma. Service is generally respectful, and the surroundings are certainly more elegant than your usual falafel stand. In fact, they're fit for a pasha.

ALLEGRIA ITALIAN 13/20

22821 Pacific Coast Hwy, Malibu 90265
310-456-3132, *Lunch & Dinner daily, $$*

Allegria may not have the benefit of an ocean view like many of its Malibu neighbors—it sits on the "wrong" side of PCH. But it is undeniably romantic, its main dining room aglow with a golden light that makes everyone look beautiful. The fare includes cracker-thin pizzas with unique toppings such as tomato, mozzarella, speck (smoked prosciutto ham) and Brie, terrific salads, and a dozen pastas including homemade tortelloni in a velvet asparagus sauce.

ALTO PALATO ITALIAN 14/20

755 N. La Cienega Blvd., W. Hollywood 90069
310-657-9271, *Lunch Fri. & Sat., Dinner nightly, $$*

Where many of the city's best Italian chefs come for pizza. Alto Palato looks like a sleek trattoria right out of design-conscious Milan: blond woods and concrete, soaring ceilings, bold modern art, strings of ultra-modern lights and a two-level bar/café where Armani models would fit right in. The crisp-crusted pizzas are divine, as are the pastas and such specialties as New Zealand snapper with tomato, almond, basil and olive oil baked in phyllo, or pork filet with figs and spiced red wine sauce. Close your eyes when you taste their gelati; you'll swear you're in Italy.

ANGELI CAFFÈ ITALIAN 13/20

7274 Melrose Ave., Melrose-La Brea 90046
323-936-9086, *Lunch Mon.-Sat., Dinner nightly, $$*

A hip, ultra-modern spot where the sound-level can be ear-splitting and the very reasonably priced Italian cuisine is perfect for grazing. Share a plate of Sicilian deep-fried rice-and-potato croquettes, or a crisp-crusted pizza topped with pesto, onions, pine nuts and cheese, or sometimes only olive oil and garlic. Then move on to chef/owner Evan Kleiman's simple pastas or her succulent lemon-and-garlic roasted chicken. Frankly, we're happy with the panini sandwiches, served on deliciously chewy pizza bread.

ANTONIO'S MEXICAN 12/20

7472 Melrose Ave., Melrose-La Brea 90046
323-655-0480, *Lunch & Dinner Tues.-Sun., $$*

For thirty years, Antonio's has been one of L.A.'s most popular Mexican eateries, in part because of its warm hospitality and colorful surroundings. The menu veers away from the usual enchiladas and tacos, and offers specialties from Mexico's diverse regions, such as chicken mole, carne asada, pork in green chile sauce and pollo Yucateco.

ARNIE MORTON'S OF CHICAGO STEAKHOUSE 14/20 

435 S. La Cienega Blvd., W. Hollywood 90048
310-246-1501, *Dinner nightly, $$$*

This clubby, leather-booth-lined restaurant is part of a national chain started by the father of Peter Morton, whose own Morton's (on Melrose) is a Hollywood heavyweights' hang-out. The stars at Arnie Morton's aren't celebs—they're the huge cuts of aged, prime, grain-fed beef. There are also giant Maine lobsters, whole grilled chickens and monster-sized cuts of swordfish and salmon. To-go-withs include baked potatoes the size of footballs. Beware: if the waiter gives you a show-and-tell spiel instead of a menu when you order, you may end up alarmed by the bill.

ASAKUMA JAPANESE/SUSHI 13/20 

11701 Wilshire Blvd., W. L.A. 90025
310-826-0013, *Lunch & Dinner daily, $$*

A big, clean-lined and colorful Japanese restaurant that is usually packed—especially at the boisterous (and fun) sushi bar. In addition to sushi and sashimi, you can order tempura and sukiyaki, and more unusual dishes like seafood bouillabaisse with udon noodles in sake-soy broth. The service is harried, the prices relatively high, but this is a reliable bet for good Japanese food on the Westside.

ATLANTIC CALIFORNIAN 12/20

8256 Beverly Blvd., Melrose-Fairfax 90036
323-295-1949, *Dinner Mon.-Sat., $$$*

Those who know say this place is decorated like one of Madonna's houses. Maybe that's because the designer for each (and Atlantic's co-owner) is Madonna's brother, Christopher Ciccone. The swank 1940s-ocean-liner look—burgundy walls, backlit mirrors and a huge mahogany bar—make a perfect stage setting for the celebs who gather here, everyone from Sharon Stone to the Material Girl herself. As for the food, choose the ahi tuna carpaccio over the calamari, and stick with such simple entrées as grilled swordfish or the New York steak with bourbon-devil sauce.

AUNT KIZZY'S BACK PORCH SOUTHERN 13/20 

4325 Glencoe Ave., Marina del Rey 90292
310-578-1005, *Lunch & Dinner daily, Brunch Sun., $*

The recipes at this down-home Southern spot hail from Texas and Oklahoma. Try the farm-raised catfish and hush puppies, the ultra-crunchy fried chicken, the chicken-and-sausage jambalaya, the short ribs and the smothered pork chops, all served with monster-sized quantities of red beans and rice, black-eyed peas, collard greens or candied yams. Fresh-squeezed lemonade is served in a mason jar; for dessert, feast on peach cobbler and sweet-potato pie.

AUTHENTIC CAFÉ SOUTHWESTERN/ECLECTIC 13/20

7605 Beverly Blvd., Melrose-La Brea 90036
323-939-4626, *Lunch & Dinner daily, $*

Chef/owner Roger Hayot cooks, answers the phone and mans the cash register in his eclectic café, best described as New Mexicanish. Much of the menu runs to nachos, tamales and other Southwestern fare, but there are also curious pizzas, pastas and good Chinese dishes, including great Szechuan dumplings. Is the Authentic Café authentic? We're not sure, but from the lines of customers usually waiting outside to get in, it doesn't matter.

BARNEY GREENGRASS DELI 12/20

Barneys New York, 9570 Wilshire Blvd., Beverly Hills 90211
310-777-5877, *Breakfast, Lunch & Dinner daily, $$*

If you can afford to shop at this bastion of New York chic, you'll appreciate the smoked salmon and sturgeon flown in from where else? Located on the store's top level, this is definitely a designer deli—which means a vodka-and-caviar bar, as well as extraordinary cold cuts and salads from the glassed-in case. This is a popular power-breakfast spot for agents from nearby William Morris, who love the imported-from-New York bagels and lox.

THE BELVÉDÈRE CALIFORNIAN 16/20

The Peninsula Hotel, 9882 Santa Monica Blvd., Beverly Hills 90212
310-788-2306, *Breakfast, Lunch & Dinner daily, Brunch Sun., $$$$*

Agents from nearby CAA power-breakfast on cholesterol-free omelets—or banana-stuffed brioche french toast at this ultra-posh hotel dining room. Executive Chef Bill Bracken is one of those young American wunderkinds who not only smokes his own salmon, but does wonders with everything from fresh duck livers and taquitoes to steak. Sample such innovations as a grilled portobello mushroom-and-artichoke sandwich on toasted brioche, lobster tacos, potato-crusted Chilean sea bass, or a porcini-dusted veal T-bone with angel-hair pie. The warm sour cream cheesecake is a to-die-for dessert.

BERNARD'S NEW AMERICAN 14/20

Regal Biltmore Hotel, 506 S. Grand Ave., Downtown 90071
213-612-1580, *Dinner nightly, $$$$*

Bernard's dark wood and clubby decor provides a soothing retreat from downtown's hustle and bustle. It's a plush, split-level room, where the service is pampering, good for celebrating a business merger or an anniversary. We favor the grilled New York steak rubbed with Armagnac and crushed pepper, served with a pillow of garlicky mashed potatoes. Duck, chicken, lamb and veal are other best bets. And after dessert, at least peruse the Cognac cart—it holds treasures that date back to the turn of the century.

BISTRO K — FRENCH — 15/20 

267 S. Beverly Dr., Beverly Hills 90212
310-276-1558, *Lunch Mon.-Sat., Dinner nightly, $$*

French bistro fans rejoice: this is the real thing. Set in a brick cottage that once housed Chez Hélène, Bistro K has the ochre-painted walls, the brass trim and the butcher paper-covered tables that you'd find in Paris. It also has a delightful patio. The new chef/co-owner, Lionel Deniaud, cooked years back at the Hollywood Canteen and more recently at New York's tony Ici. He makes a lusty pâté maison, along with such supernal starters as ahi tuna tartare and grilled portobello mushrooms with goat cheese. We're mad for his peppercorn-spiked ahi tuna, lemony seared swordfish and warm molten chocolate cake. And we're grateful for the reasonable prices.

BISTROT PROVENÇAL — FRENCH — 13/20 

829 N. La Cienega Blvd., W. Hollywood 90069
310-360-9064, *Lunch Tues.-Fri., Dinner nightly, $$*

A spin-off of Jean-François Meteigner's La Cachette, this warm, rustic bistro offers authentic French Provençal cuisine at reasonable prices. We recommend any of the pizzas, pissaladières or meats cooked in the wood-burning oven. We've also enjoyed the braised lamb shank with dried figs and apple-raisin polenta and the bourride of seafood. The tree-shaded patio is perfect for a romantic supper.

BOMBAY CAFÉ — INDIAN — 14/20 

12113 Santa Monica Blvd., W.L.A. 90025
310-820-2070, *Lunch Tues.-Fri., Dinner Tues.-Sun., $*

In a bright, ambitious little spot is a mini-mall, Bombay Café serves a light and exotic cuisine which some have dubbed "Cal-Indian." Start with sev puri, a quintessential bit of Indian street food consisting of little crisps topped with chopped onions, potatoes, cilantro and piquant chutney; the tasty, burrito-like frankies stuffed with chicken, lamb or cauliflower, or the crispy shrimp dish called haldi jhinga. Other standout dishes: the eggplant-and-yogurt purée, the tandoori chicken sausages and the tandoori chicken salad. Meg Ryan and Dennis Quaid love their tandoori so much, they have it flown in to their Montana ranch.

BOMBAY PALACE — INDIAN — 12/20

8690 Wilshire Blvd., Beverly Hills 90211
310-659-9944, *Lunch & Dinner daily, $$*

A far cry from your hole-in-the-wall Indian, Bombay Palace has high ceilings, a sweeping marble bar, plush banquettes and a gallery of niches on the walls holding gilded Indian figurines. Classic Indian dishes are well executed: chicken, lamb, fish and traditional Indian breads cooked in the tandoor oven, along with curries, vegetarian specialties and basmati rice pilafs. For the iron-hearted, there are several firey dishes such as seafood vindaloo, and ginger-chicken- pepper fry. There's a daily buffet lunch.

BORDER GRILL MEXICAN 14/20 

1445 Fourth St., Santa Monica 90401
310-451-1655, *Lunch Fri.-Sun., Dinner nightly, $$*

Experience the Latin-spiced cuisine of Mary Sue Milliken and Susan Feniger—the "Too Hot Tamales"—at this raucous, funky and intensely colorful Mexican joint. You can spend $13 and up for such sophisticated dinner entrées as the grilled pork chop with a tamarind-apple sauce or the roasted garlic-stuffed grilled prime rib chop. Or graze (and save money) on a selection of green corn tamales, black-bean-stuffed panuchos and griddled tacos filled with everything from potato and rajas to roasted lamb. Bring a pair of earplugs if you hate noisy restaurants.

BOURBON STREET SHRIMP CAJUN 12/20

8454 Melrose Ave., W. Hollywood 90069
323-653-2640, *Dinner nightly, $*

Now that the Cajun craze is over and there are only a few L.A. restaurants still serving this zesty Louisiana cuisine, we're glad that Bourbon Street Shrimp is here, sultry red walls, dart board, patio and all. Most nights the place is jammed with regulars who swear by the shell-on shrimp, the etouffeés, the scrumptious jambalaya and the lemony dill chicken. The chef will turn up the heat on request.

BOXER CALIFORNIAN 14/20 

7615 Beverly Blvd., Los Angeles 90036
323-932-6178, *Lunch Mon.-Fri., Dinner Mon.-Sat., $$$*

This plain but high-style spot doesn't have a wine-and-beer license, but you can stop in next door at restaurateur Steve Arroyo's wine shop and pick up a bottle. Chef Michael Plapp prepares such provocative fare as cucumber-basil soup concealing a stack of tomatoes and fresh mozzarella, or a silken tuna tartare salad. Entrées might include the goat cheese-and-fennel-crusted swordfish with herbed couscous, or the meaty grilled Numidian hen (descended from African game birds but raised in Seattle) in a truffled mushroom broth. On a night we dined, the chocolate cake was a bit dry, but the pear tarte was perfection.

BRASSERIE CALIFORNIAN 12/20

Wyndham Bel Age Hotel, 1020 N. San Vicente Blvd., W. Hollywood 90069
310-854-1111, *Breakfast, Lunch & Dinner daily, Brunch Sun., $$*

With its dazzling view of the city lights, its subdued decor—and excellent live jazz Tuesday through Saturday nights—this is much more than an ordinary brasserie. They do good pizzas, pastas and sandwiches, along with salads and such entrées as pork filet mignon with honey-mustard sauce, roasted apples and mashed potatoes. There are even a few low-cal dishes, such as an ahi tuna steak sandwich. If you spend over $20 per person on dinner, there's no cover charge for the jazz.

BROADWAY DELI — DELI/ECLECTIC — 13/20

1457 Third St. Promenade, Santa Monica 90401
310-451-0616, *Breakfast, Lunch & Dinner daily,* $$

This cavernous, high-tech space features roomy booths, an open kitchen fronted by a dining counter and cappuccino bar, and a continual crush of people. Traditional deli standards are available, but the best dishes are those you'd find in a French bistro or an American mom's kitchen: macaroni and cheese, savory lamb shank, French onion soup, a tangy Caesar salad and crisp, salty fries. The fresh-baked breads and desserts are swell.

THE BUFFALO CLUB — NEW AMERICAN — 14/20

1520 Olympic Blvd., Santa Monica 90404
310-450-8600, *Lunch Mon.-Fri. & Dinner Mon.-Sat.,* $$$

Writer/Producer Tony Yerkovich, creator of Miami Vice, opened this upscale bar and eatery for those in his circle of players. If you're not in the biz, you may encounter some attitude, but don't be discouraged. Chef Patrick Healy's fare—braised Maine lobster with morel mushrooms, pecan pie-crumble sundae—is just about worth the humiliation you'll be made to feel if you arrive sans entourage.

CA'BREA — ITALIAN — 14/20

346 S. La Brea Ave., Melrose-La Brea 90036
323-938-2863, *Lunch Mon.-Fri., Dinner Mon.-Sat.,* $$

This lively, hip—and noisy—hot-spot serves terrific Northern Italian food to a terrific-looking crowd. You'll find the usual carpaccios, pastas and veal dishes, but we advise trying the more unusual (for Los Angeles) specialties such as baked pancetta-wrapped goat cheese served on a bed of garlicky spinach, and roasted breast of duck with a Barolo-and-dried-cherry sauce. Finish with crème caramel or the warm apple tart with a sweet "balsamic" sauce.

THE CADILLAC CAFÉ — AMERICAN — 12/20

359 N. La Cienga Blvd., L.A. 90048
310-657-6591, *Lunch & Dinner daily, Breakfast Sat. & Sun.,* $

Imagine a punked-up retro-1950s diner in neon colors, its sidewalk patio shaded by awnings that look like panels left over from a visiting alien spaceship. Funky? Yes, but funky with pretty good food and service. Order deviled eggs just like grandma used to make, zesty turkey chili or a turkey "sundae" (roasted turkey slices leaning against a tower of mashed potatoes that's dripping with gravy and crowned with cranberry sauce) that tastes better than it looks. Share a sampler plate and soak up the wacky scene.

CAFÉ DELL 'OPERA — ITALIAN — 11/20

1714 N.Vermont Ave., Los Feliz 90027
323-661-7133, *Lunch & Dinner Tues.-Sat.,* $

Professional singers stroll through this old-fashioned café, belting out arias and schmaltzy Italian love songs. Most of the food is old-fashioned Italian: caprese salad, linguini with seafood, roasted chicken with kalamata olives and sausage and peppers. The desserts are from the bakery next door. This is a great spot for both casual dining and—what with the singers to serenade you—special occasions.

CAFÉ DES ARTISTES FRENCH 12/20

1534 N. McCadden Pl., Hollywood 90028
323-461-6889, *Lunch Mon.-Fri., Dinner Mon.-Sat., Brunch Sun., $$*

Behind a wall of ficus, this charming coverted bungalow serves quite good French bistro fare at reasonable prices. Begin with the escargots, a plate of sausage, pâté, smoked salmon and cheese, or the endive-Roquefort salad with Champagne vinaigrette. Among the entrées, we suggest the salmon en papillotte with mango, the chicken with figs and the marinated fresh vegetable lasagne. The garden terrace is an ideal setting for weddings.

CAFÉ DEL REY PACIFIC RIM 13/20

4451 Admiralty Way, Marina del Rey 90292
310-823-6395, *Lunch & Dinner daily, Brunch Sun., $$$*

A

The view of the Marina is sensational; the design is open, bright and airy. The menu? Dining at Café del Rey is like wandering around a bazaar where there's something for everyone—usually with a Pacific Rim twist. The results can be very good—or overconceived. Chef Katsuo Nagasawa serves such starters as hamachi carpaccio, curried chicken spring rolls and a "parfait" of ahi and smoked salmon. You'll always find pastas (e.g. penne with wild bacon and caramelized onions), and such entrées as pecan-crusted rack of lamb with mushroom-Gorgonzola bread pudding, and blackened swordfish with saffron-coconut rice. The hesitant diner can get a good steak.

CAFÉ LA BOHÈME ASIAN/MEDITERRANEAN 12/20

8400 Santa Monica Blvd., W. Hollywood 90069
323-848-2360, *Dinner nightly, $$$*

A

Picture a dining room gussied up like a flamboyant neo-Baroque opera house with heavy draperies on the walls, a roaring fireplace and a crystal chandelier worthy of *Phantom of the Opera*. Bordering the mezzanine is a dining balcony from which spectators can observe the scene—and it can be a scene—below. The "French/Italian/Japanese" cuisine translates into such dishes as beef carpaccio with oba-miso chutney, wild mushrooms en papillote with ponzu, and Chilean sea bass with stir-fried tofu and cardamon-infused lobster-cream sauce. Sound like weird food to you? Stick to the simpler dishes, but don't stay away—this place is a ton of fun.

CAFÉ MAURICE FRENCH 11/20

747 N. La Cienega Blvd., W. Hollywood 90069
310-652-1609, *Dinner nightly, $*

A

Café Maurice is popular because it is what it is—a place to gather with friends for good simple food and inexpensive wine—and it doesn't try to be more. Basically a dark room of booths and wood with a few etched-glass mirrors and Toulouse Lautrec-era prints, this rustic bistro serves dishes including a first-class salade niçoise, grilled salmon in saffron sauce, shepherds pie, chicken Normande and lamb ribs roasted Provençal-style. The pastas, however, can be bland and the service sometimes erratic.

CAFÉ PINOT FRENCH 15/20 

700 W. Fifth St., Downtown 90071
213-239-6500, *Lunch Mon.-Fri., Dinner nightly, $$*

Joachim Splichal's modern, mostly glass restaurant near the L.A. Public Library is one of the most attractive restaurants downtown, especially at night, when diners look out at glimmering lights of the surrounding high-rises. You can count on the quality of nearly every California-French bistro dish here: mustard-crusted rotisserie-roasted chicken with sublime french fries, salmon with artichoke ravioli, and on Fridays, suckling pig with crunchy cracklings. Kids under ten eat free, but we're inclined to leave the kids at home when we dine at this sophisticated spot. Since Café Pinot provides free shuttle service to the Music Center, it's perfect for pre-theater dining.

CAFÉ RODEO CALIFORNIAN 13/20

Summit Hotel, 360 N. Rodeo Dr., Beverly Hills 90210
310-273-0300, *Breakfast, Lunch & Dinner daily*

Get a ringside seat for people-watching on Beverly Hills' most famous shopping street. Thanks to chef Michael Shaheen, who at one time cooked at Spago and Morton's, the food is worthy of the location. Start with a spinach salad jazzed up with Bleu cheese, apple chunks and candied walnuts, and move on to one of the inventive entrées, such as grilled Hawaiian ono with pearl pasta or wild mushroom-stuffed chicken breast. Nice wines by the glass.

CAMPANILE CALIFORNIAN/MEDITERRANEAN 16/20 

624 S. La Brea Ave., Melrose-La Brea 90036
323-938-1447, *Lunch Mon.-Fri., Dinner Mon.-Sat., Brunch Sat.-Sun., $$$*

The setting—Charlie Chaplin's old digs—is attractive, the service is (usually) attentive, the wine list is eclectic and the cuisine ranges from very good to dazzling. Owner/chef Mark Peel does such rustic French or Italian-influenced dishes as brandade with warm cherry tomatoes, scallions and grilled batard, grilled swordfish with beluga lentils, spinach, currants and pinenuts, and prime rib with olive tapenade, flageolet beans and sautéed bitter greens. Nancy Silverton's pastries are sublime, as are her La Brea Bakery breads and such brunch treats as homemade granola, pecan sticky buns and bagels.

CASITA DEL CAMPO MEXICAN 11/20

1920 Hyperion Ave., Silverlake 90027
323-662-4255, *Lunch & Dinner daily, $*

With its soft lighting, comfy booths, two patios and a gigantic rubber tree that covers the entire top of the restaurant, this 36 year-old Mexican eatery is "in" with the Silverlake artsy set.

The food is a cut above the usual Mexican fare, and includes such standout dishes as the succulent chile Colorado, the chile verde and taquitos dolloped with fresh-made guacamole. Live music adds excitement on most evenings, and on frequent Saturday nights, an outrageous drag show that spoofs soap operas takes over the downstairs theater.

CAVA SPANISH 13/20 

Beverly Plaza Hotel, 8384 W. Third St., W. Hollywood 90048
323-658-8898, *Breakfast, Lunch & Dinner daily, $$*

Cava features chef/owner Toribio Prado's innovative take on Spanish cuisine, and an upstairs supper club with live music and dancing on some nights. The cozy dark red dining room with its taped flamenco music reminds us of Madrid. Share tapas like grilled asparagus wrapped in smoked salmon, ceviche, and baked marinated artichokes with garlic croutons. There are sumptuous paellas brimming with seafood, chicken and sausage. In addition, Prado creates dishes embodying flavors from Latin American, such as chicken sautéed with mango chutney and Brazilian spices, and black pepper shrimp simmered in beer butter.

CHA CHA CHA CARIBBEAN 12/20

656 N. Virgil Ave., Silverlake 90004
323-664-7723, *Breakfast, Lunch & Dinner daily, $*

L.A.'s original all-Latin, all-funky, color-splashed café looks like it belongs on a sunny beach in the Caribbean instead of on the border of Hollywood and Silverlake. We enjoy its cheerfully exotic ambience, infectious island music and good eats. Start with an assortment of jerk pork, tiny corn tostadas filled with black beans and chicken, and sautéed mushrooms marinated in sherry and garlic. For lunch, try a "rasta wrap": grilled shrimp, avocado, pineapple and black beans in a tortilla. Pass up the pastas for the vibrant Brazilian or Jamaican chicken dishes, the St. Bart's curried shrimp or one of the robust paellas.

CHAN DARA THAI 13/20

1511 N. Cahuenga Blvd., Hollywood 90028
323-464-8585, *Lunch Mon.-Fri., Dinner nightly, $*

One of the first hip Thai restaurants in L.A., Chan Dara has spawned two offshoots, both as good-looking—and with just as good-looking young Thai waiters and waitresses. They do the typical Thai dishes extremely well: crunchy, not-too-sweet mee krob, chewy phad Thai noodles, various vegetable stir-fries, spicy beef and commendable satays. The barbecued chicken is a mainstay, as are such seafood specialties as basil-and-chili-sauced "rock and roll" clams and deep-fried catfish. **Also in Hancock Park (310 N. Larchmont Blvd., 323-467-1052) and West L.A. (11940 W. Pico Blvd., 310-479-4461).**

CHAO PRAYA THAI 12/20

6307 Yucca St., Hollywood 90028
323-466-6704, *Lunch & Dinner daily, $*

Open since 1971, this is one of the first Thai restaurants in the U.S. At its worst, the food can be greasy and the service impossible. But it is rarely at its worst. In fact, Chao Praya does most of the Thai standbys well: satays, yum yai salads, hot-and-sour soups, fried Thai noodles, curries, and pork, chicken or beef with mint leaves and chili. The best dishes are probably their sweet, crunchy and spicy barbecued chicken and the fried whole catfish with curry sauce. Beware: when they say hot they mean hot.

CHAYA BRASSERIE JAPANESE/MEDITERRANEAN 14/20 

8741 Alden Dr., W. Hollywood 90048
310-859-8833, *Lunch Mon.-Fri., Dinner nightly, $$$*

At this perpetually hip restaurant, there's lots of black—the chairs, the tile floors, the trendy dress of the customers—tilting wall mirrors and a stand of bamboo reaching toward a skylight in the high ceiling. Stellar starters include Chinese duck-and-mango salad, warm goat cheese and portobello mushrooms and ahi tuna-tempura roll. We love the spaghetti with Japanese eggplant, the home-smoked crispy white fish, the seared soy-marinated Hawaiian tuna and the Chaya steak with three-peppercorn butter sauce and perfect pommes frites. Chaya rocks.

CHAYA VENICE JAPANESE/MEDITERRANEAN 14/20 

110 Navy St., Venice 90291
310-396-1179, *Lunch Mon.-Fri., Dinner nightly, Brunch Sun., $$$*

This high-style (and pricey) bistro, with its supple leather booths, modern Japanese art and happening bar scene, is very Venice. Even on a rainy night, it's filled with artists and yuppies who hang out, graze on sushi from the sushi bar (until 2:30 a.m.), or order from a menu featuring international seafood dishes. Share popcorn shrimp and spicy seafood springrolls to start, then move on to such sumptuous entrées as roasted Dungeness crab with black pepper and garlic, saffron-scented bouillabaisse or squid ink paella. Or, as at Chaya Brasserie, stick with the grilled rib-eye steak with three-peppercorn butter sauce.

CHECKERS CALIFORNIAN 14/20 

Wyndham Checkers Hotel, 535 S. Grand Ave., Downtown L.A. 90071
213-891-0519, *Breakfast, Lunch & Dinner daily, Brunch Sun., $$$*

An elegant hideaway in downtown's most charming boutique hotel, with complimentary transportation to the Music Center for pre-theater diners. Sink into a sumptuous booth, and be pampered while dining on dramatically presented (think stacked) contemporary cuisine. At lunch, choose an entrée salad—chilled steamed sea scallops with corn, celery and fresh peach in Reisling-papaya coulis—or such hearty dishes as pancetta-wrapped salmon. For dinner, we've enjoyed the crabcakes with tomato-basil-spinach chutney, followed by the medallions of veal with a napoleon of yucca root and ratatouille, and the rack of lamb.

CHEZ JAY CONTINENTAL 12/20

1657 Ocean Ave., Santa Monica 90401
310-395-1741, *Breakfast, Sat. & Sun., Lunch Mon.-Fri., Dinner nightly, $$*

A high-class dive that's been a refuge for beach bums, writers and artists for decades. Even though owner Jay Fiondella is no longer always here, mirth and mayhem still mingle in this dark and cozy refuge from the California sunshine. Though known more for the rough-and-ready ambience than the food, the food is pretty good: steak au poivre, shrimp curry and sand dabs—with a side of potatoes baked with bananas (Spock's favorite dish in the official *Star Trek* cookbook.)

CHEZ MIMI FRENCH 12/20

246 26th St., Santa Monica 90402
310-393-0558, *Lunch & Dinner daily, Brunch Sun., $$$*

Mimi Hébert, the former owner of Chez Hélène (now Bistro K), has opened Chez Mimi on the site of the former Camelion's, a wonderfully cozy and romantic cottage-and-patio setting that looks as if it belongs in Provence. Expect many of the traditional bistro favorites from Chez Hélène, including the feuilleté de chèvre, roasted chicken with lemon, fresh trout with almonds, bouillabaisse, steak au poivre with pommes frites and a classic tarte tatin. Book very early for Valentine's Day.

CHIANTI ITALIAN 13/20 

7383 Melrose Ave., Melrose-La Brea 90046
323-653-8333, *Dinner nightly, $$*

Still elegant at 60, Chianti retains a reserved, romantic old-world atmosphere. Seating is in discreet high-backed booths and the light level is so low, your attentive waiter may offer you a penlight for reading the menu. Many of the dishes are now considered "classics"—veal scaloppini or boneless breast of chicken sautéed with white wine and lemon sauce, for example. You can also find unusual pastas, such as pheasant-filled ravioli, and such straightforward entrées as the mixed seafood grill or grilled rack of lamb with fresh thyme oil. The wine list offers many excellent Californian and Italian bottles.

CHIANTI CUCINA ITALIAN 13/20 

7383 Melrose Ave., Melrose-La Brea 90046
323-653-8333, *Lunch Mon.-Sat., Dinner nightly, $$*

Cucina began as the brightly lit, casual baby brother of Chianti, and quickly became a formidable restaurant with its own loyal following. The visuals are great; you watch dishes for both restaurants being prepared in the open kitchen and hustled off to tables. The weekly changing menu appeals with juicy turkey osso buco and several satisfying pastas and risottos. As befits the best Italian food, simple dishes such as thinly seared tuna, spinach tagliolini, and luscious veal chops are offered.

CHIN CHIN CHINESE 12/20

8618 Sunset Blvd., W. Hollywood 90069
310-652-1818, *Lunch & Dinner daily, $*

Yuppie dim-sum mania was born at this modern, noisy and always-jammed sidewalk café. Though the quality can be inconsistent, the food can be delicious: Max's noodle soup, good Chinese chicken and noodle salads, plump potstickers and comforting bao buns, crisp spring rolls and succulent roasted Hunan chicken. You can order low-cal versions of many of the dishes, but we don't recommend it. **Also in Beverly Hills (206 S. Beverly Dr., 310-248-5252, Brentwood (11740 San Vicente Blvd., 310-826-2525) and Marina del Rey (13455 Maxella Ave., 310-823-9999.)**

CHINOIS ON MAIN — CHINESE/FRENCH 16/20

2709 Main St., Santa Monica 90405
310-392-9025, *Lunch Wed.-Fri., Dinner nightly, $$$$*

Chinois remains near the top of not only our "Favorite Wolfgang Puck Restaurants" list, but our "Favorite Restaurants" list. Invariably crowded and noisy, this striking Barbara Lazaroff-designed eatery features such inspired dishes as stir-fried lamb with wok-fried Maui onion rings in radicchio leaves, sizzling sea scallops with potato strings and barbecued salmon with marinated black-and-gold noodles. The whole sizzling catfish with ginger, the crispy quail and the lobster ravioli in a black bean-truffle-oil sauce, help remind you that Puck—Austrian-born, French-trained—is perhaps the most talented chef of his generation.

CIAO TRATTORIA — ITALIAN 12/20

815 W. Seventh St., Downtown 90017
213-624-2244, *Lunch Mon.-Fri., Dinner Mon.-Sat., $$*

Located in downtown's historic Fine Arts Building, this unique trattoria's ornate, barrel-vaulted ceiling and rich woods offer a look that would not seem out of place on Rome's chic via Candotti. And its striking Romanesque-style lobby, available for private parties, would make any affair quite memorable. Despite its stunning decor, however, Ciao serves the usual L.A. trattoria fare: calamari, caprese salad, pastas, veal picatta and tiramisu. The service is accommodating, the location good for pre-theater dining.

CICADA — ITALIAN 13/20 

617 S. Olive St., Downtown 90014
323-655-5559, *Lunch Mon.-Fri., Dinner Tues.-Sat., $$$*

It doesn't get much more glamorous than this. Located in the historic—and gorgeous—art-deco Oviatt Building, the moved-from-Melrose Cicada has filled the void left when the elegant Rex, Il Ristorante closed after owner, Mauro Vincenti's death. New are the gold-leaf ceiling and oversized leather booths. Sofas and leather club chairs invite guests to relax in the swank upstairs bar, with its beautiful marble dance floor. Some of the best dishes include the fried zucchini flowers stuffed with striped bass, the lobster salad, the pumpkin ravioli in an almond Amaretto sauce and the grilled veal chop with truffle-mashed potatoes. Pre-theater diners are whisked to the Music Center.

CITRUS FRENCH 15/20

6703 Melrose Ave., Melrose-La Brea 90038
323-857-0034, *Lunch Mon.-Fri., Dinner Mon.-Sat., $$$$*

The Great Richard the First no longer reigns at Citrus, where he established his authority and his fame. (Michel Richard now spends nearly all his time at his new Washington D.C. restaurant). Richard's imprint is still visible on the dramatically presented dishes offered by his successors. While the specialties are pleasing to the eye and well executed, however, they lack Richard's magic touch. On a short menu, the chanterelle-crusted seabass and rack of lamb pleased us; the tepid peppered tuna tournedos did not. The highlight, not surprisingly, were the pastries, a legacy from Richard's days as a master pâtissier.

THE CLAY PIT INDIAN 12/20

Chapman Market, 3465 W. Sixth St., Mid-Wilshire 90020
213-382-6300, *Lunch & Dinner daily, $$*

Tucked away in a handsomely restored 1920s marketplace, this high-tech café appeals with a lovely brick courtyard, splashing fountains, and superb Indian cuisine. The most memorable dishes: garlic naan, onion-stuffed kulcha bread, rich spinach-and-cheese sag paneer and all sorts of mesquite-broiled tandoori dishes, from succulent baby rack of lamb and ahi tuna to vegies. **Also Downtown (939 S., Figueroa St., 213-689-4489) for lunch only.**

COBALT CANTINA CALIFORNIAN/MEXICAN 12/20

616 N. Robertson Blvd., W. Hollywood 90069
310-659-8691, *Lunch Mon.-Sat., Dinner nightly, Brunch Sun., $*

This establishment's setting—airy, modern and casual—is only part of the reason for its popularity. The eclectic menu is the real draw: coconut onion rings with horseradish-mango sauce, shrimp empanadas in avocado sauce, sweet potato-corn tamales and crabcakes with garlic-ginger aïoli. The walls are hung with modern art, and the daily Happy Hour is suitably festive. **Also in Silverlake (4326 Sunset Blvd., 213-953-9991).**

COCO PAZZO ITALIAN 13/20

Mondrian Hotel, 8440 Sunset Blvd., W. Hollywood 90069
323-848-6000, *Breakfast, Lunch & Dinner daily, $$$*

Coco Pazzo looks like a New Yorker's fantasy of an L.A. restaurant, perhaps because it's owned by "in" New York restaurateur Pino Luongo. (The designer, Phillipe Starck, however, is French.) The white-on-white dining room is outfitted with sumptuous white leather chairs, and on the terrace, tables are sheltered by ficus trees in whimsically oversized flower pots. The dreamy view of the city is a perfect backdrop for the serious posing that goes on here. Choose the beef carpaccio over the ho-hum tuna carpaccio, the shrimp risotto over the bland spaghetti with duck confit. While one evening the sautéed duck breast was a tad overcooked and the striped bass "acqua pazza" plain, however, the veal chop was succulent. Perhaps the name Coco Pazzo, which translates as "crazy chef," has something to do with the unevenness of the kitchen.

COLEY'S PLACE JAMAICAN 12/20

5035 W. Slauson Ave., South-Central 90056
323-291-7474, *Lunch & Dinner Mon.-Sun., Brunch Sun.*, $

At this friendly spot, co-owners Veda and Don Coley greet customers and Don doubles as the chef. Seafood is popular, notably the extraordinary shrimp St. James—lots of tender shrimp and okra in a subtly spicy coconut-cream sauce—and conch fritters as crisp and light as tempura. Savory Jamaican patties are stuffed with beef and shrimp. The chicken Lockerton, a huge, deep-fried, banana-stuffed chicken breast, is the antithesis of nouvelle cuisine, but it is irresistible. And the sweet peach cobbler is pure nostalgia.

CRAZY FISH SUSHI 12/20

9105 W. Olympic Blvd., Beverly Hills 90212
310-550-8547, *Lunch Mon.-Fri., Dinner nightly*, $$

Add your name to the list posted outside the door of this frenetic little spot that has captured the hearts of neighborhood sushi fanatics. Once inside, squeeze in at the bar or seize one of the tiny tables, and pin down one of the fast-paced servers. All the usual sushi varieties here by the (rather expensive) piece, plus such only-in-Beverly-Hills specialties as "oy vey" salmon sashimi with garlic.

CRUSTACEAN VIETNAMESE/EURO-ASIAN 14/20 

9646 Santa Monica Blvd., Beverly Hills 90210
310-205-8990, *Lunch Mon.-Fri., Dinner Mon.-Sat.*, $$$

From the aquarium-wall at the entrance to the plexiglass-covered stream that undulates through the bar and into the dining room, this is a sumptuous recreation of a French-Colonial Vietnamese club/restaurant as could only exist in Beverly Hills. Owners Helene An and family, who are descendents of Vietnamese royalty, serve such appetizers as shrimp crisps, rice-paper shrimp rolls and steamed dumplings, along with entrées devised from secret family recipes including roasted Dungeness crab in pepper-garlic sauce, five-spice-roasted game hen with whiskey, and giant grilled tiger prawns lounging on garlic noodles that have a hint of sweetness and are positively addicting.

DA PASQUALE ITALIAN 13/20 

9749 Santa Monica Blvd., Beverly Hills 90210
310-859-3884, *Lunch Mon.-Fri., Dinner Mon.-Sat.*, $

We could live on the bread alone—soft, puffy disks of pizza dough baked in the wood-burning oven—at this charming little family-run trattoria. We adore it turned into sandwiches filled with marinated chicken and arugola, or turkey breast, goat cheese, avocado and peppers. Pasquale came from Italy to be the first pizza chef at Angeli. At this Tuscan-rusticized double storefront, he not only makes terrific pizzas, but also sublime marinated vegetables and such daily-changing pastas as linguine with lobster tail, garlic and hot pepper, gnocchi with smoked cheese and pappardelle with sausages. Very reasonable prices.

THE DAILY GRILL — AMERICAN — 12/20

11677 San Vicente Blvd., Brentwood 90049
310-442-0044, *Lunch & Dinner daily, $*

Spin-offs of The Grill on the Alley in Beverly Hills, these clean-and-simple American eateries are fashioned after someone's fantasy of a '40s restaurant, right down to the white-tiled floors, dark wooden booths and "Blue Plate Specials." The food is pretty good—burgers, grilled fish and chicken, meatloaf, Caesar salads—and the prices are reasonable. **Also in the West Hollywood (100 N. La Cienega Blvd., 310-659-3100).**

DAN TANA'S — ITALIAN — 12/20

9071 Santa Monica Blvd., W. Hollywood 90069
310-275-9444, *Dinner & Late Supper nightly, $$$*

Hollywood moguls, actors, screenwriters—and wannabes of all of the above—have been jamming this place since 1964. They can't be here because of the decor: red dining rooms, red leatherette booths, Chianti bottles hanging from the rafters. And we doubt they're here for the old-fashioned food: spaghetti with meat sauce, fettuccini Alfredo, veal scaloppine, shrimp diavolo and chicken cacciatore—at quite high prices. Still, old and young continue to flock here, making this great for people-watching.

DAR MAGHREB — MOROCCAN — 12/20

7651 W. Sunset Blvd, Hollywood 90046
323-876-7651, *Dinner nightly, $$$*

Plates and spoons are by request only at this exotic, fun, rowdy, eat-with-your-fingers Casbah-like party palace. The belly dancers may be more intriguing than the food, but the b'stilla is delicious, and it's a great place to share a six-course feast (around $30 per person) with friends. Reserve a private party room for your next big birthday.

DC3 — CALIFORNIAN — 12/20

2800 Donald Douglas Loop, Santa Monica 90405
310-399-2323, *Lunch Mon.-Fri., Dinner Tues.-Sat., $$$*

At this strikingly modern restaurant, there's plenty to catch your eye, whether it's the planes landing on the runway of the Santa Monica Airport, the contemporary art, the bold design or the singles bar scene. The menu tends towards appetizers with various ethnic twists: seafood wontons with a garlic-ginger sauce, crabcakes with cilantro mayonnaise and a reliable Caesar salad. Entrées run from grilled shrimp with saffron rice and Cajun-spiced rib-eye steak to braised lamb shank with roasted garlic. Ask about "Kids' Nights," when the restaurant provides free babysitting and dinner for the kiddies in a separate room—giving mom and dad the chance to enjoy a "civilized" meal.

DELMONICO'S SEAFOOD 13/20 

9320 W. Pico Blvd., W.L.A. 90035
310-550-7737, *Lunch Mon.-Fri., Dinner nightly, $$*

A clubby neighborhood spot that looks like it belongs in old San Francisco, with its semi-enclosed wooden booths lining two walls and a handsome antique bar. Their seafood dishes—Boston clam chowder, various grilled fish and pan-sautées—are fine, especially the Maine lobster. In addition, choose from steaks and chops, osso buco, herb-garlic-roasted chicken and pastas. There's a good wine list as well.

DIAGHILEV RUSSIAN/FRENCH 14/20 

Bel Age Hotel, 1020 N. San Vicente Blvd., W. Hollywood 90069
310-854-1111, *Dinner Tues.-Sat., $$$$*

This sumptuous Franco-Russian restaurant is a perfect setting in which to propose marriage. The décor—mirrors, long-stemmed roses in silver vases, paintings from some of Diaghilev's peers—is elegant. To boot, there is melancholy piano and balalaika music, cozy loveseat seating, unctuous service and an extensive selection of caviar to be paired with one of the chilled flavored vodkas. Share a selection of smoked fish and other Russian cold appetizers; try the hot beet borscht served with delicate pirozki turnovers, and the chicken Kiev finished with a nontraditional but sublime truffle sauce. The desserts are opulent, and Dimitri, the manager, deserves a "Most Gracious Host" award.

DIVINO ITALIAN 13/20 

11714 Barrington Ct., Brentwood 90049
310-472-0886, *Lunch & Dinner daily, $$*

Goran Milic charmed his customers when he greeted them at Giorgio and Toscana. They've been flocking to his own colorful trattoria since it opened in May, 1996. Hidden in the back of the Barrington Court shopping area, the café looks so tiny from the outside, you're surprised when you walk in to discover a colorful high-ceilinged, columned space, with green walls, skylights and an open kitchen. Order from a reasonably priced menu of pristine salads and pastas, and pizzas with marvelously thin crusts.

DRAGO ITALIAN 16/20 

2628 Wilshire Blvd., Santa Monica 90403
310-828-1585, *Lunch Mon.-Fri., Dinner nightly, $$$*

Celestino Drago sets new trends at this simple yet elegant restaurant serving the rustic dishes of his beloved Sicily along with such sophisticated creations as seafood and spaghetti baked in parchment. We're partial to his carpaccios, spaghetti with fresh sardines, risotto with pheasant and papparadelle with wild rabbit ragu. There is always fresh fish and usually a grilled veal chop, along with a mighty T-bone steak served with sautéed rapini and porcini mushroom sauce. When he is not off checking on his other restaurants (Il Pastaio and the new L'Arancini in Beverly Hills, and Celestino in Pasadena), Drago regularly emerges from the kitchen to chat with regulars.

DRAI'S — FRENCH — 13/20

730 N. La Cienega Blvd., W. Hollywood 90069
310-358-8585, *Dinner Mon.-Sat., $$$*

This brash Hollywoody bistro is rooted on the spot once occupied by that serene temple to French haute cuisine, L'Ermitage. Talented chef Claude Segal pays homage to the French-brasserie basics: steak tartare, osso buco, calf's liver and seven-hour leg of lamb with mashed potatoes. He turns out splendid California-ized fare as well, including the toasted filo-and-smoked-salmon appetizer, ravioli of fresh lobster and glazed Chilean sea bass with soy sauce, garlic and ginger. The place is often so packed that after the main course, you may be moved to the lounge/bar for dessert. That's okay; it's a perfect spot from which to watch the glamorous kissy-huggy scene here.

DUKES AT MALIBU — CALIFORNIAN/HAWAIIAN — 12/20

21150 PCH, Malibu 90265
310-317-0777, *Lunch & Dinner daily, Brunch Sat.-Sun., $$*

Named after Duke Kahanamoku, the "father of surfing," this ocean-side restaurant must hold a record for the longest stretch of windows with a view. Start in the outdoor barefoot bar, with its palm-thatched tables and sandy floor, and you'll feel like you're in Maui. Try the sushi or sashimi, or the panko-breaded calamari served with guava cocktail sauce to start. The Caesar salad and fishermen's chowder make a filling combination; the pork ribs and Thai chicken pizza are also good. On buffet brunch features pineapple-refreshed ceviche, prime rib, mahi mahi-topped salads and made-to-order omelets.

DYNASTY ROOM — NEW AMERICAN — 13/20

Westwood Marquis Hotel, 930 Hilgard Ave.
Westwood 90024, 310-208-8765, *Dinner nightly, $$$$*

This sumptuous restaurant is good for an impress-your-date (or business associate) dinner. The service is old-fashioned formal, but the menu will suit current tastes. Appetizers run from a chopped salad with marinated mozzarella and Peking-style roasted quail, to seared foie gras with a fruit-and-onion marmalade. Among the entrées, swordfish is baked in a tapenade crust, Maine lobster tail and sea scallops are served with risotto and asparagus-lime butter, and grilled ostrich tenderloin (a whopping $33) comes with spinach spaetzle.

EAST INDIA GRILL — INDIAN — 13/20

345 N. La Brea Ave., Melrose-La Brea 90036
323-936-8844, *Lunch Mon.-Sat., Dinner nightly, $*

This modern, high-tech café has helped reshape L.A. restaurant-goers' perception of Indian food. Naan, for example, the wonderfully puffy bread that is baked in the clay tandoor oven, here comes stuffed not only with the traditional potatoes, but also with garlic and basil, cheese, chicken or shrimp. You'll find such expected Indian dishes as samosa turnovers, curries and tandoori chicken—all done expertly.

But we recommend also trying the tandoori-roasted baby back ribs in a mango-soy marinade and crispy whole pomfret fish topped with a garlic-chile sauce.

EL CHAVO MEXICAN 12/20

4441 W. Sunset Blvd., Hollywood 90027
323-664-0871, *Lunch & Dinner daily, $*

No Cards

This dark, old-fashioned Mexican restaurant has a passionately devoted following. The menu ranges from enchiladas to more imaginative creations. We recommend anything with mole sauce. The poached Sonora chicken can be dry, but its saving grace is a well-balanced sauce of tomato, bacon, onion, olives and chiles. Pork dishes are succulent, but watch out for the fiery pork chile verde. The classics—tostadas, enchiladas, chile rellenos—are all terrific, and the tasty margaritas are automatically poured as doubles.

EL CHOLO MEXICAN 12/20

1121 S.Western Ave., Mid-Wilshire 90006
323-734-2773, *Lunch & Dinner daily, $*

El Cholo has been around since 1927, and it's still great fun. USC students love the incredible margaritas (they serve over 1,000 a day!) and festive atmosphere. But the food is good too: the taco tray, a make-your-own meal of tortillas, chicken, beef, sauces and beans; chicken breasts in flour tortillas with guacamole and zucchini; salsa-verde crab enchiladas; the Sonora-style enchilada topped with a fried egg; and the famous homemade green corn tamales from June to September. **The new El Cholo in Santa Monica (1025 Wilshire Blvd., 310-899-11016) has the same colorful decor, atmosphere and food.**

EL FLORIDITA CUBAN 12/20

1253 N.Vine St., Hollywood 90038
323-871-8612, *Lunch & Dinner daily, $*

A

In this downscale version of an old Havana supper club, the drinks are cool, the food is hot and so is the live salsa music. Their signature cocktail, the mojito, is a heady mix of mint, lime juice and rum. Start with croquetas filled with chicken or ham and served with plantain chips and garlic sauce, or potato balls stuffed with ground beef. The entrées include grilled red snapper, beef with potatoes and olives and jumbo shrimp in garlic-wine sauce. The service is friendly, and there's music and dancing on weekends.

EMPRESS PAVILION CHINESE/DIM SUM 14/20 

988 N. Hill St., Ste. 201, Downtown 90012
213-617-9898, *Breakfast, Lunch & Dinner daily, $*

Awesomely large, with an assortment of sliding walls that open to accommodate 500 diners, this ornate, bustling Hong Kong-style restaurant looks like it was plucked right out of...well...Hong Kong. Despite the volume of business, the food is good, and thanks to a complex network of servers, dishes zoom across the room sizzling and steaming. Among the nearly 200 choices on the menu, choose first from those listed as "Gourmet Selections," such as sautéed prawns with honey-glazed walnuts, steamed Dungeness crab with flat noodles and shrimp and chicken with black-bean sauce. Round up a table of ten and order one of the reasonably priced ten-course banquet menus.

ENGINE CO. NO. 28 AMERICAN 12/20

644 S. Figueroa St., Downtown 90017
213-624-6996, *Breakfast & Lunch Mon.-Fri., Dinner nightly, $$*

Situated in a beautifully restored 1912 landmark firehouse, this classic American bar and grill sports an ornate tin ceiling and dark mahogany booths along with the firehouse's original red brick floor and brass fire pole. Downtown business types flock here for power breakfasts, lunch and after-work cocktails. With free shuttle service to the Music Center, the restaurant is a good choice for pre-theater dining. The menu features all-American favorites: juicy hamburgers, crabcakes, Cobb salad, chicken pot pie, meatloaf, a meaty New York steak and robust whisky-fennel sausages.

THE FARM OF BEVERLY HILLS CALIFORNIAN 12/20

439 N. Beverly Dr., Beverly Hills 90210
310-273-5578, *Lunch and dinner daily, Brunch Sat. & Sun., $$*

This casual Beverly Hills spot features a rustic farmhouse decor, a sidewalk café and a celebrity's kid—Benjamin Ford, son of Harrison—as chef. Too bad we're not crazier about the food. We found the prices high for what you get: simple salads and pastas and grilled fish. On a recent visit, the french-fried onions left a puddle of oil in the bottom of the serving bowl and the Caesar salad was ho-hum. The cheeseburger, however, was a boffo smash, the thick beef patty topped with oven-roasted tomatoes, caramelized onions and arugula. Breakfasts are good too.

FENIX CALIFORNIAN NO RATING

Argyle Hotel, 8358 Sunset Blvd., W. Hollywood 90069
323-654-7100, *Lunch & Dinner daily, Breakfast Sun., $$$$*

We can't vouch for the cuisine since founding chef Ken Frank left for greener pastures in Napa Valley. But the view of the city lights is spectacular, as is the swank art deco design. Frank's culinary legacy lingers: porcini-crusted scallops with lobster-crushed potatoes and saffron, daikon-sesame salad with lobster and toasted salmon skin, triple duck salad with seared foie gras, duck prosciutto and confit, and New York steak with Jack Daniels-pepper sauce.

FINS OF MALIBU CALIFORNIA/ASIAN/SEAFOOD 13/20 

3835 Cross Creek Rd., Malibu 90265
310-456-5464, *Lunch & Dinner daily, Brunch Sun., $$*

Formerly Bambu, this Malibu "in" spot features a nifty Asian decor, and serves a range of innovative dishes: ceviche, sushi, steamed clams, wok stir-fries, spicy seafood salad, and such tantalizing entrées as macadamia nut-crusted halibut with Thai peanut sauce. On weekend evenings and during Sunday brunch, there's live jazz or blues. The outdoor patio doubles as a cigar lounge. **Also in Westlake Village (982 S. Westlake Blvd., 805-494-6494) and Calabasas (23504 Calabasas Rd., 818-223-3467.)**

FOUR OAKS RESTAURANT CALIFORNIAN/FRENCH 16/20 

2181 N. Beverly Glen Blvd., Bel Air 90077
310-470-2265, *Lunch Tues.-Sat., Dinner nightly, Brunch Sun., $$$$*

A sycamore-shaded cottage nestled in Beverly Glen Canyon, this is a charming and unique haven from the city whether you're seated on the patio or before the fireplace in the wood-paneled back dining room. Chef/owner Peter Roelant's considerable talent shows in such appetizers as house-smoked lavender salmon, veal sweetbreads with date-and-apple salad and caviar with brioche toast and lemon-vodka shavings. His cream-free soups magically taste like the essence of whatever vegetable they're made of. He braises monkfish with saffron, grills salmon with sesame seeds and soy-ginger glaze and serves pan-roasted venison with cinnamon-and-port-poached pears. Prepare to pay dearly for these culinary inspirations, but then, the setting is quite inspiring in itself.

410 BOYD ECLECTIC 12/20

410 Boyd St., Downtown 90013
213-617-2491, *Lunch Mon.-Fri., Dinner Tues.-Fri., $*

At this extremely cool Little Tokyo spot, local suits lunch on twists on such classic dishes as a lobster club sandwich with lemon aïoli or crabcakes with chipotle remoulade. But in the evening, artists and neighbors from the nearby lofts settle down at the bar with a glass of Sierra Nevada (on tap), an appetizer of crispy polenta sticks with Gorgonzola mayo and perhaps a juicy hamburger on rosemary bread. You won't find the pre-theater crowd here, though it's perfectly good for a little pre-drama sustenance.

FRITTO MISTO ITALIAN 12/20

601 Colorado Ave., Santa Monica 90401
310-458-2829, *Lunch Mon.-Sat., Dinner nightly, $*

This friendly neighborhood trattoria serves simple, very reasonably priced Italian food—in generous portions. Mix-and-match your choice of sauce with your choice of pasta, then toss in anything from shrimp to sun-dried tomatoes to caramelized onions. For a restaurant with such bounteous portions, it's amusing that they offer to make any dish "lite," using less or no oil or cream. But as the menu warns: what you give up in calories you may also give up in flavor.

GADSBYS CALIFORNIAN 14/20

672 S. La Brea, Melrose-La Brea 90036
323-936-8471, *Lunch Mon.-Fri., Dinner Mon.-Sat.*, $$

One of this city's most artistic chefs, Robert Gadsby constructs stunning-to-behold dishes of unexpected combinations of ingredients, and the sum of the various parts is often dazzling. Consider Yukon gold potato ravioli with mushrooms and dried sage, asparagus-and-goat-cheese terrine with smoked salmon or such entrées as oatmeal-and-dill-crusted ahi tuna with white bean coriander pistou. If you want to stop at this small, modern restaurant for a bite at lunch, order from the café menu featuring soups, salads, pastas and a reasonably priced three-course tasting menu.

GARDEL'S ARGENTINE 12/20

7963 Melrose Ave., Melrose-La Brea 90046
323-655-0891, *Lunch Mon.-Fri., Dinner Mon.-Sat.*, $$

Gardel's serves large helpings of savory Argentine cuisine, which is heavy on red meat and abounds—we warn the faint of heart—with garlic. Start with the matambre (a flank steak rolled around a melange of pimientos, hard-cooked eggs and herbs), and ajo al horno (a head of baked garlic, the interior of which you squeeze onto thick slices of bread). To sample a variety, order the mixed grill of skirt steak, sweetbreads, sausages and short ribs.

THE GARDEN ROOM CALIFORNIAN 12/20

Westwood Marquis Hotel, 930 Hilgard Ave., Westwood 90024
310-208-8765, *Breakfast, Lunch & Dinner daily*, $$$

This bright room, with its latticework and green carpet is indeed very garden-like, and a pleasant setting for a light meal. Breakfast and lunch always draw a good crowd of locals and businesspeople; dinner is a more serious and ambitious affair, with choices from monkfish to steak.

GARDENS CALIFORNIAN 15/20 

Four Seasons Hotel, 300 S. Doheny Dr., Beverly Hills 90048
310-273-2222, *Breakfast, Lunch & Dinner daily, Brunch Sun.*, $$$$

An elegant retreat from a frenzied, cellular phone-filled world, Gardens is ideal for doing business and yet perfect for romance, thanks to its series of intimate dining rooms, flattering lighting and profusion of flowers. Chef Carrie Nahabedian prepares innovative California cuisine, such dishes as foie gras with spiced sweet potatoes and shallots, tartare of salmon, ahi tuna and caviar, black walnut-crusted veal rib-eye with cauliflower gratin, hot glazed-and-smoked salmon with lentils and caramelized onions and a sirloin steak with goat cheese-glazed potatoes. The "spa" dishes include snapper Mediterranean with fingerling potatoes, fennel and artichokes. The wine list specializes in Californian Cabernets and Merlots and has an extensive choice by the glass.

GARDENS ON GLENDON CALIFORNIAN 11/20

1139 Glendon Ave., Westwood 90024
310-824-1818, *Lunch & Dinner daily, $$*

Set in one of the oldest buildings in Westwood, this brick-walled restaurant features ficus trees arching to the skylights, terra-cotta floors and a pleasant, airy ambience. A pianist serenades dinner guests while eager young waiters make guacamole at a tableside cart. Dinners and cocktails are generous, service is good, and the menu offers many choices, from pizza and pastas for under $15, to sophisticated entrées for twice that price.

GAUCHO GRILL ARGENTINE 12/20

7980 Sunset Blvd., L.A. 90046
323-656-4152, *Lunch & Dinner daily, $*

Yet another Latin chain, this time representing Argentina. The chicken dishes are good, but as everyone knows, Argentines are best at steak and beef dishes. **Also in Brentwood (11754 San Vicente Blvd., 310-447-7898), Santa Monica (1251 Third St. Promenade, 310-394-4966) and the Beverly Center (101 N. La Cienega Blvd, 310-657-9104).**

GAYLORD INDIAN 13/20

50 N. La Cienega Blvd., W. Hollywood 90211
310-652-3838, *Lunch & Dinner nightly, Brunch Sun., $$*

The Gaylord chain goes back to 1941, when its first restaurant opened in New Delhi. The Los Angeles Gaylord restaurant is conservatively elegant, thick with mauves, pinks, grays and mirrored walls. The graciously served food includes all the usual Northern Indian choices—mulligatawny soup, fine tandoori dishes, reliable kebabs—good dishes that have, over the years, become old friends.

GENGHIS COHEN CHINESE 11/20

740 N. Fairfax Ave., Melrose-Fairfax 90046
323-653-0640, *Lunch Mon.-Fri., Dinner nightly, $*

Genghis Cohen cleaned up its act since it made the CBS "grunge" (unsanitary) list in November, 1997. The consciously hip have long gathered here for creative Chinese cooking in a sleek and contemporary setting where there's good recorded jazz and sometimes live entertainment. Crispy fried chicken wings come with every dinner, along with respectable hot-and-sour soup. The pan-fried dumplings are meaty and juicy, and the three-flavor mu shu, filled with shrimp, chicken and pork, is marvelous.

GEORGE PETRELLI'S STEAKHOUSE STEAKHOUSE 12/20

5615 S. Sepulveda Blvd., Culver City 90230
310-397-1438, *Lunch Mon.-Sat., Dinner nightly, $*

They've been doing what they do since 1931: serving good, generously portioned steaks at very low prices. It looks like the quintessential California roadhouse, with a big bar, country-western entertainment, and a kitchen that churns out hundreds of meals a day. Petrelli's serves hand-cut steakhouse staples: New York steak, filet mignon, T-bone steak, roasted chicken and fried shrimp. You can also order such golden oldies as breaded veal cutlets; kids can order from a big children's menu.

GEOFFREY'S CALIFORNIAN 14/20

27400 PCH, Malibu 90265
310-457-1519, *Lunch & Dinner daily, Brunch Sun., $$$*

Perched on a hillside, Geoffrey's is the restaurant with the most spectacular view of the curving Southern California coastline, and its flower-filled patio is a sublime spot for a candlelight dinner or Sunday brunch. So don't even consider driving out here without a reservation. We've enjoyed the eggs with caviar for brunch. For dinner, we recommend the crab-and-roasted-corn chowder or the artichoke tart with sun-dried tomatoes, the seafood pasta, the lamb chops stuffed with feta cheese, sun-dried tomatoes and mint, and the lobster tart with black truffles. Check out which of Geoffrey's friends scribbled the pictures on the inner walls (yes, that's "Robert" as in De Niro, "Whoopie" as in Goldberg and "John" as in Travolta.)

GEORGIA SOUTHERN 12/20

7250 Melrose Ave., Melrose-La Brea 90046
323-933-8420, *Dinner nightly, $$*

The taste here may be Southern, but Georgia's heart is in hip Hollywood. Throughout, the liberal use of mahogany—the floors, the bar, and the shutters on the French doors that open onto a palm-filled patio—lends the restaurant warmth. These are elegant digs indeed for a restaurant serving such down-home Southern favorites as smothered pork chops and fried chicken. We recommend the crayfish-and-crabmeat strudel, the crabcakes, the broiled salmon with honey-mustard glaze and fried green tomatoes and the New York steak with bourbon-peppercorn sauce. Save room for the warm peach cobbler.

THE GETTY CENTER RESTAURANT CALIFORNIAN 12/20

The Getty Center, 1200 Getty Cen. Dr., Brentwood 90049
310-440-7300, *Lunch Tues.-Sun., Dinner Thurs.-Fri., $$$*

The Getty Center is L.A.'s hottest new attraction, which means that getting a reservation in its stunningly modern, white-on-white restaurant is nearly impossible. But if you're visiting the Getty, try to book a table as a walk-in—it's worth a shot. What you'll get for your (top) dollar are table-settings worthy of a museum, beautiful-to-behold contemporary cuisine (sea scallops with caponata; chicken with butternut squash-bread pudding) that isn't always as good as it looks. The view, however, is the most breathtaking in L.A,—especially at sunset.

GILLILAND'S — CALIFORNIAN/IRISH — 13/20 

2424 Main St., Santa Monica 90405
310-392-3901, *Lunch Mon.-Fri., Dinner nightly, Brunch Sun., $$*

California/Irish cuisine in a homey, contemporary setting. Steadfast dishes on Gerri Gilliland's ever-changing menu include the zesty cheese-and-onion tart, Irish potato cakes with gravlax and a traditional Irish beef stew served with champ (a chopped potato-and-onion concoction). Just to keep you on your toes, Gilliland throws in such exotic dishes as tandoori chicken with pumpkin chutney, Moroccan vegetable couscous and black linguini with sea scallops. Watch out for those Irish cocktails.

GINZA SUSHI-KO — SUSHI — 15/20 

218 N. Rodeo Dr., Beverly Hills 90210
310-247-8939, *Lunch Tues.-Sat., Dinner Tues.-Sat., $$$$*

With neighbors like Tiffany, Vuitton and other equally-posh purveyors of luxe, Ginza Sushi-Ko is one of L.A.'s most exclusive restaurants. It is also the most expensive. Like restaurants in Tokyo, privacy is Ginza Sushi-Ko's cachet and that, plus the perfection of the sushi, is what attracts both Madonna and Japanese executives alike. If you somehow manage to get in, a meal will cost you a samurai's ransom. The setting is aesthetically pure: just a polished wood sushi counter and a few tatami rooms. Since there's no menu, it is hard to tell exactly what is being served, but every slice of fish—shipped in daily from Tokyo—every dot of roe, every grain of rice is presented as artfully as can be.

GIOVANNI'S TRATTORIA — ITALIAN — 12/20

10026 Venice Blvd., Culver City 90232
310-839-1757, *Lunch Mon.-Fri., Dinner Mon.-Sat., $*

If the Jersey restaurant featured in the movie The Big Night had a Culver City counterpart, this would be it. Start with the bruschetta or the grilled eggplant with ricotta cheese, pine nuts, herbs and tomatoes, followed by such pastas as the spicy arrabbiata with garlic or the rigatoni with savory chicken-and-turkey meat sauce. The pizzas and calzones are scrumptious, too.

GIRASOLE — ITALIAN — 13/20 

2251/2 N. Larchmont Blvd., Hancock Park 90004
323-464-6978, *Lunch Tues.-Sat., Dinner Wed.-Sat., $*

We're charmed by this modest Larchmont Village trattoria that refuses to adopt a predictable formula-driven menu. There's no liquor license, but you won't be charged a corkage fee for wine purchased at the nearby Larchmont Wine & Cheese Shop. Friendly servers deliver wonderful non-dairy puréed soups, pumpkin ravioli, farfalle with smoked salmon, turkey Marsala, gnocchi and a masterful chocolate tart. The quality and value will bring you back for more, to the chagrin of neighborhood patrons who want to keep this their own little secret.

GLADSTONE'S 4 FISH MALIBU SEAFOOD 11/20

17300 W. Pacific Coast Hwy., Pacific Palisades 90272
310-GL4-FISH, *Breakfast, Lunch & Dinner daily, $$*

Bring out-of-towners here to show off the sweeping coastline view. Expect a long wait in sunny weather, potent beach-party drinks and cheerful service. The menu is enormous and so are the portions of fresh fish, crab and lobster. Stick with the basics and you'll be okay: chowder, salads and mesquite-grilled seafood. The foot-high chocolate cake is great for later cocktail-party conversation but usually a bit dry (a huge scoop of vanilla ice cream helps.) Even if you don't eat at Gladstone's, you can relax on the outdoor deck, which allows free public access.

GRANITA CALIFORNIAN 14/20 

23725 W. Malibu Rd., Malibu 90265
310-456-0488, *Dinner nightly, Brunch Sat.-Sun., $$$$*

Wolfgang Puck's Spago-by-the-Sea is where celebs come to dine when they're weekending at their Malibu beach houses. Barbara Lazaroff's exuberant undersea design contributes to the fun. Puck fans will feel right at home with the open kitchen, wood-burning oven and a menu of designer pizzas and pastas along with such sophisticated fare as a sautéed foie gras "sandwich" with spiced Asian pears, roasted monkfish with eggplant, fava beans and roasted garlic, lavender-honey-glazed lamb, and quail with raviolini, figs, glazed beets and bufala ricotta.

THE GRILL ON THE ALLEY AMERICAN 14/20 

9560 Dayton Way, Beverly Hills 90210
310-276-0615, *Lunch Mon.-Sat., Dinner nightly, $$$*

Traditional American bar-and-grill in ambience and cuisine—and Beverly Hills in price—the Grill features high-backed wooden booths, professional and efficient service, and a menu that features all the old-fashioned favorites. Start with an excellent Caesar salad, and you can always rely on the New York or porterhouse steaks with french-fried potatoes and crispy fried onions. On Sundays, the special roast prime rib rivals that at Lawry's. For dessert, choose the brownie sundae over the not-quite-baked apple pie. This is the place that spawned the Daily Grill chain.

HAL'S BAR & GRILL NEW AMERICAN 14/20 

1349 Abbot Kinney Blvd., Venice 90291
310-396-3105, *Lunch Mon.-Fri., Dinner nightly, Brunch Sat.-Sun., $$*

A friendly neighborhood hangout where neighbors like Chuck Arnoldi and Laddie Dill hang their art on the walls. The weekly-changing menu includes such imaginative dishes as risotto with smoked scallops, shrimp, calamari, sun-dried tomatoes, garlic and tarragon, or a salad of roasted guinea hen, mesclun, Gorgonzola cheese, pistachios and seckle pears. We recommend the grilled T-bone steak, the grilled chicken with mustard-tarragon sauce and the hamburger—especially when served with Hal's extra-crispy french fries. On weekends, a basket of biscuits and muffins is served with the leisurely brunch. If you're having a private party, check out Hal's handsome private dining room.

HAROLD & BELLE'S SOUL FOOD 14/20

2920 W. Jefferson Blvd., South-Central L.A. 90018
323-735-9023, *Lunch & Dinner daily, $$*

At Harold & Belle's, the quality of the soul food is as impressive as the gargantuan quantities. Therefore, this place is always full. A heaping plate of Louisiana-style hot links sparkles with fire, thanks to a four-alarm dipping sauce. There's much to choose from: po-boy sandwiches, fried catfish, soft-shell crabs, breaded Louisiana oysters, shrimp Creole and plentiful down-home desserts.

HAVANA ON SUNSET CUBAN 12/20

5825 Sunset Blvd., Hollywood 90028
323-464-1800, *Lunch Mon.-Sat., Dinner nightly, $*

A

This Hollywood establishment is one of the better looking Cuban eateries in town, with an Old Havana supper-club ambience and cozy tables set amidst leafy banana trees and murals evoking the surf at famed Varaderó Beach. Menu highlights include empanadas, bacalao (salt cod) fritters, grilled snapper, chicken marinated in citrus, ropa vieja and authentic Cuban sandwiches served with crispy plantain chips. Desserts include a winning flan.

HOLLYWOOD CANTEEN CONTINENTAL/SUSHI 12/20

1006 Seward St., Hollywood 90038
323-465-0961, *Lunch Mon.-Fri., Dinner Mon.-Sat., $*

It's still hip with a clubby back room and some modern twists on the bar-and-grill basics, plus there's sushi. This is one cool place to gather with friends in one of the roomy burgundy booths. The building is one of those little Hollywood classic stucco jobs from the '30s, but the '90s are evident in the kitchen's use of organic foodstuffs and the sushi is very fresh. We're also fond of the thick corn chowder, the rack of lamb with Cabernet sauce over mashed potatoes, chicken Canteen-style with Dijon mustard and the cioppino. For dessert, try the homemade panacotta, a white gelatin-like flan with raspberry sauce.

HORNBLOWER YACHT CRUISES CALIFORNIAN 12/20

13755 Fiji Way, Marina del Rey 90292
310-301-9900, *Dinner Fri. & Sat., Brunch Sun., $$$*

A

Experience a charming departure from the ordinary and dine on a yacht, while it cruises around the world's largest man-made marina—it's perfect for a special-occasion celebration. Sip cocktails on deck, then enjoy such appetizers as the fresh prawn cocktail or a tangy pasta. The set menus change regularly, but may include filet mignon and salmon with garlic potatoes, and the service is impeccable. Order ahead for chilled Champagne, balloons, a special cake or a window table. Reservations are a must. You can bet that many a marriage proposal has been offered while dining aboard one of Hornblower's yachts.

THE HOTEL BEL AIR DINING ROOM CALIFORNIAN 15/20 

Hotel Bel-Air, 701 Stone Canyon Rd., Bel Air 90077
310-472-1211, *Breakfast, Lunch & Dinner daily,* **$$$$**

Located in the city's most luxurious hotel, the Hotel Bel-Air Dining Room is an elegant, flower-filled room in which the service is formal and usually attentive, allowing for serene, pampered dining. Executive Chef Gary Clauson's Californian-French cuisine is sometimes a bit fussy but often spectacular. A dinner here often begins with a sculptured rabbit holding caviar and smoked salmon canapés, and a demitasse of lobster bisque. Among the best entrées are the luscious mustard-crusted filet of salmon with large grain couscous, filet of beef on a Stilton cheese potato cake with port wine sauce and fried leeks and duck breast with rhubarb tart and a port-sun-dried cherry sauce. On sunny days, lunch on the bougainvillea-bowered patio is sublime.

HUGO'S ITALIAN 13/20 

8401 Santa Monica Blvd., W. Hollywood 90069
323-654-4088, *Breakfast & Lunch daily,* **$$**

Hugo's looks like a chic butcher shop where Hollywood-heavyweights hang out— especially over breakfast: eggs scrambled with prosciutto, bacon and scallions; and Pasta Mama, a hearty jumble of fresh pasta and Parmesan-laden scrambled eggs. The lunch menu is composed of exotic and traditional antipasti, salads, pastas and veal dishes.

HU'S SZECHWAN RESTAURANT CHINESE 13/20

10450 National Blvd., W. L.A. 90034
310-837-0252, *Lunch Mon.-Sat., Dinner nightly,* **$**

There's almost always a wait for a table at Hu's, because the food has made a name for itself: fiery Szechuan dumplings, tender kung pao chicken, pungent shrimp with a Szechuan tomato sauce, savory dried-fried string beans with ground pork and a Mandarin chicken salad that is a perfect foil to all the spicy dishes. How much chili is used depends on the chef's whim; don't be shy to ask for more. Bottom line: Hu's serves the best Chinese food in Palms.

I CUGINI ITALIAN 12/20

1501 Ocean Ave., Santa Monica 90401
310-451-4595, *Lunch & Dinner daily,* **$$**

Grab a patio table if you can—you'll have a view of the ocean. The interior is festive, with murals on the walls and many colorful Tuscan touches. There is good fritto misto (deep-fried seafood), but we're happiest with their thin, crisp-crusted pizzas—like the one with marinated tuna and anchovies—and the pastas.

IL CIELO — ITALIAN — 12/20

9018 Burton Way, Beverly Hills 90211
310-276-9990, *Lunch & Dinner Mon.-Sat.,* $$$

Il Cielo means "the sky," and that is exactly what you see when you look heavenward from the lovely brick patio, where water trickles from the mouth of a stone lion, plants run riot and lovers draw close. While dining al fresco, or before the fireplace in the cozy interior of the Tuscan-style cottage, try the carpaccio with bits of white truffle, smoked scamorza cheese with baked eggplant, porcini risotto, lobster grilled with garlic and lemon or any preparation of veal. Call to make sure they're open, for this is a coveted site for weddings and private parties.

IL FORNAIO — ITALIAN — 12/20

301 N. Beverly Dr., Beverly Hills 90210
310-550-8330, *Breakfast, Lunch & Dinner daily,* $

Beverly Hills loves this sunny Italian trattoria where newspapers are available at the espresso bar, plump chickens turn on the rotisserie, and fresh bread is baked in the back twice daily. Enjoy the focaccia and breadsticks, and stick with the Italian basics: salads, pastas, and yes, the rotisserie-roasted chicken. **Among the many other locations, the new Il Fornaio in Santa Monica (1551 Ocean Ave., 310-451-7800) offers an ocean view from the patio.**

IL FORNO — ITALIAN — 12/20

2901 Ocean Park Blvd., Santa Monica 90405
310-450-1241, *Lunch Mon.-Fri., Dinner Mon.-Sat.,* $$

This friendly neighborhood trattoria packs them in because it offers good regional Italian cooking at reasonable prices. Start with arancini di riso, little deep-fried porcini-and-cheese-filled rice croquettes, or share a crisp-crusted rustica pizza with sun-dried tomatoes, smoked cheese, basil and olive oil. In addition to the usual Italian favorites, the menu features such spa dishes as fettuccine with yogurt, ricotta cheese and chicken consommé, steamed seafood bouillabaisse and low-fat-cheese pizza.

IL GRANO — ITALIAN — 13/20

11363 Santa Monica Blvd., W.L.A. 90025
310-477-7886, *Lunch, Mon.-Fri., Dinner nightly,* $$

This clean-lined, sparsely decorated restaurant with a handsome granite bar serves contemporary Italian cuisine. Among our favorite dishes: grilled halibut, tomato consommé with baby vegetables, grilled escolar on a thick slice of Italian bread with tomatoes and basil, and pork chops with cherry pepper sauce and mashed potatoes. Go all out with the Monte Vesuvio dessert, a volcano of raspberry and chocolate mousse with burning rum dripping down it.

IL MORO ITALIAN 13/20 

11400 W. Olympic Blvd., W.L.A. 90064
310-575-3530, *Lunch Mon.-Fri., Dinner nightly, $$*

A terrific Italian restaurant in a part of town that desperately needed one. In addition to the large, high-ceilinged dining room with its open kitchen, there's a lovely outdoor garden. We favor the tuna carpaccio, the seafood mousse-stuffed calamari, any of the crisp-crusted pizzas and such pastas as the tortelloni stuffed with lobster and crab in a saffron sauce and the fettuccine sautéed with ragout of wild pheasant. The wine list offers inexpensive to moderately priced Californian and Italian wines.

IL NIDO ITALIAN 12/20

3009 Main St., Santa Monica 90405
310-399-1843, *Dinner nightly, $$*

Santa Monica's Main Street is home to several of L.A.'s best eateries, such as Röckenwagner and Chinois. Il Nido represents the less-celebrated establishments that further enhance this street's appeal as a dining destination. The short menu includes excellent beef carpaccio, rigatoni in Gorgonzola sauce and simple Mediterranean-style salmon. The desserts are noteworthy, including a marvelous chocolate tart. Candlelight makes this narrow, sparsely decorated dining room almost romantic.

IL PASTAIO ITALIAN 14/20

400 North Canon Dr., Beverly Hills 90210
310-205-5444, *Lunch & Dinner Mon.-Sat., $$*

A

Reasonably priced antipasti, pasta and dolci—everything but the main course—are the draw at Celestino Drago's casual but handsome spin-off of Drago, the star chef's superb Italian restaurant in Santa Monica. Drago's carpaccio—beef, venison, and smoked swordfish—are luscious; Sicilian specialties like arancini (fried rice croquettes oozing beef and cheese) are practically habit-forming. Drago's fresh pastas alone make a trip here worthwhile: penne with swordfish and fennel seed; risotto with wild mushrooms and Mascarpone cheese and pappardelle with duck ragout. Drago's tiramisu is tops.

IL SOLE ITALIAN 12/20

8741 Sunset Blvd., W. Hollywood 90069
310-657-1182, *Lunch Mon.-Sat., Dinner nightly, $$*

Just down the street from the Sunset Plaza outdoor-café madness, Il Sole delivers authentic Northern Italian food in a calm and pretty, antique- and modern art-filled setting. The service can be leisurely, but we recommend any of the pastas and risottos, and we like the sidewalk terrace.

INDOCHINE VIETNAMESE 13/20 

8225 Beverly Blvd., L.A. 90048
323-655-4777, *Dinner nightly, $$*

The Hollywood branch of the New York original attracts the same good-looking model-heavy crowd, with the occasional young celeb thrown in. Against a sexy backdrop of banana-leaf murals, green-leather banquettes and booths framed in bamboo wainscoting, try delicate steamed Vietnamese ravioli and spring rolls, crispy salmon with lemon grass and braised red cabbage, grilled prawns wrapped in lettuce leaves and striped bass with coconut milk steamed in a banana leaf. Add an order of sticky rice and you've still got a healthy and relatively low-cal meal. Perfect if you're into high-fashion black.

INTERMEZZO ITALIAN 12/20

6919 Melrose Ave., La Brea-Melrose 90038
323-937-2875, *Lunch Tues.-Fri., Dinner Tues.-Sat., $*

Dine at the bar which faces the open kitchen, watching the cooks and perusing the movie reviews that patrons add to a large board on the wall. You can also dine on the tree-shaded patio. In either case, you'll enjoy the casual ambience here, and the reasonably priced fare that runs from sandwiches, quiches, pizzas and salads to such pastas as chicken ravioli with cilantro and hazelnuts, and linguine with seafood. There are plenty of reasonably priced French and Californian wines on their well-chosen list.

THE IVY AMERICAN 14/20 

113 N. Robertson Blvd., W. Hollywood 90048
310-274-8303, *Lunch & Dinner daily, Brunch Sun., $$$*

One of L.A.'s most intense power-meal boîtes, as well as one of its prettiest. The utterly charming patio is just one of the many design elements created by co-owner/designer Lynn von Kersting. Roses bloom everywhere, the chintz upholstery is lovely and the plates are hand-painted. From the kitchen comeslarge portions of California-ized Americana—Caesar salad, crabcakes, savory meatloaf, succulent Cajun prime rib, black-pepper shrimp, Louisiana soft-shell crab, and even a bang-up burger. Co-owner Richard Irving started out as a pâtissier and his desserts are divine, from the chocolate-chip cookies to the tarte tatin. The only problem here is the attitude.

THE IVY AT THE SHORE AMERICAN 13/20 

1541 Ocean Ave., Santa Monica 90405
310-393-3113, *Lunch & Dinner daily, Brunch Sun., $$$*

Ivy at the Shore has a decor resembling a sophisticated beach shack, and it's packed to the bamboo rafters every night. Owners Lynn von Kersting and Richard Irving haven't strayed too far from the original Ivy's menu: crabcakes, Cajun pizza, Louisiana soft-shell crabs and meatloaf are all just fine, as are sides of crackling Maui-onion rings and crispy french fries. The tropical drinks pack a punch; the desserts are luscious. Enjoy Sunday brunch on the glassed-in patio, with a view of the ocean.

J.R. SEAFOOD RESTAURANT CHINESE 13/20

11901 Santa Monica Blvd., W.L.A. 90025
310-268-2563, *Lunch & Dinner daily, $*

One of the first big Monterey Park-style restaurants to open on the Westside, J.R. has a plain decor, but its Cantonese seafood specialties are tops. In the gurgling tanks, choose from clams, jumbo shrimp, crabs, lobsters and a variety of seawater and freshwater fish, all priced by the pound. (You may not know the damage until the bill is presented.) The shrimp with spicy salt is so irresistible that only the cruelest of cardiologists would forbid it. For the adventurous, there's jelly fish with or without octopus. **Also in Santa Monica (102 Santa Monica Pl., 310-260-8855).**

JAKE & ANNIE'S AMERICAN 12/20

2700 Main St., Santa Monica 90405
310-452-1734, *Lunch Mon.-Fri., Dinner nightly, Brunch Sat.-Sun., $*

Set in a Victorian building and decorated with pop-neon signs and modern art, this Main Street hangout could just as easily be in San Francisco as Santa Monica. We like the colorful bar scene, the piano music in the evenings and the eclectic menu that ranges widely in selection and price. This is a good place for crabcakes and a salad, penne with chicken and grilled eggplant or such down-home American specialties as fried chicken with black-eyed peas and mashed potatoes. As at chef-owner Gerri Gilliland's other restaurants, you get your money's-worth.

JAMES' BEACH NEW AMERICAN 13/20

60 N. Venice Blvd., Venice 90191
310-823-5396, *Lunch Wed.-Fri., Dinner nightly, Brunch Sat. & Sun., $$*

What was once the terminally hip West Beach Cafe has been turned into a friendly and casual neighborhood spot, complete with a pool table in the cottage out back. You can get everything from a "beach club" sandwich (salmon, pancetta, lettuce, tomato and avocado) to fresh sand dabs to a grilled Iowa pork chop with candied-sweet potatoes and collard greens. For Sunday brunch, try the French toast made with thick sourdough bread.

JIMMY'S CALIFORNIAN/FRENCH 12/20

201 S. Moreno Dr., Beverly Hills 90212
310-552-2394, *Lunch Mon.-Fri., Dinner Mon.-Sat., $$$*

Since 1978, Jimmy's has been a stage for the drama (or is it the comedy?) of Beverly Hills high society. The sumptuous decor is touched with a warm bit of kitsch and the bar, with its live music, is busy until late. Whether seated in the formal dining room or the solarium, choose from a broad menu or ask the chef to prepare something plain and simple. We recommend the warm goat cheese salad, the smoked Irish salmon and the crabcakes. Dinner entrées include everything from filet of John Dory with portobello mushrooms to a traditional beef en croûte with truffle sauce. Jimmy Murphy's son, Sean, now manages the restaurant, but Jimmy is often on hand to meet-and-greet.

JIRAFFE — CALIFORNIAN — 16/20 

502 Santa Monica Blvd., Santa Monica 90401
310-917-6671, *Lunch Tues.-Fri., Dinner nightly, $$*

Childhood friends and a chef team since 1991, Josiah Citrin and Raphael Lunetta dazzle guests in this charming restaurant they opened in 1996. With a balcony dining area, ultra-high ceilings and lots of wood, it's a great looking—but high-decibel—spot and service can be slow. Still, we return to sample dishes far more complex than they appear, that astound with wonderful and unexpected tastes. On the oft-changing menu, we've enjoyed sea-scallop carpaccio, lobster soup with roasted eggplant, orzo and basil purée, spaghetti with roasted cauliflower and portobello mushrooms, rabbit with polenta gnocchi and oven-dried tomatoes, coriander-crusted tuna and a veal chop with roasted-and-glazed root vegetables. Ask the chef to compose a tasting menu of a half dozen mini-courses, paired with wines from the well-chosen wine list.

JITLADA — THAI — 13/20 

5233 W. Sunset Blvd., Hollywood 90027
323-667-9809, *Lunch & Dinner Tues.-Sun., $*

Expect dishes spicy enough to set your mouth blazing. This cozy little restaurant in a tacky Hollywood mini-mall, serves such starters as peppery barbecued chicken, deep-fried fresh squid, and minced pork marinated in lemon juice, ginger and shallots. Soups are excellent, particularly the poh-taek, a hot-and-sour broth loaded with seafood. Outstanding dishes include beef tamarind, fried catfish with green curry and giant shrimp served in the shell.

JOE'S — CALIFORNIAN — 15/20 

1023 Abbot Kinney Blvd., Venice 90291
310-399-5811, *Lunch Tues.-Fri., Dinner Tues.-Sun., Brunch Sat.-Sun., $$*

This small, cramped but stunning ultra-modern space packs them in. (Many regulars swear Joe's has the best food in town.) Owner/chef Joe Miller's innovative cuisine is reasonably priced for its level of sophistication. Choose from among such appetizers as the pistachio-crusted goat cheese, roasted pear and red leaf-and-endive salad, the grilled tuna and seared foie gras, or the warm onion, walnut and chanterelle mushroom tart. Entrées range from the pan-Asian—spice-crusted ono with spicy eggplant and lemon grass broth—to the down-home—crispy chicken with butternut squash purée, glazed nuts and onions. If you like roast beef, try Joe's version served with sublime mashed potatoes, portobello mushrooms and spinach.

JOSS — CHINESE — 14/20 

9255 Sunset Blvd., W. Hollywood 90069
310-276-1886, *Lunch Mon.-Fri., Dinner nightly, $$*

Cecile Tang Shu Shuen, who runs this serene, minimalist restaurant, has distilled Chinese cuisine down to its essence. The sophisticated menu offers a wide selection of dim sum—skillet-toasted, steamed or crisp—crispy Peking duck, lusty

Mongolian lamb and noodles, plus a myriad of sophisticated dishes you won't find in your everyday Chinese restaurant. Consider the delicate five-mushroom napoleon, the savory duck dumplings or chicken-and-fig soup, the apricot spare ribs or such entrées as Riesling-marinated ostrich medallions and clay pot-roasted free-range venison with glazed ginger. The reasonably priced wine list is well suited to match these distinguished specialties.

JOZU PAN-ASIAN 16/20 

8360 Melrose Ave., W. Hollywood 90048
323-655-5600, *Lunch Tues.-Fri., Dinner Mon.-Sat., $$*

The joint effort of owner Andy Nakano and chef Suzanne Tracht, formerly of Campanile, Jozu is a success in both a design and culinary sense. Nakano warmed up a rather stark space with carpeting, bamboo window dressings and attractive light fixtures. Tracht's dishes are attractive, exotic and often inspired. We've enjoyed the crisp marinated quail with tangerine sauce, the sweetbreads with tamarind, the Thai flat noodles and mushrooms, the roasted sea bass with ponzu and cabbage salad and the grilled chicken with guava sauce, sweet-onion salad and jasmine rice. Guests are served a chilled glass of sake when they're seated, and the wine list features moderately priced bottles from off-the-beaten-track vintners, as well as many choices by the glass. Our one complaint: only two tables for two.

KACHINA GRILL SOUTHWESTERN 12/20

Wells Fargo Center, 330 S. Hope St., Downtown 90071
213-625-0956, *Lunch Mon.-Fri., Dinner Mon.-Sat., $$*

This rambling, noisy place is mobbed at lunch, convivial at happy hour and dead on weekends, the common curse of downtown restaurants. You can stick with such traditional Mexican dishes as soft tacos, enchiladas and fajitas, or sample innovative specialties including citrus-and-chipotle-marinated chicken, the grilled salmon-and-goat-cheese burrito or the gulf shrimp-stuffed green corn tamale. We can't seem to get enough of the sweet corn pudding. At lunchtime, we like to eat outside on the patio, surrounded by the granite-and-glass towers of downtown.

KASS BAH CALIFORNIAN 13/20 

9010 Melrose Ave., W. Hollywood 90069
310-274-7664, *Lunch Mon.-Fri., Dinner Mon.-Sat., $$*

The casual Café Figaro that occupied this converted cottage for years, is no more. In its place, Kass Bah's white-walled and dark wood-paneled interior is far more elegant. For starters we like the baby green salad with Montrachet cheese and piquant balsamic reduction, the ahi tuna tartare with avocado and the pan-fried scallop salad. There are pizzas and pastas, and such entrées as chicken Dijon, filet mignon with baby artichokes and seared Chilean sea bass in a sesame crust. The intimate Kass Bah bar is rapidly becoming a hot gathering spot. A mambo band plays on Monday nights.

KATE MANTILINI AMERICAN 12/20

9101 Wilshire Blvd., Beverly Hills 90210
310-278-3699, *Breakfast, Lunch & Dinner daily, Brunch Sun.*, $$

Serving until 3 a.m. on weekends, this high-tech steakhouse offers a menu of dressed-up truck-stop food, circa 1947. In the dramatically stark interior, you'll pay dearly for simple food that is decent without being brilliant: juicy rotisserie chicken, baked potatoes with all the trimmings or even such late-breakfast (make that early breakfast) specials as the calves' brains omelet. You can tell this is an industry hangout: there are over a dozen "healthy alternative" dishes, plus a "Wildly Wonderful Cannes Film Festival Salad" featuring smoked salmon, organic greens and a fire-grilled sourdough spear slathered with duck pâté.

KATSU JAPANESE 14/20 

1972 Hillhurst Ave., Los Feliz 90027
323-665-5703, *Lunch Mon.-Fri., Dinner Mon.- Sat.*, $$

The austere, art gallery-like Katsu was once way ahead of its time, though the world of L.A. sushi restaurants has done a lot to catch up. Katsu's sushi is utterly above reproach: perfect slices of richly flavored yellowtail (hamachi), silky sea bass (shiromi), blood-dark tuna (both maguro and the highly prized fat-marbled toro), exquisitely oily mackerel (saba), crunchy jumbo clam (mirugai) and sea urchin (uni) that's like a mouthful of the sea itself.

KATSU 3RD JAPANESE/SUSHI 13/20 

8636 W. Third St., W. Hollywood 90048
310-273-3605, *Lunch Mon.-Fri., Dinner Mon.-Sat.*, $$

Don't look for the name on the door. All there is to denote that this is a restaurant is a carved wooden fish. Open since 1990, this stark, windowless spin-off of Katsu is where Katsu Michite, the owner of both restaurants, spends most of his time these days, preparing some tempura and teriyaki dishes but mostly sashimi and sushi. Ask for omakase, the chef's choice.

KNOLL'S BLACK FOREST INN GERMAN 11/20

2454 Wilshire Blvd., Santa Monica 90403
310-395-2212, *Lunch Tues.-Fri., Dinner Tues.-Sun.*, $$

The enduring popularity of Knoll's Black Forest Inn proves that Angelenos are not only interested in arugula salads and pizzas, but also in the hardy richness of German food. The front of the restaurant mimics a tavern in the Black Forest, with beer steins and waiters and waitresses in native costume. Best bets among the authentic dishes: bratwurst, knockwurst and schnitzels, particularly when paired with one of the good German Reislings, and the hazelnut torte or chocolate truffle cake for dessert.

KOUTOUBIA — MOROCCAN — 12/20

2116 Westwood Blvd., W.L.A. 90025
310-475-0729, *Dinner Tues.-Sun., $$*

Lounge on one of the soft-cushioned seats arranged around circular brass tables. The waiter prepares you for the first course by pouring warm water over your hands, since these are what you will be eating with. The walls, draped with fabric to imitate a Moroccan tent, create an effect of mystery. When the kitchen is on target, the best dishes are the b'stilla, a light, flaky pie filled with chicken and almonds and topped with powdered sugar, the spicy merguez sausage with couscous, the roast chicken with preserved lemons and olives and the lamb tagine. Koutoubia will cater a Moroccan feast in your own home—complete with Moroccan tent.

LA BRUSCHETTA — ITALIAN — 13/20

1621 Westwood Blvd., W.L.A. 90024
310-477-1052, *Lunch Mon.-Fri., Dinner Mon.-Sat., $$*

In business since 1984, La Bruschetta has won a loyal neighborhood following. The simple yet handsome dining room can be romantic, yet meets the demands of a business meeting or a family affair. The kitchen prepares a wide range of intriguing pasta dishes—some hearty, some delicate, most delicious. Expect classic Northern Italian entrées, most for under $20, from veal scaloppine to osso buco. The staff is attentive, the wine list impressive.

LA CACHETTE — FRENCH/CALIFORNIAN — 14/20

10506 Santa Monica Blvd., Century City 90025
310-470-4992, *Lunch Mon.-Fri., Dinner nightly, $$*

Chef Jean-François Meteigner gets better and better. At his charming eatery, he prepares French dishes that reflect a light, California influence. He perfumes the romaine-endive-walnut-roquefort-potato salad with truffle vinaigrette, and wraps foie gras in cabbage then glazes it with dried cranberry sauce. Foie gras shows up again in the ravioli that accompany the succulent farm-raised venison with Cabernet sauce and blueberries. We're fans of Meteigner's sautéed squab served with tiny puffs of potato and his renditions of such classics as braised lamb shank and cassoulet. Meteigner's tarte tatin wins prizes—deservedly.

LA CABANA — MEXICAN — 12/20

738 Rose Ave., Venice 90291
310-392-6161, *Breakfast, Lunch & Dinner daily, Brunch Sun., $*

Don't be put off by La Cabana's kitschy Mexican decor, because the food is quite wonderful. Start with a quesadilla oozing cheddar cheese and potatoes sautéed with fresh tomatoes, red onion and a piquant chili pasilla. Follow with the delicious shrimp in chipotle sauce, the burritos, or the soft, plump and savory fish tacos. The margaritas are top-notch, as are the handmade tortillas and the flan.

LA LUNA RISTORANTE ITALIAN 13/20 

113 N. Larchmont Blvd., Larchmont Village 90004
323-962-2130, *Lunch Mon.-Sat., Dinner nightly, $$*

The walls of this stylish neighborhood trattoria are adorned with Italian Renaissance reproductions, its tables illuminated by candles. The wooden chairs, however, are not conducive to lingering too long over a meal. Refreshing appetizers include the caprese salad and the carpaccio duet of sea bass and salmon. The pastas can be intriguing, such as chitarrina (a kind of spaghetti) loaded with wild mushrooms in a light sauce, and rigatoni with Mascarpone cheese, spinach and prosciutto. Entrées include hearty dishes like bacon-wrapped filet of beef sautéed in port wine. **In Santa Monica, La Luna Mare (119 Broadway, 310-656-2424), focuses on seafood dishes.**

LA PARRILLA MEXICAN 13/20 

2126 Caesar Chavez Ave., E.L.A. 90033
323-262-3434, *Breakfast, Lunch & Dinner daily, $*

Little English is spoken at this authentic Mexican restaurant decorated with earthenware bowls and Mexican tiles, in the heart of the barrio. The tortillas are handmade, and the fresh salsa is thick with crisp onions and cilantro. Mexican seafood is outstanding here: a massive, deep-fried red snapper topped with a light tomato-and-olive sauce, wonderful camarones al mojo de ajo and a seafood parrillada for two. Pozole and tamales are made fresh on weekends. Occasional mariachis add to the fun. **Also in Silverlake (3129 W. Sunset Blvd., 323-661-8055).**

LA SERENATA MEXICAN 14/20 

10924 W. Pico Blvd., W.L.A. 90064
310-441-9667, *Lunch & Dinner daily, $*

This friendly offshoot of La Serenata de Garibaldi serves the same terrific fresh mahi mahi tacos, gorditas bursting with shrimp and quesadillas stuffed with mushrooms, poblano peppers and cheese. Fresh tortillas are wrapped around shredded beef with a dash of salsa, or are served as a side to any of the stellar Mexican seafood dishes. You can eat for cheap here, but for $19.95 you can get juicy giant Mexican shrimp with luscious mojo de ajo sauce—one of the best shrimp dishes in town. They don't take reservations but everyone waits—it's worth it. **Opening soon in Santa Monica.**

LA SERENATA DE GARIBALDI MEXICAN 14/20 

1842 E. First St., East L.A. 90033
323-265-2887, *Lunch & Dinner Tues.-Sun., Brunch Sun., $*

Until it opened sister restaurants on the Westside (see above), this fun, unpretentious Mexican restaurant, entered by a back passageway filled with wicker baskets spilling fresh produce, was the place to go for the best fish tacos in town. At lunch, diners opt for gorditas, miniature pitas stuffed with chicken, pork or shrimp. Dinner features many Mexican seafood choices, made with the likes of mahi mahi, sea bass and shrimp. Fresh soups are paired with rice and black or pinto beans.

L'ARANCINO ITALIAN 16/20

8908 Beverly Blvd., W. Hollywood 90048
310-858-5777, *Lunch Mon.-Fri., Dinner nightly, $$$*

Celestino Drago's latest restaurant, a cozy skylit spot with a back patio that features dishes from Drago's native Sicily (arancini are luscious deep-fried rice croquettes that ooze melted cheese when you take a bite). We're crazy about the delicate pastas and such entrées as whole baby chicken roasted with fennel and rack of veal with mint-almond pesto. The luscious breads—and even the filtered sparkling water—are made right here.

LAVANDE FRENCH/CALIFORNIAN 16/20

Lowes Santa Monica Beach Hotel, 1700 Ocean Ave., Santa Monica 90401
310-576-3181, *Breakfast, Lunch & Dinner Mon.-Sat., Brunch Sun., $$$*

A

Discreetly operating for years under the banner of mega-chef Michel Richard, Alain Giraud is now flying on his own at Lavande, a beautiful but relaxed restaurant with an ocean-view that doesn't quit. Here, the Provence-born Giraud has achieved a synthesis of the Mediterranean and the Pacific with a simplicity that proves his talent and self command. The cuisine is appropriate to the lovely location right on the Santa Monica beach—easy to understand (and to swallow), unpretentious but still very civilized. The sautéed foie gras, for example, comes with just a hint of balsamic and Vidalia onion, and garlic enhances rather than overwhelms the bourride of monkfish. Don't miss Giraud's veal stew or remarkable desserts, like the vacherin glacé with lavender ice cream.

LAWRY'S THE PRIME RIB AMERICAN 13/20

100 N. La Cienega Blvd., Beverly Hills 90211
310-652-2827, *Dinner nightly, $$$*

A

Lawry's The Prime Rib has been serving huge slabs of savory prime rib cut to order, and simple, crowd-pleasing accompaniments, for decades. Owner Lawrence Frank has built a small empire by sticking with the basics. The prime rib is truly outstanding, marvelously tender and rich in taste and aroma. Accompaniments include creamed spinach, baked or mashed potatoes and creamed corn. And since this is the late '90s, the red-meat-averse can order fresh fish. Service is friendly but often slow.

LE CHARDONNAY FRENCH 15/20

8284 Melrose Ave., Melrose-La Brea 90046
323-655-8880, *Lunch Tues.-Fri., Dinner Tues-Sun., $$$*

A

The ownership changed in 1996, but Le Chardonnay remains a gorgeous art-nouveau vision of gleaming woodwork and sparkling mirrors—and one of the most romantic restaurants in town. If anything, the French bistro fare, now prepared by Chef Jean-Pierre Lemanissier, is better than ever. You can get such classic dishes as onion soup grantinée or rotisserie-roasted rack of pork, chicken or duck—with perfect pomme frites—along with such California-ized selections as roasted sea bass with Parmesan crust and sun-dried-tomato pesto and sautéed shrimp with tagliatelle. While the main dining room is a perfect setting in which to propose marriage, the skylighted, flower-filled Garden Room is great for a private party of up to 35.

LE CHINE WOK CHINESE/SOUTHEAST ASIAN 12/20

2958 Beverly Glen Circle, Bel Air 90077
310-475-1146, *Lunch & Dinner daily, $*

A pretty little restaurant with flattering lighting, colorful Chinese lanterns and a ficus-bordered patio, Le Chine Wok prepares Chinese and Southeast Asian dishes with a light touch—as might be expected in this fashionable and health-conscious neighborhood at the top of Beverly Glen Canyon. We particularly like the delicate Vietnamese spring rolls, the Thai-style fried catfish and the peppery soft-shell crabs. There's dim sum on the weekends. **Also in the Fairfax-La Brea area (7458 Beverly Blvd., 323-937-2100).**

LE COLONIAL VIETNAMESE 13/20 

8783 Beverly Blvd., W. Hollywood 90048
310-289-0660, *Lunch Mon.-Fri., Dinner nightly, $$*

The drinking, posing, shmoozing and smoking go on until late in the upstairs lounge. A nostalgic recreation of a glamorous French-Vietnamese club in '30s Saigon, this clone of the New York Le Colonial is a stage set of Asian tiles, rattan chairs, hammered ceilings and plenty of palms. The sophisticated cuisine is full of surprising contrasts of salty, sweet and spicy. Try the spring rolls, the stir-fried vegetables on a bed of crispy noodles, the Chilean sea bass delicately steamed in a banana leaf with lemon grass and the buttery filet mignon sautéed with yams and string beans. The shrimp chips are more addictive than potato chips.

LE DÔME FRENCH 14/20 

8720 Sunset Blvd., W. Hollywood 90069
310-659-6919, *Lunch Mon.-Fri., Dinner Mon.-Sat., $$$*

This Sunset Strip-glam fixture still draws a star-studded clientele—some of whom were investors when it opened in 1978. The handsomely decorated rooms have flattering lighting—all the better to show off the pretty, polished and powerful crowd. Celebs, agents and lunching ladies opt for the warm-duck salad, smoked salmon or the fresh Florida stone crab (available from October through May). We recommend the fresh fish entrées and the whole roasted chicken as well as such solid bistro dishes as calf's liver, leg of lamb and cassoulet. You will rarely find fault with your meal or the professional service.

LE PETIT BISTRO FRENCH 12/20

631 N. La Cienega Blvd., W. Hollywood 90069
310-289-9797, *Lunch Mon.- Fri., Dinner nightly, $*

If you ever fantasize about sitting in a lively little bistro on the Left Bank, you'll love Le Petit Bistro. The narrow, crowded little space has the dark woods, the old French ad posters, the tightly squeezed butcher-paper-covered tables—and lots of people speaking French. We appreciate the authentic French bistro food—at very reasonable prices: a sublime eggplant-and-tomato tart, roast chicken with crisp pommes frites and moist blackened salmon atop a green salad. There's buttery bread pudding and a classic crème caramel for dessert.

LES DEUX CAFÉS FRENCH 13/20

1638 N. Las Palmas, Hollywood 90028
323-465-0509, *Dinner Mon.-Sat., $$$*

This place is so "in," you'll have a hard time finding it—unless you're among the hipper-than-thou who know where it is. At the back of a Hollywood parking lot, behind an unmarked door, is a garden patio that evokes a town square in Provence. French designer and hostess extraordinaire, Michelle Lamy, moved a Hollywood bungalow to this spot and invited all her friends to come pose and dine, and then hang out in the lounge where there's live music until late. As sensuous as the garden is, we find the cozy wood-paneled dining room also appealing. The service is distracted and slow, the French food expensive and unexciting—pan-fried soft shell crabs, skate in brown butter, chicken breast in tarragon-cream sauce. But then, no one's here for the food and service.

LES FRÈRES TAIX FRENCH 11/20

1911 Sunset Blvd., Silverlake 90026
213-484-1265, *Lunch & Dinner daily, $*

This Silverlake landmark, with its ornate plaster ceiling, has been serving pretty decent traditional French fare for 70 years—escargots, sautéed mushrooms, chicken bordelaise. Most of the guests have been old (and getting older) regulars who swear by the cozy atmosphere, excellent service and perfect martinis. Recently, however, members of the trendy Silverlake and Los Feliz set seem to be forsaking the overpacked Dresden Room for this place, which may mark a renaissance for Les Frères Taix. Live entertainment.

LIMBO RESTAURANT CALIFORNIA CARIBBEAN 13/20

8338 W. Third St., W. Hollywood 90048
323-866-8258, *Lunch Mon.-Sat., Dinner nightly, Brunch Sun., $$*

Limbo's blue, yellow and purple walls are hung with splashy paintings, and the lounge is a swank spot to pose with a martini or rum-punched tropical drink. The menu features Californiaized takes on such Jamaican favorites as jerk chicken—here filling ravioli or served with risotto cake. Our favorite dishes: the grilled vegetable salad with goat-cheese-and-guava vinaigrette, the plantain-crusted sea bass lounging on garlic-mashed potatoes and the seared ahi tuna with mango salsa. The small wine list features reasonably priced boutique labels. Frequently, a calypso or steel band sets the joint jumping.

THE LITTLE DOOR MEDITERRANEAN 13/20

8164 W. Third St., L.A. 90048
323-951-1210, *Dinner nightly, $$*

Signage is not a priority for a restaurant like this one that caters to an exclusive crowd. The industry-heavy clientele knows the unmarked, weather-worn little door, behind which lies a romantic courtyard with a burbling fountain and candles flickering in the breeze. The frequently changing menu reflects the aroma of garlic, lavender and saffron wafting out of the kitchen. Among the specialties are pistou soup, roasted garlic tart, pistachio-crusted scallops in grapefruit-star anise sauce and lamb tajine. We wish all wine lists were as progressive as theirs, which offers every selection by the glass.

LOCANDA DEL LAGO ITALIAN 13/20 

231 Arizona Ave., Santa Monica 90401
310-451-3525, *Lunch Mon.-Fri., Dinner nightly, Brunch Sat.-Sun., $$*

A serene refuge from the chaos of the Third Street Promenade, with ringside seats from which to watch it. We like the neo-Tuscan decor: yellow walls hung with brightly colored china, paintings and artifacts depicting scenes of Bellagio and tall green-trimmed windows. The menu combines Italian standards with the less familiar dishes of the Lake Como region. Select antipasti from the appealing buffet, share a pizza or pasta, and try such entrées as the grilled scampi, the osso buco or the roasted salmon. Several nights of the week there is live music, and cigars are available to smoke on the sidewalk patio.

LOCANDA VENETA ITALIAN 15/20 

8638 W. Third St., W. Hollywood 90048
310-274-1893, *Lunch Mon.-Fri., Dinner Mon.-Sat., $$*

Close your eyes and let the tiny—often celebrity-filled—Locanda Veneta transport you to the cobbled streets and canals of Venice. From the kitchen you can smell the olive oil being poured over the carpaccio, hear the sizzle of roasting lamb. We recommend any of the pastas, from the penne in a spicy tomato sauce to the saffron-scented lobster ravioli. Also stellar on the small menu: the duck-and-chicken dumpling sautéed with onion-confit marmalade, the shrimp cakes, the succulent rosemary-and-garlic veal chop and, when they have them, the sweet, smoky and juicy grilled langoustines.

LOLA AMERICAN 12/20

945 N. Fairfax, Melrose-Fairfax 90046
323-736-5652, *Dinner nightly, $$*

This late-night spot is known more for its bar scene than its food. For a celeb hang-out where you might find Keanu Reeves and Courtney Love vying for a spot at the pool table, however, the food and service are pretty darn good. Owner Lola Dunsworth keeps the good times rolling with exotic martinis (the "Cirque du Soleil" is made with sake, vermouth, ginger and edible glitter), and describes the fare as "food you can eat"—everything from barbecued ribs, pastas and a turkey burger with fries, to cherry cobbler. The kitchen serves until midnight daily, the club/restaurant keeps jumping until much later.

L'ORANGERIE FRENCH 17/20 

903 N. La Cienega Blvd., W. Hollywood 90069
310-652-9770, *Dinner Tues.-Sun., $$$$*

Los Angeles' most elegant restaurant, L'Orangerie is also one of its best, an incomparably grand and romantic setting in which to enjoy exquisite, impeccably served French nouvelle cuisine. Executive Chef Ludovic Lefebvre prepares such luxurious appetizers as caviar-topped scrambled eggs served in the shell, foie gras-plumped ravioli and Maine lobster on a bed of marinated potatoes with red-wine vinegar, shellfish oil and tagliatelles of celery root with pistou. Among the sublime entrées are the caramelized monkfish with bell peppers, marinated tomato and coulis of olive-and-lemon confit, the rotisserie-roasted chicken stuffed with dates and the roasted breast of woodland duck with fresh orange powder, poached pear and fig purée. End your très chic—and très cher—dining experience with a cloud of chocolate soufflé and petits fours.

LOUIS XIV FRENCH 12/20

606 N. La Brea Ave., Melrose-La Brea 90036
323-934-5102, *Dinner nightly, $$*

A self-consciously hip—and very loud—restaurant, Louis XIV has a kitschy romantic flair, with a cozy loft, sponge-painted walls and heavy wooden tables bearing statuesque candles. There are some vegetarian dishes, but the backbone of the menu is French bistro: warm goat cheese salad, escargots, steak pommes frites, filet mignon bordelaise, along with such pastas as spinach cannelloni, and spaghetti with tomato, zucchini and black olives. If you can bear the crush of long-haired French and Italians, the très slow service—and the attitude—you can enjoy a rollicking bistro meal here.

LULA CUCINA MEXICANA MEXICAN 11/20

2720 Main St., Santa Monica 90405
310-392-5711, *Lunch Mon.-Fri., Dinner nightly, Brunch Sat.-Sun., $*

We like the bright, convivial dining room and patio filled with colorful Mexican folk art. We also like the margaritas, especially served with crisp fresh-made chips, tasty salsas and chunky guacamole. The menu features popular Mexican dishes along with more unusual specialties: squash blossoms stuffed with cheese, green corn tamales, sweet corn pudding and a fiercely hot mini-chile relleno made with a stuffed jalapeño pepper.

LUNARIA FRENCH/CALIFORNIAN 15/20 

10351 Santa Monica Blvd., Century City 90025
310-282-8870, *Lunch Mon.-Fri., Dinner Tues.-Sat., $$$*

Bernard Jacoupy is one of L.A.'s great hosts, the man who made his namesake Bernard's so extraordinary in the early '80s. In this handsomely modern setting, he has created one of the Westside's most welcoming restaurants—and a formidable jazz club. We like the square, marble-topped bar and the relaxed elegance of the dining room, with its lovely watercolor paintings and glass-walled kitchen. Among the appetizers, go for the smoked salmon or tomato confit tart. The entrées are stellar: "40-garlic-clove" chicken, seven-hour leg-of-lamb ravioli, bouillabaisse and pearl pasta "paella". After dinner, move into the lounge for the live jazz, and you'll understand why Lunaria is such a special place.

MADEO ITALIAN 13/20 

8897 Beverly Blvd., W. Hollywood 90048
310-859-4903, *Lunch Mon.-Fri., Dinner nightly, $$$*

Sophia Loren has been spotted dining at this very authentic Italian restaurant. At lunch, the roomy booths and tables are sprinkled with industry types, who choose from such antipasti as the bresaola (paper-thin strips of cured beef), steamed clams and mussels, creamy buffalo mozzarella and excellent risotto. The menu features first-rate carpaccio, pizzas with such toppings as Gorgonzola and porcini, thick Tuscan soup made with bread and cabbage and branzino-filled ravioli. Don't be put off by the below-street-level setting. It makes Madeo a perfect hideaway.

MAMAGAYA ECLECTIC 12/20

401 N. La Cienega Blvd., W. Hollywood 90048
310-659-4999, *Dinner nightly, $$*

At this posh supper club, with its bamboo ceiling, polished wood floor and animal print banquettes, the beautiful people gather like exotic animals around a jungle watering hole. Part of the draw is the entertainment—salsa, Brazilian or reggae music. The food is better than it need be for such a place: crab "cigars" with spicy curry mayo and tomato marinara, filet mignon-wrapped asparagus spears, seared tuna salad, lobster ravioli, roasted duck and Chilean sea bass in lobster sauce.

MANDALAY FRENCH-VIETNAMESE 13/20 

611 N. La Brea Ave., Melrose-La Brea 90036
323-933-0717, *Dinner daily, $*

Delicate French-Vietnamese cooking at prices considerably lower than those at Indochine, Crustacean or Le Colonial. The trendy, high-ceilinged storefront is softened by potted palms and rubber trees. Occasional dishes can be bland, but in general the food is quite good, redolent with garlic, lemon grass, ginger, curry and that all-important Asian ingredient, fish sauce. Try the addictively tangy salad of cabbage, chicken, and shrimp, and the chao tom, savory shrimp wrapped around sugarcane sticks and grilled. Other good choices include the brochettes of chicken with a delicate apricot-plum sauce, the grilled catfish filet and the fried bananas tucked inside crisp pastry wrappings.

MANDARETTE CHINESE 13/20 

8386 Beverly Blvd., W. Hollywood 90048
323-655-6115, *Lunch & Dinner daily, $*

Young hipsters in black or blue jeans join chopsticks with local families at this stylish Chinese café. The lure? Dishes ranging from Cantonese dim sum to Szechwan noodles, including such standouts as Chilean sea bass steamed in a shiny banana leaf "package," crispy sesame beef and classic lemon chicken. The interior is simple enough: high ceilings, a kimono on one wall, a gold-and-black screen towards the rear. And it's not a place for quiet conversation—a medium din is the norm. **Also in Beverly Hills (9513 Little Santa Monica Blvd., 310-385-1188).**

THE MANDARIN CHINESE 15/20 

430 N. Camden Dr., Beverly Hills 90210
310-859-0926, *Lunch Mon.-Fri., Dinner nightly, $$$*

Since 1975, a well-heeled clientele has made this lovely restaurant a Beverly Hills institution. Begin with the marvelous dish of glazed walnuts served on a bed of fried spinach leaves. The chicken salad with red ginger, the dumplings and the scallion pancakes are excellent, and the Peking duck remains a superior interpretation of the classic dish (call ahead to order it). At lunchtime, the banquet room becomes The Noodle Shop featuring lower-priced noodle dishes and other simple Chinese comfort foods.

MANHATTAN WONTON COMPANY CHINESE 13/20 

8475 Melrose Pl., Los Angeles 90069
323-655-6030, *Lunch Mon.-Fri., Dinner nightly, $$*

Paul Heller calls his place New York Chinese, but a better definition might be Hollywood Chinese, since it's usually full of industry types confabing over martinis and drunken chicken. The several small dining rooms are ultra-modern yet comfy, and the multi-level patio is one of the prettiest around. Like tortilla chips in a Mexican restaurant, fried wontons are set down on each table to go with drinks. Frankly, we find them too greasy, and prefer to go right to the menu of all the usual Chinese favorites, done very well.

MAPLE DRIVE CALIFORNIAN/MEDITERRANEAN 14/20 

345 N. Maple Dr., Beverly Hills 90210
310-274-9800, *Lunch Mon.-Fri., Dinner Mon.-Sat., $$$$*

A hot spot for jazz in the evenings, Maple Drive is a lunchtime favorite among entertainment-industry types. The ultra-modern multilevel space features several patios, a wall of secluded wooden booths and a bird's-eye maple bar that becomes the focus of action during "Happy Hour." Leonard Schwartz's simple yet sophisticated cuisine includes contemporary versions of meatloaf, matzo ball soup, a chopped Chinese chicken salad and kick-ass chili. We recommend the filet mignon with wild mushrooms and the baby chicken. And where else can you get a filet-mignon taco for $18?

MARIO'S PERUVIAN SEAFOOD PERUVIAN 12/20

5786 Melrose Ave., Melrose-La Brea 90038
323-466-4181, *Lunch & Dinner daily, $*

When Pizarro landed in Peru in the sixteenth century he was looking for gold but found potatoes instead. This plain, brightly-lit restaurant charged with the sounds of South American music has taken that staple of the Incan diet and put it into such wonderful dishes as huancaina (an egg-and-potato salad). But Mario's is really about seafood. Try such delicacies as the cold squid salad, steamed mussels buried beneath a mass of pickled onions, and the luscious stir-fry of shrimp, squid, octopus, onions and tomatoes.

MARIX TEX MEX CAFÉ MEXICAN 11/20

1108 N. Flores, W. Hollywood 90069
323-656-8800, *Lunch & Dinner daily, Brunch Sat.-Sun., $*

This trendy cantina is always packed to the gills. Count on a party atmosphere and a long wait for a table. The food is informal, low-priced and tasty: fajitas made with either beef, chicken or shrimp; heavy chalupas and chimichangas from New Mexico; margaritas and Mexican beer; salsas both mild and fiery. **Also near the beach in Santa Monica (118 Entrada Dr., 310-459-8596).**

MAROUCH MIDDLE EASTERN 13/20 

4905 Santa Monica Blvd., L.A. 90029
323-662-9325, *Lunch & Dinner Tues.-Sun., $*

This little restaurant offers a nice selection of Lebanese, Armenian and other Middle Eastern dishes—among the best in town. The pita bread is baked in the wood-burning oven and the menu includes everything from shwarma to falafel to a succulent whole barbecued chicken with creamy garlic sauce. We suggest making a meal of assorted appetizers: a $75-selection for six people includes over two dozen items, from hummus to frogs' legs.

MATSUHISA JAPANESE 15/20 

129 N. La Cienega Blvd., Beverly Hills 90211
310-659-9639, *Lunch Mon.-Fri., Dinner nightly, $$$$*

Chef Nobu Matsuhisa has given new dimensions to such Japanese clichés as tempura, and when he wraps a shiso leaf around a sea urchin you begin a culinary voyage you won't soon forget. These days, Nobu spends much of his time at his restaurants in New York and Las Vegas, but his staff nobly carries on. The sushi is as good as it gets, as are such specialties as the salmon in pepper sauce, the squid "pasta" (a paper-thin shaving of buttery squid with garlic sauce) or the sea scallops filled with black truffles and topped with caviar. Beware: you can get so excited tasting one marvelous small dish after another, you'll forget to notice that your bill is skyrocketing.

MAURICE'S SNACK 'N CHAT SOUTHERN/SOUL FOOD 11/20

5549 W. Pico Blvd., Mid-Wilshire 90019
323-931-3877, *Lunch & Dinner daily, $*

Okay, so the service can be eccentric, the decor tacky and the food uneven. Still we like this joint—it's fun and unpretentious, and there are plenty of good things to eat: heavy but tasty fried chicken, messy short ribs, wonderful yams, honest liver and onions, and such comforting desserts as coconut cake and fruit cobbler.

McCORMICK & SCHMICK'S SEAFOOD 13/20 

206 N. Rodeo Dr., Beverly Hills 90210
310-859-0434, *Lunch & Dinner daily, $$*

A

The Pacific Northwest takes its seafood restaurants seriously. The Southland branches of a Portland, Oregon mini-chain feature wood-paneled walls, spacious booths and stained-glass ceilings. The menu offers seafood from throughout the world, but we're always happiest with those caught in Pacific Northwest waters: oysters, Dungeness crab and, when it is in season, Copper River salmon baked on a cedar plank. The restaurants buzz during lunch and Happy Hour, when fresh oysters are washed down with regional beers. **Also Downtown (633 W. Fifth St., 213-629-1929).**

MEXICA MEXICAN 12/20

7313 Beverly Blvd., Melrose-La Brea 90036
323-933-7385, *Lunch Mon.-Fri., Dinner nightly, $*

The high ceiling, neon wall clock, roomy booths and '30s and '40s music don't scream Mexican restaurant, but the tilework, masks and vivid wall murals do. Despite the touches of trendiness in the decor, the food is authentic: carne asada, sweet green corn tamales and creamy flan. Best bets are the savory quesadillas filled with zucchini flowers or potato and chorizo, the grilled skewer of juicy marinated shrimp and anything with the flavorful mole sauce.

MI FAMILIA MEXICAN 12/20

8222-1/2 West Third St., Los Angeles 90048
323-653-2121, *Lunch Mon.-Fri., Dinner Nightly, $$*

This cozy 60-seat restaurant, with its charming interior patio, offers classic dishes of Central Mexico, sometimes embellished. Among our favorite entrées are the beef stew in a bold red wine sauce, the lamb shank with plum sauce and apricots served over mashed potatoes and the beef tongue in tomato-and-spinach sauce. Most entrées are served with simple boiled pinto beans, a refreshing change from the refried beans served elsewhere. The tortillas are handmade in the restaurant, and in addition to a good wine list, you'll find a variety of fresh fruit coolers.

MICHAEL'S — CALIFORNIAN — 14/20

1147 Third St., Santa Monica 90403
310-451-0843, *Lunch Tues.-Fri., Dinner Tues.-Sat., $$$$*

One of the pioneers of California Cuisine, Michael's has endured for over two decades and has even spawned a branch in New York. Today, Michael McCarty's ode to modern cuisine and modern art still offers one of the most spectacular patios in town, and some of the most innovative food. The seasonally changing menu describes dishes in minute detail, right down to naming the origins of the baby greens (the San Fernando Valley). But the dishes aren't as complicated as they sound: risotto with Manila clams, black mussels, Maine lobster and Nantucket Bay scallops is just seafood risotto; Grandma Moses' BBQ Guss pork tenderloin with jalapeño-cilantro-lime salsa is just pork. If such entrées as the Hawaiian ahi tuna with Hudson Valley foie gras and crispy sweet onions isn't filling enough, go for as the veal porterhouse or the two-pound Maine lobster.

MIMOSA — FRENCH — 14/20

8009 Beverly Blvd., Fairfax-La Brea 90048
323-655-8895, *Lunch Mon.-Fri., Dinner Mon.-Sat., $$*

Silvio di Mori, one of Hollywood's favorite restaurateurs, who wowed them at such Italian restaurants as Tutto Bene, is now playing host at this small and charming French bistro—arguably his best restaurant yet. With co-owner/chef Jean Pierre Bosc in the kitchen, the fare includes such homey bistro favorites as duck confit casserole, steak frites and bouillabaisse, along with superb pastas including spaghettini with roasted garlic, sun-dried tomatoes, pine nuts and watercress, and penne with smoked chicken, peas, corn and Gorgonzola cheese—at quite reasonable prices. We're crazy about Bosc's delicate tomato tarte tatin appetizer, and his warm apple tarte for dessert.

MIRABELLE — CALIFORNIAN — 12/20

8768 Sunset Blvd., Sunset Strip 90069
310-659-6022, *Breakfast, Lunch & Dinner daily, Brunch Sun., $$*

At this late-night Sunset Strip hangout, it's still the Seventies—from the hanging plants to the rough-wood paneling to such celeb regulars as Sean Connery and Peter Falk. The bar—where the action is—has a retractable ceiling, and the kitchen serves until 1:30 a.m. every night. The dishes include the sophisticated likes of escolar wrapped in a potato crust with lobster sauce, but we suggest sticking to the simpler fare: angel-hair pasta with tomato-basil sauce and grilled fish and steaks.

MISS GREGORY'S — AMERICAN — 12/20

7986 Sunset Blvd., W. Hollywood 90046
323-822-9057, *Lunch Tues.-Fri., Dinner Tues.-Sun., Brunch Sat.-Sun., $*

Comfort food drives the menu at this stuck-in-a-minimall eatery, and entrées including turkey meatloaf and chicken pot pie come with a choice of soup or salad, plus such vegetables as spinach cakes, maple-whipped acorn squash and garlic-chive mashed potatoes. At brunch, strong coffee and warm biscuits serve as the perfect prelude to the lamb-and-cheddar cheese omelet or the caramel-apple flannel cakes. Do schedule a post-brunch nap—you'll need it.

MODO MIO ITALIAN 13/20

15200 Sunset Blvd., Pacific Palisades 90272
310-459-0979, *Lunch Mon.-Fri., Dinner daily,* $$

The simple, country cuisine of Rimini, near Venice, dominates the menu. We've enjoyed the papa pomodoro, an intensely flavored tomato soup with hunks of chewy bread, and pappardelle al porcini, a satisfying combination of wide, fat noodles with meaty mushrooms. Seafood is plentiful: cioppino Adriatico, a generous plate of assorted seafood—swordfish, ahi tuna, green-lipped mussels, calamari, shrimp and scallops—drizzled with a light tomato stock. The wine list is laden with Italian varietals. Don't leave without ordering the luscious tiramisu.

MON KEE CHINESE/SEAFOOD 13/20

679 N. Spring St., Downtown 90012
213-628-6717, *Lunch & Dinner daily,* $$

This Chinatown favorite always seems to have a line out the door waiting for tables. In fact, it is this restaurant that introduced many L.A. restaurant-goers to the joys of Chinese seafood cooking, which is uniformly tasty here: juicy shrimp coated with rock salt, stir-fried rock cod in a sweet-and-sour sauce, double-fried scallops, steamed rock cod with soy sauce, and best of all, the generous, messy crab in either black bean or ginger sauce. **Also in Brentwood (111677 San Vicente Blvd., 310-826-8287).**

MONROE'S CALIFORNIAN/ECLECTIC 13/20

6800 Westward Beach Rd., Malibu 90265
310-457-5521, *Dinner nightly, Brunch Sun.,* $$$

Cherished by locals for its excellent food and cozy, romantic setting, Monroe's offers one of the prettiest views on the coast. Tucked under the cliffs on a quiet strip of beach south of Zuma, Monroe's is a friendly spot run by Richard and Donna Monroe, transplants from Liverpool, England. We've enjoyed the plump crabcakes and carrot-pear soup, the eggplant stuffed with artichoke and mushrooms, and the linguini with clams and such entrées as veal with roasted garlic and lamb with a sweet-sour mint sauce. The banana cake with custard sauce is a scrumptious finale.

MONSOON CAFÉ PAN-ASIAN 12/20

1212 Third St. Promenade, Santa Monica 90404
310-576-9996, *Lunch & Dinner daily,* $$

Bali on the Third Street Promenade. Monsoon is an over-the-top homage to the exotically tropical, with a lily pond, Balinese masks on the bamboo walls, semi-private booths and lots of beach shack-bar action. The menu ranges from

Vietnamese spring rolls to dim sum to Thai curry dishes, all good for grazing while sipping a potent tropical drink. The jazz and (sometimes) salsa music continues upstairs in the lounge until 1 a.m. on weekends.

MONTEGO BAY CARIBBEAN/JAMAICAN 12/20

1031 Abbot Kinney Blvd., Venice 90291
310-450-1933, *Lunch Tues.-Fri., Dinner Tues.-Sun., Brunch Sat.-Sun., $$*

This Caribbean (mostly Jamaican) restaurant has a colorful "islands" setting, from the brightly painted furniture to the tropical foliage that shades the back patio. Order a daiquiri or Red Stripe beer, then sample jerk chicken ravioli, vegetable patties with tomato-cinnamon chutney, and such exotic entrées as curried goat with crisp sweet potato or jerk chicken with banana fritters. Call in advance to find out when there is live steel drum music; it will make you feel as you're in Montego Bay.

MORTON'S AMERICAN 13/20

8764 Melrose Ave., W. Hollywood 90069
310-276-5205, *Lunch Mon.-Fri., Dinner Mon.-Sat., $$$*

A

Owned by Peter Morton, the co-creator of the Hard Rock Café, and run by his twin sister, Pamela, Morton's is a high-energy hangout for Hollywood's heaviest of hitters. The menu changes from time to time, but you might run into starters like spicy tuna sashimi, or a shrimp-and-black-bean quesadilla. Main courses are simple but exceptional: Chesapeake Bay crabcakes with a frisky mustard aïoli, various fresh grilled fish, succulent grilled lime chicken, superb steaks, one of the best grilled, roasted and steamed vegetable plates in town and a dynamite hot fudge sundae. Great California red wines too, and an impressive (if expensive) list of Bordeaux.

MOUSTACHE CAFÉ FRENCH 12/20

8155 Melrose Ave., Melrose-Fairfax 90069
323-651-2111, *Lunch Mon.-Sat., Dinner nightly, $$*

This French café is stuck in the '70s—which is when it opened—and frankly, we're amazed by its staying power. We suppose the Moustache's success comes from the fun atmosphere, the wide selection of dishes—and the reasonable prices. The covered patio, the hanging plants and the thousands of pin lights are still the same. But today you can order pasta as well as crêpes, and a Yucatan chicken salad along with the classic Niçoise. Stick with the simple basics: roasted chicken, omelets, the "French Disaster" hamburger topped with ratatouille and the chocolate soufflé. **Also in Westwood (1071 Glendon Ave., 310-208-6633).**

MUSE CALIFORNIAN 13/20

7360 Beverly Blvd., Melrose-La Brea 90036
323-934-4400, *Dinner Tues.-Sat., $$*

After a dozen or so years, this hip industrial-looking spot remains one of L.A.'s best-kept secrets. It's virtually signless, with a blank concrete exterior on one of the busiest streets in town. The menu features California cuisine with Pacfic-Rim overtones: Peking-duck egg roll and chicken- lettuce tacos, spicy Thai rigatoni and charbroiled hickory-smoked pork chops. The desserts—toasted coconut bread pudding, cinnamon-crusted pippin apple brown betty—are exemplary. You're likely to spot a celeb or two.

MUSSO & FRANK'S GRILL CONTINENTAL 10/20

6667 Hollywood Blvd., Hollywood 90028
323-467-7788, *Breakfast, Lunch & Dinner Tues.-Sat.*, $$

You're in Raymond Chandler territory at Musso's. A Hollywood landmark since 1919, this place has the clubby look and feel to which newcomers like The Grill aspire. If nothing else, come for a Manhattan at the bar. When dining, expect brusque service and such old-fashioned favorites as grilled steaks and chops, beef stroganoff, sauerbraten, chicken pot pie, short ribs and cannelloni. The all-day breakfast menu includes omelets and flannel cakes. You haven't been to Hollywood if you haven't been to Musso's.

NAWAB OF INDIA INDIAN 12/20

1621 Wilshire Blvd., Santa Monica 90403
310-829-1106, *Lunch Mon.-Fri., Dinner nightly, Brunch Sat. & Sun.*, $

This popular and reliable Indian restaurant has wonderful service and an appealing menu of all the usual Northern Indian dishes, many cooked in an authentic clay tandoor oven. Some of the curry dishes are perhaps too mildly spiced, but we've enjoyed the puffy tandoori breads, the rice pilafs, the tandoori chicken and the soothing saffron-flavored ice cream with pistachios for dessert.

THE NEWSROOM CAFÉ ORGANIC/CALIFORNIAN 12/20

120 N. Robertson Blvd., W. Hollywood 90048
310-652-4444, *Breakfast, Lunch & Dinner daily*, $

Shine-and-dine at this busy vegetarian-friendly hot-spot that draws celebs, Designer-Row shoppers, and doctors from nearby Cedars-Sinai. From 8 to 3 Mondays through Saturdays, the resident shoe-shiner will polish your shoes while you eat. The huge menu offers everything from organic oatmeal and spirulina smoothies to tandoori chicken salad, red chile-honey-glazed fresh grilled chicken, and the "ultimate" Maui veggie burger, their best-selling dish. We get a kick out of seeing hipsters at one table chugging double shots of wheatgrass juice, while nearby, junior sophisticates knock back double martinis.

NICOLA NEW AMERICAN 13/20 

601 S. Figueroa, Downtown 90017
213-485-0927, *Lunch Mon.-Fri.*, $$

Nicola is a wild adventure in metal and wood, a post-Blade Runner setting where the "ethnic-influenced American" food is as hip as the design. Grilled wild mushrooms are presented between thin sheets of filo dough; among the noodle and rice options, the pan-fried rice noodles with roast duck is well worth ordering. Desserts include a memorable chocolate semifreddo with pralines. A number of good wines are available by the glass, and a section of the intriguing wine list is devoted to the bottlings of Bonny Doon Vineyards. Open for private parties evenings.

NIC'S AND THE MARTINI LOUNGE ECLECTIC 12/20

453 Canon Dr., Beverly Hills 90210
310-550-5707, *Lunch & Dinner Mon.-Sat., $$$*

A force in the L. A. dining scene since he opened L.A. Nicola in Silverlake in 1980, Larry Nicola offers his artistic, Latin- and Asian-influenced cuisine in this swank supper-club setting. The best dishes include the chow fun noodles with duck and cranberries, the spinach salad with grapefruit, pancetta and goat cheese, and the sea bass with caramelized tangerines. Campechana, a seafood combination in a spicy, gazpacho-like broth, exemplifies Nicola's ability to add his imprint to something as familiar as a seafood cocktail. In the adjoining Martini Lounge, try the martinis that combine spiced fruits and various liquors.

NOUVEAU CAFÉ BLANC FRENCH/JAPANESE 13/20 

9777 Santa Monica Blvd., Beverly Hills 90210
310-888-0108, *Lunch & Dinner Tues.-Sat., $$*

In this tiny white jewel box of a room, foodies and worshippers of the Japanese aesthetic look to Chef Tommy Harase for beautifully presented and usually tasty food. At lunch, far and away the bargain meal here, we found the salmon-scallop tartare was short on flavor, but the monkfish liver terrine was sublime. The prix-fixe multi-course dinners might include roasted sweetbreads with Pinot Noir sauce or seared Norwegian salmon with basil vinaigrette, both good examples of Harase's culinary creativity.

OBACHINE PAN-ASIAN 14/20 

242 N. Beverly Dr., Beverly Hills 90210
310-274-4440, *Lunch & Dinner daily, $$*

Maybe because Spago Beverly Hills opened just a block away, Wolfgang Puck's and Barbara Lazaroff's high-style homage to Asian cuisine took awhile to catch on. It's a beautiful two-level complex, with the bar, satay bar and patio on the street level, and the restaurant and open kitchen upstairs. The menu is all over the map of Asia, featuring Puck's renditions of everything from sushi and Thai noodles to Indian tandoori. We highly recommend the warm sesame seed-crusted oysters, the spicy minced lamb, the lemon-and-ginger chicken, the whole roasted red snapper and the delicate rice pudding napoleon.

OCEAN AVENUE SEAFOOD SEAFOOD 13/20 

1401 Ocean Ave., Santa Monica 90401
310-394-5669, *Lunch & Dinner daily, Brunch Sun., $$*

This bustling, upscale seafood restaurant/oyster bar is just across the street from the Santa Monica bluffs and commands a terrific view of the ocean. The atmosphere is cheery, the decor modern and the oyster bar features fresh picks from Washington state, Nova Scotia—even as far away as Chile. Good clam chowder and crabcakes, plus all the usual fresh fish dishes, from Hawaiian ahi tuna to Ecuadorian mahi mahi and Maine lobster. Stick with the simplest preparations and you can't go wrong.

OCEAN SEAFOOD CHINESE/DIM SUM 13/20 

750 N. Hill St., Downtown 90012
213-687-3088, *Breakfast, Lunch & Dinner daily, $*

One of Chinatown's best Cantonese seafood houses, this huge, mildly glitzy Hong Kong-style eatery is famed for some of the best dim sum—and fresh seafood—in town. The seafood is gleaned from giant tanks filled with lobsters, crabs, all sorts of finned fish and, most wonderfully, shrimp, which are served five different ways. The best way to eat here is with a group, banquet-style: deep-fried shrimp on bamboo sticks, braised whole abalone, pan-fried lobster with ginger, baked crab with black bean-and-chili sauce and deep-fried whole fish.

OFF VINE CALIFORNIAN 13/20 

6263 Leland Way, Hollywood 90028
323-962-1900, *Lunch Mon.-Fri., Dinner nightly, Brunch Sun., $$*

A chic little restored Hollywood bungalow with white-washed walls, a fireplace, Herb Ritts photos and Adirondack chairs dotting the front lawn. You can get everything from a cheeseburger or a blackened-chicken chopped salad to Chinese shrimp pasta. Brunch is big here, with industry types lingering over their lox omelets. We love the blueberry crumble pie for dessert.

ON CANON ITALIAN 12/20

301 N. Canon Dr., Beverly Hills 90210
310-247-2900, *Lunch & Dinner daily, $$*

In a town that has more than its share of Italian restaurants, this casual-but-chic trattoria (owned by the Il Forno folks from Santa Monica) is a reliably good spot for pizza, pastas and people-watching. Adam Tihany designed the high-ceilinged space for a much fancier restaurant (the late Bice), and we appreciate getting all that high style for such reasonable prices. Start with a crisp-crusted pizza, pasta or carpaccio. Then forget everything you've read about red meat; the thinly sliced grilled filet mignon topped with arugula salad is heavenly. Like the service, the food can be uneven. Bottom line: we recommend On Canon for the scene and the comfort more than for the food.

ONE PICO NEW AMERICAN 13/20 

Shutters on the Beach, One Pico Blvd., Santa Monica 90405
310-458-0030, *Lunch & Dinner daily, $$$*

One Pico brings a little of Cape Cod and a lot of Ralph Lauren to the beach in Santa Monica—and offers a stunning ocean view. But One Pico is not just a "view" restaurant. The New American cuisine is simple yet well prepared. Among our recommendations: corn chowder with smoked shrimp, steamed mussels with Chardonnay and herbs, applewood-smoked salmon, herb-crusted rack of lamb and the pressed free-range chicken with spinach.

THE ORIGINAL SONORA CAFÉ SOUTHWESTERN 13/20 

180 S. La Brea Ave., Melrose-La Brea 90036
323-857-1800, *Lunch Mon.-Fri., Dinner nightly, Brunch Sun., $$$*

Located in a high-ceilinged industrial-chic space on trendy La Brea, Sonora serves oceans of blue-corn tortillas and salsas made with obscure chiles. The menu features superb Southwestern dishes: confit of duck tamales, tequila-marinated smoked salmon, whitefish with spicy mango-peanut-curry sauce and fresh corn pudding, and chile-charred ahi with vegetable chimichanga. You'll find a couple of lusty Texas-style entrées too: barbecued pork chops with sweet potato tamales and a South Texas mixed grill of ranch antelope, quail and venison sausage.

ORSO ITALIAN 13/20 

8706 W. Third St., W. Hollywood 90048
310-274-7144, *Lunch & Dinner daily, $$*

With its bushy ficus trees and Italian-rusticized stucco walls, Orso's patio is divine—one of the most beautiful settings for al fresco dining in town. The interior, with its warm woods and soft angles, is also attractive though often noisy. We love Orso's pizzas with their crisp, crackly crusts—or the pizza bread alone—as well as the pastas, the mixed seafood grill with saffron risotto and the sautéed sole with wilted spinach and roasted mushrooms. Try a side of white beans, roasted shallots and rosemary. Service can be slow, but hey, if you're seated on the patio on a pleasant night, you feel as if you have all the time in the world.

OSTERIA NONNI ITALIAN 12/20

3219 Glendale Blvd., Atwater Village 90039
323-666-7133, *Lunch Tues.-Fri., Dinner nightly, $*

Knockout pizza dough is at the core of the ten or so pizzas, the lunchtime panini and that basket of warm bread on your table. The rest of the menu runs to simple starters, including an excellent antipasti assortment, modest and sometimes dull pastas (spaghetti marinara, spaghetti with butter and Parmesan), grilled entrées like the whole baby chicken and tiramisu. The wine selection is adequate, and the caffè lattes are frothy and the prices are a steal.

PACIFIC DINING CAR AMERICAN 13/20 

1310 W. Sixth St., Downtown 90017
213-483-6000, *Open 24 hours daily, $$$*

A veritable Los Angeles dining institution, the original Pacific Dining Car has built up a loyal following through sheer longevity. The front room looks like a railway car from the halcyon days of the Union Pacific, with a clubby ambience. Breakfasts and appetizers are good here, and so, for that matter, is the service. The chile is exceptional, spareribs are smoky, and the french-fried zucchini is addictive. With the downtown location open daily round-the-clock, the **Santa Monica location (2700 Wilshire Blvd., 310-453-4000)** open til 2 a.m., either is a good spot in which to satisfy a craving for red meat in the middle of the night.

THE PALM STEAKHOUSE 14/20 

9001 Santa Monica Blvd., W. Hollywood 90069
310-550-8811, *Lunch Mon.-Fri., Dinner nightly,* $$$

With its walls plastered with celebrity caricatures, its personable, in-your-face waiters and a sound level akin to that of a raucous New York cocktail party, the Palm doesn't take itself all that seriously—except when it comes to its steaks and lobsters. Both the 18-ounce prime-aged eastern New York steaks and the three-pound-and-up Nova Scotia lobsters are among the biggest—and best—you'll get in L.A. The bread and salads are nothing to write home about, but some of the side dishes are stellar, including the thick-cut cottage fries. The New York cheesecake is a must.

PANE E VINO ITALIAN 13/20 

8265 Beverly Blvd., W. Hollywood 90048
323-651-4600, *Lunch Mon.-Sat., Dinner nightly,* $$

Pane e Vino is all warm earthen tones and Tuscan-ish details with a courtyard patio filled with flowers and climbing vines. You'll find simple salads and good appetizers—try the grilled shrimp with feta cheese and mint leaves or the risotto cake with wild mushrooms. Our favorite entrée is the garlic-haunted clay-roasted chicken dripping with juices, and the sausages and peppers with polenta. And you can count on such pastas as the capellini al pomodoro and the penne with porcini mushrooms and pancetta.

PANGAEA NEW AMERICAN/JAPANESE 15/20 

Hotel Nikko, 465 S. La Cienega Blvd., Beverly Hills 90048
310-246-2100, *Breakfast, Lunch & Dinner daily, Brunch Sun.,* $$

With tables set wide apart on two levels, the Hotel Nikko's elegant restaurant is perfect for business—or romantic—dinners. As this is a Japanese-owned hotel, expect such well executed Japanese standards as udon noodles, teriyaki-style chicken and Japanese-style curries. New American Cuisine-inspired dishes result from the creative chef's continuing search for the best—and unique—ingredients. We've enjoyed the roasted Colorado rack of lamb over spaghetti-squash primavera with roasted shallots and minted spaetzle, the mustard-crusted New York strip steak and the sublime roasted banana tiramisu for dessert.

PASTINA ITALIAN 12/20

2260 Westwood Blvd., L.A. 90064
310-441-4655, *Lunch & Dinner Mon.-Sat.,* $$

On a stretch of Westwood Boulevard that's been nicknamed "Little Tehran" for its wealth of Persian restaurants, this understated trattoria—with its reasonable prices and friendly service—stands out. Starters include carpaccio, scampi, calamaretti fritti and a spirited Caesar salad. We enjoy the pastas, such as penne alla arrabbiatta and linguine alla puttanesca, along with the osso buco, chicken in porcini sauce and veal specialties.

PASTIS FRENCH 12/20

8114 Beverly Blvd., Melrose-Fairfax 90048
323-655-8822, *Dinner Mon.-Sat., $$*

This charming little Provençal bistro is authentic right down to the use of a "," instead of a decimal point in the prices. We love the rustic ambience, the warm colors, the candlelight and the flowers. We're just sorry that sometimes we've run into snail-paced service. Start with mussels in garlic-and-shallots sauce, a tartine of Roquefort cheese with walnuts and Cognac or a fresh-tomato tart. The simple entrées include grilled tuna on a bed of ratatouille, roasted chicken breast with olives and bouillabaisse. Go on a warm summer night, when the tables spill out onto the sidewalk and tout le monde seems to be speaking French.

PATINA FRENCH/CALIFORNIAN 18/20

5955 Melrose Ave., Melrose-La Brea 90038
323-467-1108, *Lunch Tues.-Fri., Dinner nightly, $$$$*

Even though chef/owner Joachim Splichal's restaurant empire has grown—along with his family—over the past few years, with Pinots from Pasadena to the Napa Valley, the simple yet sublimely elegant Patina remains L.A.'s top spot for innovative—nearly flawless—cuisine. Start with corn blini draped with fennel-marinated salmon, crème fraîche and red bell pepper sauce, or escalope of sweetbreads with artichoke and fried artichoke spaghetti. Move on to crispy whitefish with "not fried" French fries, roasted garlic cloves and brandade, or roasted rabbit leg stuffed with spinach and dried plums served on grits. Splichal performs miracles with potatoes, from his potato roll of scallops to his potato truffle chips. There is a 5-course "Crustacean Menu" (picture millefeuille of polenta chips with yams, Santa Barbara shrimp and red curry sauce), and a 5-course vegetarian "Garden Menu" (think roasted winter squash risotto with black-and-gold chanterelle mushrooms). With so many wonders to choose from, we suggest you order one of the four- or five-course "tasting menus," which might include such unique dishes as wild pigeon and honey-poached quince. Patina's wine list is distinguished, as befits Splichal's sophisticated cuisine.

PEDALS CAFÉ CALIFORNIAN 10/20

Shutters on the Beach, One Pico Blvd., Santa Monica 90405
310-458-0030, *Breakfast & Lunch Mon.-Fri., Dinner daily, Brunch Sat.-Sun., $$*

This sunny and upscale—and noisy—hotel café opens right onto the boardwalk, and is a great stopping-point for weekend bike-riders and in-line-skaters. They don't take brunch reservations on the weekends, and it's hard to get on the patio. We liked the herbed asparagus omelet, the spiced-walnut pancakes and the Belgian waffles better than the eggs Benedict. For dinner, try the linguine with mussels and clams or the meatloaf. Celebrities and industry people love this place, so keep an eye out.

PIAZZA RODEO — ITALIAN — 11/20

208 Via Rodeo, Beverly Hills 90210
310-275-2428, *Lunch & Dinner daily, Brunch Sun., $$*

Piazza Rodeo sits at the top of the Beverly Hills equivalent of Rome's Spanish Steps on Via Rodeo, a faux-European street with its impressive assortment of ultra high-ticket shops. It's a perfect spot for people-watching, while nursing an espresso or a glass of wine, or sampling such simple delights as toasted rosemary bread with tomatoes and basil, chicken salad made with sun-dried tomatoes and pancetta, a grilled vegie sandwich on rosemary bread, tuna with fennel and bow-tie pasta with sugar-snap peas.

PIER VIEW CAFÉ & CANTINA — AMERICAN/SEAFOOD — 11/20

22718 PCH, Malibu 90265
310-456-6962, *Breakfast, Lunch & Dinner daily, $$*

Pier View has about the most popular deck in town—it's perched right over the ocean. The place is always crowded with surfers and beach babes, but if you can get in, try the blackened chicken with tequila-lime sauce or the grilled swordfish with fresh salsa, followed by the homemade apple pie. What a grand place to watch the sunset. For weekend breakfast, we recommend the huevos rancheros and reservations long in advance.

PINOT HOLLYWOOD — FRENCH — 13/20 

1448 N. Gower St., Hollywood 90028
323-461-8800, *Lunch Mon-Fri., Dinner Mon-Sat., $$*

Joachim Splichal's handsome restaurant in the heart of Hollywood features a swank dining room with high ceilings, skylights and dark woods—sort of Left Bank meets California. In back is a bar and lounge where you can sip martinis from the comfort of overstuffed sofas. Expect Splichal's splendid French bistro fare, pastas, and meats done on the grill. We're partial to his corn blinis with marinated salmon, roasted mustard chicken with garlic and fries, and citrus-marinated whole fish with thyme-roasted potatoes. If it's Tuesday, this must be roasted suckling pig with braised cabbage, new potatoes and spicy mustard.

PIZZICOTTO — ITALIAN — 14/20 

11758 San Vicente Blvd., Brentwood 90049
310-442-7188, *Lunch Mon.-Sat., Dinner nightly, $*

A terrific place for a quick fix of Italian hospitality, this café/market features Italian gourmet-food products, authentic antipasti, pastas and pizza, and such sophisticated entrées as grilled salmon, whitefish filet with a horseradish-pistachio crust and spicy grilled lamb sausages with sautéed mushrooms and cannellini beans served over a bed of soft polenta. Take a seat in the loft dining room, order a bottle from the reasonably priced Italian/California wine list, and share a "Centro Tavolo" (for the center of the table) dish, such as roasted portobello mushrooms served over slices of Parma ham and roasted peppers.

POLO LOUNGE CALIFORNIAN 14/20 

Beverly Hills Hotel, 9641 Sunset Blvd., Beverly Hills 90210
310-281-2916, *Breakfast, Lunch & Dinner daily, $$$*

The "Pink Lady's" power-breakfast, power-lunch and power-cocktails spot has a new chef—Suki Katsuo Sugiura—who uses herbs from the garden he planted outside the restaurant. If you're somebody—or want to pretend you are—come for impeccable service in sumptuous surroundings that are part of Hollywood history. We like the forest-green wheeling-and-dealing bar by night, the pepper-tree-shaded patio by day. The menu features such Polo Lounge traditions as the Dutch apple pancake, the McCarthy salad and steak tartare, along with such pure '90s dishes as potstickers with grilled portobello mushrooms, honey-pepper-rosemary-cured smoked salmon and potato-crusted sea bass on yellow lentils. As befits a luxe hotel in Beverly Hills, you'll also find caviar—and low-cal spa dishes.

PORTER'S CALIFORNIAN 15/20 

11690 San Vicente Blvd., Brentwood 90049
310-826-1446, *Lunch Mon.-Fri., Dinner nightly, $$$*

A small (57-seat) and attractive neighborhood restaurant where the owner—Alex Resnik—plays host and the chef—Jeff Perlman—mans the stove. We appreciate their hands-on approach: the service is good and what comes out of the kitchen is sublime. Try such inventive starters as molasses-cured salmon, sesame-ginger salmon tartare or truffled Yukon ravioli with oxtail stew, followed by the grilled salmon napoleon with fennel purée, the crispy white fish with horseradish potatoes or the seafood risotto. Perlman's strong suit is desserts. Case in point: his chocolate-truffle-banana bread pudding with banana ice cream.

PREGO ITALIAN 13/20 

362 N. Camden Dr., Beverly Hills 90210
310-277-7346, *Lunch Mon.-Sat., Dinner nightly, $$*

Beverly Hills' first modern Italian trattoria is still one of its best. When you enter, you'll notice not only the chic crowd, but a wood-burning pizza oven spewing fire and smoke and disgorging excellent thin-crusted pizzas. You'll find a great bar and chummy service, and dishes that need no introduction: carpaccio, waist-watching salads, agnolotti filled with lobster and ricotta in a lemon-lobster sauce and wonderful grilled fish and meats.

PRIMI — ITALIAN — 14/20

10543 W. Pico Blvd., W. L.A. 90064
310-475-9235, *Lunch Mon.-Fri., Dinner Mon.-Sat., $$*

The casual-chic cousin of Valentino, Primi is jammed with movie studio executives at lunchtime. At dinner it draws diners who crave Piero Selvaggio's take on modern Italian cuisine (as executed by chef Hector Lopez, who has been with Selvaggio for over 20 years.) The emphasis here is on "primi" (first) courses: duckling crespella with cremona mustard or seafood risotto are good choices. But we're tempted by the main courses too, especially the Italian veal meatloaf, the osso buco and the crispy sweetbreads with artichokes and Marsala-truffle sauce.

REAL FOOD DAILY — VEGETARIAN/HEALTH FOOD — 12/20

514 Santa Monica Blvd., Santa Monica 90404
310-451-7544, *Lunch & Dinner daily, $*

What began as a home-food delivery service in Malibu (for such high-profile clients as Barbra Streisand and Al Pacino), is now a comfy and pleasant restaurant near the Third Street Promenade. Though Ann Gentry's organic cuisine is prepared with no animal or dairy products, cholesterol, eggs, fats, sugars or refined flours, it draws raves for flavor. In fact, such dishes as the black bean tostadas and tempeh enchiladas illustrate how surprisingly good vegetarian food can be when it's properly prepared.

REBECCA'S — MEXICAN — 12/20

2025 Pacific Ave., Venice 90191
310-306-6266, *Dinner nightly, $$*

It's usually jam-packed and head-splitting noisy; portions are small, and there's a two-hour limit at the tables. But if you want a trendy bar scene, over-the-top architecture and great homemade taco chips washed down with margaritas, Rebecca's is for you. The menu offers fresh-made ceviche, oyster shooters with tequila, tacos nestling everything from carne asada to halibut, along with such entrées as mesquite-grilled spare ribs, Mexican seafood paella and, on Fridays and Saturdays, cabrito (baby goat).

RED — CALIFORNIAN — 13/20

Californian, 7450 Beverly Blvd., Beverly-Fairfax 90036
323-937-0331, *Breakfast, Lunch & Dinner daily, $$*

Coffee shops don't come much hipper than this corner spot near CBS. It's always abuzz with twenty-something hipsters and mogul wannabe's, schmoozing, sipping mega-martinis and chowing down on food that's a lot better than it needs to be for this crowd. At lunch, we crave the portobello mushroom, roasted pepper and fresh mozzarella cheese sandwich. At night, we look beyond the turkey burger and meatloaf to the polenta-crusted sea bass, the red-chile-coated filet mignon or the grilled peppercorn salmon. The service is friendly but distracted. The color scheme of the decor at Red may be red, but the color most guests wear is black. **Also in Santa Monica (101 Broadway, 310-260-1100).**

THE REEL INN SEAFOOD 12/20

18661 Pacific Coast Highway, Malibu 90265
310-456-8221, *Lunch & Dinner daily, $*

Grab a spot at one of the wooden picnic tables, knock back a beer and chow down on huge portions of steamed clams or deep-fried oysters, followed by pretty decent (and definitely fresh) grilled or deep-fried ono, ahi, mahi mahi or wahoo. On busy weekends, you have to line up to order from the blackboard menu at this funky beach-adjacent café. We're particularly fond of the grilled Cajun shrimp, the creamy cole slaw and the zingy Cajun rice. **They've managed to create the same chaotic beach-shack look at the cavernous Reel Inn on the Third Street Promenade, Santa Monica (310-395-5538).**

THE REGENT DINING ROOM CALIFORNIAN/FRENCH 15/20 

Regent Beverly Wilshire Hotel, 9500 Wilshire Blvd., Beverly Hills 90212
310-274-8179, *Breakfast daily, Lunch Mon.-Sat., Dinner nightly, $$$$*

You can dress to the nines for this stunning hotel dining room. It is classical yet modern, formal yet comfortable and perfect for business or romance with its trompe l'oeil murals, burnished woods, a glassed-in kitchen and gracious, impeccable service. The cuisine is gorgeous and reliable: crusted foie gras and air-dried duck, ahi tuna tart in phyllo pastry, potato-crusted sea bass with braised leeks, wild mushroom risotto with white asparagus, along with such old favorites as French onion soup and filet mignon au poivre. On weekday mornings, you'll see William Morris agents power-breakfasting on bagels and egg-white omelets. On weekend nights, the lights are dimmed and the Arthur Hanlon Trio plays jazz and swing standards for dancing.

REMI ITALIAN 14/20

1451 Third Street Promenade, Santa Monica 90401
310-393-6545, *Lunch & Dinner daily, $$$*

Step away from the Third Street Promenade crowds and you're in a serene, modern bastion of Venetian cooking. Start with the arugula with sweet-and-sour shallots, walnuts, and black-olive dressing, the bacon-wrapped grilled quail with polenta or the smoked- goose prosciutto with truffle oil. We've enjoyed such pastas as whole wheat spaghetti with caramelized onions and anchovies, fresh-tuna-stuffed ravioli and linguini with scallops and broccoli rabe. Remi prepares excellent seafood entrées, such as the whole striped sea bass with sautéed vegetables, but we're also partial to the grilled and sliced New York steak served with shallots and roasted potatoes.

RESTAURANT SPAIN SPANISH 12/20

1866 Glendale Blvd., L.A. 90026
323-667-9045, *Lunch & Dinner Tues.-Sun., $*

Don't be put off by this eatery's awkward location at the end of the Glendale Freeway or its big tacky sign. Just inside the door are shelves stocked with Spanish products (e.g. marzipan, olive oil, saffron), a case of meats and empanadas ready-to-go. Further inside lies a charming dining room filled with paella pans, Spanish travel posters and smartly dressed tables. The tapas here include empanadas, fried smelt and calamari, respectable croquetas, Manchego cheese and chorizo. The main attraction here is the generously portioned but bargain-priced paella.

RICE MAN — PACIFIC RIM — 12/20

1401 Ocean Ave., Santa Monica 90401
310-458-4771, *Lunch Tues.-Fri., Dinner Tues.-Sun., $$*

All blonde woods and sleek surfaces, Chef Sejii "Waka" Wakabayashi's restaurant (he cooked at Spago and Café del Rey) is casual enough to lure away Third Street Promenaders, but sophisticated enough for a romantic dinner. Waka's dishes are lovely to behold, and most deliver in taste: "lobster and crabmeet," for example, a melange of lobster and crab meat, vegetables and sweet ginger cream, the "sandwich" of barbecued New York steak medallions, caramelized onions, avocado, tomatoes and pommes frites, green tea spaghetti or the roasted duck breast with Camembert bread pudding and apple chutney.

RINCON CHILENO — CHILEAN — 12/20

4354 Melrose Ave., Melrose-La Brea 90029
323-666-6075, *Lunch & Dinner Tues.-Sun., $*

This tiny restaurant serving Chilean cuisine exudes warmth and conviviality. The menu features mostly seafood, everything from sea urchin to fried smelts to imported-from-Chile congrio—fried, stewed or sautéed with wine and garlic. The namesake dish, a spicy white broth filled with clams, crab, shrimp and fish, is the best thing here, and tastes good washed down with Argentinean Santa Fe beer.

THE RITZ-CARLTON DINING ROOM — FRENCH — 14/20 

The Ritz-Carlton Hotel Marina del Rey, 4375 Admiralty Way, M.D.R. 90292
310-823-1700, *Dinner Tues.-Sat., $$$$*

Through the windows of this formal dining room, you can glimpse a California dream of white sails on blue water and gulls streaking through the sky. New Executive Chef Mark Ehrler plans to open those windows to bring in the fresh breeze—just as he is bringing fresh new tastes to the Provençal menu. Among his specialties are a timbale of escargots, garlic hazelnuts and parsley butter, an eggplant-and-swordfish napoleon and a single côte de boeuf with bone marrow flan. For a taste of the sea, try the $55 bouillabaisse dinner—the lusty and aromatic Provençal fish soup is preceded by a niçoise salad and followed by dessert.

RIX — ECLECTIC — 13/20

1413 Fifth Street, Santa Monica 90401
310-656-9688, *Lunch Mon.-Fri., Dinner Mon.-Sat., $$$*

The real excitement at this modern Santa Monica restaurant is upstairs in the patio bar, where the late-night trendy Gen-X action takes place. Cutting-edge chef Neil Frazier has designed a menu featuring such eclectic entrées as rice-crusted Chilean sea bass, venison and grilled vegetable tian. Although we found the lamb shank a bit fatty, we highly recommend the porterhouse steak and the warm St. Agur cheese tart appetizer. The caramelized banana tart with chocolate crème brûleé is exquisite. There is often live music to make the upstairs scene even livelier.

RÖCKENWAGNER CALIFORNIAN 15/20 

2435 Main St., Santa Monica 90405
310-399-6504 ,*Dinner nightly, Brunch Sat.-Sun., $$$*

The bastion of one of L.A.'s most talented chef/bakers, this handsome and modern restaurant in the Frank Gehry-designed Edgemar complex offers a small but always intriguing selection of Hans Röckenwagner's inspired and expertly executed dishes. Among his "classics" are the crab soufflé with sliced mango, the "short stack" of smoked salmon, potato chips and caviar and the roasted air-dried duck. We're keen, too, for such inventions as prosciutto and grilled pears with melted foie gras and port wine reduction, pumpkin-seed-crusted salmon and grilled scallops on coconut-mashed sweet potatoes. Weekend brunch revolves around his superb German-style breads. Anytime, if you come alone, you'll eat well—and make friends—at the single-diners' table.

R-23 JAPANESE/SUSHI 13/20 

923 E.Third St., Downtown 90013
213-687-7178, *Lunch Mon.-Fri., Dinner Mon.-Sat., $$*

A favorite of visiting Japanese businessmen, this well hidden eatery in the loft district near Little Tokyo is hard to find even for locals, yet many regard the sushi here among the very best in town. The stark, high-ceilinged neo-industrial setting consists of whitewashed walls with contemporary art and funky chairs upholstered with cardboard. There's a menu of cooked specialties, but we've found them generally disappointing. The way to make the most of R-23 is to stick to what it does best: exquisitely fresh sushi served on boldly emblazoned platters or striking marble slabs. The fish is of premier quality and the resident sushi chefs execute their craft with finesse and artistry.

RUTH'S CHRIS STEAKHOUSE STEAKHOUSE 14/20 

224 S. Beverly Dr., Beverly Hills 90212
310-859-8744, *Dinner nightly, $$$*

Think juicy red meat sizzling on a platter and dripping in butter. That's the big draw at this steakhouse, one of a national chain born in New Orleans. You can order veal, lamb, chicken or fish, but we suggest you stick with Ruth's Chris' hand-cut U.S. prime mid-western filet mignon, rib-eye, New York strip, T-bone or porterhouse-for-two steaks, accompanied by one of seven preparations of potatoes. After, try the bread pudding with whiskey sauce, another rich-and-luscious New Orleans specialty.

SABOR — LATIN AMERICAN 12/20

3221 Pico Blvd., Santa Monica 90405
310-829-3781, *Lunch Mon.-Fri., Dinner nightly, $$*

While the adobe-style walls are covered with masks and folk crafts that could be from exotic Central American villages or a Zuni reservation, the cuisine borrows elements from Louisiana, El Salvador, the Caribbean and Brazil—all with a touch of whimsy that could only happen in L.A. Appetizers include baby cactus salad, pupusas and coxinhas, pastry balls stuffed with a creamy chicken mousse. Entrées run from lamb chops in a mulato chile-and-Roquefort sauce, and Jamaican jerkspiced filet mignon, to a terrific mesquite grilled salmon enhanced with molasses, ginger, sesame and lime. Sabor's globetrotting wine list is modestly priced.

SCHATZI — NEW AMERICAN 13/20

3110 Main St., Santa Monica 90405
310-399-4800, *Lunch Mon.-Fri., Dinner nightly, Brunch Sat.-Sun., $$$*

Okay, so Arnold Schwarzenegger and Maria Shriver own this place. Don't think celebrity haunt. Focus instead on the kitchen, which puts out consistently good food with an Austrian twist. Mostly the food is sophisticated renditions of home-style cooking: maple-Dijon sauced salmon, crabcakes, pizzas and pastas. We like the wienerschnitzel, bratwurst and knockwurst best—and the handsome beer-hall-meets-California decor. When Maria's cousin, JFK, Jr. is in town, he sometimes brunches on the patio.

SEOUL JUNG — KOREAN 13/20

Omni Los Angeles Hotel, 930 Wilshire Blvd., Los Angeles 90017
213 688-7880, *Lunch & Dinner daily, $$*

At the entrance to this exotic temple of refined Korean cuisine in the Korean Airlines-owned Omni Hotel, a two-ton marble sphere gently floats on a cushion of water, an impressive display of tranquility. State-of-the-art grills are set in the center of each polished granite tabletop, where guests barbecue their own well-seasoned meats, shrimp and chicken, Korean-style. (A special exhaust system draws the smoke up completely away from the tables.) The setting—and moderate prices—make this an excellent exotic downtown dining destination. Great lunchtime specials.

17TH STREET CAFÉ — CALIFORNIAN 12/20

1610 Montana Ave., Santa Monica 90403
310-453-2771, *Breakfast, Lunch & Dinner daily, $$*

A favorite Montana Avenue dining destination for years, this cozy eatery offers moderate prices and an array of intriguing dishes and reasonably priced wines. Its unflashy, earth-toned dining room is a pleasant refuge for many of the café's high-profile regulars steering out of the fast lane for an evening of straightforward fare. Big salads—Chinese chicken, blue cheese-walnut, yellowtail—California pizzas and pastas are popular, along with such entrées as orange-curry chicken, pesto-marinated salmon and steak.

72 MARKET STREET CALIFORNIAN/FRENCH 14/20 

72 Market St., Venice 90291
310-392-8720, *Lunch Mon.-Fri., Dinner nightly,* $$$$

A hip, high-tech place in the heart of the Venice art scene. Stellar chef Roland Gibert turns out cuisine as impressive as the restaurant's soaring, glass-and-concrete, art-filled interior (even the earthquake support pole is decorated with a Robert Graham relief sculpture). We find the chairs a bit uncomfortable, the tables a bit cramped, but the action at the oyster bar is something to behold and the fare is memorable. In addition to fresh seafood galore, good starters include the artichoke-and-truffle bouillon with grilled prawns and orange confit, and stuffed zucchini blossoms with mushrooms and truffle sauce. Entrées range from linguini with lobster and shiitake mushrooms and a so-so pan-seared John Dory, to a lusty cassoulet. The wine list is extensive, eclectic and expensive.

SHAHRZAD PERSIAN 12/20

1422 Westwood Blvd., Westwood 90024
310-470-3242, *Lunch & Dinner daily,* $

Consistently good Persian food at reasonable prices. The lamb tahchin, saffron- and yogurt-marinated lamb on tah dig (a crispy yogurt, egg and rice base), is good. Savory other choices are the beef, chicken and veal stews: fesenjan covers the meat in a rich walnut-and-pomegranate paste. Don't pass up the mast o'khiar, a yogurt dipping sauce studded with crushed herbs, walnuts and raisins.

SHANGHAI REDS CALIFORNIAN 13/20 

23813 Fiji Way, Marina del Rey 90292
310-823-4522, *Lunch & Dinner daily, Brunch Sun.,* $$

This was the first restaurant built in the marina—nearly forty years ago—and it's still a lively spot for watching the boats and the sunset. Enter over a trellis-covered bridge that spans the koi ponds, then into the spacious Victorian setting. We like the garden patio on warm days; the bar has a fireplace for cold nights. Nearly every table in the series of dining areas has a marina view. Start with the steamed clams and dip the fresh-baked focaccia rolls into the buttery lemon broth. We recommend the shrimp with mango salsa and the prime rib, or design your own seafood pasta from a selection of sauces. Take advantage of the budget "Sunset Suppers" before 6 p.m.

SHARK BAR SOUTHERN/SOUL FOOD 12/20

826 N. La Cienega Blvd., W. Hollywood 90048
310-652-1520, *Dinner nightly,* $$

You'll see stars from the worlds of TV sitcoms, rap music and pro sports at this clubby Chicago-born spot—if you can get in. There's always a crush of gorgeous—mostly African-American—Gen-Xers waiting to crowd into the lounge or pose at the long bar. Down-home comfort food is served in the dining room: crabcakes, catfish, gumbo, barbecued ribs and fried chicken, with all the trimmings.

SHIBUCHO JAPANESE 12/20

333 S. Alameda St., #317, Downtown 90013
213-626-1184, *Lunch & Dinner daily, $$$*

There's an elegance to eating at Shibucho that's uniquely Japanese. The sushi is fresh and quite fine, particularly the belly cut of tuna called toro (in season). Ask for omakase, "chef's choice," and you'll be rewarded with the best morsels the chef has on hand. **Also in the Melrose-La Brea area (3114 W. Beverly Blvd., 213-387-8498).**

SIAMESE GARDEN THAI 12/20

301 Washington Blvd., Marina del Rey 90292
310-821-0098, *Lunch Mon.-Fri., Dinner nightly, $*

This tiny gem of a converted cottage houses a wonderfully intimate Thai restaurant. Stoop through the tiny doorway into the candlelit dining room. Once inside, you'll feel as if you've discovered a wonderful secret. There are a few tables and very private booths concealed behind gauzy curtains. Try the yam yai salad, the succulent ginger fish, the deliciously spicy beef salad, the sinus-declogging Thai sausage and any of the noodle dishes. The homemade coconut ice cream is marvelous.

SIAMESE PRINCESS GINGER GRILL THAI 12/20

8048 W. Third St., W. Hollywood 90048
323-653-2643, *Lunch Fri., Dinner Tues.-Sun., $$*

More expensive than most Thai eateries, the former Siamese Princess now boasts Thai dishes found nowhere else in Los Angeles, like chicken with walnuts, pork tossed with crisply fried noodles and duck-and-escargots-filled dumplings, as well as other favorites like mee krob in peanut sauce. As the name implies, the Siamese Princess exudes royalty, with countless framed photographs of the Thai-royal family on the walls.

SOFI GREEK 13/20

8030 3/4 W. Third St., W. Hollywood 90048
213-651-0346, *Lunch Mon.-Sat., Dinner nightly, $$*

Dining on the bougainvillea-shaded patio will make you think you're in Mykonos. Sitting in the two-level interior, you'll feel you're a guest in a gracious Greek home. Share an array of such appetizers as fresh feta cheese doused with olive oil and oregano, tzatziki (yogurt and cucumbers), octopus salad and spanakopita, crisp little phyllo-dough spinach turnovers. We enjoy Sofi's moussaka, souvlaki, and lemony baked chicken. In fact we like most of the down-home Greek food here.

SPAGO BEVERLY HILLS CALIFORNIAN 16/20 

176 N. Canon Dr., Beverly Hills 90210
310-385-0880, *Lunch Mon.-Sat., Dinner nightly, $$$$*

Larger and with a more stunning décor—by Puck's wife and partner, Barbara Lazaroff— than the original Sunset Strip Spago, this is a gorgeous, exciting—and noisy—spot to see-and-be-seen. Puck has departed from his designer pizza-and-pasta formula, presenting a menu that was inspired by cuisines from all over the globe. We have enjoyed the tempura soft-shell crabs with black bean sauce, the thickly sliced côte de boeuf with a potato-garlic-cheese purée, the grilled whole fish with artichokes, lemon and coriander—and for dessert, the apple strudel. Try to get a table on the patio, which is shaded by two century-old olive trees and sports a fountain inscribed with "passion" in twenty languages. On the other hand, unless you're somebody, be grateful if you can get a table anywhere in the restaurant—without calling months in advance.

SPAGO HOLLYWOOD CALIFORNIAN 15/20 

1114 Horn Ave., W. Hollywood 90069
310-652-4025, *Dinner Tues.-Sat., $$$*

Overlooking Sunset Strip, this restaurant isn't just filled with Spago B.H. overflow or those who aren't tony enough to get a reservation at the new digs. Many old Spago regulars actually prefer this smaller, more casual—and compared to the B.H. location, calmer—restaurant. Besides, unlike at the new Spago, you can get Puck's signature wood-burning-oven pizza here. Puck is far from being a nightly presence, but he trains good people, and you can dine well without being either rich or famous. In addition to the pizzas, we've always been partial to such dishes as the lobster spring roll, the chopped Chino farm salad, the roasted whole fish, the lobster with fettuccine and the Cantonese duck with whatever sauce Puck dreams up. The desserts get better and better, as does the remarkable wine list.

STEPPS ON THE COURT ECLECTIC 12/20

Wells Fargo Center, 350 S. Hope St., Downtown 90071
213-626-0900, *Lunch Mon.-Fri., Dinner nightly, $$*

Stepps' "vibe" is popular with Downtown's young urban professionals, and so is the food. Pastas, salads and daily fish specials are mainstays, as are such "share" dishes as fried gouda cheese with apples and smoked lamb ribs. We appreciate their fresh-baked focaccia. The open dining area is packed at lunch, so making reservations is a must; even dinnertime can be lively—a rarity downtown.

SUSHI-KO JAPANESE 13/20

2932 1/2 Beverly Glen Circle, Bel Air 90077
310-475-8689, *Lunch Mon.-Fri., Dinner nightly, $$*

Hidden away in the tiny and tony shopping center at the top of Beverly Glen Canyon, this chi-chi sushi bar is a favorite with celebs who don't want to see-and-be-seen. The fresh sushi is first-rate, but you pay for what you get.

SUSHI ROKU JAPANESE 14/20

8445 W. Third St., W. Hollywood 90048
323-655-6767, *Lunch Mon.-Fri., Dinner nightly, $$*

This Matsuhisa wannabe is a favorite with the Gen-X movie-industry set. In sleekly modern surroundings, share such delicate and exotic appetizers as tuna tataki salad, monkfish pâté and rock shrimp popcorn tempura, followed by every manner of sushi including a roll filled with shrimp and deep-fried jalapeño peppers, and the sea bass with shredded deep-fried yams. Wash it all down with sake or such potent specialty drinks as the "Tokyo Rose," a blend of sake, plum wine, triple sec and a splash of cranberry juice.

SUSHI SASABUNE — SUSHI — 14/20

11300 Nebraska St., W.L.A. 90025
310-268-8380, *Lunch Mon.-Fri., Dinner Mon.-Sat., $$*

Okay, so Sasabune looks like it was plopped down in what was an old Mexican restaurant, and without a reservation you'll have to wait an hour for a table. The regular crowd of sushi mavens puts up with it—and with the slow service—to dine on some of the best sushi in town. Don't expect the chef to customize your sushi to suit your taste. At Sasabune, what the chef makes is what you get.

TAHITI — ECLECTIC — 14/20

7910 W. Third St., Melrose-Fairfax 90048
323-651-1213, *Lunch Mon.-Fri., Dinner Mon.-Sat., $$*

Giant pillows invite guests to lounge on the faux leopard-skin banquettes; peacock feather-covered light fixtures hang from the ceiling; a fringe of thatch borders the glassed-in kitchen where chef/owner Tony Di Lembo and crew turn out his lusty and exotic cuisine. We're mad for the crabcakes puffed up with crispy angel hair pasta, any of the pizzas, the pasta with mussels and white beans, the sesame-seed-encrusted rare ahi tuna and the chewy but flavorful T-bone steak topped with fabulous beer-battered onion rings. Start with a drink on the bamboo-bordered patio, and finish off with the rich chocolate-pudding cake.

TAIKO — JAPANESE/NOODLES — 13/20

11677 San Vicente, Ste. 302, Brentwood 90049
310-207-7782, *Lunch & Dinner daily, $*

This architecturally stunning little noodle shop would be a sleeper except for one thing: it's been discovered, and they've added sushi and sashimi to the menu. We like the combination specials served with a choice of either hot or cold soba or udon noodles. For those who want to design their own noodle bowl, Taiko offers a list of eighteen extras to add; among these are Japanese mountain vegetables, fried soy bean curd, tempura batter, cod roe, and grated raw Japanese yam. There are daily bento-box specials.

TAKAO — JAPANESE/SUSHI — 14/20

11656 San Vicente Blvd., Brentwood 90049
310-207-8636, *Lunch Mon.-Sat., Dinner nightly, $$*

Takao, the chef/owner, was a chef at Matsuhisa—need we say more? Not to be confused with Taiko, the Brentwood Japanese noodle restaurant described above, this clean-and-spare Brentwood storefront specializes in sushi and innovative Japanese preparations from fish bone chips to fresh seaweed salad. The servers treat you like family when you come by yourself—and when you come back with all your friends. This is a perfect spot for a small bite, but beware of a big check if you have a hearty appetite.

TALESAI THAI 14/20

9043 Sunset Blvd., W. Hollywood 90069
310-275-9724, *Lunch Mon.-Fri., Dinner Mon.-Sat.,* **$$**

Talesai is the most upscale Thai restaurant in town, and you may see rockers from the nearby Roxy supping before their set in this sleek, all-white setting. The "heavenly" barbecued chicken—marinated in coconut milk and spiced with ginger and turmeric—justifies its name. We love the shrimp curry served in a pineapple shell, the Thai salmon, and the pad Thai noodles tossed with chicken and shellfish in a punchy peanut sauce.

TAM O'SHANTER INN ENGLISH/AMERICAN 12/20

2980 Los Feliz Blvd., Atwater Village 90039
323-664-0228, *Lunch Mon.-Fri., Dinner nightly, Sun. Brunch,* **$$**

This Lawry's operation has been around since 1922, and features a fun Scottish pub atmosphere. House specialties include Scotch rarebit, toad in the hole and prime rib, as well as hard-to-resist sides of creamed spinach and creamed corn. The service is friendly and efficient, the Sunday brunch is one of the best-kept secrets in town, and on Bobbie Burns birthday, they bring out the bagpipers and the haggis. The Happy Hour is lively.

TAMAYO MEXICAN 11/20

5300 E. Olympic Blvd., E. Los Angeles 90022
323-260-4700, *Lunch Mon.-Fri., Dinner Mon.-Sat.,* **$**

Owned by an influential non-profit community organization—and a shining example of successful economic development in East L.A.—this rambling great-looking establishment is named after the great Mexican painter, Rufino Tamayo. Located in a converted historic home, Tamayo's spacious dining room reflects the fine Spanish hacienda-style architecture of the late 1920s. The menu is not particularly exciting, but the kitchen does a commendable job with fajitas, enchiladas and other favorites. Worth a trip for the Old L.A. ambience alone.

TAVERNA TONY GREEK 12/20

23410 Civic Center Way, Malibu 90265
310-317-9667, *Lunch & Dinner daily,* **$$**

This friendly Malibu eatery serves traditional dishes reminiscent of the Greek Isles—moussaka, roasted baby lamb and whole grilled striped bass scented with olive oil, garlic and herbs. Start with the flaming saganaki cheese or the spanakopita, and try some of the homemade Greek sweets with your coffee.

TERRAZZA OF BEL AIR ITALIAN 14/20 

2960 Beverly Glen CircleBel Air 90077
310-475-7404, *Lunch & Dinner daily,* **$$**

Located in the most exclusive strip mall in L.A. (at Beverly Glen Boulevard near Mulholland), where you're likely to see movie stars picking up their dry-cleaning, this tiny but sleek trattoria features a warming hearth, a ficus-tree-bordered patio and terrific California-ized Italian cuisine. Start with a garlicky grilled portobello mushroom bruschetta or a salad of arugula and pear, followed by ahi tuna on a bed of three-grain salad or salmon with herb-accented polenta.

TESORO TRATTORIA ITALIAN 12/20

300 S. Grand Ave., Downtown 90071
213-680-0000
Lunch Mon.-Fri., Dinner Mon.-Sat., $$

Tesoro is one of those places that many downtown high-rise workers and theater-goers regard as their own little secret. Located in the picturesque fountain court of California Plaza, this trattoria is stylishly decked out in polished mahogany, etched glass and tasteful artwork. The Tuscan-inspired menu offers an array of familiar specialties such as calamari fritti, tuna carpaccio, Caesar salad, pizzas, veal Marsala and tiramisu, all very respectably prepared. It's an easy walk from here to the Music Center.

THAI HOUSE THAI 11/20

8657 W. Pico Blvd., W. L.A. 90035
310-274-5492, *Lunch Mon.-Sat., Dinner nightly, $*

Where to go if you want to dress in black and nibble on delicious chicken satay, squid salad or spicy-and-sour seafood soup. This stark, postmodern Thai café offers a few unique specialties like the "Eight Musketeers," sautéed scallops, shrimp, squid, chicken, snow peas, bamboo shoots and fresh greens in a spicy house sauce. **Also in Westwood (1049 Gayley Ave., 310-208-2676).**

TOMMY TANG'S THAI 14/20

7313 Melrose Ave., Melrose-La Brea 90046
323-937-5733, *Lunch & Dinner daily, $$*

One of L.A.'s trendiest Thai restaurants is still one of its best. Sit on the plant-filled patio or inside the casual but attractive dining room, and order the signature "Tommy duck," two-pepper salmon or grilled prawns with curry. Also terrific: the chicken satay, the zesty Malaysian clams and the spicy mint noodles. On Tuesday nights, waiters dress in drag and the place becomes a gender-bender glam spot, with music and videos to match.

TOP OF FIVE INTERNATIONAL 12/20

The Bonaventure Hotel
Fifth & Figueroa Sts., Downtown 90071
213-612-4743, *Lunch Mon.-Fri., Dinner nightly, $$$*

Perched atop the five towers (hence the name) of the still futuristic Bonaventure Hotel, Top of Five is a ring of dreams, 360 degrees of glass and steel and the romance is on its way. The decor has a soft touch of nostalgia, with well-separated booths ideal for lovers. Sit on the west side and watch a glorious sunset, after which the fairy electricity spells its magic on the City of Angels. The dishes display an international accent—baked East Coast oysters, steamed New Zealand mussels, Indonesian rack of lamb, Pacific bouillabaisse.

TOSCANA ITALIAN 14/20 

11633 San Vicente Blvd., Brentwood 90049
310-820-2448, *Lunch Mon.-Sat., Dinner nightly, $$*

Before there was Ago and the Rösti chain, there was Toscana. Agostino Sciandri's clubby little trattoria in Brentwood is still always jam-packed. You have to make reservations a week in advance, and when you get here you have to wait, but the food is worth it: thin-crusted pizzas, chewy focaccias and pastas, aromatic steaks seasoned with olive oil and sizzling veal chops. We're crazy about Sciandri's signature pollo al mattone, rosemary-and-garlic-kissed chicken that's grilled under a weight.

THE TOWER CONTINENTAL 11/20

1150 S. Olive St., Downtown 90015
213-746-1554, *Lunch Mon.-Fri., Dinner Mon.-Sat., $$$*

L.A.'s answer to New York's Window on the Worlds restaurant atop the World Trade Center, this "view" restaurant on the 32nd floor of the Transamerica Building does a big corporate and special-occasion business. Which means the service is old-fashioned formal and the menu tends towards Continental classics: chilled shrimp, onion soup or a Caesar salad to start, followed by such entrées as grilled beef tenderloin and roasted rack of lamb. There are more fanciful dishes, such as miso-marinated sea bass and seared ahi tuna in a sesame crust, but they're not reason to come. It's all about that spectacular, sparkling-light view.

TRADER VIC'S POLYNESIAN 12/20

Beverly Hilton, 9876 Wilshire Blvd., Beverly Hills 90210
310-274-7777, *Dinner nightly, $$$*

This upscale Tahitian beach shack, with its hanging "Tiki" longboat and a view of a lush, tropical garden, has been a Beverly Hills fixture forever. These days, it's not just old-money types dining here, but young up-and-comers who fancy the kitschy decor and the fun bar scene. Who needs martinis when you can choose from over 75 tropical rum drinks? Share a selection of Trader Vic's "tidbits," everything from spareribs and crab Rangoon to pancake-wrapped ham-and-cheese "bings" and rumaki. This being the late 90's, there's even sushi. Our favorites among the entrées are the squab, salmon and rack of lamb roasted in the Chinese wood-fired ovens.

TRATTORIA AMICI ITALIAN 14/20 

469 N. Doheny Dr., Beverly Hills 90210
310-858-0271, *Lunch Mon.-Fri., Dinner Mon.-Sat., $$*

A nondescript motel is hardly the place you'd expect to find an Italian restaurant as good as this one, but here it is. We appreciate the warm, homey atmosphere and the generous portions of superb—reasonably priced—rustic Italian cuisine. Start with bundles of smoked salmon-wrapped shoestring potatoes, a bracing salad of raw baby artichokes and hearts of palm, or a crisp-crusted pizza. Move on to such hearty pastas as the rigatoni with chicken and sun-dried-tomato sausage. And by all means, order the tender garlic-kissed whole (yes, whole) grilled chicken.

TRATTORIA FARFALLA ITALIAN 13/20 

1978 Hillhurst Ave., Los Feliz 90027
323-661-7365, *Lunch Mon.-Fri., Dinner nightly, $*

This cramped but homey neighborhood spot is so good, there's usually a wait. (Old regulars actually prefer it to the newer more spacious Farfalla on La Brea.) The roasted chicken is simple perfection and the pizzas are sublime, as are such pastas as tagliolini with shrimp, garlic and zucchini. We love their creamy tiramisu.

TRAXX CALIFORNIAN 12/20

Union Station, 800 N. Alameda St., Downtown 90012
213-625-1999, *Lunch Mon.-Fri., Dinner Mon.-Sat., $$$*

There's now a serious restaurant in the historic Union Station. Traxx's sleekly designed dining room embodies the romance of train travel, with seating under the station's dramatic 50-foot arch, as well as in a courtyard under a canopy of jacaranda trees. On the small, frequently changing menu, we've enjoyed the crabcakes with chipotle chile rémoulade, the grilled lamb chops with basil-pesto risotto and the house-cured double-cut pork chop with prosciutto and polenta. The rosemary bread pudding topped with a cinnamon-raspberry sauce is sublime.

2424 PICO ECLECTIC 13/20 

2424 Pico Blvd., Santa Monica 90405
310-581-1124, *Lunch Mon.-Fri., Dinner Tue.-Sun., $$*

This out-of-the-way spot, "in" with those who know, features unadorned mustard-and-burgundy walls, roomy booths, striped banquettes and an open kitchen in which chef David Wolfe draws inspiration from every corner of the globe. We love his rendition of a Greek salad: a large timbale covered with cucumbers and layered with roasted red peppers, feta cheese and a pungent kalamata olive tapenade. He makes Korean "tacos" with ground rib-eye steak stuffed in romaine leaves, prepares sea bass with a ginger-lemon grass-cilantro crust and glazes game hens with honey and pomegranate. The wine list includes selections from some boutique California wineries.

TYPHOON PACIFIC RIM 14/20 

3221 Donald Douglas Loop South, Santa Monica 90405
310-390-6565, *Lunch Sun.-Fri., Dinner nightly, Brunch Sun., $$*

Celebs like John Travolta have been known to fly their own planes to this hip, high-tech restaurant on the edge of the Santa Monica Airport, where the walls showcase customers' pilot licenses like the caricatures of movie-star clients at The Palm. The exhibition kitchen features dishes from throughout Asia, which means you can make an exotic, tasty mix-and-match meal of Japanese pot stickers, Chinese dim sum, Thai coconut-chicken curry and Indonesian stir-fried noodles. You can gaze out the Cinemascope windows at the planes taking off and landing, but it's so noisy inside, you'll never hear them. In warm weather, the rooftop becomes an Asian beer garden.

VALENTINO ITALIAN 17/20 

3115 W. Pico Blvd., Santa Monica 90405
310-829-4313, *Dinner Mon.-Sat.*, $$$

It's on a bleak stretch of Pico where you'd never expect to see Mercedes and other luxury vehicles heading into a restaurant parking lot. But there they are every night. Dedicated followers of owner Piero Selvaggio swear that this is the best Italian restaurant in town. Ignore the menu (and prepare not to look when you see the tab) and ask Selvaggio to order for you. He will undoubtedly come up with some stellar pasta (pappardelle with duck ragout), a starter like rabbit with mushrooms and some stunning entrée involving veal, lamb or fish. In season, order the celestial risotto with white truffles, which Selvaggio calls "The Lord's Porridge." Even though Selvaggio lost 20,000 bottles of wine in the last big earthquake, he still has one of the best wine lists in California.

VERSAILLES CUBAN 12/20

10319 Venice Blvd., Culver City 90034
310-558-3168, *Lunch & Dinner daily*, $

Prices are low at these noisy, hipster-filled Cuban restaurants, and the decor is nondescript. Still, prepare to wait for a table. The reason: the roast chicken, served with sweet raw onions and fried plantains on white rice is luscious to the max. **Also in W.L.A. (1415 S. La Cienega Blvd, 310-289-0392), Encino and Manhattan Beach.**

VICTOR HODD'S AMERICAN/ECLECTIC 12/20

7953 Santa Monica Blvd., W. Hollywood 90046
323-822-9652, *Dinner nightly, Brunch Sun.*, $$$

What was formerly a picnic-tabled seafood joint is now a stylish supper club, with muted colors, ceiling fans and jazz. Chef Daly Thompson's menu offers an appealingly eclectic cuisine featuring dishes that often reflect his Southern heritage, such as grilled chicken and andouille sausage skewers, Creole shrimp cakes and Cajun-style barbecued pork loin. His wife, pâtissière Liz Thompson, bakes scrumptious rolls and desserts.

VIDA ECLECTIC 14/20

1930 Hillhurst, Los Feliz 90027
323-660-4445, *Dinner nightly*, $$$

Chef/owner Fred Eric never met a pun he didn't like—they're all over the menu at his high-tech beyond-hip restaurant. ("Rolling Along" is a thin-and-crispy spring roll; "Mr. French II" is a caramelized leg of lamb with fresh pappardelle pasta.) Despite the humor of the dishes' names, Eric's cooking style is no joke. You can count on gorgeous presentations and creative combinations of flavors. Wines are listed by adjective ("ripe, intense, rich, spicy") rather than varietal or region.

VINCENTI RISTORANTE ITALIAN 16/20

11930 San Vicente Blvd., Brentwood 90049
310-207-0127, *Dinner Tues.-Sun., $$$*

This sleekly modern trattoria, the effort of Maureen Vincenti and chef Gino Angelini, is all marble counters, blond woods and stunning modern Italian light fixtures. The menu consists of the simple yet sublime cuisine that Angelini did so well at the late Rex, Il Ristorante (which was owned by Maureen and her late husband, Mauro Vincenti): grilled scallops with tomato-mint sauce, sautéed zucchini and ricotta cheese, cheese-fondue-and-almond ravioli with spinach-and-mushroom sauce, potato gnocchi with pigeon ragu, and, especially, succulent, fork-tender meats from the wood-burning rotisserie and the wood-burning oven. As at Rex, the wine list is impressive, and the desserts—caramelized apple purée in caramel cake with green-apple sorbetto, for example—are divine. Mauro would be proud.

V.I.P. HARBOR SEAFOOD CHINESE 13/20 

11701 Wilshire Blvd., W.L.A. 90025
310-979-3377, *Lunch & Dinner daily, $$*

An offshoot of a popular Chinese restaurant in San Gabriel, V.I.P is a gift to Westsiders who love Cantonese seafood. As its a great place for a multi-course Chinese banquet, you'll usually see lots of parties of six or more dining in these rather dressy surroundings. Go for the dim sum during the day. But at night, try such specialties as crab with black bean sauce, crispy fish with ginger-and-scallion sauce and shrimp on a skewer with spicy salt. This is one of those rare local restaurants where you can rely on the quality of such delicacies as shark's fin soup and Peking duck, dramatically carved at tableside.

WARSZAWA POLISH 13/20 

1414 Lincoln Blvd., Santa Monica 90401
310-393-8831, *Dinner Tues.-Sun., $$*

Polish cuisine has never been considered sexy. That, coupled with the fact that it's hardly considered health food, has put it at a distinct disadvantage in the L.A. market. Still, Warszawa has lasted longer than dozens of trendsetters. A charming bungalow whose intimate rooms are decorated with Polish poster art, the restaurant serves such traditional dishes as borscht, country pâté and dried plums wrapped in bacon, roasted duck with delightfully crispy skin and pierogi stuffed with cheeses, meats and vegetables. For dessert, try the vanilla crêpes.

WATER GRILL SEAFOOD 13/20 

544 S. Grand Ave., Downtown 90071
213-891-0900, *Lunch Mon.-Fri., Dinner nightly, $$*

An ocean of money went into this dark and clubby art-deco dining room and bar, a sophisticated haven in the heart of downtown. The Maine lobsters and Dungeness crabs are plucked, live, from the restaurant's tanks. You can also get such hard-to-find fresh fish as wild Columbia River sturgeon, Arctic char, white Mexican shrimp and New Zealand daurade. The clam chowder is silken.

WASHINGTON STREET BAR & GRILL AMERICAN 11/20

3016 Washington St., Marina del Rey
310-823-9898, *Dinner nightly, $$*

Gerri Gilliland is busy running three successful restaurants in Santa Monica—Gilliland's, Lula Cucina Mexicana, and Jake and Annie's—which may be why we found the food and service at her newest endeavor a bit off. We like the look of the place: mahogany wainscoting, beamed ceilings, a mixture of banquette and table seating. However, we found that the Caesar salad had a timid dressing, and the steaks—cooked over the special Santa Maria-style barbecue—were a bit tough.

WOLFGANG PUCK CAFÉ CALIFORNIAN 13/20 

8000 Sunset Blvd., Los Angeles 90046
323-650-7300 , *Lunch & Dinner daily, $*

Casual, colorful spin-offs of Spago, these cafés serve Puck's wood-fired pizzas and pastas, bounteous salads, good rotisserie-roasted chicken and a few Pacific Rim dishes inspired by Chinois. Barbara Lazaroff's appealing decor uses lots of tiles, ceramic art pieces and various other flights of whimsy. When they offer such dinner specials as grilled ahi tuna and wienerschnitzel, go for it—they're almost as good as Spago's but only half the price. **Also in Santa Monica (1323 Montana Ave., 310-393-0290).**

WOODSIDE NEW AMERICAN 14/20 

11604 San Vicente Blvd., Brentwood 90049
310-571-3800, *Lunch Mon.-Fri., Dinner nightly, $$*

With its exposed-brick walls, ironwood tables and chairs, and a long, dark wood bar enclosing the open kitchen, this newish neighborhood bistro looks like it has been here forever. The service is friendly and attentive. The seasonally changing cuisine is sophisticated, imaginative—and often inspired. We recently found the beet purée soup tasty but a bit tepid, but we were knocked out by a salad of julienned pears, Gorgonzola cheese, endive, rocket and spiced pecans, and such entrées as the rare tuna steak atop a crispy rice cake stacked with braised daikon and shiitake mushrooms, and the fork-tender veal shank tufted with savory mixed sprouts. For dessert, both the persimmon pudding and apple pie were sensational.

XI-AN CHINESE 12/20

362 N. Canon Dr., Beverly Hills 90210
310-275-3345, *Lunch & Dinner daily, $$*

On a sunny day, the sidewalk patio at Xi-an abounds with fashionable ladies and businessmen doing lunch. At this sleekly modern Beverly Hills spot, the fare is Chinese food for the California palate, and in many cases, waistline. About one-third of the dishes are preceded by those telltale American Heart Association hearts, including a pretty tasty chopped chicken salad and foil-wrapped chicken. While the succulent duck dishes are "heartless," the true health fanatic can order something called "Power Zone Rice" made with brown and wild rice and egg whites.

YUJEAN KANG'S CHINESE 16/20 

8826 Melrose Ave., W. Hollywood 90069
310-288-0806, *Lunch & Dinner daily, $$*

At this simple yet elegant restaurant, Yujean Kang dazzles guests with translucent pork-and-shrimp dumplings, gossamer crêpes stuffed with prawns in pickled cabbage and blackened chilies, and astoundingly delicate—and delicious—Beijing duck. Kang's presentations are breathtaking, his combinations of flavors inspired. It's hard to choose among such specialties as duck-and-mushroom soup garnished with a savory meringue, Chinese noodles with beef, sun-dried tomatoes and chili oil, fresh prawns with fava beans, mushrooms, tomato, garlic and ginger, and Szechwan-style flank steak with sweet bell peppers and anise seed. Ask the chef to plan your menu and your wines—about which he is also an expert.

ZENZERO PACIFIC RIM 15/20

1535 Ocean Ave., Santa Monica 90401
310-451-4455, *Lunch Mon.-Fri., Dinner nightly, $$*

This ultra-modern restaurant facing the Pacific dramatically combines California and Asian influences in its decor: tile-and-wood floors, a mural that is part Renaissance Italy, part Japan. Chef Fred Iwasaki presents generous portions of gorgeous, vibrantly flavored Pacific Rim cuisine: stir-fried spicy chicken scooped up in leaves of radicchio, wok-fried calamari tossed in a vegie salad, Chilean sea bass dusted with crushed Chinese black beans and zested with red-and-yellow-tomato salsa. The Chinese air-dried duck with plum wine-orange reduction is crisp-skinned perfection. Come at sunset, when the view of the ocean is spectacular.

ZOOMA SUSHI JAPANESE/SUSHI 13/20 

29350 PCH, Malibu
310-457-4131, *Dinner nightly, $$*

The light and airy dining room overlooks a Japanese garden and koi pond, and is usually filled with locals who seem to know everyone there. Try the rainbow rolls and spider rolls, the deep-fried calamari, tempura dishes and the grilled chicken or crispy shrimp. The apple or banana tempura, and the tempura green-tea ice cream, are desserts you won't find many other places. And for a tiny little restaurant, they have a surprisingly impressive wine list. Mid-week, the specials are $2 less than on weekends.

AND ALSO...

BARFLY — CALIFORNIAN

8730 W. Sunset Blvd., W. Hollywood 90069
310-360-9490, *Dinner nightly*, *$$$*

There's pretty good Wolfgang Puck-ish food here—the chef, Kazuto Matsuka, came from Puck's Chinois on Main via Paris' Buddha Bar. But that's not the reason the glitzy starlet-studded crowd flocks here. Talk about a bar scene! Unless you're gorgeous or rich or *someone,* you can't get into the seen-and-be-seen place after ten, when a deejay pumps up the volume from the balcony. Okay, Barfly is hot—but will it last?

BEAU RIVAGE — MEDITERRANEAN

26025 Pacific Coast Hwy., Malibu 90265
310-456-5733, *Dinner nightly, Brunch Sun., $$$*

This bougainvilla-adorned cottage across PCH from the sea, reminds us of a French or Italian villa. Come for the Continental food, the ambience and the view.

BEL-AIR BAR & GRILL — CALIFORNIAN

662 N. Sepulveda Blvd, Bel Air 90049
310-440-5544, *Lunch & Dinner daily, Brunch Sat.-Sun., $$*

New when we went to press, the Bel-Air Bar & Grill is a good choice if you're en route to the Getty Center nearby. (The restaurant provides free shuttle service.) Expect carpaccio, pastas, grilled fish and meats. The bar is lively until late.

BROADWAY BAR & GRILL — AMERICAN

1460 Third St., Santa Monica 90401
310-393-4211, *Lunch & Dinner daily, Brunch Sat.-Sun., $$*

Even before it was surrounded by the Third Street Promenade, this red-brick walled San Francisco-style bar and grill was reason enough to come to Santa Monica. You'll find one of the city's best burgers, topped with Irish bacon, a dynamite Caesar salad and reliable desserts.

CASA ESCOBAR — MEXICAN

14160 Palawan Way, Marina del Rey 90292
310-822-2199, *Lunch & Dinner daily, $*

A favorite with long-time Marina residents, the Casa has been serving up its South of the Border nightclub ambience and okay Mexican food in the Southland for over 50 years. In the large bar, there's music and dancing on weekends. **Also in Santa Monica (2500 Wilshire Blvd., 310-828-1315).**

CASABLANCA MEXICAN/SEAFOOD

220 Lincoln Blvd.,Venice 90291
310-392-5751, *Lunch & Dinner daily, $*

The quasi-Moroccan decor is right out of the movie, but the food is strictly Mexican: good seafood and wonderful homemade tortillas. We like the festive ambience.

THE CHART HOUSE AMERICAN

18412 Pacific Coast Hwy., Malibu 90265
310-454-9321, *Dinner nightly, Brunch Sun., $$*

A

Perched over the beach, this Chart House has a spectacular ocean and coastline view. But it features the same salad bar, steaks, and grilled fish as at every Chart House in this multi-state chain. Expect a long wait. **Also in Marina del Rey (13950 Panay Way, 310-822-4144).**

CHASEN'S AMERICAN/CONTINENTAL

246 N. Canon Dr., Beverly Hills 90210
310-858-1200, *Lunch Mon.-Fri., Dinner nightly, $$$*

A

Grady Sanders may have purchased the name and some of the memorabilia of the venerable Chasen's, but this place isn't Chasen's. What Sanders has created in the old Bistro space is a distinctive forties-style, multi-level supper club and lounge. Several chefs have come and gone, so we can't give you a money-back guarantee on the food. Stick with such simple dishes as the broiled white fish or the cold poached salmon. The food, however, is irrelevant. The real draw is the crowd.

EPICENTRE CALIFORNIAN

Kawada Hotel, 200 S. Hill St., Downtown 90012
213-625-0000, *Lunch Mon.-Fri., Dinner nightly, $$*

A

The Japanese, familiar with earthquakes, opened this restaurant in the renovated Kawada Hotel. The decor—tempting fate—tries to simulate post-quake chasms in concrete panels, and the menu is full of earthquake-related terms. "Epitizers" include "San Andreas soup" and "epi salad." The "curry on the Richter scale" entrée allows you to choose chicken or shrimp and the desired degree of hotness by picking a number on the scale measuring a quake's magnitude. If you can get past the theme, Epicentre is a respectable addition to this neighborhood.

456 CARETTA CONTEMPORARY/CONTINENTAL

456 N. Bedford Dr., Beverly Hills 90210
310-858-7000, *Lunch & Dinner Mon.-Sat., $$*

On a street known mostly for its Beverly Hills doctors' offices, this charming little café is easily overlooked. Egon Naday, who formerly cooked at the Hotel Bel-Air, does his thing in the open kitchen. Among his classically grounded but inventive dishes: tuna tartare, an arugula salad with prosciutto "bark", shiitake risotto, rack of lamb with tomato-chipotle sauce, ricotta cheese-and-spinach-stuffed squid and wonderful thin-crusted pizzas.

GIGI FRENCH

Hotel Sofitel, 8555 Beverly Blvd., W. Hollywood 90048
310-278-5444, *Breakfast, Lunch & Dinner daily, Brunch Sun., $$*

Located in the French-owned Sofitel, the former La Cajole is a cheerful French bistro with white-tiled floors, dark-wood paneling and French posters. The menu features such traditional French bistro dishes as escargots, crêpes and quiche Lorraine, plus a good steak frites. There's a reasonably priced three-course Sunday Champagne brunch.

GOTHAM HALL CALIFORNIAN

1431 Third Street Promenade, Santa Monica 90401
310-394-8865, *Dinner nightly, $$*

Industry folk like to talk shop over spring rolls and eight balls at this high-end billiard club. Hip's the thing.

IL PICCOLINO ITALIAN

350 N. Robertson Blvd., W. Hollywood 90048
310-659-2220, *Lunch Tues.-Fri., Dinner Tues.-Sun., $*

A charming enclosed patio is the focal point of this casual Italian eatery, which thrived in its first location on Melrose for 11 years. Good pizzas, pastas and such entrées as grilled scampi, along with sandwiches served on rosemary focaccias with great french fries.

INN OF THE SEVENTH RAY HEALTHY/VEGETARIAN

128 Old Topanga Road, Topanga 90290
310-455-1311, *Lunch Mon.-Sat., Dinner nightly, Brunch Sun., $$*

This New Age, outdoorsy hideaway overlooking a creek in Topanga Canyon, has managed to survive despite countless surrounding brush fires. Come for homemade bread, vegetarian entrées and even a few non-vegie dishes such as mango-papaya duck under the oaks. It's often closed for weddings.

KYOTO JAPANESE

Omni Los Angeles Hotel, 930 Wilshire Blvd., Downtown 90017
213-896-3812, *Lunch & Dinner Mon.-Fri.*

A

This smart-and-elegant new restaurant on the hotel's mezzanine level, with its 600-gallon saltwater fish tank, boasts both a sushi and a tempura bar. We recommend the sashimi platter where you may sample not only the expected maguro, but conch and striped-bass, too.

LUCY'S CAFÉ EL ADOBE MEXICAN

5536 Melrose Ave., Hollywood 90038
323-462-9421, *Lunch & Dinner Mon.-Sat., $*

A

Lucy's used to be a pit-stop for famous names (former Governor Jerry Brown and Linda Ronstadt for examples), but the food is just run-of-the-mill Mexican. The margaritas and the dark ambience may explain Lucy's success.

LUMPY GRAVY ECLECTIC

7311 Beverly Blvd., La Brea-Beverly 90036
323-934-9400, *Lunch Mon.-Sat., Dinner nightly, $$*

In highly surreal surroundings—get a load of the zeppelin suspended from the ceiling—enjoy surreal comfort food such as peanut-butter turnovers, macaroni 'n cheez, Zombie-Woof chicken wings and a dessert called the bananagasm. There is live entertainment nightly in this fun spot, everything from jazz to poetry readings.

MILKY WAY KOSHER

9108 W. Pico Blvd., Fairfax District 90035
310-859-0004, *Lunch Mon.-Fri., Dinner Sun.-Thurs., $*

One of L.A.'s most famous Jewish mothers, Mama Spielberg (yes, as in Steven) has been pleasing the crowd long before her son got into the biz. Homemade cheese blintzes, kosher pizzas, potato pancakes and pastas, in a warm family atmosphere.

MOODY'S AMERICAN

The Sheraton Grande Hotel, 333 S. Figueroa St., Downtown 90071
213-617-1133, *Lunch Mon.-Fri., Dinner nightly, $*

A polished wood, San Francisco-style pub inside a major downtown hotel. It's a comfortable, reasonably priced spot for discussing business over a Caesar salad and a steak sandwich. The "Happy Hour" rocks.

OOMASA JAPANESE/SUSHI

100 Japanese Village Plaza Mall, Downtown 90012
213-623-9048, *Lunch & Dinner Wed.-Mon., $$*

With its thatched-bamboo interior, this is an excellent spot to enjoy sushi in the heart of Little Tokyo. We also recommend the deep-fried soft-shell crab and soybeans.

MOONSHADOW BAR & GRILL SEAFOOD

20356 PCH, Malibu 90265
310-456-3010, *Lunch & Dinner daily, $$*

A 🚗 📷 🏃

With the waves crashing on the rocky shore just beneath the window, this place has one great view. We can vouch for the seafood chowder, the fresh broiled salmon and the ahi tuna.

ORIENTAL SEAFOOD INN CHINESE

4016 Lincoln Blvd., Marina del Rey 90292
310-306-9088, *Lunch & Dinner daily, $*

Yuppies who don't want to venture as far as Chinatown, let alone Monterey Park, come here for a fix of Hong Kong-style Chinese seafood and Cantonese standards.

PERESTROYKA RUSSIAN

5468 Wilshire Blvd., Mid-Wilshire 90036
323-934-2215, *Lunch & Dinner daily,* $

The hearty, lamb-based cuisine of the country of Georgia is featured at this ornate restaurant, where a band plays on weekends and the vodka always flows freely. A favorite with Russian emigrées, who dress up to celebrate here.

ROYAL STAR SEAFOOD CHINESE SEAFOOD

3001 Wilshire Blvd., Santa Monica TK
310-828-8812, *Lunch & Dinner daily,* $$

The owners of Monterey Park's venerable Ocean Star, have brought an authentic Cantonese seafood restaurant to the Westside, teeming fish tanks and all. In one of three big dining rooms, savor one of the many fresh crab, shrimp or crayfish specialties. There are chicken and meat dishes as well, but this is one of those places where you should go with a gang of friends, roll up your sleeves and hunker down over plates of eat-with-your-fingers shellfish in a myriad of Chinese sauces.

SOMETHING'S FISHY SUSHI/SEAFOOD

18753 PCH, Malibu 90265
310-456-0027, *Lunch & Dinner daily,* $

Right across the street from the ocean on PCH, Something's Fishy is usually bustling with beach folk. The sushi is fresh, the tempura light and crispy and the prices reasonable. Try the combination specials—tempura and sushi or chicken teriyaki and sushi—plus a California roll or two.

360 CALIFORNIAN

6290 Sunset Blvd., Penthouse, Hollywood 90028
323-871-2995, *Dinner nightly, Brunch Sun.,* $$

Sure you can get steaks, seafood and vegetarian dishes, but the reason to take the elevator up here is the spectacular 360-degree view from the top of this high-rise at Sunset and Vine. And when you're not looking out at the Hollywood sign, you can watch the trendy Gen-X scene that heats up this beyond-hip supper club and bar.

TRA DI NOI ITALIAN

3835 Cross Creek Rd., Malibu 90265
310-456-0169, *Lunch & Dinner daily,* $$

This hideaway is a favorite of Malibu locals who satisfy their pasta cravings with such specialties as linguine with grilled chicken and rigatoni with clams and mushrooms. Pizzas and entrées including grilled salmon on a bed of steamed spinach and polenta cooked in Grappa served with fontina cheese and roasted quail.

A Tranquil Getaway From the Surrounding City

Set in the heart of the city's financial district, the New Los Angeles Marriott provides a welcome escape for the hurried business person, conference attendee or leisure traveler.

Our 469 guestrooms and suites are among the most spacious in the downtown area. Each commands a view of the dynamic city skyline.

Dining at the hotel can best be described as diverse. From our informal garden room, the BACK PORCH, to the casual pub atmosphere of MOODY'S BAR & GRILLE. For dinner, try the contemporary cuisine of THREE THIRTY THREE.

Telephone 213.617.1133

333 S. Figueroa Street, Los Angeles, CA 90071

LOS ANGELES Marriott DOWNTOWN

WAIKIKI WILLIES ROCK & ROLL SEAFOOD SEAFOOD/ECLECTIC

13535 Mindanao Way, Marina del Rey 90292
310-574-3932, *Dinner nightly, Brunch Sun., $$*

This place is pure Marina-singles scene, with spirited servers, a rowdy sports bar, dancing to live music on the weekends and outrageous tropical drinks. Expect hearty portions of everything from fresh seafood to prime rib, a "Crab Fest" on Wednesday nights and a tropical seafood brunch on Sundays.

ZUMAYA'S MEXICAN

5722 Melrose Ave., Hollywood 90038
323-464-0624, *Lunch Mon.-Fri., Dinner nightly, $*

Fairly classy Mexican chow at fairly reasonable prices is served in this charming little spot near Paramount Studios and Hancock Park.

QUICK BITES

AMERICAN: COFFEE SHOPS, BURGERS & DINERS

THE APPLE PAN

10801 W. Pico Blvd., W. L.A. 90064
310-475-3585, *Lunch & Dinner Tues.-Sun.*
No Cards

Great burgers and legendary apple pie. The cooks/waiters at this tiny and always crowded spot race around inside the horseshoe-shaped counter, turning out orders as fast as they can. Those waiting for seats will stare ravenously at you, making sure you devour your food pronto. Take home an apple pie for your freezer.

BLUEBERRY

510 Santa Monica Blvd., Santa Monica 90404
310-394-7765, *Breakfast & Lunch daily*
No Cards

A cute little spot for breakfast—blueberry pancakes, a malted waffle with vanilla-rum butter—where a white picket fence marks off the upstairs mezzanine, and rows of hand-canned vegies line the shelves on the walls. Lots of omelets and egg dishes, sandwiches and salads at lunch, and blueberry pancakes with blueberry syrup and blueberry ice cream any time of the day.

CASSELL'S HAMBURGERS

3266 W. Sixth St., Mid-Wilshire 90020
213-480-8668, *Lunch daily*
No Cards

At lunchtime, you'll have to stand in line with the local pinstripe-suit set to order what many call the best hamburger in town: a simple, large hamburger made with freshly ground beef, a huge bun, homemade mayonnaise and fresh lettuce, tomatoes and pickles. No decor, no ambience—just great burgers.

DINAH'S

6521 S. Sepulveda Blvd., Culver City 90045
310-645-0456, *Breakfast, Lunch & Dinner daily*
A

Dinah's is that sprawling, tacky-looking coffee shop that you pass on the way to LAX, the one with the sign announcing its daily breakfast special for $2.95. Since 1959, the restaurant has served over 100 million pieces of its secret-recipe fried chicken, but the real draw here are their over-the-top pancakes, especially the huge, puffy, skillet-baked German apple pancake with a cinnamon glaze.

THE FARMERS' MARKET

Third & Fairfax Sts., Melrose-Fairfax 90036
Breakfast & Lunch daily
No cards

We didn't quite know how to categorize this L.A. sightseeing landmark, for it has a Dupar's coffee shop along with assorted food stalls selling everything from crab cocktails to tostadas. There are also tchotchkies and "I Love L.A." T-shirts galore, along with purveyors of fine produce, meat, fish, candy, nuts and baked goods. Choose whatever you feel like eating, grab one of the tiny metal tables, and you're in for some fine people-watching. Mixed in with the tourists and seniors who have been coming here forever, are hopeful out-of-work actors and the occasional celeb. Some stalls are closed on Sundays.

FRED 62

1850 N.Vermont, Los Feliz 90027
323-557-0062, *Open 24 hours daily*

"Eat Now, Dine Later" is the motto of Fred Eric's avante-garde, open-all-night coffee shop next door to his popular Vida restaurant. Expect to see multi-pierced club types stopping in for bowls of udon noodles and/or corn-flake-crusted French toast at 4 a.m. The "Juicy Lucy" burger is a "fatty patty" of fresh-ground beef with cheese.

HAMPTONS HOLLYWOOD CAFÉ

1342 N. Highland Ave., Hollywood 90028
323-469-1090, *Breakfast, Lunch & Dinner daily*

Hamptons has been serving great burgers—topped with everything from Swiss cheese and chili to sour-plum jam, peanut butter and Dijon mustard—for decades. Recently spruced up, the place also serves sandwiches, clam chowder, garlic cheese bread, salads, ribs, scampi and even ostrich. There's a bounteous salad bar, rich desserts and a one that's not so rich: fat-free chocolate brownie covered with fat-free vanilla ice cream and fat-free fudge.

JODY MARONI'S SAUSAGE KINGDOM

2011 Ocean Front Walk, Venice 90291
310-306-1995, *Open daily*
No cards

Even if Jody Maroni's little stand wasn't located right on zany Venice beach it would be worth driving to—from any part of town. Jody usually has about a dozen varieties of dogs available to eat at the stand, from old favorites (knockwurst, Italian sausage) to his own fanciful inventions (Mexican jalapeño sausage, Indian sausage). **Also at Universal CityWalk and LAX.**

JOHN O'GROATS

10516 W. Pico Blvd., W. L.A. 90064
310-204-0692, *Breakfast & Lunch daily, Dinner Wed.-Sat.*

Bring along the newspaper to read when you come for breakfast on Sunday morning, for there is likely to be a wait. The owners visited the tiny Scottish town of John O'Groats, and were so impressed that they named their restaurant after it. They will feed you well, with crisp, nongreasy fish and chips, omelets stuffed with spinach or homemade salsa, biscuits, home fries and tasty soups. Since the kitchen is tiny and the staff is small, expect a lag time between ordering and eating. Be patient.

THE MALIBU INN

22969 PCH, Malibu 90265
310-456-6106, *Breakfast, Lunch & Dinner daily*

The decor is "Hollywood saloon," with 200 photos of screen stars on the walls, and surfboards hanging from the ceiling. Pick up a crayon and doodle on the menu while you wait. Order a juicy burger or a sandwich, then splurge on an ice-cream sundae. Breakfast is served all day, and there's a large ocean-view patio where a band plays on weekends.

MALIBU MUTTS

3835 Cross Creek Rd., Malibu
310-456-1211, *Lunch & Dinner daily*

Mutts features hot dogs and hamburgers served with big steak fries, as well as tuna pitas, grilled chicken sandwiches, falafels and tamales with chile-bean sauce.

MEL'S DRIVE-IN

8585 Sunset Blvd., L.A. 90069
310-854-7200, *Open 24 hours daily*

Googie architecture prevails! Ben Frank's, a popular Sunset Strip all-night-hangout in the '50s and '60s, narrowly escaped the wrecking ball and has been restored to its former splendor. The jukebox features such classics as "Peppermint Twist" and "Rock Around the Clock," but the diner menu has been brought into the '90s: In addition to burgers, shakes and fries, you can get vegetarian and low-cal dishes as well. We just wish there was car-door service, like back in the '50s. **Also in Sherman Oaks.**

MILLIE'S

3524 W. Sunset Blvd., Silverlake 90026
323-664-0404, *Breakfast & Lunch daily*
No Cards

No cell phones allowed. Millie's is a real insider's place, where musicians, artists and assorted neighborhood folk hang out, trading jokes and insults with owner Magenta and her wacky crew. The decor is bare-bones retro diner, and the countertop jukebox music is always great. The food is hearty, homemade, cheap and good. Heavy biscuits and gravy are the thing to get here, along with eggs and seriously spicy home-fried potatoes. The "Devil's Mess," a zesty egg-and-turkey sausage dish, is the house specialty.

NETTY'S

1700 Silverlake Blvd., Silverlake 90026
323-662-8655, *Lunch & Dinner Mon.-Sat.*

The prison-like chain-link fence surrounding Netty's is off-putting, but inside you'll find great food, from cold salads and pastas to tamales and pesto bread. Netty runs a thriving take-out and catering business from this little storefront. Call 665-DISH for daily lunch and dinner menu choices, which often include gazpacho, flank steak sandwich with pea pods and tomatoes, warm seafood salad with oranges, blackened tuna salad, linguini with artichokes, and various Cajun and Latin American dishes, such as Salvadoran-style tamales.

ORIGINAL PANTRY

877 S. Figueroa St., Downtown 90017
213-627-6879, *Open daily 24 hours*
No Cards

Mayor Riordan is the proud owner of this downtown landmark. It's no surprise, then, that the mayor and his circle of top L.A.-business men and women can often be seen here. Those who swear by this place love the charbroiled steaks, the oversized pork and lamb chops, and daily specials like macaroni and cheese. Breakfasts are legendary: enormous omelets, very good bacon and pan-fried potatoes, and thick sliced breads. The bake shop next door is tiny, but the breakfasts are the same feasts, and there are sticky buns, cinnamon rolls and brownies. This place keeps going all night long, and it's worth a visit for a taste of downtown L.A. history.

PAPA JAKE'S

9527 Santa Monica Blvd., Beverly Hills 90210
310-276-7823, *Lunch & Dinner Mon.-Sat.*

The huge jars of pickled peppers come from Jersey, as does the mix for the bread that's baked here every fifteen minutes. This little joint with a few stools and a counter, is the best place on the Westside to get authentic Philly cheesesteaks, chicken cheesesteaks and other "hotties." The thick and sloppy, 12-inch long sub sandwiches are made to order. If you can't find a combo on the menu that you like, you can design your own. **Also in Manhattan Beach (312 Rosecrans Ave., 310-796-0470).**

PHILIPPE'S ORIGINAL SANDWICH SHOP

1001 N. Alameda St., Downtown 90012
213-628-3781, *Open daily*
No Cards

The decor of this cavernous landmark is early-fast-food: sawdust on the floors and high stools along shared tables. But since 1908, people have been lining up at the huge counter to order wonderful beef, pork or lamb french-dip sandwiches. The signature French dip sandwich at Philippe's goes for $3.55, which is hard to beat. Round out your sandwich with a decent potato salad and one of the many imported beers, or try Philippe's coffee, still Depression-priced at ten cents a cup.

PICNIK

1431 Ocean Ave., Santa Monica 90401
310-394-0044, *Breakfast, Lunch & Dinner daily*

We really enjoy dining while watching the roll and heave of the ocean, and this is an ideal spot to do just that. For breakfast on the weekends, try one of the many varieties of eggs Benedict. The kitchen manages to work the scrumptious white chicken chili—their signature dish—into every meal. Other worthy items are the smoked chicken pasta, the filet mignon with mashed potatoes and the smoked chicken pizza. The wine and beer bar, with its cushy sofas, is charming and cozy.

PINK'S HOT DOGS

709 N. La Brea Ave., Melrose-La Brea 90038
323-931-4223, Open daily
No Cards

Much ado has been made about Pink's chili dogs, which are so tasty that throngs of customers put up with dirty tables, an unsavory Hollywood neighborhood, and often-lukewarm sodas. Still, the all-beef hot dogs (served with lots of messy all-beef chili) make Pink's worth a visit.

RAE'S

2901 Pico Blvd., Santa Monica 90405
310-828-7937, *Breakfast, Lunch & Dinner daily*
No Cards

This small, turquoise-blue joint is a classic '50s diner—the real thing, not a re-creation like Mel's Drive-In. As at most of L.A.'s good breakfast spots, patrons line up outside on weekends, waiting for Rae's frenetic waitresses to serve them pancakes, french toast, omelets and biscuits with gravy.

SILVER SPOON RESTAURANT

8171 Santa Monica Blvd., W. Hollywood 90046
323-650-4890, *Breakfast, Lunch & Dinner daily*

This coffee-shop-plus is one of the most enduring spots in W. Hollywood. The menu consists of the usual burgers, steaks, sandwiches, salads and daily comfort-food specials, all definitely a cut above Denny's. At breakfast, the eggs are so fresh they taste as if the cook just plucked them from a henhouse in the parking lot. The bacon is crispy, the potatoes are never greasy and the pancakes and waffles are as light as air. Try for a seat on the patio.

SNUG HARBOR

2323 Wilshire Blvd., Santa Monica 90404
310-828-2991, *Breakfast & Lunch daily, Dinner Mon.-Sat.*

Snug Harbor is a tiny box of a diner with a secret: a charming back patio. The thin honey-nut pancakes and enormous omelets bring in the likes of Uma Thurman and Ethan Hawke, plus small hoards of neighbors who wait for their names to be called by the casual, catch-a-wave host. For lunch, there's a satisfying tostada salad, as well as a real Philadelphia cheese steak sandwich and a spicy chicken sandwich on pesto-painted sourdough. Service can be slow, but the waitresses are very sunny.

TAIL O' THE PUP

329 N. San Vicente Blvd., W. Hollywood 90048
310-652-4517, *Breakfast & Lunch daily*
No Cards

One of the few remaining examples of L.A.'s roadside-pop architecture of the twenties, the landmark Tail of the Pup is little more than a huge stucco hot dog, and it's worth a visit just for a look at this rare gem of programmatic design. While you're studying the architecture, try one of the good hot dogs or juicy hamburgers.

TOMMY'S

2575 W. Beverly Blvd., L.A. 90057
213-389-9060, *Open daily 24 hours*
No Cards

We don't dare criticize Tommy's, or an army of its incredibly devoted fans will surely burn every one of these books in print. So we'll say this: the burgers themselves aren't much, but the topping is a glob of impressively tasty chili that seems to have magical addictive powers. No matter what hour, you'll find a crowd eating chiliburgers along the makeshift counter lining the parking lot. **Also in Westwood, Eagle Rock, Hollywood and Santa Monica.**

TULSA

112 S. La Brea Ave, L.A. 90036
323-938-6335
Breakfast, Lunch & Dinner daily
No Cards

You can get breakfast until four in the afternoon at this trendy La Brea spot: steak and eggs, huevos rancheros or eggs, bacon and pancakes. At night, the "home cooking" extends to spaghetti and meatballs, meatloaf, fried chicken, burgers and pork chops, followed by apple pie as good as mom used to make.

Bagel Shops

Ten years ago, you had to go to an authentic Jewish delicatessen to get good bagels. Now, there are almost as many bagel shops in Los Angeles as there are gourmet coffee shops (in fact, wherever you find a **Starbuck's**, there's likely to be a **Noah's Bagels** next door). And most of them serve a variety of bagel sandwiches—or at least bagels and shmeers (cream cheese flavored with everything from lox to strawberry).

But there are bagels and there are *bagels*. Ideally, a bagel is crusty on the outside and soft and yielding on the inside—a texture that is achieved by quickly dropping the raw bagels in boiling water before baking them. Not all bagel shops do this. (Noah's, for example, sprays hot water on the raw bagels before baking them.)

The Best: We were amazed to discover the Southland's very best bagel shops in the San Gabriel Valley, an area not exactly known for its Jewish delicatessens. But here's our favorite: **Goldstein's Bagel Bakery** (86 W. Colorado Blvd, Pasadena, 818-792-2435; 412 N. Santa Anita Ave., Arcadia, 818-447-2457, 1939 Verdugo Blvd., La Cañada. 818-952-2457). Goldstein's makes their bagels the authentic New York way, boiling them before baking them, and uses no oils, fats or preservatives, to attain results that approach bagel-nirvana. They offer all the latest flavors in addition to the traditional egg, water and onion, and they make scrumptious bagel sandwiches. Their specialties that we swoon for, however, are the stuffed bagels—bagels filled with the likes of a kosher hot dog, turkey and jack cheese, veggies and cheddar cheese—even strawberries and cream cheese.

The Next Best: We don't like their occasional attitude, but we do love the near-perfect bagels at Brentwood's **New York Bagel Company** (11640 San Vicente Blvd, 310-820-1050). The usual varieties, plus rosemary and the "El Greco" with feta cheese and sun-dried tomatoes. The bagels at the **Bagel Nosh** (Beverly Hills, Santa Monica and other locations) are by far the largest in town, and usually achieve a perfect ratio of crusty outside and soft inside, but come in traditional flavors only. Like Starbuck's, **Bueller's Bagels** (10840 Olympic Blvd. W.L.A., 310-474-6064), originated in Seattle. The bagels are perfectly textured and come in offbeat flavors such as jalapeño and chocolate. We're partial to the garlic-and-tomato bagel pizza.

The Best of the Rest: St. Urbain Street Bagels (449 N. Beverly Dr., Beverly Hills, 310-288-0219) Named after a famous bagel-baking street in Montreal, this shop bakes a bagel with a crust we find a bit wimpy, but we appreciate the wide variety of flavors (cranberry and blueberry are great in the morning.) **Manhattan I & Joy Bagel Company** (numerous locations) A national bagel chain took over what had been a local family-run operation, but you can still count on these shops to have good fresh bagels throughout the day. **Noah's Bagels** (numerous locations). Though from the pictures on the wall, Noah's Bagels seem to be imported from New York, they actually originated in Berkeley. We're not crazy about the crust (see introduction), but we like the friendly service, the variety and the frequency with which they bake fresh bagels daily (a bagel over a few hours old is a *stale* bagel.)

Bakery-Cafés

DOUGHBOYS BAKERY

8136 W. Third St., Los Angeles 90048
323-651-4202, *Breakfast & Lunch daily*

Stop in for coffee and a luscious mega-muffin in the morning, or, for the rest of the day, for a salad, pizza, or a sandwich on one of their crusty, pesto-dusted baguettes: chopped artichokes with diced tomato, green onion and shredded asiago cheese, prosciutto with camembert or roast beef. We predict you'll leave with at least one loaf of their dense and flavorful breads, most probably the rosemary and roasted garlic, three-cheese onion or Italian fruit.

LA CONVERSATION

638 N. Doheny, W. Hollywood 90048
310-858-0950, *Breakfast & Lunch daily*

This tiny shop bakes fresh buttery croissants, an outstanding Italian cheese-and-spinach torte, rich chocolate cakes, luscious cookies and mini-tarts. At breakfast, neighbors pop in for French toast made with fresh sourdough. For lunch order sandwiches on their fresh baguettes or focaccia bread.

LA PROVENCE

8950 W. Olympic Blvd., Beverly Hills 90211
310-888-8833, *Breakfast, Lunch, Early Dinner Mon.-Sat.*

At his adorable bakery/café, European-trained Farshid Hakim turns out refined French pastries, crumbly biscuits and scones, and homemade strawberry butter. He does impeccable soups, quiches, pâtés, salads and sandwiches—baked turkey moist with apple—too. His ice-blended mochas, made with house-roasted coffee and specially blended chocolates, are the best in town and for special occasions and weddings—diet alert!—he goes all out with a Viennese sweet table guaranteed to do you in.

LE PETIT FOUR

8654 Sunset Blvd., W. Hollywood 90069
310-652-3863, *Breakfast, Lunch & Dinner daily*

What began as a tiny French pâtisserie has grown into a lovely sidewalk café and restaurant, usually crowded with the beautiful people who like to see-and-be-seen at Sunset Plaza. To-go items include quiches, feuilletés and pâtés, along with their French pastries.

MÄNI'S BAKERY

519 S. Fairfax Ave., Melrose-Fairfax 90036
323-938-8800, *Breakfast & Lunch daily*

A

You can have your cake and eat it too at Mäni's, known for its wide variety of healthy desserts made with unrefined sugars and a minimum of fat. Along with his "faux nuts" (baked donuts available in six flavors), there are fat-free desserts including muffins and tortes topped with crunchy oatmeal-meringue. For breakfast, you can get omelets, pancakes and scrambled eggs with lox. Throughout the day, sandwiches are made on their own rosemary or nine-grain breads. Also yummy are non-dairy mousses and hand-rolled truffles dusted with cocoa. Good lattes too. **Also in Santa Monica (2507 Main St., 310-396-7700) and West Hollywood (8801 Santa Moica Blvd., 310-659-5955).**

MICHEL RICHARD

310 S. Robertson Blvd., W. Hollywood 90048
310-275-5707, *Breakfast, Lunch & Dinner daily*

The peripatetic chef hasn't owned this place in years, but the refined French breads and pastries he introduced to L.A. decades ago are still baked fresh here daily. The crowd includes French expats, industry-types and others who crave an authentic croissant and a big cup of cappuccino while perusing Daily Variety. There are several different quiches, salads and omelets as well.

Q BAKERY

16605 Sunset Blvd., Pacific Palisades 90272
310-459-3564, *Breakfast & Lunch daily*

They bake bread here, along with an assortment of very French pastries, from Napoleons and chocolate eclairs to buttery-crusted fresh fruit tarts. There are a few tables where you can enjoy a sandwich—egg salad, tuna, turkey, ham and cheese—on their olive, ciabatta, multi-grain or jalapeño-and-cheddar breads.

SWEET LADY JANE

8360 Melrose Ave., W. Hollywood 90069
323-653-7145, *Breakfast & Lunch Mon.-Sat.*

Everything at this European-style café and bakery, from the brownies to the dreamy desserts, is made from the freshest ingredients. Sweet Lady Jane is acclaimed for its cheesecakes, decorated cakes and lemon-meringue tarts. Don't miss the English fruitcakes with "royal icing" during the holidays. Grab one of the tiny tables and enjoy a croissant and coffee at breakfast, a sandwich at lunch—or a cup of tea and a luscious scone in the late afternoon.

THE VIENNA CAFÉ

7356 Melrose Ave., Melrose-La Brea 90046
323-651-3822, *Breakfast, Lunch & Dinner daily*

Adjoining the Melrose Baking Company, this café serves its own dense and hearty Austrian-style breads and rolls (rosemary, walnut, olive and sourdough). You can order breakfast omelets all day long, along with sandwiches (smoked salmon club, herbed chicken), pizzas and pasta.

Barbecue

BENNY'S BARBECUE

4077 Lincoln Blvd., Marina del Rey 90292
310-821-6939, *Lunch & Dinner daily*

You can smell the good, mostly take-out food cooking at Benny's from at least two blocks away, especially the superb ribs bathed in a fiery sauce and what may be the best hot links in town, with lots of peppercorns and plenty of bite.

Bars & Pubs

BARNEY'S BEANERY

8447 Santa Monica Blvd., W. Hollywood 90069
323-654-2287, *Breakfast, Lunch & Dinner daily*

Not for the indecisive, Barney's offers some 150 hamburgers, 20 hot dogs, 50 sandwiches, 90 omelets, 25 scrambled egg dishes and 65 variations of chili. It's all edible, but you don't come to Barney's for the food—you come for the appealingly scruffy atmosphere and the fantastic beer selection. The place is a maze of pool tables, coffee shop-like booths, video games and a long, dark bar.

O'BRIEN'S PUB

2941 Main St., Santa Monica 90405
310-396-4725, *Dinner nightly*

There's a wee bit of the Irish at this jolly place, where you can get good pub grub—shepherd's pie, roast beef in green-peppercorn sauce—for under $10 and there's live music on weekends.

RED ROCK ON SUNSET

8782 Sunset Blvd., W. Hollywood 90069
310-854-0710, *Lunch & Dinner daily*

A

This wonderfully funky pub, just beyond the Sunset Strip, is always crammed. The drinks are reasonably priced, even the more upscale martinis, and they also offer 18 varieties of domestic and imported beer on tap. We recommend the lamb burger, the pizzas and pastas, and the English bangers and mash.

TEASER'S IN THE MARINA

4445 Admiralty Way, Marina del Rey 90292
310-823-4534, *Breakfast Sat.-Sun., Lunch & Dinner daily*

A

This cavernous sports bar is Yuppie heaven, with a wall of big TV screens extending across the room showcasing all the games of the season. The crowd participates and the mayhem drowns out all but the loudest. Not a place for conversation—go for the scene, the specialty drinks and appetizers. The dining room is somewhat separate and offers a view of the marina.

Cafés

BACK ON THE BEACH

445 Pacific Coast Highway, Santa Monica 90405
310-393-8282, *Breakfast, Lunch & Dinner (April-September)*

No kidding—this place is right on the beach. Walk, bike or skate here from the Santa Monica Pier, then wiggle your toes in the sand while dining on a feta cheese-tomato-spinach omelet or the breakfast pasta. We've enjoyed the barbecued chicken pizza, the homemade soup and the tangy chicken-potato salad. Most of all, we've enjoyed the unique beach-restaurant setting.

CAFFÈ LUNA

7463 Melrose Ave., Melrose-Fairfax 90046
323-655-8647, *Breakfast, Lunch & Dinner daily*

What started out as a hole-in-the-wall for terrific lattes, has turned into a major scene for hip young actors and models—at all hours of the day and night. Pretty good things to eat too, from the marinated-chicken Waldorf salad to the gnocchi. The best people-watching is in the back courtyard (yes, that's the cast of *Friends*). Service can be...well...leisurely, but then this is a place to hang. And after late-night partying, where else can you get French-toasted panettone at four in the morning?

CHEESECAKE FACTORY

4142 Via Marina, Marina del Rey 90292
310-306-3344, *Lunch & Dinner daily*

Like all the outlets of this chain, "Factory" is the operative word, as they churn out bounteous salads, sandwiches and entreés–and gigantic slabs of cheesecake–from a menu that offers something for everyone. This Cheesecake Factory has a marina view–which means you'll have to wait even longer than at most of these restaurants. **Numerous other locations including Brentwood (11647 San Vicente Blvd., 310-826-7111,) Beverly Hills (364 N. Beverly Dr., 310-278-7270), and Pasadena (2 W. Colorado Blvd., 626-584-6000).**

THE COFFEE TABLE

2930 Rowena, Silverlake, 90039
323-644-8111, *Breakfast, Lunch & Dinner daily*

Some regulars call the chef Silverlake's version of the Seinfeld soup Nazi, and his spicy corn chowder, tomato lentil, vegetarian split pea, chicken curry and vegetable soups are much in demand. The works of Silverlake artists hang on the walls of this neighborhood comfort-food stop. For breakfast, try a frittata, an Italian turkey sausage frittata or the breakfast burrito. Lunch features sandwiches and salads, and dinner includes such specials as pot roast and crabcakes. The scones, muffins and cookies are hard to resist and the coffee concoctions are tops.

EAT PANINI

2715 Main St., Santa Monica 90405
310-399-9939, *Breakfast, Lunch & Early Dinner daily*

One small storefront, a patio and thirteen sandwiches—it doesn't get much more basic. But it doesn't get much better either. Consider grilled portobello mushroom, roasted red peppers, Parmesan and arugula, or roast beef, melted Brie, sliced red onion, watercress and Dijon mustard, both on toasted La Brea Bakery bread. All sandwiches come with a mini Chinese to-go container of fancy mixed greens with a balsamic vinaigrette. And for dessert, comfort on toast: warm chocolate Nutella.

FLORA KITCHEN

460 S. La Brea Ave., Melrose-La Brea 90036
323-931-9900, *Breakfast, Lunch & Dinner daily*

This appealing café offers selections from an ever-changing Mediterranean-ish roster, like citrus roasted peppers with goat cheese, spinach-and-feta-cheese-filled phyllo purses and torte Milanese. For breakfast, try the Scottish smoked salmon with bagels and cream cheese.

KING'S ROAD

8361 Beverly Blvd., W. Hollywood 90048
323-655-9044, *Breakfast, Lunch & Dinner daily*
No Cards 

The sidewalk tables are always crowded at this West Hollywood haunt, where, conveniently, there's an adjacent outdoor newsstand. Great breakfasts—eggs baked with goat cheese, sweet risotto with dried figs—as well as salads, antipasti and crisp pizzas.

MAISON ET CAFÉ

148 S. La Brea Ave., Melrose-La Brea 90036
323-939-9860, *Breakfast & Lunch daily*

A few tables and a lovely old antique bar comprise this café (officially named Café 148) in the back of a wonderful, cavernous store selling country French home furnishings from armoires to cappuccino cups. Sip an espresso, or try one of the baguette sandwiches (we love the mozzarella cheese and eggplant) while deciding which Pierre Deux fabric to buy for those pillows that need re-covering.

LA POUBELLE

5907 Franklin Ave., Hollywood 90028
323-465-0807, *Dinner nightly*

La Poubelle is a genuine French neighborhood café, and the food, like the somewhat shabby decor, is basic, comforting and unexceptional—the omelets, crêpes, onion soup, salads and simple entrées are tasty and reasonably priced.

MARMALADE

710 Montana Ave., Santa Monica 90403
310-395-9196, *Lunch & Dinner daily*

You'll find American regional favorites and gourmet goodies from around the world at these deli/cafés that with their rustic woods and hanging plants look like a throwback to the Sixties. In addition to fresh scones and muffins, you'll find bounteous salads, sandwiches and pastas. **Also in Malibu (3894 Cross Creek Rd, 310-317-4242).**

THE ROSE CAFÉ

220 Rose Ave., Venice 90291
310-399-0711, *Breakfast & Lunch daily, Dinner Fri. & Sat.*

Quintessentially Venice for nearly twenty years, the Rose Café is at once a bohemian coffeehouse, a beachy self-service café, a bakery and a charming brunch spot. If you sit in the cavernous interior and walk up to the counter to order, you can linger over your cappuccino and croissant for as long as you wish. If you prefer service, there's a sunny side patio with a full menu and attentive service. The salads, quiches and pastries are unfortunately secondary to the atmosphere, but in this case, that's more than all right.

SIDEWALK CAFÉ

1401 Ocean Front Walk, Venice 90291
310-399-5547, *Breakfast, Lunch & Dinner daily*

The best seat on the Venice boardwalk. Dining on this crowded outdoor patio can be immensely entertaining, especially on weekends, when the passing parade of humanity turns into a virtual freak show. Unfortunately, to enjoy this you'll have to put up with humdrum food and a truly dingy interior. Keep your choice as simple as possible—a no-frills omelet or burger.

SWEET BASIL CAFÉ

7994 Sunset Blvd., W. Hollywood 90039
323-656-5022, *Lunch & Dinner daily*

A

This pleasant spot is conveniently located in the strip mall next to the Sunset Five Plaza. With its open kitchen, deep vermilion walls, rustic tables and profusion of plants, the atmosphere is distinctly Tuscan. The service is terrific; so is the reasonably priced food: chicken-and-spinach ravioli, vino blanco lime fettuccini with chicken and roasted poblano chilies in a lime-cream tequila sauce, crispy gourmet pizzas. The wine list has good low-priced offerings.

TAVERN ON MAIN

2907 Main St., Santa Monica 90405
310-392-2772, *Lunch & Dinner daily, Brunch Sat.-Sun.*

Santa Monica's busy Main Street suffers from no lack of nosheries and cafés, but one of the better contenders is Tavern on Main, a fine-looking boîte serving up revisionist Americana food in pleasant surroundings. The '30s-era grill decor features a long bar, tiled floors and lots of dark wood. There's also a charming outdoor patio, especially nice for brunch and lunch. The food: generous sandwiches on French rolls, meatloaf and chili, along with terrific waffle-cut french fries.

26 BEACH CAFÉ

26 Washington Blvd., Venice 90291
310-821-8129, *Breakfst, Lunch & Dinner daily*

Join the locals on this funky patio and you'll catch up on the latest hip beach jargon. The crowd here chows down on big burgers and fries, and a variety of hearty pasta dishes.

VENICE BISTRO

323 Ocean Front Walk, Venice 90291
310-392-3997, *Lunch & Dinner daily*

A favorite for people-watchers—it's right on the Venice Boardwalk—this little café is fine for sandwiches, salads, burritos and quesadillas. The Champagne mimosas are made with fresh orange juice.

Cajun/Soul Food

GAGNIER'S CREOLE KITCHEN

1315 Third St., Santa Monica
310-319-9981, *Lunch & Dinner daily*

Lost, perhaps, behind a Wolfgang Puck Express on the second floor of a Third Street Promenade food court, this little spot serves authentic Creole comfort food, from Cajun popcorn and jambalaya to breaded oysters and catfish. Try the bread pudding with whiskey sauce for dessert.

THE GUMBO POT

Farmer's Market, 6333 W. Third St., Melrose-Fairfax 90036
323-933-0358, *Lunch & Dinner daily*

No need to spend $20 to $40 a head at a Cajun restaurant—not when you can come to the Gumbo Pot in touristy Farmer's Market and get great Cajun/Creole food for a fraction of that price. The best things here are the incredible muffelata sandwiches and the flavorful gumbo yaya with chicken, shrimp and andouille sausage.

ROSCOE'S HOUSE OF CHICKEN 'N' WAFFLES

1514 N. Gower St., Hollywood 90028
323-466-7453, *Breakfast, Lunch & Dinner daily*

The name may sound offbeat, but we assure you that this down-home combination really works, with sweet cinnamon-flavored waffles complementing crispy fried chicken. Try the oniony stewed greens on the side, but steer clear of the gravy, which often turns to paste as it cools on the plate. **Also in Mid-Wilshire (5006 W. Pico Blvd., 323-934-4405), South-Central (106 W. Manchester Ave., 213-752-6211) and Pasadena (830 N. Lake Ave., 626-791-4890).**

ROYCE'S CAFÉ ORLEANS

10916 W. Pico Blvd., W. L.A. 90064
310-441-7427, *Lunch Mon.-Fri., Dinner nightly*

Barbecue king Rick Royce and former owner of the now-defunct Orleans Café, Mary Atkinson, have joined forces to bring us the city's newest big time Cajun-Creole spot. The dining room is spare but decorated with works by Cajun artist Rodrigue. The tri-tip and rib platters are excellent, as is the sherried crawfish. Pass on the indifferent Caesar salad, but the house-baked jalapeño-cheddar rolls are delectable.

Chicken

KOO KOO ROO

435 N. Beverly Dr., Beverly Hills 90210
310-859-3434, *Lunch & Dinner daily*

These sensational fast-food joints serve chicken grilled simply over an open flame—with or without the skin—after being marinated in a vibrant blend of vegetable juices and spices. It's served with a lavosh-like bread, and side orders which we think they should improve. New items: rotisserie-roasted chicken, roast turkey and various salads. **Numerous other locations including Brentwood (11650 San Vicente Blvd., 310-207-3232), Downtown (255 Grand Ave., 213-620-1800), Hancock Park (310 N. Larchmont Blvd., 323-962-1500), Santa Monica (2002 Wilshire Blvd., 310-453-3722), West Hollywood (8520 Santa Monica Blvd., 310-657-3300, Venice (255 Main St., 310-452-3722) and W.L.A. (11066 Santa Monica Blvd., 473-5858.)**

ZANKOU CHICKEN

5065 W. Sunset Blvd, Hollywood 90028
323-665-7845, Lunch & Dinner daily
No Cards

See review in "SAN GABRIEL VALLEY—Quick Bites."

Chinese

ABC SEAFOOD

205 Ord St., Downtown 90012
213-680-2887, *Lunch & Dinner daily*

At night, fresh Cantonese seafood is the specialty. During the day, young women work the large, open room, hawking open-faced meat dumplings, shrimp hidden in thick rice noodles, barbecued pork, baked and steamed bao buns and all manner of other exotic dishes. The selection is broader than at most Chinatown dim sums, and the quality is much better than average.

FEAST FROM THE EAST

1949 Westwood Blvd., W.L.A. 90025
310-475-0400, *Lunch & Dinner Mon.-Sat., $*

This is a teeny place with just a few tables inside and outside, but don't be put off by its size or you'll risk missing out on their terrific Chinese chicken salad, a bounteous melange of chicken, ginger, wide crispy noodles, scallions and lettuce with a knockout sesame dressing.

MANDARIN DELI

727 N. Broadway, Ste. 109, Downtown 90012
213-623-6054, *Lunch & Dinner daily*
No Cards

The pan-fried dumplings come to your table still steaming and are best eaten flavored with a bit of hot chili oil and a splash of white vinegar. There are also boiled-fish and pork dumplings. The savory noodle soups work especially well if coupled with the Mandarin-style cold noodles, which are bathed in a richly spiced sesame sauce. Atmosphere is nonexistent at the Chinatown branch, but the **Little Tokyo branch (356 E. Second St., 213-617-0231)** boasts comfortable booths and an attempt at a décor and takes major credit cards.

TAIPAN

7075 Sunset Blvd., Hollywood 90028
323-464-2989, *Lunch & Dinner daily*

The setting is almost space-age with its white-tile walls, decorative red tubing and open kitchen. The cha siu bao (pork buns) are especially luscious—among the best in town. We also highly recommend the sizzling shrimp, the tart lemon chicken and the catfish with black bean sauce.

Coffeehouses & Tea Rooms

CAFFÈ LATTE

6254 Wilshire Blvd., Mid-Wilshire 90048
323-936-5213, *Breakfast & Lunch daily*

The coffee roaster is front-and-center at this classic coffee house, popular not only with neighborhood residents but with designers, writers and other creative sorts. The decor is homey, and what's on the menu is enticing: egg-and-sausage dishes and pancakes for breakfast, sandwiches and pastas for lunch. Their fresh-roasted coffee is excellent, so buy some to go.

CHADO

8422 1/2 W. 3rd St., W. Hollywood 90048
323-655-2056, *Breakfast & Lunch Mon.-Sat.*

In this charming shrine to the Camellia sinensis, the walls are lined floor-to-ceiling with large jars of more than 200 varieties of tea from around the world. Green teas, smoked black teas, herbal tisanes and more hail from unexpected places such as Africa, Turkey and Russia, as well as from throughout Asia and England. You can buy tea by the ounce or the pound, and it's a treat to sit and enjoy a steaming potful and a scone or mini-sandwich while perusing the endless "menu," a virtual encyclopedia of tea.

COFFEE BEAN AND TEA LEAF

11698 San Vicente Blvd., Brentwood 90049
310-442-1019, *Open daily*
No Cards

Now there are over 30 of these pleasant, vaguely '60s (warm woods and plants) coffee shops throughout the Southland.

Many varieties of coffee beans to choose from, plus great espresso drinks, muffins and cakes. Some people swear their blended-iced-mocha concoction is unbeatable. **Numerous other locations.**

PADDINGTON'S TEA ROOM

355 S. Robertson Blvd., Beverly Hills 90211
310-652-0624, *Lunch & Afternoon Tea daily*

Fake flowers, tchotchkes galore, English sweets and yes, Paddington teddy bears, fill this cutesy tea room. Come for scones, crumpets, omelets, bounteous salads and sandwiches or savory steak-and-kidney pie throughout the day. From 2 p.m until 5:30 p.m. tea is served in fine bone china, to accompany the traditional finger sandwiches, pâté, scones with Devonshire cream and tiny pastries. In keeping with the times, they also serve gourmet coffees.

PREBICA

4325 Glencoe Ave., Marina del Rey 90292
310-823-4446, *Open daily*

This funky café is also the retail outlet for Allan Chemtob's Café au Lait and Paradise Tropical Teas (passion fruit, kiwi, papaya, mango), which wholesale to some of the top hotels and restaurants in the country. Over 40 types of coffee, including flavored and decaffeinated.

SEATTLE'S BEST COFFEE (S.B.C.)

9475 Santa Monica Blvd., Beverly Hills 90210
310-275-2053, *Open daily*

Like Starbucks, S.B.C. is another Seattle import, but it doesn't pack the same punch. They make terrific iced mochas, latte granitas and coffee milkshakes, however. And to go-with, you can get Il Fornaio breads and an assortment of croissants, cinnamon buns and cakes. **Numerous other locations.**

STARBUCKS

Beverly Connection, 100 N. La Cienega Blvd., W. Hollywood 90048,
310-289-7815, Numerous other locations, *Open daily*

Can't start your day without your nonfat, half-caf, grande latte? Rainy Seattle started the gourmet coffee craze that's swept the nation, all because of the folks at Starbucks. At the modern yet comfy outlets of the now ubiquitous roaster/retailer, the service is always friendly and efficient, and you can choose from among dozens of varieties of consistently good coffee, from Indonesian Sulawesi to Arabian-Mocha Java to decaffeinated Viennese, along with coffee-making paraphernalia and mugs, bulk teas, assorted baked goods and sometimes even sandwiches. Here in sunny So Cal, we like their iced and frappéed coffee drinks, as well as their rich coffee ice creams, and new Chai tea. "Starbucks" doesn't just mean a cup of coffee anymore—it's become a way of life. **Numerous other locations.**

Delis

CANTER'S

419 N. Fairfax Ave., Melrose-Fairfax 90036
323-651-2030, *Open daily 24 hours*

This Fairfax District mainstay got slammed in the November, 1997 CBS TV exposé regarding unsanitary practices in L.A. restaurant kitchens (turkeys left out of the fridge, plus more yucky tidbits.) Still, regulars swear by Canter's in-your-face waitresses, the gargantuan sandwiches and the chicken soup. If nothing else, Canter's deserves praise for staying open 24 hours a day.

GREENBLATT'S

8017 W. Sunset Blvd., W. Hollywood 90046
323-656-0606, *Breakfast, Lunch & dinner daily*

This full-service deli not only has all the requisite super-sandwiches, blintzes and matzoh-ball soup, but also a spectacular wine shop, offering a huge selection of wines and champagnes, Cognacs, and Armagnacs (some dating to the 1800s), single-malt scotches, and grappas. Receive a 20 percent case discount or plunk down a dollar or two for a taste from the Cruvinet.

JERRY'S FAMOUS DELI

8701 Beverly Blvd., W. Hollywood 90048
310-289-1811, *Open 24 hours*

Craving pastrami at three am? Ignore the fact that it was one of the eateries caught in the Channel 7 "dirty restaurants" net at the end of 1997, and head to Jerry's. The menu is enormous, the waitstaff friendly and efficient, and the hefty—and heftily priced—sandwiches keep folks coming back. **Numerous other locations including Westwood (10925 Weyburn Ave., 310-208-3354 and Marina del Rey (13181 Mindanao Way 310-821-6626.)**

LANGER'S

704 S. Alvarado St., Downtown 90057
213-483-8050, *Open Mon.-Sat.*

A sign in the window reworks an old adage: "When in doubt, eat hot pastrami." Wise advice, especially if you eat Langer's legendary pastrami, which is lean, delicious and copiously served. We counted nearly 30 pastrami dishes on the extensive menu, the rest of which lists all the deli classics: blintzes, lox, chopped liver, gefilte fish and so on. Despite the bad neighborhood and the dismal atmosphere, Langer's is one of our favorite delis in L.A.

NATE 'N' AL'S

414 N. Beverly Dr., Beverly Hills 90210
310-274-0101, *Breakfast, Lunch & Dinner daily*

Forget having Sunday breakfast here without a wait. Though bagel shops are opening all around it, this plain-and-simple deli holds its own. The bagels are only so-so and the decor is down-at-the-heels coffee shop, but the huge sandwiches, matzoh-ball soup, blintzes, pickles and smoked-fish plates are everything they should be and more.

NEW YORK BAGEL COMPANY

11640 San Vicente Blvd., Brentwood 90049
310-820-1050, *Breakfast and Lunch daily*
No cards

On weekend mornings, this place is Brentwood Yuppie Central. A metal sculpture of the Chrysler Building hangs from the ceiling, and along with bagels, deli specialties and the like (see entry under "Bagels"), we like their Mexican breakfast dishes, especially chorizo with eggs).

STAGE DELI

Century City Shopping Center, 10250 S.M. Blvd., Century City 90067
310-553-3354, *Breakfast, Lunch & Dinner daily*

On the up side, the L.A. version of the New York original is a good-looking place, cavernous and decorated with old movie posters. Not only that but the food is generally decent, as long as you stick to the sandwiches, salads, and such standards as potato pancakes, blintzes and stuffed cabbage. On the down side, the soups can be bland and the desserts often seem tired. And the ambience pales in comparison to that of its noisy, jam-packed New York cousin.

Ethiopian

ROSALIND'S

1044 S. Fairfax Ave., Melrose-Fairfax 90019
323-936-2406, *Lunch & Dinner daily*

A friendly spot on Fairfax's "Ethiopian Row," Rosalind's is perfect for a group of friends open to sharing exotic dishes. Try the ground-nut stew, the Nigerian-style spinach, the Sengalese lemon-and-onion-marinated chicken, the Ghanian-style eggplant, the Liberian-style cabbage along with a highly spiced Ethiopian dish or two, scooped up with a thick Ethiopian millet pancake.

Healthy

JAMBA JUICE

474 N. Rodeo Dr., Beverly Hills 90210
310-247-7828, *Breakfast, Lunch & Dinner daily*
No cards

Jamba Juice started the current juice-bar craze that's sweeping the nation, and you can definitely make a meal of one of their delicious and good-for-you smoothies. Mix and match fresh juice flavors (from beet to watermelon) with "boosts" (from biloba to vegetarian protein) and frozen yogurt. The "Coldbuster," made of freshly squeezed orange juice, peaches, banana, raspberry sherbet and ice, gives you 2500% of your daily requirement of Vitamin C and has only 460 calories. Numerous other locations.

THE FIGTREE

429 Ocean Front Walk, Venice 90291
310-3923-4937, *Breakfast, Lunch & Dinner daily*

A favorite for healthy fare in Venice, this little café tops focaccia with chicken, avocado, spinach or jack and feta cheese, and makes a low-fat cocoa cake. For breakfast, try the grilled organic polenta with maple syrup or the latkes with herbed chicken sausage, sour cream and apple butter. For lunch, we've enjoyed the veggie stir-fry or the penne with wild mushroom ragout. The service can be slow, but hey, kick back and relax—you're in laid-back Venice.

Ice Cream & More

AL GELATO

806 S. Robertson Blvd., Beverly Hills 90211
310-659-8069, *Lunch & Dinner daily*
No Cards

Sublime Italian gelato—the best in L.A—in over seventy different flavors (there are usually twenty available at a time). Plus sensational homemade Italian breads, and resulting sandwiches, along with pastas and warming soups. The crowd's a mix of Beverly Hills types and homesick Italians, who hang out here 'til one a.m. on weekends.

THE BIGG CHILL

10850 Olympic Blvd., W.L.A. 90025
310-475-1070, *Open daily*
No Cards

We just wish they had a bigger parking lot at this Mecca for soft-frozen yogurt fans. You'll find many flavors to choose from, and they taste richer than 31's or Penguin's—even though most are low-fat or fat-free. The servings here are enormous, and there are plenty of toppings to choose from, along with fat-free muffins and cookies.

CHARLY TEMMEL

1241 Third St. Promenade, Santa Monica 90401
310-394-7253, *Breakfast, Lunch & Dinner daily*
No Cards

Austrian ice cream? Yep, that's the specialty here: creamy, richly flavored ice creams and sorbets, many, they claim, with just a smidgin of fat. The story is that the ultimate Austrian, Arnold Schwarzenegger, is the one who coaxed Austria's ice cream king to open shops here. We like the funky '50s-meets-outer space decor, and such goodies as the ice cream hamburger. There are sandwiches, pizza and salads too. Expect to see more of these popping up.

DOUBLE RAINBOW

7376 Melrose Ave., Melrose-Fairfax 90046
323-655-1986, *Open daily*
No Cards

Clean-brightly-lit and adorned with original art, these parlors have the look and feel of an upscale Baskin Robbins. The flavors, however, taste far richer and more complex than those of America's favorite chain—the white pistachio, coffee bean, and Heath Bar crunch are outstanding examples. There is also a rotating roster of excellent nonfat yogurt flavors and decent espresso. **Also in W.L.A.**

EIGER

124 S. Barrington Pl., Brentwood 90049
310-471-6955, *Open Fri.-Sun.*
No Cards

Rich, dynamite-flavored homemade ice cream, along with rich-tasting low-fat frozen yogurts, soft and hard. The coffee ice cream and yogurt will you give you a caffeine buzz. Expensive but worth it.

Indian

CHAMIKA CATERING

1717 N. Wilcox Ave., Hollywood 90028
323-466-8960, *Lunch & Dinner Tues.-Sun.*

Chamika features the cuisine of Sri Lanka, an island off the southern coast of India, where there are strong Indian, Portuguese, English and Dutch culinary influences. After you devour the complimentary basket of crackly papadams, try one of the many curries—pumpkin, eggplant, okra, cashew, chicken, shrimp and lamb. We also recommend the biriyani, pittu, string hoppers, roties (maybe the original wrap) and the exotic sweets and drinks, scarcely any of which even approach $10.

Italian

C&O TRATTORIA

31 Washington Blvd., Marina de Rey 90292
310-823-9491, *Breakfast, Lunch & dinner daily*

This place has been a well kept secret since the '60s, and when you see the prices, you'll think they haven't changed in over 35 years. Imagine paying $6.96 for a plate of pretty good spaghetti that's easily big enough for two. Throw in a couple of killer garlic rolls (be sure that everyone in your party eats one), help yourself to the honor wine bar and sing along when the waiters belt out *That's Amore* at least once every wild-and-crazy evening. Just a block from the beach, this is a great spot to carbo-load on linguine-with-scrambled-eggs before taking off on the bike path.

CHARLIE'S TRIO

5769 Huntington Dr. North, Los Angeles 90032
323-223-3871, *Lunch & Dinner daily*

See review in "SAN GABRIEL VALLEY—Quick Bites"

IL TRAMEZZINO

454 N. Canon Dr., Beverly Hills 90210
310-273-0501, *Breakfast, Lunch & Early Dinner daily*

This casual little Italian cafe, where the staff is notably nice, is justly popular. Their chicken Dijon sandwich alone would justify its existence. But there are also a dozen or so fresh salads and some very satisfying pastas. Try the eponymous penne Tramezzino made with Buffalo mozzarella, sun-dried tomatoes, basil and sautéed mushrooms in a light marinara sauce. Or stop by for a good espresso and a flaky croissant, as the ladies from the Aida Thibiant spa across the street do; they've even been known to jaywalk for one of Il Tramezzino's fresh fruit smoothies.

FABIOLUS CAFÉ

5750 Melrose Ave., Hollywood 90038
323-462-1549, *Lunch & Dinner daily*

The proximity to the studios, and the servings of large and steamy pasta dishes, and huge salads makes this trendy restaurant chain high on the lunch-crowd list. The panini are hearty, and you can get fish, lamb chops, chicken and steak entrées served with pasta or salad. The decor is practical, with high ceilings and lots of wood; the candlelight at dinner does wonders. **Also at 5255 Melrose (open only for lunch), 5255 Melrose Ave., 323-464-5857, and 6270 Sunset Blvd., 323-467-2882.**

PORTA VIA

424 N. Canon Dr., Beverly Hills 90210
310-274-6534, *Open Mon.-Sat.*

We love this tiny sidewalk café/take-out/catering spot, whose Italian-trained chef turns out earthy wild-mushroom-and-spinach lasagna, moist rotisserie chickens, and a polenta poundcake that is absolutely addictive. Their dense, flavorful scones are among the best in town.

RÖSTI

908 S. Barrington Ave., Brentwood. 90049
310-447-8695, *Open daily*

The owners of Toscana opened these good-looking Italian trattoria/take-out spots, which feature their sensational rosemary-scented, flattened and grilled chicken. You'll always find a tempting array of antipasti (we like the white beans with Italian tuna), along with fresh pastas of the day, pizzas and Italian sandwiches. **Also in Beverly Hills (233 S. Beverly Dr., 310-275-3285), Melrose-Fairfax (7475 Beverly Blvd., 323-938-8335) and Santa Monica (931 Montana Ave., 310-393-3236).**

Japanese

ASHAI RAMEN

2027 Sawtelle Blvd., W. L.A. 90025
310-479-2231, *Lunch & Dinner Fri.-Wed.*
No Cards

This popular little shop always seems to have customers waiting at the door. The draw? Fresh Japanese noodles cooked appealingly al dente and served with a variety of toppings in a light but flavorful meat broth. The gyoza—little, crescent-shaped potstickers with a finely textured, gingery pork filling—are excellent.

ASIAN NOODLE HOUSE

8393 Beverly Blvd., LA 90048
323-782-0039, *Lunch & Dinner Mon.-Sat.*

Hiro and Yasu Obayashi hope to follow the success of Hirozen, their nearby sushi bar, with this noodle house, patterned after the train-stop eateries in Japan. Try the noodles in soup or pan fried, along with salads, rice dishes and such specialties as Mongolian beef on a bed of mashed potatoes and soba crêpes with oyster sauce.

THE CURRY HOUSE

163 N. La Cienega Blvd., Beverly Hills 90211
310-854-4959, *Lunch & Dinner daily*

In a clean and pleasant setting, this eclectic eatery serves curry dishes, Japanese dishes and gourmet burgers, too. All are worthy, but the chicken and the seafood curries are standouts and the wiener-vegetable curry is downright exotic. We also recommend the spicy shrimp spaghetti with the tomato cream sauce. **Also in Little Tokyo (123 S. Onizuka St., 213-620-0855, Torrance (21215 Hawthorne Blvd, 310-540-8980), and Gardena (310-323-7017).**

MISHIMA

11301 Olympic Blvd., #210, W.L.A. 90064
310-473-5297, *Lunch & Dinner daily*

Frankly, we wonder why these noodle shops have customers lining up outside. Yes, the wheat or buckwheat noodles are made fresh here. But those we've sampled seemed bland, the broth they floated in was thin, and portions—as noodle houses go—were small. **Also in West Hollywood (8474 W. Third St., 323-782-0181.)**

SHABU HANA

7916 Sunset Blvd., L.A. 90046
323-845-9395, *Lunch Mon.-Fri., Dinner nightly*

In Japanese, shabu shabu means swish-swish. That's exactly what you do in this modern, cozy setting. Once you're seated in a banquette or at the horseshoe bar, your server will light the burner before you, bring a pot of braised seaweed broth and ask for your choices—chicken, seafood, Kobe beef, fresh vegetables or any combination. When the pot boils, swish them around until they're cooked. Shabu is made even more delicious accompanied by Kubota, Shabu Hana's private label sake. If you aren't in the mood to "swish," there are many other traditional Japanese dishes—sashimi, teriyaki, tataki—too.

TODAI

Beverly Center, 8612 Beverly Blvd., W. Hollywood 90048
310-659-1375, *Lunch & Dinner daily*

For Homer Simpson, this would be pig heaven. A neon-lit industrial cavern next to the Hard Rock, Todai is a veritable food factory of hot-and-cold Asian dishes and sushi. Okay, so the quality isn't up to that at Matsuhisa, but the prices for the all-you-can-eat buffet are unbeatable: For $11.95 at lunch, $18.95 at dinner—and $1 more on weekends and holidays—you can pack it away. **Also in Brentwood, Studio City, Woodland Hills, Glendale and Cerritos.**

UMEMURA

123 S. Onizuka St., #303, Downtown 90012
213-620-9023, *Lunch & Dinner Wed.-Mon.*
No Cards

There's no pretension in this noodle shop's plain white walls and wooden tables and chairs. The service is swift and absolutely charming, and the selection of ramen is astoundingly good. We've enjoyed their subtly flavored fresh noodles with clear meat broth, soy-doused broth, and robust miso broth, topped with anything from stir-fried vegetables to boiled pork wontons, barbecued pork to spicy Korean-style pickled cabbage.

YOKOHAMA RAMEN

11660 Gateway Blvd., W.L.A. 90064
310-479-2321, *Lunch & Dinner Wed.-Mon.*

The noodles at this small, efficient-looking café are terrific, whether stir-fried with a variety of ingredients, such as barbecued pork and vegetables, pan-fried, or served cold. Also good pan-fried dumplings, as well as a terrific version of Chinese chicken salad.

Korean

SOOT BULL JEEP

3136 W. Eighth St., Koreatown
213-387-3865, *Dinner nightly*

Of the hundreds of Korean barbecue restaurants in L.A., this is one of the best. It's smoky, it's noisy, but you'll enjoy barbecuing your own dinner over the charcoal grill right in the middle of your table. Cook short ribs, pork loin, baby octopus and other morsels to your liking, then wrap them in scraps of lettuce leaf with a bit of marinated scallion and perhaps fermented-bean paste. If you have a bad case of garlic-breath when you leave (and at a Korean restaurant, that's most likely), grab a piece of the perfumed Korean chewing gum they offer guests.

Kosher

NESSIM'S

8939 W. Pico Blvd, W.L.A. 90035
310-859-9429, *Lunch Sun.-Fri., Dinner Sat.-Thurs.*

Kosher sushi? You bet, plus trout amandine, chicken dishes, and dinners for well under $10 at this friendly "Kosher Kanyon" eatery.

PICO KOSHER DELI

8826 W. Pico Blvd., W.L.A. 90035
310-273-9381, *Breakfast, Lunch & Dinner daily*

A

The place doesn't look like much, but they serve terrific corned beef and pastrami sandwiches, plus other deli favorites

Mexican & Latin American

THE CORAL BEACH CANTINA MEXICAN

29350 PCH, Malibu 90265
310-457-5503, *Lunch & Dinner daily*

Ready for a good wine margarita, or a homemade micro brew? Order a pitcher and settle on the tree-shaded patio, snacking on nachos and chicken quesadillas. The Cantina's moderately priced Mexican fare draws a loyal local crowd, including a movie star or two. Put your quarter in the oldies jukebox and order regional plates, combinations, or specials from the grill. The crab and avocado tostado is luscious, as are the tamales and chili rellenos. Finish with a Cantina-style hot fruit turnover.

DON FELIX PERUVIAN

305 N. Virgil Ave., L.A. 90004
323-663-1088, *Breakfast, Lunch & Dinner Wed.-Mon.*

A

From coastal regions to the Andes high country, Peru's cooking is incredibly diverse, borrowing from the cuisines of

Spain, Italy, China and Japan. This bare-bones setting is a good place to sample it. Specialties include an array of ceviches, ocopa (appetizer of potato and eggs with an addictive walnut sauce), papas huancainas, beef milanesa, fried chicken, beef teriyaki and even pastas. Try a glass of the chicha morada, Peru's famous punch tinted with purple corn. **The newer Hollywood location (4435 Fountain Ave. 213-669-7575) is a more spacious restaurant.**

EL COYOTE MEXICAN

7312 Beverly Blvd., Melrose-La Brea 90036
323-939-2255, *Lunch & Dinner daily*

The decor at El Coyote is a combination of fake-peeling-plaster and authentic Mexican folk art. What draws thousands of people to this unpretentious landmark, including fraternity guys, blue hairs and Hollywood rockers? It can't be the food—countless gallons of refried beans and rice laden with glutinous orange cheese. It must be the margaritas, the fiesta ambience and the prices. Those bent on finding good food are well advised to pass by El Coyote's overflowing combination plates, and its tostadas piled with mountains of canned peas and carrots.

EL TEPAYAC CAFÉ MEXICAN

812 N. Evergreen Ave., E.L.A. 90033
323-267-8668, *Breakfast, Lunch & Dinner Weds.-Mon.*
No Cards

Burrito lovers from all over the city make pilgrimages to East L.A.'s El Tepayac. The menu lists lots of Mexican standards, most of which are good, but burritos are the thing here. They're huge beyond belief, stuffed full of all kinds of delicious goodies: machaca, chile verde, beans, rice, guacamole and more. Beware the seriously hot salsa.

GUELAGUETZA MEXICAN/OAXACAN

11127 Palms Blvd., Palms 90066
310-837-8600, *Breakfast, Lunch & Dinner daily*
A

A friendly little establishment with authentic—perhaps the city's best—Mexican cuisine from the state of Oaxaca which is sometimes referred to as "the land of seven moles." The tables are communal, the music is sweetly raucous, the empanadas are terrific and the pizza-like clayudas are the specialty. **Also Downtown (3337 1/2 W. Eighth St., 213-427-0601).**

HANNAH'S CANTINA MEXICAN

18763 PCH, Malibu 90265
310-456-8800, *Breakfast, Lunch & Dinner daily*

This funky shack looks like it belongs on the beach in Baja, but serves Mexican fare without the lard it's cooked in south of the border. For breakfast, the huevos rancheros are good. Other favorite dishes include the seabass potato-chip style (thin-sliced with lemon, pepper and garlic), the chili rellenos and the chicken salad with lime-cilantro dressing. The wine list is a nice surprise, and includes some good selections. This place is always packed.

ITANA BAHIA — BRAZILIAN

8711 Santa Monica Blvd., W. Hollywood 90069
310-657-6306, *Lunch & Dinner Tues.-Sun., Brunch Sun.*

Diners at this colorful new place can request their table not by location, but by the postcard image of one of the 16 orixas, or spirits, that's posted there. The room is a repository of musical instruments and symbols from Salvador da Bahia, the colonial city that has a unique Afro-Brazilian culture and produces sensational music and food. Specialties like vatapá (fresh seafood in a sauce of manioc flour), acarajé, bean rolls with fried shrimp and moqueca, a stew of shrimp or fish in coconut milk, are intensely flavorful and seldom found outside Bahia. For dessert, the coconut flan goes well with a strong cup of Brazilian coffee.

LA PLANCHA — NICARAGUAN/SALVADORAN

2814 W. Ninth St., Downtown 90006
213-383-1449, Lunch & Dinner daily

Expect fine Nicaraguan food at rock-bottom prices. Order the empanada and the nacatamal, and owner Milton Molina will push more on you: "What, you don't want the fried cheese? It comes special in 40-pound blocks, all the way from San Francisco." The cheese is remarkable. Nacatamales are like grown-up tamales filled with chicken, pork, whole chiles, carrots, tomatoes and even prunes. Among the many meat dishes, choose chopped or shredded ones over the often-tough grills. The decor is dreary, but Milton's personality could brighten a crypt.

LA SALSA — MEXICAN

11075 W. Pico Blvd., W.L.A. 90064
310-479-0919, *Breakfast, Lunch & Dinner daily*

We know a New York food writer who always stops here on her way into town from the airport. This popular taco chain features great soft tacos and burritos stuffed with succulent beef and chicken, which you can then douse with a variety of fresh salsas from a well-stocked salsa bar. One plus here for those who yearn for the real thing: the salsas marked "hot" really are. **Numerous other locations, including Malibu, Beverly Hills and Brentwood.**

MEXICO CITY — MEXICAN

2121 Hillhurst Ave., L.A. 90027
323-661-7227, *Lunch Wed.-Sun., Dinner nightly*

The pierced-and-tattooed Silverlake crowd flocks to this superfly Mexican, sister restaurant to Mexica, for gooey queso fundido, green corn tamales and fresh guacamole. There's also a decent selection of fresh seafood and vegetarian dishes, including spinach enchiladas and shrimp in garlic sauce. The interior is groovy Nuevo Mexican: a couple of piñatas, bright primary colors and a bar where the bartender whips up "Horny Margaritas." And what other Mexican has the good sense to serve tarte tatin? Follow the Beck-lookalikes to this locals-only spot.

MONTE ALBAN — MEXICAN/OAXACAN

11927 Santa Monica Blvd., W.L.A. 90025
310-444-7736, *Lunch & Dinner daily*

This family enterprise in a strip mall, turns out a parade of moles—tomato, black, red, green and yellow—most served over succulent chicken breasts. Also good: tilapia in garlic sauce, chicken chile relleno with tomato, raisins and almonds, stewed goat and plenty of warm fresh chips. Wash it all down with a fresh fruit agua fresca, atole (corn drink) or horchata (rice drink).

POQUITO MAS — MEXICAN

8555 Sunset Blvd., W. Hollywood 90046
310-652-7008, *Lunch & Dinner daily*

Poquito Mas makes incomparable carnitas, which go into generous, delicious burritos and soft tacos. Tasty fish tacos are usually offered, and the tostadas are perfection. You can eat inside in a tiny room, or outside on a patio.

SEÑOR FISH — MEXICAN

424 E. First St., Downtown 90012
213-625-0566, *Lunch & dinner daily*
No Cards

See review in "SAN GABRIEL VALLEY—QUICK BITES"

TORTILLA GRILL — MEXICAN

1357 Abbot Kinney Blvd., Venice CA 90292
310-581-9953, *Breakfast Sat.-Sun., Lunch Mon.-Fri., Dinner nightly*

Tired of the recent influx of "authentic" Mexican joints that fail to meet your expectations? Then sample some of the zesty dishes at this neighborhood establishment where the tostada shells are made right before your eyes and the bounty of fresh ingredients line the counter. Owner David Gurtz doesn't use lard, MSG or sulfites, and sticks with extra-lean steak and pork, skinless chicken breasts and 100% cholesterol-free canola oil. We recommend the homemade black bean soup and the muy grande "macho burrito," washed down with freshly squeezed watermelon juice. **Also near the Venice beach (46 Windward Ave., 310-452-5751).**

YUCA'S HUT — MEXICAN

2056 N. Hillhurst Ave., Los Feliz 90027
323-662-1214, *Lunch & Dinner Mon.-Sat.*
No Cards

We know New Yorkers who land at LAX and head straight for Yuca's, which sits in the parking lot between a liquor store and a real estate office. Dora and her family dispense some of the best carnitas and carne asada tacos and burritos we've ever tasted. Get a Dos Equis from the liquor store, grab one of the rickety tables, order a couple of tacos, and enjoy one of L.A.'s great small pleasures.

Middle Eastern

SUNNIN

1779 Westwood Blvd., W.L.A.
310-477-2358, *Lunch & Dinner daily*

Homesick expats from Lebanon, Iran and Egypt are regulars at this tiny Lebanese place. Try the foul, a staple of fava beans liberally seasoned with garlic and spices, the shanklish, a mixture of ground homemade cheese, onions and tomatoes, shish tawook and skewers of chicken with a garlic spread we'll pit against any garden-variety vampire. Once you taste the ashta, an irresistible homemade sweet made with bananas, honey and pistachios, you'll be a regular, too, even if your home town is L.A.

Pizza

ABBOT'S PIZZA COMPANY

1407 Abbot Kinney Blvd., Venice 90291
310-396-7334, *Lunch & Dinner daily*

We're crazy about their pizza—made with bagel-dough crusts! Thin in the center but not soggy, and crispy on the edges, the crusts are best when ordered with onion, garlic, sesame, poppy or hot-spicy. Choose from one of the twelve inventive toppings, including sweet onions, cheese and pesto sauce, mushrooms and pesto and goat cheese. You can order them by the slice, so you can mix-and match. Pizza lovers and ex-pat New Yorkers don't mind eating at counters set against the walls, or taking their slices to go, because Abbot's is a must.

CALIFORNIA PIZZA KITCHEN

207 S. Beverly Dr., Beverly Hills 90212
310-275-1101, *Lunch & Dinner daily*

Wolfgang Puck invented "designer" pizzas. CPK brought them to the masses. In these bright, yellow-black-and-white high-tech settings, you can get hearth-baked pizzas topped with everything from barbecued chicken to hoisin duck, wontons and portobello mushrooms. We advise sticking to the basics—cheese, pepperoni, or fresh tomato, basil and garlic—along with their generous salads. **Numerous other locations including the Beverly Center (121 N. La Cienega, 310-854-6555), Marina del Rey (13345 Fiji Way, 310-301-1563) and Downtown (330 Hope St., 213-626-2616).**

IL BUCO

107 N. Robertson Blvd., Beverly Hills 90211
310-657-1345, *Lunch Mon.-Fri., Dinner Mon.-Sat.*

A Drago (as in Giacomino, younger brother of Celestino,) is baking thin-crusted pizzas at this little place when he's not behind the stoves at nearby Il Pastaio. We like the traditional Italian toppings, and are glad they're adding rustic Neapolitan dishes to the menu.

JACOPO'S

490 N. Beverly Dr., Beverly Hills 90210,
310-858-6446, *Lunch & Dinner daily*

The brick-walled Beverly Hills Jacopo's is cozy to some and cramped and uncomfortable to others, and the other branches are rather cold and prefab looking. The service can be shaky, too, so we prefer to get take-out. (They do good delivery.) Despite this, Jacopo's is extremely popular with the designer-sweatsuit crowd, who seem to love the very cheesy pizza—or non-fat—cheese-pizza. **Also in West Los Angeles (11676 Olumpic Blvd, 310-477-2111), Pacific Palisades (15415 Sunset Blvd., 310-454-8494), and West Hollywood (8166 Sunset Blvd., 323-650-8128).**

MULBERRY STREET PIZZERIA

240 S. Beverly Dr., Beverly Hills 90212
310-247-8100, *Lunch & Dinner nightly*

Around the corner from the William Morris Agency, this is the cheapest place to "do lunch" with "an agent in training." Forget about the salads and go straight to the New York-style pizza, topped with a choice of everything from pepperoni and cheese to chicken Parmesan. The secret to this succulent pie is in the sauce—we dare you to stop at just one slice. **Also in Beverly Hills at 347 N. Canon Drive (310-247-8998) and in Encino (17040 Ventura Blvd., 818-906-8881).**

PALERMO

1858 N. Vermont Ave., Hollywood 90027
323-663-1430, *Lunch & Dinner Wed.-Mon.*

Locals and fans from across the city don't mind the long wait here, as long as the house keeps the free industrial-strength wine flowing. The big draw is the thick-crusted, Sicilian style pizza, marvelously spicy and flavorful and loaded with toppings. True, it's too heavy for more refined palates, but what a taste! The heavy pastas are also good in a rustic way, but avoid anything even slightly fancy, particularly the scampi and the veal.

VITTORIO!

16646 Marquez Ave., Pacific Palisades 90272
310-459-3755, *Dinner Tues.-Sun.*

The best-kept secret in the Palisades, Vittorio! is hidden just off Sunset Boulevard and serves good food in an ambience of utter Italian chaos. Not only will your waiter be an aspiring actor, he'll probably sing to you as he sprinkles Parmesan on your pasta. You can get good, classic spaghetti with meatballs and crispy New York-style pizzas with all the old-fashioned ingredients, from pepperoni to sausage.

Russian

CASPIAN CUISINE

205 Broadway, Santa Monica 90401
310-395-5695, *Lunch & Dinner Tues.-Sun.*

A handpainted map of the Caspian Sea, pinpointing Azerbaijan, Kazakhstan, Persia, Russia and Turkmenistan, the destinations that inspire the food here, stretches across the ceiling like Michaelangelo's fresco in the Sistine Chapel. Sample an appetizer sampler of borani (spinach in yogurt), garlicky eggplant, Russian patties—sort of a cross between moussaka and potato kugel lamb-and-beef dumplings. Nearly everyone orders the fessenjon duck in sweet-sour pomegranate-and-walnut sauce or one of the unusual kebabs, say the quail or Cornish hen or venison.

ROBERT'S CUISINE & GRILLE

16031 1/2 N. La Brea Ave., Hollywood 90028
323-851-4202, *Lunch & Dinner daily*

Catering to the Russian immigrants who have settled in the Hollywood area, this friendly spot has a big-screen TV mounted on the wall but no liquor license. (There's no corkage fee if you bring your own bottle.) Start with one of the eggplant dishes prepared either Armenian or Israeli style, than choose from among such traditional Russian dishes as borscht, chicken Kiev, beef Stroganoff, shashlik, grilled sturgeon or marinated rack of lamb. Try the non-alcoholic drink called Tann, a foamy, white and tangy mixture of unsweetened yogurt and seltzer water.

UZBEKESTAN

7077 Sunset Blvd., Hollywood 90028
323-464-3663, *Lunch and dinner daily, Brunch Sun.*

A ☎

Don't be put off by the kitschy mauve walls, carpets and minaret-shaped booths. Traditional Russian dishes like beef Lagman, lamb Plov and chicken Kiev are very good, along with such Uzbek dishes as pirogi filled with juicy lamb, baked dumplings and Ugra dumpling soup. Uzbekistan serves a variety of heady vodka concoctions, one named "Drunk Ivan." Friday through Sunday there is live entertainment provided by an engaging and talented one-man band, and the place is packed with Russian emigrées.

Seafood

FROGGY'S TOPANGA FRESH FISH MARKET

1105 N. Topanga Canyon Blvd., Topanga 90290
310-455-1728, *Dinner nightly*

This ramshackle fish market serves some of the best seafood in Southern California, along with killer spuds and crunchy coleslaw. The fish chowder is stellar; so are the swordfish, scallops, shrimp, and lobster. Anarchy seems to reign here, but somebody must be in charge—the food's just too good.

MALIBU SEAFOOD

25653 Pacific Coast Highway, Malibu 90265
310-456-3430, *Lunch & Dinner daily*

This funky little place is a genuine slice of California beach culture, straight out of the Sixties. Bring your own wine or beer, place your order at the counter, and grab a table on one of the three levels of patio while waiting for your number to be called. We appreciate the unpretentious fresh seafood—fish and chips, New Zealand mussels, grilled snapper—at very reasonable prices. This is a perfect, laid-back spot to watch the sun set on another perfect day in paradise.

Thai

THE KING & I

272 S. La Cienega Blvd., Beverly Hills 90211
310-652-9845, *Lunch & Dinner daily*

A popular and friendly little Thai eatery that's been here forever. Fine preparations of all the Thai favorites—pad Thai noodles, mee krob, curries and seafood cooked in a pot—at very reasonable prices.

L.A. FOOD COURT

Thailand Plaza, 5321 Hollywood Blvd., Hollywood 90027
323-993-9000, *Lunch & Dinner daily*

On top of a Thai supermarket is this gargantuan space with Formica tables, TV monitors, and a huge stage where a rock band plays every night except Wednesday—and Kavee, the "Thai Elvis", belts out the king's tunes. You'll be amazed at the staggering choice of over four hundred dishes offered by eight different Thai kitchens surrounding the dining area. We recommend the spicy green-papaya salad, coconut soup with fish balls, red curry with chicken and glass noodles and the garlic-basil beef.

PINK PEPPER

1638 N. La Brea Ave., Hollywood 90028
323-461-2462, *Lunch & Dinner daily*

On the outside, this appears to be but another storefront Thai restaurant, but the rose-toned interior is quite romantic. And the food is consistently good. Among our favorite dishes: "Pink Pepper rolls," light-as-air rice sheet wraps filled with basil, vermicelli, vegetables and tofu; spicy eggplant with black bean sauce and garlic; a stir-fried seafood combo and cashew chicken.

ROSALYNN THAI RESTAURANT

2308 Lincoln Blvd.,Venice 90291
310-397-2647, *Lunch Mon.-Sat., Dinner nightly*

A

Pass on the lengthy menu at this tiny Thai, and choose from the seasonal blackboard specials, most of which are very mildly spiced unless you request otherwise. We've enjoyed the green papaya salad with shrimp, the duck salad, the shrimp curry and such noodle dishes as the lard nah in a sweet bean sauce. Try the ginger fish, a whole crispy-fried pompano slathered with ground pork, tomatoes and peppers.

THAI BEER

7513 Sunset Blvd., Hollywood 90046
323-883-1805, *Lunch & Dinner daily*

Although this is another storefront Thai place, it's very clean, the service is brisk and friendly and the food is very special. Pad Thai includes shrimp so fresh and crunchy they pop in your mouth. A few of the standout dishes are roast duck curry, green curry chicken or beef and spicy fried rice with mint leaves. The chefs are happy to spice up or cool down any dish. Visit the restaurant during the holidays and you will see one of the most festively decorated Christmas trees around.

THAI SEAFOOD

5615 Hollywood Blvd., Hollywood 90028
323-462-7678, *Lunch & Dinner daily*

A tiny Thai place with terrific food: egg rolls served so crispy and hot from the fryer they may burn your mouth, fish cakes, fried mussels, steamed rainbow trout with ginger and noodle dishes like those sold by riverboat-vendors in Bangkok. With a $15 minimum order, you get egg rolls or Thai iced tea.

WILD ORCHID

7669 Beverly Blvd., L.A. 90036
323-937-3100, *Lunch & Dinner daily*

We find this quirky little hole in the wall quite charming, right down to the purple orchid mural on the back wall. The Thai (with Chinese overtones) food is fresh and commendable, especially the crab Rangoon with cream cheese in won ton wrappers, the spider rolls with crab, avocado, cucumber and rice sushi, the succulent chili prawns in red curry sauce and the catfish. They don't serve beer and wine, but if you bring your own there is no corkage fee.

Theme Restaurants

DIVE! SUBMARINE

Century City Shopping Center, 10250 Santa Monica Blvd., 90067
310-733-DIVE, *Lunch & Dinner daily*

A

Not one of Steven Spielberg's greatest hits, this submarine-themed restaurant has never quite surfaced among the ranks of the Hard Rock and Planet Hollywood. Maybe that's because patrons care more about rock and roll and movie memorabilia than submarines. Maybe it's because the food just isn't very good: submarine sandwiches, burgers and other kid-friendly food with cutesy names. **Also in Las Vegas.**

ED DEBEVIC'S — FIFTIES DINER

134 N. La Cienega Blvd., Beverly Hills 90211
310-659-1952, *Lunch & Dinner daily.*

This campy '50s diner may lack authenticity, but it makes up for it in zany fun. In-your-face waitresses with big hair and bobby socks serve decent but lifeless diner standards (milkshakes, burgers, chili, french fries) while busboys clown and sing along with blaring rock oldies. Teens and kids, especially, can't seem to get enough of this theme spot—Debevic's is packed night and day.

HARD ROCK CAFÉ — ROCK 'N ROLL

Beverly & La Cienega Blvds., W. Hollywood 90048
310-276-7605, *Lunch & Dinner daily*

So what are we doing here, being jostled by Japanese schoolgirls dressed in Hard Rock T-shirts? We're having great fun—checking out the Cadillac plunging through the roof, the loud, energetic rock-and-roll, the fantastic collection of movie-and-music memorabilia and the hopping bar. Surprisingly, the food is pretty good, especially the succulent, lime-grilled chicken, various burgers, chili and apple pie à la mode. **Also in Universal CityWalk and Newport Beach.**

HOUSE OF BLUES — SOUTHERN

8430 Sunset Blvd., W. Hollywood 90069
323-848-5100, *Lunch Mon.-Sat., Dinner nightly, Brunch Sun.*

Blues, of course, is the big draw at this colorful place, where the biggest names draw the biggest crowds. The menu includes Cajun, Creole and downhome Southern specialties, as well as a smattering of Thai and Indian. Visiting "star" chefs add their own specials monthly. The high-energy Sunday Gospel Brunch features homemade sausage, fried catfish nuggets and corn bread among its many other Southern delicacies.

PLANET HOLLYWOOD — MOVIES

9560 Wilshire Blvd., Beverly Hills 90212
310-275-7828, *Lunch & Dinner daily*

This noisy, glitzy, Hollywood movie-paraphernalia-filled eatery may be owned by celebrities (Sly, Demi and Bruce among them), but you're more likely to encounter tourists here. All-American junk food, plus, at the Beverly Hills location, healthy "For the Industry" specialties, such as the "Wilshire Salad" and the angel-hair pasta with fresh tomato and basil.

San Fernando Valley

SAN FERNANDO VALLEY

Encompasses **Burbank, Calabasas, Chatsworth, Canoga Park, Encino, Granada Hills, North Hollywood, Northridge, Sherman Oaks, Studio City, Tarzana, Toluca Lake, Universal City, Van Nuys, West Hills** and **Woodland Hills.**

DINING

ANDALUZ — SPANISH — 12/20

7257 Topanga Canyon Blvd., West Hills 91303
818-999-4598, *Lunch & Dinner Mon.-Sat., $*

In a cleverly remodeled former fast-food facility, one can escape to the land of Quixote. Sip a sherry in the bright white-and-red-hued dining room, nibble on serrano ham, Manchego cheese, baby sautéed squid and tortilla Española tapas. We also recommend the gazpacho served, in true Andalusian style, with condiments, the paella and any of meat or fish dishes cooked with sherry and/or brandy. Prices are low—and that applies to the carefully chosen list of Spanish wines, many of which are under $20.

ARAZ — MEDITERRANEAN — 12/20

11717 Moorpark St., Studio City 91604
818-766-1336, *Lunch & Dinner Tues.-Sun., $*

A

Originally from Beirut, the owner/chef cooks assertive food, liberally using fresh and dried herbs. In addition to the usual kebabs, try the sensational-looking salad called fettouch, topped with chopped mint and a sharp berry called sumak, the juicy, marinated quail and the grilled Armenian sausages known as soujouk.

ASANEBO — JAPANESE — 14/20 

11941 Ventura Blvd., Studio City 91604
818-760-3348, *Dinner Tues.-Sun., $$*

A

The most flattering way to describe this simple and friendly mini-mall discovery is to call it a "poor-man's Matsuhisa". As at that celebrated establishment, Asanebo combines artistry with culinary proficiency in creating one imaginative composition after another. An authentic sashimi bar, it also serves a remarkable array of cooked specialties, including velvety monkfish liver in ponzu sauce, a caviar-topped lobster "cocktail" and asparagus-stuffed calamari.

BAMBOO INN CHINESE 13/20

14010 Ventura Blvd., Sherman Oaks 91423
818-788-0202, *Lunch & Dinner daily, $*

At the friendly neighborhood restaurant, the mandatory appetizers include plump fried dumplings, aromatic beef and smoked fish, or the barbecued chicken salad. Though the seafood dishes are expensive, some are worth the splurge, particularly the braised shrimp and filet of fish in black bean sauce, and the sweet-and-pungent shrimp.

BARSAC BRASSERIE MEDITERRANEAN 13/20 

4212 Lankershim Blvd., N. Hollywood 91602
818-760-7081, *Lunch Mon.-Fri., Dinner Mon.-Sat., $$*

Newly remodeled in a warmly intimate-and-romantic style, the Barsac Brasserie caters to a movie-studio crowd and offers a mix of French and Italian fare. We recommend the frisée-and-red leaf salad, the mushroom risotto and the roast duck with red wine, Curaçao and sliced citrus fruit.

THE BISTRO GARDEN AT COLDWATER CONTINENTAL 13/20 

12950 Ventura Blvd., Studio City 91604
818-501-0202, *Lunch Mon.-Fri., Dinner nightly, $$$*

Tiny white lights twinkle in the ficus trees at this lovely winter garden setting, all that's left of the Bistro/Bistro Garden glamour-restaurant family that once ruled in Beverly Hills. You can count on good service and good renditions of such updated Continental dishes as farfalle with wild mushrooms and veal sauce, ravioli with ricotta cheese, osso buco and rack of lamb with black peppercorn sauce. Their chocolate soufflé is worthy of its stellar reputation. Next door, **Bistro To-Go** sells juicy rotisserie chickens, pastas, sandwiches and yes, those sublime chocolate soufflés.

BROTHER'S SUSHI JAPANESE/SUSHI 13/20 

21418 Ventura Blvd., Woodland Hills 91364
818-992-1284, *Lunch Tues.-Fri., Dinner Mon.-Sat., $$*

Because of unspecified kitchen problems, this popular Valley spot—where nearly everyone sits at the counter—no longer serves the wonderful grilled bonito and miso asari, or the excellent soy-bean-and-clam soup. But they still serve sushi, which is definitely a cut above.

CA'DEL SOLE ITALIAN 14/20 

410 Cahuenga Blvd., N. Hollywood 91602
818-985-4669, *Lunch Mon.-Fri., Dinner Mon.-Sat., $$*

A rustic Italian spot with a series of giant-windowed dining rooms, spacious booths, a double-sided fireplace and a shaded patio, where dishes are served in big copper pans. Good starters include the bruschetta and the lobster-and-crab cakes with cannellini beans. We've enjoyed the pumpkin-stuffed pasta with sage, the free-range veal in citrus sauce, the corn-fed lemon chicken and the lamb shank slow-roasted in red wine and fresh herbs. Save room for the homemade gelati.

CAFÉ BIZOU FRENCH 13/20

14016 Ventura Blvd., Sherman Oaks 91423
818-788-3536, *Lunch Mon.-Fri., Dinner nightly, Brunch Sat.-Sun., $*

This "playful kiss" of a café has a devoted foodie following. We can't believe the oh-so-reasonable prices for such tantalizing fare as the angel hair pasta with tiger shrimp, the piquant mushroom-and-scallop tart, the crispy potato-scaled salmon swimming in a delicious port-and-white wine sauce. Here's how you really save money here: order an entrée, and soup or salad are only $1 more; and bring your own bottle of wine—the corkage fee is a mere $2.

CALIFORNIA CANTEEN CONTINENTAL 12/20

3311 Cahuenga Blvd.W., Universal City 90068
213-876-1702, *Breakfast, Lunch & Dinner daily, $*

This vivacious little spot is popular with show-biz folk from the east Valley studios. The look is Spanish, the feel is French and the fare is Italian/Continental with a California spin. The Niçoise salad with fresh tuna or the steamed mussels are good bets, as are the blackened seafood platter with angel hair, the veal stew and the penne with grilled chicken breast, pesto and goat cheese. Expect to taste plenty of garlic—and to see some faces you recognize from TV. The room next door has the look and feel of a French guinguette—it's a great place to hang out in the evening.

CHA CHA CHA CARIBBEAN 12/20

17499 Ventura Blvd., Encino 91316
818-789-3600, *Lunch & Dinner daily, Brunch Sun., $$*

A

A spin-off of East Hollywood's Cha Cha Cha, this lively establishment is wrapped in vivid murals and serves sometimes-sassy Caribbean cuisine. We've enjoyed the grilled chicken breast with Brazilian spices and pineapple, the fusilli pasta with sautéed garden veggies and herbs and the free-range veal chop.

CHAO PRAYA THAI 12/20

13456 Ventura Blvd., Sherman Oaks 91423
818-789-3575, *Lunch & Dinner daily, $*

A

See review in "L.A. AREA—Dining."

CHIN CHIN CHINESE 12/20

16101 Ventura Blvd., Encino 91436
818-783-1717, *Lunch & Dinner daily, $*

See review in "L.A. AREA—Dining." **Also in Studio City (12215 Ventura Blvd., 818-985-9090).**

CHINA STAR CHINESE/DIM SUM 13/20

9250 Reseda Blvd., Northridge, 91324
818-886-0789, *Lunch & dinner daily, $*

With celebrated chef Chi Chou Chen at the helm and three tanks of fresh fish, this establishment is offering up many items one doesn't ordinarily find in Valley Chinese restaurants. Come for the pork-rib-and-bitter-melon soup, the green onion pancakes, the Taiwanese-style duck strips, and best of all, the dim sum.

THE DAILY GRILL AMERICAN 12/20

16101 Ventura Blvd, Encino 91436
818-986-4111, *Lunch & Dinner daily, $*

See review in "L.A. AREA—Dining." **Also in Studio City (12050 Ventura Blvd., 818-769-6336).**

DELMONICO'S SEAFOOD GRILLE SEAFOOD/ITALIAN 12/20

16358 Ventura Blvd., Encino 91436
818-986-0777, *Lunch Mon.-Fri., Dinner nightly, $$*

See review in " L. A. AREA—Dining."

THE GAUCHO GRILL ARGENTINE 12/20

12050 Ventura Blvd, Studio City 91604
818-508-1030, *Lunch & Dinner daily, $*

See review in "L.A. AREA—Dining." **Also in Woodland Hills (6435 Canoga Ave., 818-992-6416).**

THE GREAT GREEK GREEK 10/20

13362 Ventura Blvd., Sherman Oaks 91423
818-905-5250, *Lunch & dinner daily, $$*

Zorba would feel at home in this taverna where great bouzouki music resounds and a line of frenzied dancers snakes across the room. Appetizers are the kitchen's main strength, particularly the Greek salad and the delicious tzatziki. Entrées include moussaka, shish kebab and other Greek favorites, as well as more intriguing items like the char-broiled jumbo "Garithes" shrimp.

HONG KONG PARADISE CHINESE 13/20

16240 Ventura Blvd., Encino 91436
818-783-7213, *Lunch & Dinner daily, $$*

A Monterey Park-style Chinese seafood restaurant finally comes to Encino, its tanks brimming with live crabs, lobsters, shrimp and fish. In addition to the generously portioned seafood dishes, we recommend the shredded duck soup, beef with black bean sauce, sensational spicy eggplant, delectable deep-fried pork chops and barbecued pork. More exotic specialties include several clay pot dishes, jellyfish, and bird's nest and shark's fin soup.

HORTOBAGY — HUNGARIAN — 12/20

11138 Ventura Blvd., Studio City 91604
818-980-2273, *Lunch & Dinner Tues.-Sun.*, $

If you are a serious carnivore, the "wooden platter" is a must: a groaning board for two piled high with spicy pork sausages, breaded slabs of veal and liver, potato salad, marinated red cabbage and a small hillock of rice. The thick goulash is topped with sour cream.

IL FORNO — ITALIAN — 12/20

22239 Mulholland Hwy., Calabasas 91302
818-222-6699, *Lunch & Dinner daily*, $

See review in "L.A. AREA—Dining."

IL TIRAMISU — ITALIAN — 12/20

13705 Ventura Blvd., Sherman Oaks 91423
818-986-2640, *Dinner nightly*, $$

This smart-looking trattoria offers a fine version of the ubiquitous Italian dessert, but there's much to enjoy before it: crunchy calamari fritti, tuna carpaccio, excellent pizzas, and intriguing pastas including gnocchi with smoked salmon and whitefish caviar in a Mascarpone cheese sauce. As a minor deviation from the signature dessert, try the delicious casalinga—Marsala-soaked ladyfingers layered with vanilla custard.

IROHA SUSHI — JAPANESE/SUSHI — 12/20

12953 Ventura Blvd., Studio City 91604
818-990-9559, *Lunch & Dinner Mon.-Sat.*, $$

Many say the single best item here is the spiced tuna: tender chopped tuna mixed with wasabe, shichimi and seven spices. There are superlative crispy salmon skin rolls and first-rate California rolls—which are surprisingly popular with visiting Japanese tourists.

JOE JOE'S — CALIFORNIAN — 14/20

13355 Ventura Blvd., Sherman Oaks 91423
818-990-8280, *Lunch & Dinner Tues.-Sun.*, $$

A spin-off of the tiny but popular Joe Joe's in Venice, this bright-and-cheery storefront has super-friendly service and sensational food at very reasonable prices. We've loved the saffron-laced eggplant soup and the grilled salmon with basil-mashed potatoes, along with such innovations as the onion tart with gravlax, the grilled shiitake mushrooms with smoked mozzarella and roasted peppers, the grilled shrimp on saffron risotto and crispy breast of chicken with a twice-baked potato. Pop in early for the budget-priced three-course prix-fixe dinner menu.

KUSHIYU — JAPANESE/SUSHI — 12/20

18713 Ventura Blvd., Tarzana
818-609-9050, *Lunch & Dinner Tues.-Sun., $$*

Featuring a kushiyaki grill imported from Japan (there are only a few in L.A.), this is a grazer's paradise. Order a myriad of barbecue sticks skewered with everything from chicken, beef, tuna, squid, smelts and quail egg, to pork-wrapped asparagus. There are also a number of delicious deep-fried Japanese snacks and—of course—sushi.

LA FINESTRA — ITALIAN — 11/20

19647 Ventura Blvd., Tarzana 91356
818-342-2824, *Lunch Tues.-Fri., Dinner Tues.-Sun., $*

At this cheerful-looking Valley trattoria, owner/chef Mario Tidu, influenced by his mother's cooking and that of ex-Adriano's chef Ueli Huegli, makes airy gnocchetti in a fresh tomato sauce, thin-crusted pizza and a lovely dish combining moist chicken with Kalamata olives, capers, fresh rosemary and tomatoes. A good spot for a tasty inexpensive dinner.

LA FRITE CAFÉ — FRENCH — 11/20

15013 Ventura Blvd., Sherman Oaks 91403
818-990-1791, *Lunch & Dinner daily, Brunch Sun., $*

The ambience is homey and the straightforward bistro fare sends us home full. For starters try the baked goat-cheese ratatouille, or the crab cake with Cajun mayonnaise. Entrée choices include a wide variety of salads and crêpes, several quiches, a number of pizzas, chicken Cordon Bleu and fresh sautéed trout amandine. **Also in Woodland Hills (22616 Ventura Blvd., 818-225-1331).**

LA LOGGIA — ITALIAN — 13/20 

11814 Ventura Blvd., Studio City 91604
818-985-9222, *Lunch Mon.-Fri., Dinner nightly, $*

People from the studios crowd this casual, intimate and cheery spot day and night. You're best off forgoing the entrées and desserts in favor of the delicious salads, antipasti, pastas and pizzas. Try the smoke-cured salmon with artichoke hearts or the black mussels steamed in white wine. The homemade whitefish cake with cucumbers and lentils is terrific. They serve late supper nightly.

LA PARRILLA — MEXICAN — 13/20 

19265 Roscoe Blvd., Northridge 91324
818-993-7773, *Breakfast, Lunch & Dinner nightly, $*

See review in "L.A. AREA—Dining." **Also in Tarzana (19601 Ventura Blvd., 818-708-7422).**

LE PETIT BISTRO FRENCH 12/20

13360 Ventura Blvd., Sherman Oaks 91423
818-501-7999, *Lunch Mon.-Fri., Dinner nightly, $$*

La Cienega's favorite French bistro has cloned itself in the Valley. The place has all the simple charm of the original: dark woods, old French ad posters, butcher-paper-covered tables. But here the tables aren't so closely squeezed together and there are a few spacious booths. We appreciate the simple, authentic French bistro food—at very reasonable prices (the top entrée price is $12.95): a sublime eggplant-and-tomato tart, aromatic mussels marnière, roast chicken with crisp pommes frites and moist-blackened salmon atop a green salad. There's buttery bread pudding and a classic crème caramel for dessert.

MALLORY'S NEW AMERICAN/IRISH 12/20

3575 Cahuenga Blvd. West, Universal City 90068
213-876-4953, *Lunch Mon.-Fri., Dinner nightly, $$*

This place started out serving well-turned New American fare: pan-seared calamari and sweet peppers in a lemon and vinegar-flavored broth, horseradish-crusted cod on garlicky mashed potatoes, rare ahi tuna with portobello mushrooms and breast of duck with a honey-balsamic sauce. As we went to press, they were introducing some Irish culinary touches—which we look forward to trying.

MISTRAL BRASSERIE FRENCH 12/20

13422 Ventura Blvd., Sherman Oaks 91423
818-981-6650, *Lunch Mon.-Fri., Dinner Mon.-Sat., $$*

People dress down for this neighborhood-bistro mainstay, as if they were Provençals dropping into their village bistro for a bite. This is one of the places to go for the steeped-in-olive-oil cooking of Provence. From the traditional pizza called pissaladière (choux-pastry crust topped with caramelized onions, olives, herbs and anchovies) through classic versions of New York steak frites, grilled entrecôte and stewed chicken, you won't be disappointed.

MONTEFRIO DE MADRID SPANISH 12/20

222 S. Glenoaks Blvd., Burbank 91502
818-954-0159, *Lunch & Dinner Tues.-Sun., $*

Though the small dining room is decidedly no-frills, diners feel pampered by the exceptional quality of the Manchego cheese, Spanish chorizo, croquetas, empanadas, Serrano ham, lemon-steamed mussels and other authentic tapas. The saffron-perfumed paella, packed with shellfish, is outstanding, as are the bacalao (salt cod) and callos a la Madrileña (beef tripe and trotters). Other dishes worth considering are fabada Asturiana, a white bean and chorizo stew from northern Spain, and brandy-flavored shrimp.

MOONLIGHT AMERICAN/CONTINENTAL 12/20

13730 Ventura Blvd., Sherman Oaks 91423
818-788-2000, *Dinner Tues.-Sun., $$*

A nightclub where most people go more for the dancing than the food, Moonlight has the look and feel of a refined '50s swing joint where one wouldn't be surprised to see the Rat Pack swagger in. Try the shellfish-and-chicken paella with chorizo sausage, the fresh Atlantic salmon with cucumber-and-tarragon Hollandaise or the roasted veal chop Marengo with garlic-mashed potatoes. Swing night is every Thursday. While dining, don't be alarmed if a conga line with singing waiters passes by.

OUT TAKE CAFÉ ECLECTIC 13/20 

12159 Ventura Blvd., Studio City
818-760-1111, *Lunch Mon.-Sat; Dinner nightly, $*

This austere and often-cramped storefront café is no longer the well kept secret it once was, but maybe upscale food at downscale prices shouldn't be a secret. The soups are great (Ukrainian borscht and vegetable wonton). So are the amazing chicken panzoti-filled pasta and the steamed mussels (40 of them, in a lemon grass-coconut milk broth). We like the spicy turkey chili and the braised lamb shank. If you order an entrée, you can add on a salad for $1 extra. There are lots of wines by the glass, and if you bring your own bottle, there's a mere $4 corkage fee.

PASION SUPPER CLUB CALIFORNIAN 12/20

12215 Ventura Blvd., Studio City 91604
818-752-7333, *Dinner Tues.-Sun., $$*

People drive from as far away as Santa Barbara to enjoy the food, music and dancing at this provocative little club hidden away in a Studio City strip mall. There are music and dancing and dance lessons, a full bar and quite good food: smoked salmon rolatini with soy-soaked cucumbers in dill-Dijon sauce, pepper-crusted ahi tuna in mint vinaigrette, Chilean sea bass and leeks in roasted red pepper sauce. This place is very sexy and perfect for a night when you want to let your hair down.

PERROCHE NEW AMERICAN 14/20 

11929 Ventura Blvd., Studio City 91604
818-766-1179, *Lunch Mon.-Fri., Dinner Mon.-Sat., $$*

The name may sound French, but Perroche is actually an English goat cheese. This compact little restaurant is run by two Brits—Grady Atkins, who cooked with The Peninsula Hotel's Bill Bracken, and Stuart Barker, formerly a chef himself—who have put together a small menu of inventive dishes here. We've been impressed with the ginger-boosted smoked trout appetizer, the pan-roasted cod on white cabbage, the sweet potato ravioli with garlic confit and the succulent whole roasted baby chicken with golden beets and tarragon sauce. End your meal with a comforting baba au rhum.

PIERO'S SEAFOOD HOUSE ITALIAN 11/20

2825 W. Olive Ave., Burbank 91505
818-842-5159, *Lunch Mon.-Fri., Dinner nightly, $$*

This Italian-seafood house offers hearty cuisine. It's a pleasant, casual setting, with good service and good food. And the prices are more than reasonable, as all entrées include soup or salad and a side dish of pasta. Best bets are the half a dozen or more nightly seafood specials. And be sure to order the tomato-bread appetizer.

PINOT BISTRO FRENCH 15/20 

12969 Ventura Blvd., Studio City 91604
818-990-0500, *Lunch Mon.-Fri., Dinner nightly, $$$*

Joachim Splichal's ultra-chic bistro is enjoying the same success as his other endeavors—Patina, Pinot at the Chronicle, Café Pinot and Pinot Hollywood. The Parisian décor is gorgeous and the classic bistro fare is always done with aplomb. Onion soup...escargots...duck confit...steak frites...braised oxtail—they're everything you would expect from a Splichal-restaurant kitchen, and there are wondrous nightly specials such as the roasted rack of pork stuffed with pine-nuts, rosemary and olives. True to its name, Pinot has a good assortment of moderately priced bistro wines.

POSTO ITALIAN 14/20 

14928 Ventura Blvd., Sherman Oaks 91403
818-784-4400, *Lunch Mon.-Fri., Dinner nightly, $$$*

Piero Selvaggio, owner of Valentino and Primi, has reason to be proud. He doesn't spend a lot of time here, but he doesn't have to. Luciano Pellegrini is an excellent and innovative chef. The wisest plan is to ignore the menu and just say, "Make my dinner...please." Your request will make Pellegrini happy, and in turn he'll make you very happy. If you're not feeling adventurous and want to stick to the menu, don't miss the rainbow trout with Sicilian pesto or the garlic-infused rabbit wrapped in smoked bacon.

PREZZO ITALIAN 10/20

13625 Ventura Blvd., Sherman Oaks 91423
818-905-8400, *Dinner & Late Supper nightly, $$*

Okay, so this spot is a popular Valley singles' bar. Perhaps surprisingly, the kitchen serves up food that is satisfying and in some instances, inspired. The isalata fagioli is good—a refreshingly crunchy mix of beans, fresh tomatoes, cucumber, green and fava beans with red onion. The pastas are good, too, and the pizza is of the Spago/California Pizza Kitchen school. Grilled dishes—salmon with a tomato-coriander sauce, as well as the marinated chicken and the swordfish—are particularly reliable. The front patio is now covered, and they offer live entertainment Tuesdays through Saturday nights.

PROSECCO ITALIAN 12/20

10144 Riverside Dr., Toluca Lake 91602
818-505-1895, *Lunch & Dinner Tues.-Sat., $$*

This Toluca Lake eatery features a homey dining room with tables clad in burgundy and white, large still-life paintings on the walls and a prominent wooden bar. We've enjoyed the anchovy-studded caprese, corn chowder, salmon in citrus-pesto sauce, grilled chicken lasagne, pepper-crusted beef tenderloin in Cabernet-butter sauce and the terrific pear turnover with chocolate and Mascarpone cheese.

RIVE GAUCHE CAFÉ FRENCH 11/20

14106 Ventura Blvd., Sherman Oaks 91423
818-990-3573, *Lunch & Dinner daily, Brunch Sat.-Sun., $$*

This little French-style café is popular among the Valley "Ladies Who Lunch." The food is simple café-French: quiches and crêpes, appetizers such as an artichoke in a saucy vinaigrette, brunch items like the salmon-and-spinach tart and a variety of salads. At dinner, the cooking is more upscale: roast duck à l'orange or the wonderfully garlicky scampi.

RIVERSIDE CAFÉ FRENCH 12/20

1221 W. Riverside Dr., Burbank 91506
818-563-3567, *Breakfast, Lunch & Dinner Tues.-Sun., $*

What was once a fast-food joint near the Los Angles Equestrian Center, is now a charming little café frequented by neighbors and nearby studio workers. The diminutive dining room has a rustic wood-beamed ceiling. You'll find such typical bistro dishes as wild boar sausage, French onion soup, beef tartare and coq au vin, along with rack of lamb, pepper steak flambéed in brandy, grilled salmon and pastas—all at budget prices.

SADDLE PEAK LODGE AMERICAN 13/20 

419 Cold Canyon Dr., Calabasas 91302
818-222-3888, *Dinner Wed.-Sun., Brunch Sun., $$$$*

Rumor has it that this beautifully reconstituted 85-year-old lodge was once a bordello. Located between Malibu and Calabasas, it has the feel of a country retreat and boasts rustic dining rooms with fireplaces, antlered-animal heads on the walls and a bar bedecked with vintage guns and fishing rods. Sit in the small room on the top floor and view the surrounding mountain peaks through French doors, or on the terrace bordered by a cactus garden. Game is the specialty of the house, and we're captivated by such dishes as the sautéed ostrich with a potato stack, the tenderloin of buffalo smothered with wild mushrooms and the chef's-choice daily game plate. The marvelous atmosphere diverts you from any lapses that might occur in the kitchen. On Sundays, go for a drive in the country and stop in for brunch—but reserve a table well in advance.

SANAMLUANG CAFÉ THAI 12/20

12980 Sherman Way, N. Hollywood 91605
818-764-1180, *Lunch, Dinner & Late Supper daily, $*

Whether or not Sanamluang is the home of the best noodles in town, as their business card proclaims, they certainly vie for the broadest variety. Several dozen noodle dishes lurk on this menu along with countless other intriguing concoctions: koo chai, rice biscuits bulging with chopped Chinese vegetables and served with a deliciously syrupy sweet-and-spicy sauce, and rahd nah, a mountain of rice noodles with chicken, pork, pork stomach, squid and shrimp, topped with a fried egg. For those with late night cravings, when nothing will do but some duck-feet stew, Sanamluang is open until four in the morning.

SHIHOYA JAPANESE/SUSHI 12/20

15489 Ventura Blvd., Sherman Oaks 91403
818-986-4461, *Lunch Tues.-Fri., Dinner Mon.-Sat., $*

At this elegant Japanese temple of dining, the sashimi appetizers of deep-fried sculpin and sharply spiced fuguzukui halibut (shaped like small rose petals) are marvelous. Lighter- textured fish include the jumbo clams, abalone, bream, salmon and crab. You can get sushi with oyster, barracuda, Spanish mackerel, sea urchin roe and the illustrious toro.

SPUMANTE ITALIAN 13/20

12650 Ventura Blvd., Studio City 91604
818-980-0734, *Lunch Mon.-Fri., Dinner Mon.-Sat., $$*

A

On a street lined with dozens of cookie-cutter trattorias, this is one that stands out. Joe Salas, who reigns from Spain rather than Italy, keeps his appealing dining room clicking, and in addition to Italian dishes, the kitchen does top-drawer tamales and lobster bisque. House specialties include colossal grilled prawns, wild mushroom soup, risotto di mare and goat cheese-filled ravioli. The dining room is casual but polished; the patio offers a somewhat more romantic setting.

SUMIYA JAPANESE 12/20

4517 Sepulveda Blvd., Sherman Oaks 91403
818-995-8580, *Lunch Mon.-Fri., Dinner nightly, $*

In Japan, yakitori bars are a common sight, usually concentrated around commuter train stations. Customers step up for succulent skewers of chicken, beef, pork, fish, turkey and even vegetables, dipped in a light glazing sauce then barbecued over charcoal. Sumiya claims to be the first yakitori bar in the San Fernando Valley. We recommend the skewers of chicken, flattened chicken wings and ground pork with onion. Sumiya also serves hand-cut sushi rolls and—for braver souls—chicken sashimi.

SUSHI NOZAWA JAPANESE/SUSHI 14/20 

11288 Ventura Blvd., Unit C, Studio City 91604
818-508-7017, *Lunch & Dinner Mon.-Fri., $$*

The source of urban legend—heard about the Sushi Nazi?—this small sushi bar isn't much to look at, but the sushi's great. Nozawa, the one and only sushi man here, doesn't make California rolls. He layers pink-and-perfect salmon with translucent seaweed noodles, steeps heavenly mussels in a rice-vinegar broth, enfolds elaborate hand rolls in toasted sheets of seaweed. Some flavors are subtly concealed, and like the proverbial Chinese puzzle box, appear magically as others vanish, awakening your taste buds to Nozawa's handiwork.

SUSHI ON TAP JAPANESE/SUSHI 12/20

11056 Ventura Blvd., Studio City 91604
818-985-2254, *Lunch Mon.-Fri, Dinner nightly, $*

Tap-dancing sushi chefs? Only when they're not wielding their knives, please. This is definitely an only-in-L.A. thing: a sushi bar where the punked-up chefs, hostess and wait-staff perform tap-dance routines for appreciative customers. It's a kick, to say the least. On top of that, the sushi is immaculate, the kitchen serves hot and cold soba and udon noodle dishes—and the prices are low.

TABU BISTRO CALIFORNIAN/FRENCH 12/20

18607 Ventura Blvd., Tarzana 91356
818-758-9368, *Lunch Mon.-Fri., Dinner nightly, $*

Taking a cue from Café Bizou, Tabu lures cost-conscious diners by offering soup or salad for only one dollar above the cost of an entrée, and charging only a $2 corkage fee if they bring their own wine. The entrées themselves top out at around $15, and include a respectable rack of lamb, potato-crusted whitefish, roast duck breast with cherry sauce, a hearty bouillabaisse and sesame-crusted grilled salmon. We like the chef's tendency to use crispy onions as a flavor garnish.

TALESAI THAI 14/20 

11744 Ventura Blvd., Studio City 91604
818-753-1001, *Lunch Mon.-Fri., Dinner nightly, $$*

We love the look of the white-on-white, neon-art-filled valley cousin of the Sunset Strip Thai eatery. See review in "L.A. AREA—Dining " for specialties.

TEMPO MIDDLE EASTERN/ECLECTIC 12/20

16610 Ventura Blvd., Encino 91436
818-905-5855, *Lunch & Dinner daily, $*

What began as a falafel stand has evolved into a restaurant and piano bar offering Middle Eastern and Israeli specialties, as well as some dishes from around the world. The casual, airy establishment is transformed into a lively supper club after dark. Among the favorites are the moist, flavorful falafel, the Israeli chicken, hummus topped with sautéed mushrooms, chicken shwarma and lamb kebabs. Believe it or not, you can also get Cajun-style orange roughy and Chinese cashew chicken here.

TERU SUSHI JAPANESE/SUSHI 12/20

11940 Ventura Blvd., Studio City 91604
818-763-6201, *Lunch Mon.-Fri., Dinner nightly, $$*

Many credit (or blame) Teru Sushi for launching the sushi craze in Los Angeles. Despite the increased local competition, the crowds here haven't abated and the place is still great fun. On weekends, plan on a wait for dishes like "tiger's eye" (salmon-stuffed squid), "sea flowers" (red snapper shaped into flower petals) and combination rolls apparently invented to appeal to the taste of sake-drenched yuppies. Teru also serves up plenty of high-quality straight stuff.

VERSAILLES CUBAN 12/20

17410 Ventura Blvd., Encino 91316
818-906-0756, *Lunch & Dinner daily, $*

See review in "L.A. AREA—Dining."

VIVA FRESH MEXICAN 10/20

900 Riverside Dr., Burbank 91506
818-845-2425, *Lunch & Dinner daily, $*

Adjacent to the Los Angeles Equestrian Center, Viva has a place outside for you to tie your horse while you're inside a pleasant, albeit clichéd, dining room experimenting with its two-dozen tequilas and traditional Mexican specialties. Entrees like the carnitas traditionale and the shrimp borracho make this place worth a short drive—or ride.

WOLFGANG PUCK CAFÉ CALIFORNIAN 13/20

Universal Citywalk, 1000 Universal Century Dr., Universal City 91608
818-985-9653, *Lunch & Dinner daily, $*

See review in "L.A. AREA—Dining." **Also in Woodland Hills (6100 Topanga Canyon Blvd., 818-710-9653).**

YAMAKAWA JAPANESE/SUSHI 12/20

10118 Riverside Dr., Toluca Lake 61602
818-763-8355, *Lunch Mon.-Sat., Dinner daily, $$*

You won't find much better sculptured sushi than Chef Yama's and he hits the fresh fish market more often than most. The kitchen's superb gyoza, yellowtail collar and black cod help keep seats here occupied.

YANG CHOW CHINESE 13/20 

6443 Topanga Canyon Blvd., Woodland Hills 91303
818-347-2610, *Lunch & Dinner daily, $*

We're very pleased that this Valley offshoot of the original downtown Yang Chow is serving the same good Szechwan won-

Vittel
MINERAL WATER
LOW MINERAL CONTENT
Bonne Source
ENHANCE
THE
Experience.

tons in a tasty, aromatic broth, as well as lamb with scallions, fine kung pao chicken and the ever-intriguing slippery shrimp. Even that old warhorse, cashew chicken, passes muster here.

AND ALSO...

ANARBAGH INDIAN

22721 Ventura Blvd., Woodland Hills 91364
818-224-3929, *Lunch & Dinner daily, $*

This Indian restaurant turns out consistently good tandoori specialties. To start, try the puffy samosas and crispy, deep-fried Indian-style onion balls that any onion-ring fancier will love. Order several of the nine varieties of naan tandoori bread. To follow, we like the mixed tandoori grill. The Anarbagh chef will be more than happy to spice your order up or down to taste, and to prepare it oil-free if you insist on low-cal.

THE BRANDYWINE CONTINENTAL

22757 Ventura Blvd., Woodland Hills 91364
818-225-9114, *Lunch Mon.-Fri., Dinner Mon.-Sat., $$*

A lace-curtained jewel with semi-private booths and guitar music in the evenings. Expect well-prepared old-fashioned Continental cuisine, everything from frog legs to bouillabaisse to roast duckling. The paella is good but requires a day's notice and is only available weekdays. For dessert, the cherries jubilee and crêpes Suzette are flambéed tableside.

FONTANA DE TREVI ITALIAN

21733 Ventura Blvd., Woodland Hills 91364
818-888-0206, *Lunch Mon.-Fri., Dinner nightly, $$$*

This pricey, pre-tiramisu-generation establishment offers satisfying food, graciously served in a romantic setting, as well as live music and dancing. We like the Trevi salad, a crisp mixture of tri-color peppers, tomato, eggplant and mozzarella. The risotto with porcini mushrooms is noteworthy and the filet mignon in Marsala, topped with truffled-duck pâté is a real feast.

FUNG LUM CHINESE

222 Universal Terrace Pky., Universal City 91608
818-763-7888, *Lunch & Dinner daily, Brunch Sun., $$*

This tourist-heavy restaurant has an extravagant decor, but the food is another story. We've liked the minced squab appetizer, tender greens with black mushrooms and fresh bamboo shoots and steamed catfish, but the steamed rice was mushy, the special lemon chicken was smothered in a cloying batter, and on and on. Avoid the duck dishes.

THE GYPSY GRILL AMERICAN/CONTINENTAL

16911 Ventura Blvd., Encino 91316
818-784-7393, *Lunch Mon.-Fri., Dinner daily, $$*

This place was once so raucous it was difficult to enjoy a meal here. All that changed when they put in carpeting, deep and comfy banquettes and acoustic padding. Dishes range from mussels and grilled ahi tuna in a pear-and-red-wine reduction, to couscous with lamb and chicken, penne with chopped chicken, pancetta, sun-dried tomatoes and mushrooms. Soup or salad is only $1 with any entrée. One of the most commendable aspects of this establishment is the constantly evolving wine list. There's an adjoining lounge with live entertainment.

LA VE LEE MEDITERRANEAN

12514 Ventura Blvd., Studio City 91604
818-980-8158, *Dinner Tues.-Sun., $$*

Only in L.A. could you find a pan-cultural experience like this: They serve Middle Eastern and Mediterranean food and feature live Brazilian jazz. Appetizers—including hummus, dolmas and tabbouleh—are all good bets. Try the La Ve Lee combo, a generous platter of lamb-and-chicken shish kebabs plus kibbee and lahmajeen.

OMINO SUSHI JAPANESE/SUSHI

20957 Devonshire St., Chatsworth 91311
818-709-8822, *Lunch Mon.-Fri., Dinner daily, $$*

The reasonable prices and friendly service are definite draws, but it's the fish that keeps regulars coming back. Many of the fish are still swimming moments before you eat them. Besides sushi, there's teriyaki and tempura too.

OUTBACK STEAK HOUSE AUSTRALIAN

18711 Devonshire St., Northridge 91324
818-366-2341, *Dinner nightly, $*

A popular nationwide chain where the service is friendly, the atmosphere is convivial and the fare is vaguely Australian—which means plentiful helpings of steak, ribs, "loaded" baked potatoes, "bush" bread and grilled shrimp. Wash it all down with a frosty mug of Honey Blonde draft brew and you'll feel like Crocodile Dundee. **Also in Thousand Oaks (137 E. Thousand Oaks Blvd, 805-381-1590.**

SISLEY ITALIAN KITCHEN ITALIAN

15300 Ventura Blvd., Sherman Oaks 91411
818-905-8444, *Lunch & Dinner daily, $*

What was once Diamond Jim's now quarters this hectic—and yes, noisy—Italian bistro, serving well-turned entrées of generous proportions. **A spin-off of the Sisley in the Westside Pavilion (10800 Pico Blvd., W.L.A., 310-446-3030.)**

THE SMOKEHOUSE AMERICAN

4420 Lakeside Dr., Burbank
818-845-3731, *Lunch Mon.-Sat., Dinner nightly, Brunch Sun., $$*

Popular with the Burbank movie-studio crowd for over fifty years, this All-American eatery serves steaks and chops, but it's most famous for its garlic-cheese bread.

SOMPUN THAI

12051-3 Ventura Pl., Studio City 91604
818-762-7861, *Lunch Mon.-Fri., Dinner nightly, $*

There are trendier and pricier restaurants on the Boulevard grabbing East Valley Thai honors, but this congenial spot with an adjacent market has a large repertoire, much of it quite good.

TANGO D'AMORE ITALIAN

19524 Nordhoff Pl., Northridge 91324
818-727-7399, *Lunch Mon.-Fri., Dinner nightly, $$*

While its kitchen yields very respectable fare, its dining room, while on the romantic side of the spectrum, doesn't go very far in trying to live up to its very sexy name. In any case, we liked the Chilean seabass sautéed with black olives and artichokes, and you can't go wrong with the fresh fusilli alla Siciliana, prepared with tomato, basil and eggplant.

THE WINE BISTRO FRENCH

11915 Ventura Blvd., Studio City 91604
818-766-6233, *Lunch Mon.-Fri., Dinner Mon.-Sat., $*

The convenience and comfort of this studio-close bistro make it a popular lunch spot with show-biz honchos, though the food remains lackluster. You'll be fine if you stay with the soups, salads and appetizers.

QUICK BITES

American: Coffee Shops, Burgers & Diners

BARRON'S FAMILY RESTAURANT

4130 W. Burbank Blvd., Burbank 91505
818-846-0043, *Breakfast, Lunch & Dinner daily*

Something of an institution in Burbank and as American as they come, Barron's has a funky-kitsch interior, friendly waitresses and reasonable, solid food.Breakfast is the big show: scrumptious french toast, pancakes, crispy baconand eggs-to-order, along with plenty of good coffee. The restaurant also provides on-camera food for television shows like Third Rock from the Sun.

DUPAR'S COFFEE SHOP

12036 Ventura Blvd., Studio City 91604
818-766-4437, *Breakfast, Lunch & Dinner daily*

A

There are branches of DuPar's all around Los Angeles, but this one is by far the best. The food is the same here, but the clientele makes this one of the hippest Valley early-morning/late-night hangouts. Studio executives, trendy-teenagers, actors and Sherman Oaks suburbanites all frequent DuPar's, drinking the good coffee and eating excellent french toast, pancakes, egg dishes and pies (the rest of the food is decent but mediocre, except for the white toast which toast-lovers swear by).

MILLIE'S COUNTRY KITCHEN

10318 Sepulveda Blvd., Mission Hills 91345
818-365-7597, *Breakfast, Lunch & Dinner daily*

A

This upscale-chain coffee shop is as homey as a calico apron, and it serves immense portions of good ol' boy food. When you've got a hankering for fried chicken with mashed potatoes, biscuits and gravy, pot roast and deep-dish pies, you could do a lot worse than Millie's. It's a great place for kids and seniors-kind of a campy bit of ex-urban America, at pre-inflation prices. **Also in Van Nuys (16840 Van Owen St. 818-785-3894)**

THE WIENER FACTORY

14917 Ventura Blvd., Sherman Oaks 91403
818-789-2676, *Lunch & Dinner daily*
No Cards

This quaint little dive, offering, quite frankly, some of L.A.'s best hot dogs, is well-worth going out of your way for. Order them to-go at the outdoor take-out counter, or devour them (devour them, you will) at the rustic indoor area with tables. The basic dog is excellent, but our unsurpassed favorite is the thick, juicy, spicy Polish dog. The operative word is addiction.

Barbecue

BIG DADDY'S KITCHEN BARBECUE

21604 Ventura Blvd., Woodland Hills, 91364
818-704-7042, *Lunch & dinner Mon.-Sat., $*

Dr. Hogly Wogly's Barbecue may be in danger of losing its title as best barbecue joint in the San Fernando Valley. At this new spot, they call their cue California rather than Texas-style; whatever you call it, it's delicious. Try the generous portions of ribs, broasted chicken and tri-tip. The chili is terrific, too.

DR. HOGLY WOGLY'S TYLER, TEXAS BARBECUE

8136 N. Sepulveda Blvd., Van Nuys 91402
818-780-6701, *Lunch & Dinner daily*

A

Named for original owner Johnny Greene, who got his nickname in 1932 when he was a chubby delivery boy for a Piggly Wiggly market in Texas, this unassuming joint's decor is a comforting melange of Early American-vinyl and Formica.

Dive into tangy Texas-hot links, way-above-average spareribs, tender chicken and juicy beef brisket. All the meat is smoked on the premises. You may be full but you'll have a tough time resisting the down-home pecan and sweet-potato pies.

MOGO'S

4454 Van Nuys Blvd., Sherman Oaks 91403
818-783-6646, *Lunch Mon.-Thurs., Dinner nightly*

Hidden away in a corner mall, Mogo's offers a buffet stocked with meats and vegetables, an open barbecue and a pile-it-as-high-as-you-can attitude. It also has a comfortable decor and relaxed service. Come for a great meal-in-a- bowl, an all-you-can-eat, create-your-own mix of beef, pork, turkey, lamb, vegetables and savory sauces.

MOM'S BAR-B-Q HOUSE

14062 Van Owen St., Van Nuys 91405
818-786-1373, *Lunch & Dinner daily*

The decor is strictly rec-room, but who cares, because Mom's serves up some of the city's best barbecue. The beef and pork ribs, chicken, hot links, fried chicken, fried chicken livers and rib tips will render you blind to your surroundings. Fantastic sides, too, especially the macaroni and cheese and the cooked-forever baked beans. Even after the mammoth portions, don't miss the pineapple-coconut cake, a cooling antidote to Mom's combustible sauce.

Cafés & Bakery-Cafés

MÄNI'S BAKERY

3960 Laurel Canyon Blvd., Studio City 91604
818-762-7200, *Breakfast, Lunch & Dinner daily*

See review in "L.A. AREA-Quick Bites."

MARMALADE

14901 Ventura Blvd., Sherman Oaks
8188-905-8872, *Lunch & Dinner daily*

See review in "L.A. AREA-Quick Bites."

OLD TOWN BAKERY

18530 Devonshire St., Northridge 91324
818-832-7744, *Breakfast, Lunch & Dinner daily.*

See review in "SAN GABRIEL VALLEY-Quick Bites."

Chicken

ZANKOU CHICKEN

5658 Sepulveda Blvd, Van Nuys
818-781-0615, *Lunch & Dinner daily*
No Cards

See review in "SAN GABRIEL VALLEY-Quick Bites."

Chinese

GOURMET 88

230 N. San Fernando Blvd., Burbank 91502
818-848-8688, *Lunch & Dinner daily*

See review in "SAN GABRIEL VALLEY-Quick Bites-Chinese"

Delis

ART'S DELI

12224 Ventura Blvd., Studio City 91604
818-762-1221, *Breakfast, Lunch & Dinner daily*

It's expensive; it's done in gold vinyl and Formica; and the food is served by no-nonsense waitresses. You'll forgive everything once you bite into one of Art's gargantuan hot- pastrami sandwiches, or taste their incredibly fresh lox, excellent smoked-fish platter or fresh-baked bagels. We agree with their motto that at Art's, "Every sandwich is a work of art."

JERRY'S FAMOUS DELI

12655 Ventura Blvd., Studio City 91604
818-980-4245, *Open daily 24 hours*

See review under "L.A. AREA-Quick Bites."

Filipino

TRYST BAR & GRILL

21352 Devonshire St., Chatsworth 91311
818-993-3043,*Lunch and Dinner daily*

Yes, there are steaks, chops, seafood, chicken, sandwiches and salads, but Filipino chef-owner Tommy Puyot cooks his native food well, allowing those who partake to enjoy his robust fare at ridiculously low prices. Just forget you ever heard of cholesterol. Start with pork soup, then choose from among such traditional dishes as pancit noodles, chicken adobo, lumpia and pork skewers. On Mondays there's a Filipino-style menudo (pork, liver, potatoes and green peppers), on Wednesdays lechon kawali (deep-fried pork backs like Mexican chicharrones)-all for under $5. Forget the mung bean mixture unless you've acquired a taste for it. Kaldereta, a beef stew with potatoes and both red and green sweet peppers is a tasty Thursday offering.

Healthy

THE NATURAL GOURMET

5242 Van Nuys Blvd., Sherman Oaks 91401
818-905-6717, *Lunch & Dinner Mon.-Fri.*

Basically a pizza, pasta and Mediterranean-style sandwich shop, this place is elbow-to-elbow at lunchtime. The cool whitewashed interior, with its brightly tiled tables is good for taking off a few degrees on a hot day in The Valley. Build a sandwich or a pizza from the deli selections. The pastas are also good, although we found the penne with roasted vegetables oily. A good sandwich is the Corfu with smoky roasted vegetables, smooth goat cheese and a mustard vinaigrette, with a side of tomato basil.

Japanese

TODAI

11239 Ventura Blvd., Studio City 91604
818-762-8311, *Lunch & Dinner daily*

A

See review in "And Also-L.A. Area." **Also in Woodland Hills (20401 Ventura Blvd., 818-883-8082).**

Italian & Pizza

FAB'S ITALIAN KITCHEN

4336 Van Nuys Blvd., Sherman Oaks 91403
818-995-2933, *Lunch Mon.-Sat., Dinner daily*

Generous pizzas and such comfort dishes as veal Marsala, eggplant Parmigiano and white-fish pizzaiola are the mainstays here. Try the respectable calamari fritti and the deliciously cheesy veal saltimbocca as well. Entrées come with a side of good spaghetti and there are a couple of decent Chiantis on an otherwise limited wine list.

JACOPO'S

16161 Ventura Blvd., Encino
818-789-9998, *Lunch & Dinner daily 91316*

See review in "L.A. AREA-Quick Bites."

LITTLE TONI'S

4745 Lankershim Blvd., N. Hollywood 91602
818-763-0131, *Dinner daily*

A

Little Toni's is the kind of nondescript neighborhood Italian restaurant one would visit only upon a recommendation. So here it is: Little Toni's makes an excellent, cheesy pizza. Get the thin crust—it's delicious and evenly crisp—with several of the generous and fresh toppings (we like bacon, onion, green pepper and sausage).

MARIA'S ITALIAN KITCHEN

23331 Mulholland Dr., Woodland Hills 91362
818-225-0586, *Lunch & Dinner daily*

There's always a wait to get into these little Italian delis and cafés. Their popularity can be attributed to two things: the low prices and the down-home, retro Italian food. This is the kind of simple Italian food that everyone loves, from pizza to linguine with pesto to meaty lasagne. **Also in Encino 16608 Ventura Blvd., 818-783-2920), Northridge (9161 Reseda Blvd., 818-341-5114) and Sherman Oaks (13353 Ventura Blvd., 818-906-0783).**

PAOLI'S PIZZERIA

21020 Ventura Blvd., Woodland Hills 91364
818-883-4136, *Lunch & Dinner daily*

Local consensus is that Paoli's makes the best pizza in the Valley; folks from in-town have been known to come over the hill for the tasty pies they bake here. The signature all' Alfredo pizza substitutes butter-rich white sauce for the usual tomato mixture and is popular without any topping or in combination with onions and spicy house-made sausage. Pasta, chicken and veal dishes here are also worthy.

PIT FIRE PIZZA COMPANY

5211 Lankershim Blvd., N. Hollywood 91601
818-980-2949, *Lunch & Dinner daily*

Barbecued pizza? Yes, that's the specialty here-pizzas and "rollzones" cooked over a hardwood-fired barbecue pit, so that the thin crust has a slightly smoky flavor. Try the Tuscan, with pit-fire chicken rosemary potatoes, caramelized onions, cheese and pesto. You'll find a variety of good pastas too-and everything is priced well under $10.

RÖSTI

16403 Ventura Blvd., Encino 91316
818-995-7179

See review in"L.A. AREA-Quick Bites." **Also in Westlake Village (160 Promenade Way, 805-370-1939).**

Mexican, Caribbean & Latin American

EL CRIOLLO CUBAN

13245 Victory Blvd., Van Nuys 91401
818-508-0865, *Lunch & Dinner Tues.-Sun.*

El Criollo is such an inconspicuous tenant of a drab Valley strip mall, that finding it is nearly as tough as getting to Cuba. But inside this delightful little eatery—a small no-frills dining room with faux windows and plastic plants—enjoy respectable sardinas Españolas, ropa vieja, marinated tongue, bacalao, squid in its own ink and chicken in a tangy tomato sauce. To drink, order a batido, sort of a Cuban smoothie made from exotic Caribbean fruits.

POQUITO MAS MEXICAN

2635 W. Olive Ave., Burbank 91506
818-563-2252, *Lunch & Dinner daily*

See review in "L.A. AREA-Quick Bites." **Also in North Hollywood (10651 Magnolia Blvd., 818-994-8226) and Studio City (3701 Cahuenga Blvd. West., 818-760-8226.)**

RESTAURANTE MORAZAN SALVADORAN

15706 Vanowen St., Van Nuys 91406
818-994-3838, *Breakfast, Lunch and Dinner daily*

If you stick with the Salvadoran antojitos (small bites), you may never get to the main courses here. They serve pupusas-large, puffy, ground corn pancakes stuffed with beans, pork, cheese or any combination thereof—with spicy pickled cabbage, and, if you request it, loroco, El Salvador's subtly flavored herblike flower. For a change of pupusa pace, ask for a "pupusa de harina de arroz" made with rice flour. We also like their pork or chicken tamals, pastelitos, Salvadoran enchiladas and chile rellenos. And a plate of pollo encebollado arrives as an impressive heap of moist chicken topped with onions and peppers for well under $10.

SHARKEY'S MEXICAN GRILL

13238 Burbank Blvd., Sherman Oaks 91401
818-785-2533, *Lunch & Dinner daily*
No cards

Stop by this eatery for fresh and luscious burritos, tacos, tostadas and quesadillas stuffed with shark, mahi mahi, shrimp, steak and chicken. **Also in Northridge (9250 Reseda Blvd., 818-772-2203) and Tarzana (5511 Reseda Blvd, 818-881-8760).**

Middle Eastern

SKEWERS

14611 Ventura Blvd., Sherman Oaks 91403
818-995-8888, *Lunch & Dinner daily*

Just as the name suggests, this tiny spot does food on skewers along with an assortment of Middle Eastern salads, pastas and sandwiches. We've found the salads inconsistent and a bit bland, so stick to the skewers, especially the pepper-and-rosemary-marinated filet mignon, the mint-curry-marinated chicken and the ahi tuna. **Also in Downtown L.A. (617 S. Central Ave., 2113-689-6900, lunch only) and West Hollywood (8939 Santa Monica Blvd., 310-271-0555.)**

Russian

RASPUTIN

13615 Ventura Blvd., Sherman Oaks 91423
818-907-6336, *Lunch & Dinner, Tues.-Sun.*

The Russian folk-art murals and tabletops, and the shot of vodka with fresh fruit juice they hand you to start with, whets our appetite for such Russian- style comfort-food dishes as potato dumplings, grilled sturgeon with pomegranate sauce, or baked with sliced potatoes and mushrooms. On weekends, the place is booked months in advance with private parties and there's more commotion than the Russian Revolution. When you leave, you get to take home a loaf of the good house-made bread.

Spanish

HOLA ESPAÑA

14054 Burbank Blvd., Sherman Oaks 91401
818-997-6604, *Lunch & Dinner daily*

Tucked into a nondescript mini-mall, like many of the city's better ethnic gems, this colorful little eatery not only offers the authentic cooking but also the spirit of sunny Spain. Tapas include moist croquetas, callos Madrileña (tripe) and Galician-style octopus. Among the entrées featured are rotisserie chicken, shrimp in garlic sauce, grilled lamb chops and-of course-paella.

Theme Restaurants

B.B. KING'S BLUES CLUB BLUES

1000 Universal Center Dr., Universal City 91608
818-622-5464, *Dinner nightly, Brunch Sun.*

A

Venerable Blues Baron B.B. King has scored a winner with this colorful new establishment where the stage is visible from each of its three levels. Although the music—blues—is the main draw, the Southern food (with catchy names we won't go into here) is pretty good: popcorn crawfish, gumbo soup, smoked chicken salad, St. Louis-style pork ribs and pan-seared catfish with green tomato tartar sauce.

THE HARD ROCK CAFÉ ROCK 'N ROLL

Universal CityWalk, 1000 Universal Century Dr., U.C. 91608
818-622-3304, *Lunch & Dinner daily*

A

The latest, glitzy addition to touristy Universal City Walk. See review under "L.A. AREA-Quick Bites".

Pasadena & the San Gabriel Valley

PASADENA & THE SAN GABRIEL VALLEY

Encompasses **Arcadia, Alhambra, City of Industry, Eagle Rock, Glendale, La Cañada-Flintridge, Monrovia, Monterey Park, Pasadena, Rosemead, San Gabriel, San Marino and South Pasadena.**

DINING

ABIENTO MEDITERRANEAN 12/20

110 S. Lake Ave., Pasadena 91101
626-449-4151, *Lunch Mon.-Fri., Dinner nightly, Brunch Sun.,* $$

Though chef/owner Rick Steffanns once cooked at New York's très French La Caravelle, his own restaurant features cuisine that is unpretentious and fun. Choose between the lively dining room with its terra-cotta floor and art-clad mustard-colored walls, or the quieter, more romantic patio. Best dishes: the smoked salmon terrine, chicken potstickers with ponzu sauce, a buttery Alsatian-leek tart, veal sausage with sweet onions and the cedar-plank-roasted salmon.

ALL INDIA CAFÉ INDIAN 13/20

39 S. Fair Oaks Ave., Pasadena 91105
626-440-0309, *Lunch & Dinner daily,* $

Once you've tasted the exotic food here, you'll find it hard to settle for the cookie-cutter menus of most Indian restaurants. Start with aloo tikki, potato pancakes topped with onions, tamarind and chutney, the uttapam, a thin griddlecake made with cream of wheat or crispy pakoras, fritters of onion, shrimp or fish. Entrées include outstanding curries, aromatic tandoori dishes and frankies, little burrito-like rolls that are sold from pushcarts on the beaches of Bombay. Even the desserts are intriguing, especially the Indian rice pudding and the mango ice cream.

ARIRANG KOREAN 13/20 

114 W. Union St., Pasadena 91105
626-577-8885, *Lunch & Dinner daily,* $$

This handsome upscale branch of a noted Hong Kong establishment is contributing to Korean cooking's transition from obscurity to trendiness in the Southland. At lacquered tables with inset gas-fired barbecues, grill a variety of meats—paper-thin marinated beef and pork, short ribs—and seafood, wrap them in lettuce leaves and enhance them with an array of condiments—including a kim chee for every palate.

ARROYO CHOP HOUSE STEAKHOUSE 13/20 

536 S. Arroyo Parkway, Pasadena 91103
626-577-7463, *Dinner nightly, $$$*

Next door to Pasadena's California-style Parkway Grill (and owned by the same folks) is this New York-style steakhouse, serving food as traditional as the Parkway's is innovative. We like the wood-and-brass-trim look, the comfy booths and the pianist. We also like the huge cuts of filet mignon, rib-eye and New York steaks served with a choice of sauces: peppercorn-sherry, béarnaise, caramelized-onion-Dijon or portobello mushroom. Prices are high but portions are generous; expect to bring home a doggy bag.

BECKHAM PLACE BRITISH/AMERICAN 12/20

77 W. Walnut St., Pasadena 91103
626-796-3399, *Lunch Mon.-Fri., Dinner nightly, $$*

A

For Pasadenans looking for a prime-rib fix but unwilling to make the trek to Lawry's, this ivy-covered replica of an old English inn is perfect. A series of gently lit, wood-paneled rooms lends a congenial ambience. Patrons slide into fireplace-warmed booths, enjoy traditional Anglo-American beef dinners and perhaps imagine they're dining at a London pub. Prime rib, accompanied by spinach soufflé, Yorkshire pudding and silken creamed corn, is the specialty; other favorites include bangers and mash.

BISTRO 45 FRENCH/CALIFORNIAN 13/20 

45 S. Mentor Ave., Pasadena 91106
626-795-2478, *Lunch Tues.-Fri., Dinner Tues.-Sun., $$*

A

At once cosmopolitan and homey, this restaurant occupies an impeccably restored art-deco structure. You'll encounter the occasional cassoulet, but the cooking here is predominantly California-French. Ever-present owner Robert Simon's menu features superlative ingredients and marvelous reduction sauces. We've enjoyed the crisp calamari served with a zippy mustard dressing, and the roasted free-range veal stuffed with wild-mushroom mousse. The wine list is among the best in Pasadena.

BLUE PYRAMID ECLECTIC 12/20

1000 E. Broadway, Glendale 91205
818-548-1000, *Lunch Mon.-Fri., Dinner Mon.-Sat., $$*

Some of the decor touches are inspired by ancient Egypt, while the main dining room is wrapped in murals that place guests in a Mediterranean fishing village. The menu exhibits equally diverse influences, enabling patrons to table-hop from Venice to Athens to Madrid to Beirut without leaving Glendale. Appetizers include calamari fritti, spanakopita and hummus, as well as Caesar and Greek salads. The Sicilian chef turns out good pastas, along with thin-crusted pizzas, kebabs and saffron-scented paella.

THE BRAE CONTINENTAL 12/20

Sheraton Hotel, One Industry Hills Pkwy., City of Industry 91744
626-854-2335, *Lunch Mon.-Fri., Dinner nightly, Brunch Sun.,* **$$$**

One of the few places left for which folks still dress up for dinner—especially in this part of town. Overlooking a golf course, the restaurant features flattering lighting, polished brass accents and tuxedo-clad waiters attending to tables set with fine crystal. Starters include traditional extravagances—caviar, gravlax, escargots—and novel dishes such as abalone bisque, curried oysters and even sautéed rattlesnake and alligator. We recommend the salmon baked on a cedar plank, the Dover sole meunière, the Peking duck and the venison.

CAFÉ BEAUJOLAIS FRENCH 13/20 

1712 Colorado Blvd., Eagle Rock 90041
213-255-5111, *Dinner Mon.-Sat.,* **$$**

Should you ever long for an authentic French bistro in Eagle Rock, this charmer is it. Housed in an old bungalow, it looks the part, with a big wooden bar, white linen-covered tables and walls covered with colorful French posters and Van Gogh reproductions. The French owners offer attentive service and the same fare you'd find at a family-run bistro on a side street in Paris: rabbit, Provençal-style salmon, duck with peppercorn sauce, stuffed chicken in mustard sauce and tarte tatin.

CAFÉ SANTORINI MEDITERRANEAN 12/20

64 W. Union St., Pasadena 91103
626-564-4200, *Lunch & Dinner daily,* **$$**

This lively café serves good Greek and Italian fare, with the pastas and kebabs among the most popular dishes. On a warm evening, we love sharing an array of appetizers such as hummus and stuffed grape leaves, sipping wine, and looking down from the brick-walled balcony on the action in Old Town. We also appreciate the succulent wood-oven-roasted boneless chicken marinated in Dijon mustard and rosemary, the souvlaki and the fricassée of seafood in a tangy marinara sauce.

CAFÉ SOLÉ ITALIAN 12/20

1929 Verdugo Blvd., La Cañada 91011
818-790-6062, *Lunch & Dinner Tues.-Sun.,* **$**

Tucked away near a movie-theater complex is this tiny family-friendly Italian café where Antoinetta Costantino plays every role, from chef to busser. Handblown bottles that formerly held Patron tequila now hold olive oil and herbs, while Chambord bottles are filled with balsamic vinegar. The food is as fresh and delightful as Antoinetta's personality: calamari, pizzas, penne arrabiatta, chicken breast with lemon and capers—all prepared to order and very affordably priced. The daily specials might include grilled Italian sausage with polenta and marinara sauce.

CAMERON'S SEAFOOD SEAFOOD 11/20

1978 E. Colorado Blvd., Pasadena 91107
626-793-3474, *Lunch & Dinner daily, $$*

While we haven't always been crazy about this old-fashioned, family-oriented fish house and oyster bar, we can't deny its value and vast selection. The cavernous 300-seat eatery, with its maritime decor and mesquite grills, turns out everything from crab cocktails and clam chowder, to Southern-style catfish, cioppino, fish and chips and Cajun-style mahi mahi. Most items are fresh and prices are lower than at more prominent seafood restaurants.

CELESTINO ITALIAN 13/20 

141 S. Lake Ave., Pasadena 91101
626-795-4006, *Lunch Mon.-Fri., Dinner Mon.-Sat., $$*

A spin-off of Celestino Drago's Drago in Santa Monica, Celestino is a homey spot serving the Italian—and Sicilian—dishes that the celebrated chef and his family do so well. We're always impressed with the pastas, and we tend towards such entrées as the rabbit in a sweet-and-sour sauce and the pork tenderloin in a Barolo-wine-and-dried-cherry sauce. The dessert table dominating the center of the dining room features everything from the requisite tiramisu to a delicious bread pudding made with panettone.

CHAMELI INDIAN/VEGETARIAN 12/20

8752 Valley Blvd., Rosemead 91770
626-280-1947, *Lunch & Dinner Wed.-Mon., $*

In an area best known for its Chinese eateries, this stark, skylighted restaurant serves vegetarian cuisine from India's northern region. The long menu of intriguing dishes at remarkably low prices includes paneer cheese, samosas, Indian-style pumpkin, black-eyed peas (a staple in northern India as in the American South), and a plethora of rice and lentil dishes. Visit the Indian gift shop next door.

CHARMING GARDEN CHINESE/DIM SUM 13/20 

111 N. Atlantic Blvd. #351, Monterey Park 91754
626-458-4508, *Lunch & Dinner daily, $$*

A

An authentic and friendly Hunan restaurant tucked away in an Asian shopping center. Rising from clay pots, platters and bowls are the heady aromas of fish, beef, pork and poultry entrées prepared spicy-hot, Hunan style, or mildly—just ask. Try the crispy taro-paste rolls, the minced date bao and the sweet soup of lotus seed and red dates. Dim sum is served daily through the lunch hours, and there is also a very reasonable lunch menu. **Also in Rowland Heights (19240 E. Colima Rd., 626-965-0202).**

CHEZ SATEAU FRENCH/CALIFORNIAN 12/20

850 S. Baldwin Ave., Arcadia 91107
626-446-8806, *Lunch Tues.-Fri., Dinner Tues.-Sun., Brunch Sun., $$*

A ☎ 🚗

Quiet middle-aged suburbanites yearning for traditional cuisine, and younger Asian couples, crowd this dignified dining room. Highly regarded Chef Ryo Sato presents reasonably priced French fare with an occasional Asian inspiration. We've enjoyed the duck-pistachio terrine with cranberry relish, the crab Louie and various renditions of fresh salmon. Refreshingly untrendy, Chez Sateau offers good value for the money and is on par with many of the Westside's higher-profile French restaurants.

CINNABAR FRENCH/PACIFIC RIM 13/20 

933 S. Brand Blvd., Glendale 91204
818-551-1155, *Lunch Tues.-Fri., Dinner Tues.-Sun.*, $$

Set in an old moving-company building, the stark, dark-toned dining room proves oddly romantic. Cinnabar's cuisine has a basis—however attenuated—in French cooking, with Pacific Rim accents. We've been impressed with the spicy lemon grass bouillabaisse in Asian lime-leaf broth, the air-dried duck in a tamarind sauce and the yellowtail millefeuille, an exciting concoction of sashimi layered between won-ton skins and a black-sesame tuile.

CLEARWATER SEAFOOD CALIFORNIAN 11/20

168 W. Colorado Blvd., Pasadena 91105
626-356-0959, *Lunch & Dinner daily, Brunch Sun.*, $

The metamorphosis of the Clearwater Café from a vegan haven to a full-blown seafood restaurant is complete. The menu features a full compliment of fresh seafood, including hard-to-get items like halibut and coho salmon. Entrées come with soup or salad and a choice of two sides, and there are plenty of pastas, salads and sandwiches, too. The patio-seating is in the Tanner Market complex.

DRAGON REGENCY CHINESE/SEAFOOD 13/20 

120 S. Atlantic Blvd., Monterey Park 91754
626-282-1089, *Lunch & Dinner daily*, $

Located on the edge of one of the many shopping centers that make up Monterey Park's burgeoning Chinatown, Dragon Regency has quite a following. The many good Cantonese seafood selections on the menu include sizzling oysters with ginger and green onions, braised noodles with black mushrooms and frog in a pungent garlic sauce. If you dare, sample the snake soup—when it's in season.

EL EMPERADOR MAYA MEXICAN 13/20 

1823 S. San Gabriel Blvd., San Gabriel 91776
626-288-7265, *Lunch Tues.-Fri., Dinner Tues.-Sun.*, $

Behind an unassuming facade lies an immaculate and adorable little dining room that is home to some of the best Yucatecan cuisine outside of Merida. Acclaimed yet humble, this establishment offers outstanding renditions of such regional specialties as cochinita pibil, citrus-flavored pork roast in a banana leaf and poc chuc, chile-rubbed pork served with black beans. Other dishes we have enjoyed are salmon marinated in achiote, chile rellenos and caballero pobre, and an elaborate bread pudding. The flan is one of L.A.'s best.

FAR NIENTE ITALIAN 12/20

204 1/2 N. Brand Blvd., Glendale 91203
818-242-3835, *Lunch Mon.-Fri., Dinner nightly, $*

The cheerful dining room is romantic at night, when candles flicker on the cozy tables. We like the fragrant rosemary bread, plus such starters as mussels in white wine, and grilled portobello mushrooms covered with pine nuts and served on a bed of arugula. Try one of the pastas or such entrées as venison with green pepper sauce.

FRESCO RISTORANTE ITALIAN 14/20 

514 S. Brand Blvd., Glendale 91204
818-247-5541, *Lunch Mon.-Fri., Dinner Mon.-Sat., $$*

Chef/owner Antonio Orlando has succeeded in separating this quiet spot from the pack of moderately priced Italian restaurants struggling to distinguish themselves in Southern California. We're particularly pleased with Orlando's risottos, and such pastas as the gnocchi di porcini or tagliolini in a pungent pesto sauce. Fresco's casually elegant dining room is one of those rare places that can be just right for any occasion.

GENNARO'S RISTORANTE ITALIAN 13/20 

1109 N. Brand Blvd., Glendale 91202
818-243-6231, *Lunch Mon.-Fri., Dinner Mon.-Sat., $$$*

For those seeking a superb Italian dining experience in a quiet setting, where the service is formal yet friendly, this understatedly elegant restaurant is a good choice. Gennaro's pastas are so well prepared, even the simplest angel hair with tomatoes and basil is memorable. Their signature risotto with mushrooms is at once rich and light. The meat dishes are solid, too, particularly those with a Cognac sauce. Desserts are satisfying but don't hit the high standards of the preceding courses.

GERLACH'S GRILL ECLECTIC 12/20

1075 S. Fair Oaks Ave., Pasadena 91105
626-799-7944, *Breakfast, Lunch & Dinner daily, $*

An extensive repertoire emerges from this cramped kitchen, which is essentially a take-out stand adjacent to a liquor store. From the Middle East comes an array of dishes such as hummus, falafel, dolmas and kebabs. And from the kitchen's equally adept Mexican soul come tacos stuffed with salmon, tuna, shrimp, scallops, sea bass or squid, in addition to chicken, lamb and beef specialties. The seafood dinners are consistently satisfying.

THE GRILL CONTINENTAL 13/20 

The Ritz-Carlton Huntington Hotel, 1401 S. Oak Knoll Ave., Pasadena 91106
626-568-3900, *Breakfast & Lunch Sun., Dinner nightly, $$$$*

In this posh and clubby restaurant accented with gilt-framed seascapes, dine on fine renditions of both classic and contemporary cuisine, such as succulent lamb chops and thick roasted sesame-seed-crusted ahi tuna. Though the service is pampering, it can be slow—especially on nights when the hotel's private-party rooms are booked for gala events. Don't leave without sampling one of the nearly two dozen special martinis and a dessert soufflé.

HARBOR VILLAGE CHINESE/DIM SUM 14/20 

111 N. Atlantic Blvd., Monterey Park 91759
626-300-8833, *Lunch & Dinner nightly, $*

Dim sum alert—the dumplings here are among the best in Southern California. At this big, boisterous restaurant in Monterey Park's Chinatown, we've also enjoyed the Mongolian beef with ginger and scallions, the marinated octopus and the crispy ribs.

HARVEST INN CHINESE/MANDARIN 12/20

550 N. Brand Blvd., Glendale 91203
818-956-8268, *Lunch Mon.-Sat, Dinner nightly, $*

Don't be put off by its location in a Glendale office building. This restaurant serves some excellent dishes, including shrimp with macadamia nuts, braised sea cucumber and sweet-and-pungent chicken. Pass on the bland Szechwan bean curd, but do try the fish head in casserole or the fish tail in brown sauce.

HOLLY STREET BAR & GRILL ECLECTIC 12/20

175 E. Holly St., Pasadena 91103
626-440-1421, *Lunch Tues.-Fri., Dinner Tues.-Sun., Brunch Sat.-Sun., $$*

Occupying a former mortuary may not seem like a winning formula for a restaurant, but Holly Street's historic setting is very much alive. A short walk from Old Pasadena, this unfussy place is enhanced by art from a local gallery, and features a charming patio for al fresco dining. The menu is all over the map: tabbouleh from the Middle East, seared ahi from the Pacific Rim and cedar plank-roasted salmon with caramelized onions from the Northwest. The "picnic" of roasted garlic, blue cheese and tapenade is très Provençale, while the pastas pay homage to Tuscany.

HUGO MOLINA RESTAURANT CALIFORNIAN 13/20 

1065 E. Green St., Pasadena 91106
626-449-7820, *Lunch Mon.-Fri., Dinner nightly, $$*

After years of cooking at the celebrated Parkway Grill, Hugo Molina has his own restaurant, a minimalist setting in which the Guatemalan-born chef can do his thing. And Molina's "thing" is inventive Latin-infused cuisine with the occasional Pacific touch. Cases in point: the poblano chile stuffed with shrimp and mushrooms, the pan-seared ahi tuna in a wasabi-soy vinaigrette, the lamb chops in a wild berry reduction and the swordfish with citrus-persimmon sauce. Pastry chef Aricia Alvarado, another Parkway Grill grad, makes terrific fruit-filled phyllo-dough "ravioli."

KUALA LUMPUR MALAYSIAN 12/20

132 W. Colorado Blvd. Ste. 16, Pasadena 91105
626-577-5175, *Lunch & Dinner Tues.-Sun., $$*

If you're keen to sample exotic Southeast Asian dishes laced with tamarind, garlic and peanuts, start here. Tucked in the back of an Old Pasadena landmark, this little restaurant specializes in the subtly spiced cooking of Malaysia and Indonesia.

LA BAMBA CARIBBEAN 13/20 

61 N. Raymond Ave., Pasadena 91113
626-584-9771, *Lunch, Dinner & Late Supper Tues.-Sun., $*

This festive spot features salsa dancing on Thursday nights. The food is an appealing mix of seafood, poultry and meat, prepared with the spicy accents of the Caribbean. We've enjoyed the tamales smothered in fresh garlic, the sautéed shrimp with cilantro and garlic and the saucy jerk chicken. The most exotic dish is the zesty melange of mussels, clams, lobster and shrimp. For dessert, try the luscious flour tortilla filled with tropical fruit, then deep-fried and crowned with whipped cream.

LA FORNARETTA ITALIAN 12/20

30 S. Raymond Ave., Pasadena 91105
626-585-9088, *Lunch Tues.-Fri., Dinner Tues.-Sun., $$*

If you think spaghetti and meatballs are out of style, you haven't experienced this Old Pasadena ristorante, where a fashionable crowd digs into rustic Sicilian fare. The unpretentious storefront dining room features terra-cotta tile floors, rust and gold colored walls, green banquettes and earth-toned tablecloths covered with butcher paper. Most of the pastas, pizzas and house specialties are topped with a crimson-hued tomato sauce bursting with fresh flavors. Also recommended: the spaghetti topped with garlicky breadcrumbs, saffron and anchovy.

LA LUNA NEGRA SPANISH 11/20

44 W. Green St., Pasadena 91105
626-844-4331, *Lunch & Dinner daily, Brunch Sun., $$*

Have you ever sat at a Madrid tapas bar, snacking on croquetas, sardines, Manchego cheese, olives and tortillas while sipping a glass of Valdapeñas? Boldly hued La Luna Negra captures at least the spirit of that tradition. Listen to some classical guitar and select from a large menu featuring bacalao (salt-cured cod), sautéed tongue, stuffed peppers, Galician scallops, garlicky mussels and squid stuffed with almonds and anchovies. Unfortunately, they all arrive on a single platter, which leads to sauces inadvertently mixing. We don't recommend the paellas.

LA PARISIENNE FRENCH 13/20 

1101 E. Huntington Dr., Monrovia 91016
626-357-3359, *Lunch Mon.-Fri., Dinner Mon.-Sat., $$*

This restaurant may not set any culinary trends, but we've had many a good meal here. Resembling a French country inn dropped in the suburbs, with its beamed ceilings and white linen-covered tables, La Parisienne serves such French comfort-food dishes as escargots, moules marnière, coq au vin, bouillabaisse and duck a l'orange.

LAKE SPRING CUISINE — CHINESE — 14/20 

219 E. Garvey Ave., Monterey Park 91754
818-280-3571, *Lunch & Dinner daily, $*

Lake Spring is perhaps the Southland's best place to sample Shanghai cuisine, much of which is pork-related: shrimp and shredded pork with bean-curd soup; salted pork with bamboo-shoot casserole; pepper-seasoned pork chops; vermicelli and ground pork; spicy eggplant and shredded pork. The big specialty here is the "pump," a sweet, anise-perfumed, fork-tender mass of delicious—and yes, fatty—pork. The menu also includes a number of "neutralize" dishes made with bean curd.

LYON — ASIAN/FRENCH — 12/20

713 E. Green St., Pasadena 91101
626-796-9501, *Lunch Tues.-Fri., Dinner Tues.-Sun., Brunch Sun., $$*

Chef Tada Matsuno outgrew the miniscule—but celebrated—Grill Lyon, and took over what was once a cozy place called Claude's. The charming French country inn ambience remains: a prominent fireplace, lace curtains, hanging copper cookware. The menu includes classics such as escargots and filet mignon au poivre, as well as such Franco-Japanese items as ahi in ginger-scallion sauce.

MARKET CITY CAFFÈ — ITALIAN — 12/20

33 S. Fair Oaks Ave., Pasadena 91105
626-568-0203, *Lunch & Dinner daily, $$*

Market City Caffè offers outdoor seating on its brick-lined patio. The menu features Southern Italian foods, many made from an owner's family recipes, plus a few Middle Eastern- and even African-influenced specialties. We often succumb to the lavish—but bargain-priced—antipasto bar and skip the menu altogether.

MARSTON'S — AMERICAN — 12/20

151 E. Walnut St., Pasadena 91103
626-796-2459, *Breakfast & Lunch Tues.-Sat., $*

If Aunt Bee had set out to conquer the Mayberry restaurant scene, she would have built a charming little cottage just like this. With its railed porch, frilly curtains and dried flowers, this homey eatery exudes warmth. The old-fashioned comfort food includes breakfasts of hollandaise-enhanced omelets, sourdough French toast breaded with cornflakes and macadamia nut pancakes. The lunch menu features terrific white chile, fish tacos, creative sandwiches and an outstanding California orange salad—chicken, greens, avocado, oranges, blue cheese, apples and candied pecans in a garlicky dressing—served with oven-fresh cheese popovers. Try the fabulous bread pudding.

McCORMICK & SCHMICK'S SEAFOOD 13/20 

111 N. Los Robles Ave., Pasadena 91101
626-405-0064, *Lunch & Dinner daily, $$*

See review in "L.A. AREA—Dining."

MI PIACE ITALIAN 12/20

25 E. Colorado Blvd., Pasadena 91105
626-795-3131, *Lunch & Dinner daily, Late Supper Fri.-Sat., $$*

This busy white-on-white restaurant in Old Town has one foot in the present and the other planted comfortably in the past. Most of the pastas, salads and Italian entrées are well prepared, and we love the crusty homemade breads from the adjacent Pasadena Baking Company. Crisp-crusted New York-style pizzas are topped with the likes of pepperoni and mushrooms, and the French-pastry-style desserts from the case are sublime. **Also in Burbank (801 San Fernando Blvd., 818-843-1111).**

MIN'S KITCHEN THAI 12/20

1040 Foothill Blvd., La Cañada-Flintridge 91011
818-790-6074, *Lunch & Dinner Mon.-Sat., $$*

If your favorite Thai restaurant is a hole-in-the-wall in Hollywood, don't be skeptical about Min's, which is located in the pristine hills of this tony community. The food is authentic and includes all the usual Thai appetizers, salads and noodle dishes, plus curries that are creamier than most. The garlic scallops are potent with the stinking rose.

NBC SEAFOOD CHINESE/DIM SUM 12/20

404 S. Atlantic Blvd., Monterey Park 91754
626-282-2323, *Lunch & Dinner daily, $$*

An ornately decorated, Hong Kong-style restaurant where dinner can be an elaborate affair featuring seafood plucked from tanks lining the gilded dining rooms. During the day, waitresses push carts overflowing with siu mai, bao, har gow, jing joon, potstickers and other exotic dumplings. They seem to have a wider variety—and to make the rounds of the dining room more frequently—than in other Monterey Park dim-sum parlors.

NIKOS GREEK 12/20

48 S. Fair Oaks Ave., Pasadena 91105
626-683-9341, *Lunch & Dinner Tues.-Sun., $$*

Pasadena's only major Greek taverna happens to be an excellent one. A distinctly Mediterranean flavor permeates a room filled with colorful murals, classic statuettes, tables cloaked in blue and white, and exuberant, plate-smashing waiters shouting "Opah!" All the traditional Greek favorites are found here: spanakopita, dolmades, souvlaki, moussaka, pasticcio, taramasalata and baklava. In addition to retsina, Nikos offers Greek wines whose mellow, fruity characteristics may surprise you.

OCEAN STAR SEAFOOD — CHINESE/DIM SUM — 12/20

112 N. Chandler Ave., Monterey Park 91754
626-300-8446, *Lunch & Dinner daily, $$*

With its mirrors and marble—and its crowds—the 800-seat Ocean Star could double as a casino, and it's almost as noisy. It's such an enormous piece of real estate, in fact, that the waiters often communicate with the kitchen via walkie-talkies. The extensive dinner menu features such delicacies as conch-and-shark fin- and bird's-nest-soups. Dinner here is an enjoyable experience, but it's the superb dim sum that keeps those 800 coming back.

PAPASHON — PACIFIC RIM — 12/20

91 N. Raymond, Pasadena 91103
626-792-6060, *Lunch Tues.-Fri., Dinner Tues.-Sun., $$*

The tasteful, dimly lit dining room features soothing colors, modern furniture, comfortable banquettes and art-deco accents. The menu has Pacific-Rim overtones, with some dishes more inspired in concept than execution. Choose from among such specialties as crispy catfish with sweet-and-sour tomato-ginger sauce, orange blinis with smoked salmon and barbecued chicken with mu-shu pancakes. **Also in Beverly Hills (8635 Wilshire Blvd., 310-360-0807) and Encino (15910 Ventura Blvd, 818-783-6664).**

PARKWAY GRILL — CALIFORNIAN — 14/20 

510 S. Arroyo Pkwy., Pasadena 91105
626-795-1001, *Lunch Mon.-Fri., Dinner nightly, $$$*

The Parkway Grill has been enormously popular since it opened in the 1980s—with good reason. Their Californian cuisine is innovative and appealing, and includes such dishes as robust black bean soup with smoked pork and lime cream, smoked pheasant on Applewood bacon hash, whole fried catfish with ginger, scallions and a lime-soy sauce, and pizza with duck and radicchio. The desserts, like bread pudding and cheesecake, hew to the American style of being substantial and sweet. The wine list is full of worthy bottles.

PINOT REST. & MARTINI BAR — FRENCH/CALIFORNIAN — 14/20 

897 Granite Dr., Pasadena 91101
626 792-1179, *Lunch Mon.-Fri., Dinner Mon.-Sat., $$*

Pinot has been doing a bustling business since Joachim and Christine Splichal revamped the space which long had been home to The Chronicle, one of Pasadena's classic restaurants. As in the Splichals' sister Pinots in Hollywood, Studio City and downtown, the menu features fine renditions of French bistro food, plus whimsical touches such as "soup of yesterday," "asparagus in metamorphosis" and a daily spa selection. We most enjoy dining in the martini bar, where there are over 50 types of martinis.

QUANJUDE BEIJING DUCK RESTAURANT CHINESE 12/20

8450 Garvey Ave., Rosemead 91770
626-280-2378, *Lunch & Dinner daily, $$*

If there is such a thing as Chinese haute cuisine, Peking Duck ("Beijing" Duck to be politically correct) qualifies. Especially here at this branch of a famous Tian-An-Men-Square restaurant. Wonderfully delicate, crispy skin is the hallmark of this specialty, and the chefs have spent over a century perfecting it at their Beijing location. In addition, every imaginable part of the duck is offered with finesse, along with some solid non-duck dishes.

RESTAURANT DEVON CALIFORNIAN 13/20 

109 E. Lemon Ave., Monrovia 91016
626-305-0013, *Lunch Tues.-Fri., Dinner Tues.-Sun., $$$*

A converted 1890s carriage house, Devon features a contemporary-styled dining room dominated by a chandelier whose long, copper tentacles extend across the ceiling like a giant octopus. Appetizers might include carpaccio of ostrich in a soy-black pepper sauce, ravioli stuffed with a turtle mousse in green peppercorn sauce or velvety foie gras with mango. The portions are sometimes petite, but the masterful sauces compensate. Among the recommended entrées: venison, monkfish in tomatillo-Grand Marnier sauce and swordfish in a balsamic reduction. There are good pastries and an impressive wine list.

RESTAURANT LOZANO SOUTHWESTERN 12/20

44 N. Baldwin Ave., Sierra Madre 91024
626-355-5945, *Lunch daily, Dinner Mon.-Sat., $$*

This charming restaurant served Southwestern cooking long before it was trendy. In a light and airy setting brightened with bold contemporary art, try the shrimp quesadillas, burritos, mango salad, Southwestern ravioli and fettuccine with shrimp and red-chile-cream sauce. In addition to the Southwestern creations, the menu is laced with influences from Asia, the Caribbean and Europe, with such items as jerk chicken, whole crisp catfish and salmon in curry sauce. Lozano's takes its wine seriously, and offers special winemaker dinners.

SALADANG THAI 12/20

363 S. Fair Oaks Ave., Pasadena 91105
626-793-8123, *Lunch & Dinner daily, $*

A hip, neo-industrial decor—high ceiling, exposed ducts, hard concrete surfaces—is softened by traditional Thai art. The result is a sleek setting for contemporary renditions of ancient recipes. Specialties such as crab curry, whole deep-fried catfish, sizzling beef in peanut sauce and salmon with coconut dressing reflect a menu that extends well beyond the usual pad Thai and barbecued chicken. Those in search of a lighter style will like the salad rolls with honey-mustard sauce. Desserts include a velvety plum-colored pudding of glutinous black rice.

SESAME GRILL FUSION/ PACIFIC RIM 12/20

108 E. Huntington Dr., Arcadia 91006
626-821-0880, *Lunch & Dinner Mon.-Sat., $$*

This Euro-Asian eatery broke new ground when it opened in Arcadia. The sleek, contemporary-styled dining room has been embraced by locals, who are thrilled with such imaginative dishes as chilled calamari in lemon-herb vinaigrette, lobster ravioli with saffron-vermouth sauce, chicken ravioli in Parmesan cream sauce, pork tenderloin with shiitake-wine reduction and salmon in an orange-grapefruit vinaigrette. The fried catfish in ponzu sauce is nearly as good as at nearby Shiro.

SHIRO FRENCH/JAPANESE 15/20 

1505 Mission St., S. Pasadena 91030
626-799-4774, *Dinner Tues.-Sun., $$*

Owner/chef Shiro has a marvelous eye for ultra-fresh fish and the facility of a superb French saucier—the resulting dishes are masterful. He offers a handful of classics, including ravioli stuffed with shrimp-and-salmon mousse in a subtle smoked salmon sauce, and such Asian dishes as sizzling catfish with ponzu and scallops in saffron sauce. Chef Shiro's eye for detail shows up in the exquisite desserts. On the wine list, you'll find several respectable bottles for under $20.

SPENCERS CONTINENTAL 12/20

70 S. Raymond Ave., Pasadena 91105
626-583-8275, *Lunch Mon.-Fri., Dinner Mon.-Sat., $$*

Opened by key staffers of the late Chronicle, this elegant restaurant draws many of the Chronicle's old regulars and has won new enthusiasts as well. The menu combines classics like escargots, sand dabs and chateaubriand with a few more contemporary California dishes. Although we have experienced some lapses in service, the owners seem anxious to please, and judicious ordering can result in a satisfying meal. The wine list does not compare with The Chronicle's legendary 74-pager, but is respectable.

STONEY POINT BAR & GRILL CONTINENTAL 13/20 

1460 W. Colorado Blvd., Pasadena 91105
626-449-9715, *Lunch & Dinner daily, $$*

One of Pasadena's best kept secrets, Stoney Point is a neighborhood haunt serving excellent Continental and Italian specialties in a green and white dining room decorated with photographs of Pasadena from an era when Harvard played in the Rose Bowl. Piano music—occasionally punctuated by a brief operatic outburst—wafts from a lively bar adjoining the dining room. Recommended dishes include the Pernod-infused escargots in mushroom caps, lamb chops with mustard sauce, any number of pastas, crab cakes in citron sauce, cioppino and grilled salmon.

SUSHI POLO — JAPANESE/SUSHI — 12/20

927 E. Colorado Blvd., Pasadena 91106
626-356-0099, *Lunch Mon.-Fri., Dinner nightly, $*

A

A narrow, soothing dining room with a sleek sushi bar, blonde wood trim, delicate screens and traditional art. For starters, the menu features such delicacies as salmon collar, soft-shell crab tempura, salmon roe sushi and octopus salad. Sushi rolls include spicy tuna, salmon skin, toro-scallion, eel and the ubiquitous California version. Salmon teriyaki, seafood tempura, unagi donburi (grilled eel over rice), filet mignon and grilled ahi tuna are rewarding entrées. Half-price sushi specials ensure good value.

TAYLOR'S STEAKHOUSE — AMERICAN — 12/20

901 Foothill Blvd., La Cañada-Flintridge 91011
818-790-7668, *Lunch Mon.-Fri., Dinner nightly, $$*

If the prices at Arnie Morton's, The Palm or Ruth's Chris make you wince, you'll love Taylor's, where you'll spend about half for a good steak. Regulars slide into the big burgundy booths to enjoy deftly prepared porterhouse, rib-eye, New York strip steaks and prime rib. The side dishes are modestly priced too. And if you enjoy a full-bodied red wine with your beef, you may pick out a decent Cabernet Sauvignon priced in the teens. Non-carnivores should note that fresh seafood is provided by one of Southern California's top fish markets.

THE TERRACE — MEDITERRANEAN — 13/20

The Ritz-Carlton Huntington Hotel, 1401 S. Oak Knoll Ave., Pasadena 91106
626-568-3900, *Breakfast, Lunch & Dinner daily, Brunch Sun., $$*

A

Overlooking the lush hotel gardens and pool, this indoor-outdoor café serves an assortment of pastas, seafoods and grilled items. On Sundays, the lavish brunch features everything from blintzes to sushi.

TOMMY TANG'S — THAI — 13/20

24 W. Colorado Blvd., Pasadena 91105
626-792-9700, *Lunch & Dinner Tues.-Sun., $$*

A

See review in "L.A. AREA—Dining."

TWIN PALMS — CALIFORNIAN — 13/20

101 W. Green St., Pasadena 91105
626-577-2567, *Lunch & Dinner daily, Brunch Sun., $$*

A

Evoking the feel of a Provençal village fair, the sprawling center patio with its towering palm trees, provides a superb al-fresco-dining venue. Although not entirely shielded from the frequent late-night musical performances on the patio, the interior dining room is quiet enough to accommodate a modicum of conversation. The menu emphasizes fresh ingredients with influences from Latin America and the Pacific Rim. Worthy dishes include a warm goat cheese salad with figs and candied walnuts in a hazelnut dressing, a crock of Maui onion soup and a pan-seared, crispy-skinned salmon filet in a citrus-infused Zinfandel reduction.

WAHIB'S — MIDDLE EASTERN/LEBANESE — 12/20

910 E. Main St., Alhambra 91801
626-576-1048, *Lunch & Dinner daily, $*

In a community dominated by Chinese restaurants, this popular spot offers one of the best Middle Eastern dining opportunities in the San Gabriel Valley. Blanketed with Mediterranean murals, arches and columns, the dining room has the air of a bustling Middle Eastern bazaar. Among the starters are stuffed grape leaves, falafel, lentil soup, creamy hummus and tabbouleh. The selection of entrées includes lamb roast, shwarma, kebabs, barbecued quail and spicy soujok sausage. Sautéed lamb's brain, frog legs and raw kibbeh are offered for the adventuresome, in addition to Greek moussaka and Egyptian mouloukhiya. Wahib's baklava is among the best in town.

XIOMARA — NUEVO LATINO — 14/20 

69 N. Raymond Ave., Pasadena 91105
626-796-2520, *Lunch Mon.-Fri., Dinner nightly, $$*

Xiomara Ardolina has transformed her stylish, contemporary French bistro into one that fuses French technique with tastes from her native Cuban and other Latin cusines. Specialties include the rock shrimp tamal with a chanterelle-shrimp cream sauce, seared foie gras on a Colombian arepa, Cuban seared pork hash, lamb shanks with malanga and mojo, and coffee-soaked tres leches cake with caramel ice cream. We find this inventive cooking quite exciting.

YUJEAN KANG'S — CHINESE — 16/20 

67 N. Raymond Ave., Pasadena 91103
626-585-0855, *Lunch & Dinner daily, $$*

This is the original restaurant opened by creative chef Yujean Kang, who manages now to oversee both this and his West Hollywood eatery. See review in "L.A. AREA—Dining."

AND ALSO...

CLANCY'S CRAB BROILER — SEAFOOD

219 N. Central Ave., Glendale 91203
818-242-2722, *Lunch & Dinner daily, $$*

With its clichéd decor, this would appear to be just another neighborhood chowder house. Initial impressions aside, Clancy's proves to be an accomplished restaurant offering many creative dishes—not to mention fabulous chowder.

DE LACEY'S CLUB 41 — AMERICAN

41 S. Delacey St., Pasadena 91105
626-795-4141, *Lunch & Dinner daily, $*

Delacey's is rife with nostalgia: high-backed wooden booths, mosaic tile floors, thick white tablecloths, burnished dark wood, hanging schoolhouse light fixtures. The menu brings to mind L.A.'s venerable Musso & Frank's, and contains all the chophouse standards, from Cobb salad to onion rings to cheesecake.

DICKENSON WEST AMERICAN

181 East Glenarm Suite 105, Pasadena 91105
626-799-5252 , *Lunch Tues.-Fri., Dinner Tues.-Sat.*, $$$

Located in a mini-mall just off Arroyo Seco Parkway, this charming dining room features a polished-wood bar and an attractive wine cabinet between the open kitchen and the dining area. A glass-walled room in the center creates a provocative atmosphere for small private parties. Among the most promising dishes on the new menu are the persimmon-cucumber-and-pear salad with curry-vanilla vinaigrette, the osso buco and the rack of lamb with grilled portobello mushrooms & peppered gnocchi. The service is efficient and friendly.

THE FRANCOS' SUNNY ITALY ITALIAN

470 S. Rosemead Blvd., Pasadena 91107
626-792-7437, *Dinner Tues.-Sun.*, $$

Sunny Italy has been around since 1953 and in some respects it hasn't left that era. Yet after being saturated by trendy trattorias, we find its supper-club atmosphere a refreshing change of pace. Cozy booths, flattering candlelight and unobtrusive entertainment enhance a room vaguely reminiscent of a piazza in a small Tuscan village. Appetizers include calamari fritti, steamed mussels and garlicky escargots. Among the better entrées are the veal Marsala and the chicken ravioli.

NICK'S CALIFORNIAN

009 El Centro St., S. Pasadena 91030
626-441-7910, *Lunch & Dinner Tues.-Sun.*, $$

We've heard of tenting a parking lot for a party. Well, chef & owner Nick Coe tented a parking lot for his promising new restaurant. There are lots of flowering plants, and such contemorary dishes as grilled shrimp salad with mango, asparagus morels and pressed chicken with garlic.

OAKS ON THE PLAZA CONTINENTAL

Doubletree Hotel, 191 N. Los Robles Ave., Pasadena 91101
626-792-2727, *Breakfast, Lunch & Dinner daily, Brunch Sun.*, $$

This hotel dining room serves good contemporary California food. For starters, there's always a pick of rich little brioche pizzas, and for the main course there are quite a few good mesquite-grilled offerings. We've enjoyed the rack of lamb with an herbed peanut crust, and the shrimp spiced with Thai peppers and pineapple-mint sauce.

THE RAYMOND AMERICAN

1250 S. Fair Oaks Ave., Pasadena 91105
626-441-3136, *Lunch & Dinner Tues.-Sun., Brunch Sat.-Sun.*, $$$

This cozy restaurant, all that's left of the historical Raymond Hotel, is set in the old caretaker's cottage. The setting—high-backed wooden booths, fireplaces in several lace-curtained rooms—is charming, the food straightforward and old-fashioned. Lunch tends towards big salads and pastas; for dinner, you can count on good fish, veal, chicken and rack of lamb.

QUICK BITES

American: Coffee Shops, Burgers & Diners

BEADLE'S CAFETERIA

825 E. Green St., Pasadena 91101
626-796-3618, *Breakfast Mon.-Fri., Lunch & Dinner daily*

A

Although now an endangered species along with drive-in theaters and five-and-dime stores, this resilient old cafeteria keeps the concept alive. Despite its location in a modern high-rise, every aspect of Beadle's reminds us of a more innocent era, from the low prices to the gracious service. Homespun favorites such as roast turkey, chicken pot pie, prime rib, macaroni and cheese and Boston cream pie are just a sampling of the selection available at this spacious, vintage '50s dining room.

BURGER CONTINENTAL

535 S. Lake Ave., Pasadena 91101
818-792-6634, *Breakfast, Lunch & Dinner daily*

In addition to charbroiled fish and prime rib, much of the food here is Greek and Armenian—huge plates of lamb kebabs and rice pilaf, moussaka, hummus with pita bread. Your order will include a salad bar and heaps of rice and vegetables. Eat out on the brick patio, where local college students put away pitchers of beer.

KATHLEEN'S

595 N. Lake Ave., Pasadena 91101
626-578-0722, *Breakfast Sat.-Sun., Lunch Tues.-Sun., Dinner Tues.-Sat.*

A

When we feel like some good old-fashioned comfort food, we head here. Behind a rustic facade, Kathleen's dining room has a modern, straightforward design, where regulars enjoy hearty breakfasts served with fabulous pumpkin-walnut bread. Among the lunch and dinner offerings are pastas, kebabs, quiches, oversized salads, overstuffed sandwiches and burgers. Consistent with the cultural diversity of the community, this all-American eatery features some solid Mexican specialties as well.

THE PHILADELPHIA CONNECTION

633 S. Arroyo Pkwy., #3, Pasadena 91105
626-304-9944, *Lunch & Dinner Mon.-Sat.*
No Cards

If you're a homesick refugee from the City of Brotherly Love, you'll feel right at home in this mini-mall eatery filled with banners from beloved "local" teams: the '76ers, Temple, Rutgers and Villanova. The Philly cheese steak is the real thing: tender strips of rib-eye, sautéed onions and molten cheese on an Italian roll flown in from a Philadelphia bakery. A chicken version is offered, along with other hoagies, plus authentic home town snacks like Goldenberg's Peanut Chews.

Argentine/Italian

EL MORFI

241 N. Brand Blvd., Glendale 91203
818-547-4420, *Lunch & Dinner daily*

Unassuming little El Morfi has fostered a loyal clientele through friendly service, low prices and good Argentine cooking. Its empanadas, blood sausage and crispy mollejas (sweetbreads) are all excellent. Try the parrillada, a typical Argentine platter of grilled meats, the chicken or beef Milanese or the Argentine pizza called fugazetta. The kitchen turns out good pastas, paellas, flans, bread pudding and crêpes with sweet dulce de leche.

Bakery-Cafés

A BIENTÔT

230 N. Brand Blvd., Glendale 91203
818-244-8822, *Breakfast, Lunch & Dinner daily*

What began as a traditional French bakery turning out wonderful croissants, brioche, cinnamon rolls, muffins, cookies, fruit tarts, cheesecake, opera cake and more, now is also a full-fledged café as well. You can also get espresso drinks, breakfast, lunch and candlelit dinners.

GOLDSTEIN'S BAGEL BAKERY

86 W. Colorado Blvd., Pasadena 91105
636-792-2435, *Breakfast, Lunch & Dinner daily*

See review in "L.A. AREA—Quick Bites" **Also in Arcadia (412 N. Santa Anita Ave., 626-447-2457) and La Canada (1939 Verdugo Blvd. 818-952-2457).**

OLD TOWN BAKERY

166 W. Colorado Blvd., Pasadena 91105
626-793-2993, *Breakfast, Lunch & Dinner daily*

At this charming Pasadena bakery-café, you'll find homey fresh-fruit pies, a three-layer raspberry-chocolate mousse and a stunning triangular bittersweet chocolate terrine decorated with gold leaf. They make good sandwiches with their homemade breads. **Also at LAX.**

PASADENA BAKING CO.

29 E. Colorado Blvd., Pasadena 91105
626-796-9966, *Breakfast, Lunch & Dinner daily*

Right next to the ever-popular Mi Piace in Old Pasadena, the Pasadena Baking Co. provides a prime opportunity for people-watching while enjoying a cup of cappuccino and a sampling the splendid cakes, tarts, pastries and breads coming out of one of the Southland's finest bakeries. There are sandwiches and omelets, too, all at very reasonable prices.

Brewery-Restaurants & Pubs

GORDON BIERSCH

41 Hugus Alley at One Colorado, Pasadena 91103
626-449-0052, *Lunch & Dinner daily*

When this brewery/restaurant opened a few years back, about the most complicated entrée on the menu was roast chicken with garlic fries. Today you'll find such exotic items as chili-tiger shrimps with snow peas and charred rare tuna steak with wasabi-mashed potatoes and sweet onion rings. Needless to say, there's a thriving bar scene, where their wonderful homemade brews are savored. We like sitting out on the porch on a warm night.

JOHN BULL ENGLISH PUB

958 S. Fair Oaks Blvd., Pasadena 91105
626-441-4353, *Lunch, Dinner & Afternoon Tea daily*

If you're interested in an authentic English pub experience, a visit to this Tudor-style inn can save you hundreds of dollars in airfare. The walls are covered with Union Jacks, dart boards and enough British kitsch to fill a duke's castle. Belly up to the massive wooden bar to enjoy one of the many British brews on tap, such as Younger's, Newcastle, Guinness or Woodpecker's Cider. Naturally, every table is stocked with Coleman's mustard, Norfolk Manor brown sauce and malt vinegar. The fish and chips, shepherd's pie, Yorkshire mixed grill and sweet fruit crumbles will make you think you're eating across the pond.

Cafés

CHELSEA

2527 Mission St., San Marino 92069
626-441-8288, *Lunch Tues.-Sat., Dinner Tues.-Sun.*

San Marino's Mission Street is a quaint collection of shops and cafés yet to be invaded by national chains—not even a Starbucks. It's just the kind of environment in which charming little Chelsea can flourish. Recommended items include the potsticker salad, the crab cakes, chicken ravioli and fettuccine in lime-jalapeño cream sauce. It's no surprise that the gourmet pizzas—barbecued chicken, Thai shrimp, lamb sausage—are first rate; owner Norman Cheng honed his skills at the Parkway Grill. **Cheng's Pizza Place California in San Gabriel (303 S. Mission St., 626-570-9622) features essentially the same menu.**

CROCODILE CAFÉ

626 N. Central Ave., Glendale 91203
818-241-1114, *Lunch & Dinner daily*

The Crocodile Café has been packed since the doors opened. Is the food worth the wait during peak dinner hours? Probably not. But if you come at an off time—a late lunch, an early dinner—you'll enjoy the tasty, inexpensive salads, pastas and pizzas. Weather permitting, skip the bright, bustling interior (replete with open kitchen, naturally) and sit on the patio. **Also in Pasadena (140 S. Lake Ave., 626-449-9900).**

JULIENNE

2649 Mission St., San Marino 91108
626-441-2299, *Breakfast & lunch Mon.-Sat.*

This quaint little café, with its marble tables spilling out onto the sidewalk, is sometimes dismissed as a place for well-heeled San Marino "ladies who lunch." However, the kitchen's considerable proficiency effectively rebuts that narrow reputation. Here one can enjoy a satisfying lunch of apricot-chicken salad with toasted almonds and rosemary-Dijon dressing, mango-lime-glazed chicken breast or pistachio-crusted salmon in citrus vinaigrette. Breakfasts are excellent and one of the area's better gourmet shops—stocked with mustards, olive oils, preserves and prepared specialties—adjoins the café.

Cajun/Creole

AUNT GUSSIE'S PLACE

2057 N. Los Robles Ave., Pasadena 91104
818-794-6024
Breakfast, Lunch & Dinner daily

A

Delicious fried chicken, spicy jambalaya, tender fried catfish, authentic po-boy sandwiches, homemade cobblers, and Southern hospitality bring the taste of the Big Easy to Pasadena. They open at 6:30 a.m.

Chicken

ROTISSERIE CHICKEN OF CALIFORNIA

712 E. Colorado Blvd., Pasadena 91101
626-405-0365, *Lunch & Dinner daily*

Rotisserie chicken has emerged as one of L.A.'s most popular meals, and here it adopts the flavors of France, Japan, Italy and the American South. The airy, glass ensconced dining room is sparingly but artfully decorated, its bright yellow walls adorned with giant Lichtenstein prints. The menu includes chicken prepared a dozen different ways: teriyaki, bourguignonne, hot & spicy and the highly recommended 32-spice variety. Steaks, fresh fish and sandwiches also take on various multi-cultural identities.

ZANKOU CHICKEN

1415 E. Colorado St., Glendale 91205
818-244-1937, *Lunch & Dinner daily*
No cards

Part of a small, Armenian family-owned chain, this fast-food outlet clips the wings off its big corporate competitors, serving what is possibly the best rotisserie chicken in the kingdom. A mere $5.45 buys you a half-chicken plate with crisp-skinned, ultra-tender rotisserie chicken, incomparable garlic sauce, hummus, pickled turnips and pita bread. You'll also find great falafel, shwarma, kebabs and sandwiches—at winning prices.

Chinese

DUMPLING MASTER

423 N. Atlantic Blvd., # 106, Monterey Park 91754
626-458-8689, *Lunch & Dinner daily*
No cards

The atmosphere of this endearing hole-in-the-wall is in sharp contrast to the lavish, marble-clad dim sum palaces just down the street. Nonetheless, a simple meal here can be a rewarding experience. Among the plethora of dumplings served, our favorites are the plump pan-fried potstickers served sizzling from the hot oil, along with the chow mein, scallion pancakes, kung pao chicken and hot Szechwan shredded pork.

G.C. RIVER

727 E. Valley Blvd., San Gabriel 91776
626-288-6182, *Lunch & Dinner daily*

Yet another tiny storefront Chinese restaurant with a giant menu and a great chef-owner from Hong Kong. Clark Ho makes such luscious dishes as lobster in sweet red sauce with garlic and ginger, deep-fried chicken wings stuffed with sticky rice, fish-cake-stuffed squid, Chinese sausage with snow peas and low-cal scrambled egg whites over broccoli that's a lot better than it sounds. Try Ho's home-baked sesame-sprinkled pocket breads stuffed with stir-fried beef and vegetables.

GOURMET 88

315 S. Brand Blvd., Glendale 91204
818-547-9488, *Lunch & Dinner daily*

Hardly an ordinary neighborhood Chinese restaurant, this establishment is a lucky find indeed (a feng shui master will tell you how desirable the number "8" is). It offers a pleasant blend of authentic regional cuisine with only minor concessions for the American palate. Our favorites: giant sea scallops in lemon sauce, Mongolian lamb, lobster in black bean sauce and a stellar sesame beef. The dining rooms are casual yet tastefully appointed and service is exceptionally gracious.

SAM WOO SEAFOOD

140 W. Valley Blvd, San Gabriel 91776
626-571-8686, *Lunch & Dinner daily*

Where chef Joachim Splichal (of Patina and several Pinot restaurants) takes his family for Chinese seafood—particularly for the crab and shrimp dishes—on Sunday nights. Need we say more?

SEA STAR — CHINESE/DIM SUM/NOODLES

2000 W. Main St., Alhambra 91801
818-282-8833, *Breakfast, lunch & Dinner daily*

Formerly New World Restaurant, Sea Star is a spacious, raucous restaurant offering terrific dim sum and rice noodles daily. The real standouts are the sweets, from sesame balls with red-bean paste to incredible coconut snowballs filled with a sweet peanut purée.

Ethiopian

IBEX

119 W. Green St., Pasadena 91105
626-793-3822, *Lunch & Dinner Tues.-Sun.*

African art decorates the maroon-and-cream walls. The food and its presentation are authentically Ethiopian. While utensils are available for patrons who don't enjoy eating with their fingers, if you want to do it the right way, fingers in tandem with torn morsels of delectable Ethiopian bread is definitely the way to go. We recommend the ye-doro watt chicken simmered for hours in a special sauce and beef awaze tibbs. Vegetarians will like the spiced pea flour simmered in a sauce of onions, garlic and berberé paste and the red lentils simmered in chili pepper sauce.

Ice Cream & More

FAIR OAKS PHARMACY AND SODA FOUNTAIN

1526 Mission St., S. Pasadena 91030
818-799-1414, Breakfast, Lunch & Dinner daily
No Cards

Since 1915, the Fair Oaks Pharmacy has been home to a traditional corner soda fountain. We feel like wide-eyed kids here, bellying up to the marble counter with its chrome stools and stained-glass cabinetry. The ice cream they use in their sundaes, shakes and sodas, is so-so, but the ambience—and the friendly service from clean-cut local teenagers—makes up for it. There's also a welcome contemporary touch: an espresso machine.

SODA JERKS

219 S. Fair Oaks Ave., Pasadena 91105
626-583-8031, *Breakfast, Lunch & Dinner daily*

With its Fifties memorabilia and old-fashioned fountain machines, this place is sure to bring back some special memories. Quality Fosselman's ice cream (a local brand) is featured, and the sandwiches—Philly cheese steak, Chicago dog, overstuffed club, veggie-burger and Reuben—are quite good. Jump up on a stool at the marble counter and replay a moment of your childhood with a big sundae or a malt.

Italian

BONA CORSO'S

655 N. Lake Ave., Pasadena 91101
818-795-6816, *Lunch & Dinner daily*

The number of old-fashioned, primarily red-sauced Italian eateries has dwindled, but when we've had enough of those trendy trattorias, this is one of our favorite destinations. The menu is extensive, and the oversized ravioli with meat sauce is as good as you'll find anywhere. The garlic bread is heavenly, and all bottles of wine are an unheard of $9.

BUCA DI BEPPO

80 W. Green St., Pasadena 91106
626-792-7272, *Dinner nightly*

We thought of categorizing this as a "theme" restaurant—the "theme" being a rollicking, roll-up-your-sleeves-and-dig-in family Italian restaurant like the ones the first Italian immigrants opened in this country around 1900. Forget delicate Tuscan cuisine. Bring a party of at least four or six (more is better) and share huge platters of spaghetti and meatballs, lasagne and chicken cacciatore consisting of a whole chicken in tomato sauce spiked with mushrooms, garlic and capers. The food is better than it need be for a restaurant that's about entertainment. Expect to bring home a shopping bag full of leftovers.

CHARLIE'S TRIO

47 W. Main St., Alhambra 91801
626-284-4943, *Lunch & Dinner daily*

A

Charlie's Trio is what neighborhood Italian eateries are all about, a place whose menu was as in style in the fifties as it is today. Loyal customers come for its solid red-sauced dishes at low prices. While you can order a chicken dinner or a rack of ribs, the menu highlights include ravioli in marinara sauce, lasagne, eggplant Parmigiano, fettuccine Alfredo and spaghetti with meatballs. Pizzas are popular items in the lively sports bar.

DINO'S ITALIAN INN

2055 E. Colorado Blvd., Pasadena 91107
626-449-8823, *Lunch Mon.-Fri., Dinner nightly*

A

Sitting on an unfashionable block of Colorado Boulevard, far from trendy Old Pasadena, Dino's is not chic. It's an old (1949), old-style Italian restaurant more likely to be found back in Brooklyn. Its red candles, red vinyl booths and thick red sauces are all pretty much out of style, but we're thrilled this old Sicilian is still kicking.

Jamaican

KINGSTON CAFÉ

333 S. Fair Oaks Ave., Pasadena 91105
626-405-8080, *Lunch & Dinner Tues.-Sat., $*

A

You may not expect to find a taste of Montego Bay in the heart of Pasadena, but this little café delivers everything but the beach. A small bungalow with intimate rooms gives customers the impression of dining in somebody's home. The main attraction here is aromatic, robustly seasoned jerk chicken. Other specialties are curried goat, stewed oxtail with navy beans, and a vegetarian plate zested with island spices. Beverages include wonderful brown sugar-infused Jamaican lemonade, carrot juice with allspice, a unique sorrel drink and Blue Mountain coffee.

Japanese

SUSHI OF NAPLES

735 E. Green St., Pasadena 91101
626-578-1123, *Lunch & Dinner daily*

You'll find skilled and friendly sushi chefs, intriguing fresh specialties, delicious hand rolls—and very reasonable prices.

TODAI

Glendale Galleria, 50 W. Broadway, Glendale 91204
818-247-8499, *Lunch & Dinner daily*
See review in "L.A. AREA—Quick Bites."

Mexican & Latin American

MAMITA — PERUVIAN

714 S. Brand Blvd., Glendale 91204
818-243-5121, *Lunch & Dinner Tues.-Sun., $*

Dwarfed by the dealerships on Glendale's auto row, this petunia of a place is easily missed but worth finding. The cozy dining room is decorated with Peruvian folk art, and the kitchen delivers L.A.'s best rendition of papas a la huancainas (boiled potatoes topped with a creamy chile-inflected cheese sauce), Peru's most famous dish. Other specialties include ceviche de mariscos, fried fish in teriyaki sauce (reflecting the Japanese influence in Peruvian cuisine), fried chicken and breaded steak.

MERIDA — MEXICAN

20 E. Colorado Blvd., # 102, Pasadena 91105
626-792-7371, *Breakfast, Lunch & Dinner daily*

If you have ever vacationed in Cancun and tried the area's authentic cuisine, you know the joys of Yucatecan dining. Merida's worn brick walls are lined with soccer posters, regional art, maps of Mexico and a few colorful neon beer signs, and there's a terrific open-air courtyard. Signature dishes include thinly sliced pork marinated in sour orange and spices and charred on a hot grill, and pork marinated in achiote and roasted in a banana leaf. Other traditional dishes worthy of consideration are the ceviche, whole fried red snapper, tamales and Yucatecan turkey.

SEÑOR FISH — MEXICAN/SEAFOOD

618 Mission St., S. Pasadena 91030
626-403-0145, *Lunch & Dinner daily*
No Cards

Devotees of this burgeoning chain wax poetically about its high quality Mexican-oriented seafood. Lines are often long, and the dining rooms are not built for comfort, but the seafood might stir memories of an exotic ceviche shack on a Mexican beach. Fish tacos, seafood burritos, crispy whole fried snapper, octopus, English-style fish and chips, scallop tacos and grilled trout are menu highlights. The house-made flan makes a perfect finale to an inexpensive seafood feast here. **Also in Eagle Rock (4803 Eagle Rock Blvd., 213-257-7167) and Alhambra (115 W. Main St., 626-299-7550).**

Pizza

CALIFORNIA PIZZA KITCHEN

99 N. Los Robles Ave., Pasadena 91101
626-585-9020, *Lunch & Dinner daily*

"See review in L.A. AREA—Quick Bites." **Also in Glendale (101 N. Brand Blvd., 818-507-1558).**

TARANTINO'S PIZZERIA

784 E. Green St., Pasadena 91101
626-796-7836, *Lunch & Dinner daily*
No Cards

This narrow storefront usually packs people in like anchovies. Many swear theirs is the best traditional pizza in the San Gabriel Valley. The Philly cheese-steak sandwich is good too.

Tea Rooms

HUNTINGTON LIBRARY & GARDENS TEA ROOM

1151 Oxford Rd., San Marino 91108
626-683-8131, *Lunch & Tea Tues.-Sun.*

Located just behind the rose garden in the Huntington Museum and Gardens, this is an idyllic place where the achievements of man and Mother Nature coexist in magnificent splendor. For just over $10, enjoy a buffet-style tea with scones, finger sandwiches and pastries; it will fortify yourbefore or after a stroll through the Huntington's magnificent grounds.

THE LIPTON TEA HOUSE

124 Colorado Blvd., Pasadena 91105
626-568-8787, *Open daily*

Not to be daunted by the current coffee craze sweeping the nation, Lipton Tea has set out to prove that Americans can develop an even greater thirst for tea. At this white-oak-and-marble shop—the prototype, Lipton hopes, for hundreds more—you can buy 51 varieties of loose-leaf Lipton tea, and sip such exotic drinks as fruit tea, tea spritzers, chocolate chai and tea lattes, while snacking on tea brownies and tea biscotti. Non-tea pastries and sandwiches too.

ROSE TREE COTTAGE

828 E. California Blvd., Pasadena 91106
626-793-3337, *Open Tues.-Sun.*

Authentically British, the Rose Tree Cottage is a bastion of gentility and a memorable place to enjoy a relaxing high tea. In its surprisingly unstuffy room, the formally attired staff serves tea in delicate bone china, along with the full compliment of fresh scones, finger sandwiches and shortbread cookies. The adjoining bungalows and gardens feature English china, books and other collectibles for sale.

Vietnamese

JASMINE TERRACE

230 S. Lake Ave., Pasadena 91101
626-792-6600, *Lunch & Dinner Mon.-Sat.*

While hardly a celebrity-packed trendsetter like L.A.'s Le Colonial and Indochine, Jasmine Terrace provides a nice introduction to beguiling Vietnamese cuisine. The menu offers traditional favorites such as goi cuon (rice paper-wrapped vegetarian spring rolls), chao tom (sugarcane wrapped in shrimp paste), bo luc lac (sizzling flank steak), fried catfish and shrimp with sweet-and-sour sauce. The dining room features floral banquettes and paintings depicting the bucolic Vietnamese countryside.

Theme Restaurants

HOLOWORLD — FUTURISTIC/LASER TAG

620 N. Lake Ave., Pasadena 91101
626-578-0009, *Lunch & Dinner daily*

Cartoon characters, holographic images and "ghosts" greet guests at this crazy, cosmic restaurant-entertainment complex. The menu varies with each dining room, whether it be the "Western Saloon," the "Jungle Room" or the "Space Alien Invasion Room." Which means dishes like "solar chicken quesadillas," a "reservation steak sandwich" or a "caveman fried chicken salad." At the Cravers Ice Cream Bar, where the theme is Australian beaches (don't ask) guests choose from 120 ice cream flavors and 150 toppings. Upstairs, there's laser tag, video and "virtuality" games and "cosmic" pool. Needless to say, Holoworld is often busy with kids' birthday parties.

SOUTH BAY

SOUTH BAY

The area known as South Bay encompasses **El Segundo, Hermosa Beach, LAX-adjacent, Long Beach, Manhattan Beach, Palos Verdes Estates, Redondo Beach, San Pedro, and Torrance.**

DINING

THE ADMIRAL RISTY SEAFOOD 13/20 

31250 Palos Verdes Dr. West, Rancho Palos Verdes 90275
310-377-0050, *Dinner nightly, Brunch Sun., $$*

Since 1966, this spot has been drawing locals who appreciate the friendly service and spectacular ocean view. A charming stained-glass whale, seashell lighting fixtures and captains chairs add to the seaside decor. In addition to fresh fish, the specialties here include a superb cioppino, home-cured gravlax, fresh oysters, a Caesar salad tossed with fresh Dungeness crab and flank steak. The hearty breads are baked on the premises.

AIMEE'S FRENCH/MEDITERRANEAN 12/20

800 S. Pacific Coast Hwy., Redondo Beach 90277
310-316-1081, *Dinner Tues.-Sun., $$*

With its spare black and white decor, its walls hung with black and white photos, Aimee's has the look of an old Parisian bistro. Owner Aimee Mizrahi serves such eclectic dishes as salmon carpaccio with olive bruschetta and grilled eggplant, tuna tartare, grilled portobello mushrooms with white beans, orrechiette with currants, bitter greens, Gorgonzola and pine nuts, Moroccan-spiced ahi tuna with wheat salad, fava beans, red lentils, raisins and lemon-curry vinaigrette and a New York steak with caramelized onion-and-mushroom potato cake.

AÏOLI RESTAURANT & TAPAS BAR MEDITERRANEAN 12/20

1261 Cabrillo Ave., Torrance 90501
310-320-9200, *Lunch Mon.-Fri., Dinner Mon.-Sat., $$*

A Mediterranean-inspired restaurant serving many dishes zipped up with aïoli, the garlic-infused mayonnaise popular in northern Spain and southern France. The eclectic menu might include seared ahi tuna with soba noodles, rack of lamb with apple bacon, Zinfandel reduction and whipped potatoes, double-cut pork chops, garlic chicken, paella, or filet mignon with Cognac-hazelnut sauce and roasted red potatoes. The wine room is elegant for parties, wonderful breads are baked in Breadstix, the adjoining bakery, and such desserts as the apple baked in a crust, delight.

ALLEGRIA SPANISH/MEDITERRANEAN 13/20 

115 Pine Ave., Long Beach 90802
562-436-3388, *Lunch Mon.-Fri., Dinner nightly, $$*

At night, downtown Long Beach has become somewhat of a happening place, in part because of Allegria, a sister restaurant to L'Opera next door. Walk into the bar with its murals of Spanish haciendas, pitchers of potent sangria and hot-and-cold tapas, and you're likely to be pulled up onto the stage where a live band plays music for flamenco dancing. In the quieter dining room, sample stuffed baby jalapeño peppers or flash-fried calamari, followed by a hearty paella and silken flan. The tempo here heats up as the night progresses.

THE AUBERGE MEDITERRANEAN 12/20

Barnabey Hotel, 3501 N. Sepulveda Blvd., Manhattan Beach 90266
310-545-5693, *Breakfast, Lunch & Dinner daily, Brunch Sun., $$*

This restaurant's Middle European cooking includes klare rindsuppe (clear beef soup) and an updated game platter of quail, venison and rabbit with blackcurrant sauce. For dessert, order the yummy chocolate chip cheese pie.

BEACH CITY GRILL ECLECTIC 13/20 

376 W. Sixth St., San Pedro 90731
Lunch & Dinner Tues.-Sat., $

Instead of linens, glass-topped beach towels cover the tables at this funky and fun spot. Owner/chef Larry Hodgson, who grew up in Aruba and served in the Peace Corps in Paraguay, draws from a myriad of ethnic cuisines when creating dishes for the oft-changing menu. We enjoy his black bean soup with cilantro and lime, blackened salmon tacos, fajitas, seafood gumbo, Cajun sweet potato fries and jambalaya pasta Aruba. Desserts include such over-the-top concoctions as the "No Fear" pie made with white chocolate, almonds, English toffee, butterscotch chips and caramel.

BISTRO OF LUNADA BAY FRENCH 13/20 

724 Yarmouth Rd., Palos Verdes Estates 90274
310-541-3316, *Dinner Tues.-Sun., $$$*

Formerly J'Adore, this charming spot is one of the South Bay's hidden treasures. The old-fashioned French dishes include such specialties as roasted duck, rack of lamb, tournedos Rossini, chocolate mousse and crème brûlée. The five-course tasting menu runs a reasonable $35.

THE BLUE MOON SEAFOOD 12/20

207 N. Harbor Dr., Redondo Beach 90277
310-374-3411, *Lunch Fri.-Sun., Dinner nightly, Brunch Sat.-Sun., $$*

A very fishy place—it says so right on the business card. Sit in one of the comfortable tiered booths under the high peaked ceiling, and enjoy the spectacular 180-degree view from Palos Verdes to the Redondo Beach pier. They play everything from Elvis to Jefferson Airplane during dinner (and there's live music on weekend nights), when steaks, lobster and fresh salmon are specialties. During the weekend Champagne brunch, the menu features the omelets, eggs Benedict and pancakes, along with Lady Alexandria grilled cinnamon-battered egg bread with powdered sugar and maple syrup.

CAFÉ PICCOLO TRATTORIA ITALIAN 12/20

403 N. Pacific Coast Hwy., Redondo Beach 90277
310-798-4688, *Dinner nightly, $$*

Dip almond biscotti into a glass of limone liqueur while sitting in the living room-like piano bar. Just a few blocks from the ocean, this friendly neighborhood trattoria could be near the Tirreno Sea in Sorrento, Italy. The rooftop patio is bordered with an herb garden. The menu changes with the seasons and might include grilled peppers, mozzarella, anchovies and capers, carpaccio with shaved parmesan, arugula, capers and artichokes, house-marinated Atlantic salmon, fresh rock shrimp with pesto, osso buco, veal or steak, along with crisp-crusted pizzas from the wood- burning oven.

CAFÉ PIERRE FRENCH/CALIFORNIAN 13/20

317 Manhattan Beach Blvd., Manhattan Beach 90266
310-545-5252, *Lunch Mon.-Fri., Dinner nightly, $$*

This popular Manhattan Beach standby has expanded its menu. In addition to the traditional steak au poivre, escargot and onion gratinée soup, you'll find such pastas as linguine with scallops, pumpkin ravioli and spaghettini California. There are burgers and other strictly American entrées as well, plus an extensive dessert list.

CHALET DE FRANCE FRENCH/CONTINENTAL 12/20

23254 Robert Rd., Torrance 90505
310-540-4646, *Lunch Tues.-Fri., Dinner Tues.-Sun., $$*

Classic French cuisine without any surprises is what you'll find here; the chef cooks by the rules and makes few mistakes, but also takes few chances. Entrées come with soup or salad and include such dishes as chicken in Champagne sauce, beef Wellington and quail with raspberry sauce. Pyrotechnic desserts—cherries jubilee, crêpes Suzette—are big here.

CHART HOUSE AMERICAN 12/20

231 Yacht Club Way, Redondo Beach 90277
310-372-3464, *Dinner nightly, $$*

The first Southland restaurant in what has become a national chain—and some say the best—the Redondo Chart House has been a community favorite for over 30 years. Built out over the ocean, it commands a spectacular view of the coastline. Business types from nearby corporations—and volleyballers—pack in nightly for simple steaks, seafood dishes and such appetizers as coconut-crusted shrimp and the herbed artichoke. The chowder is thick with clams, and the salad bar is exceptional (it often features caviar!). Ladies can enjoy a drink and dinner here and avoid the singles- bar hustle. **Also in Malibu (8412 P.C.H., 310-454-9321) and Marina del Rey (13950 Panay Way, 310-822-4144).**

CHELSEA ON THE QUEEN MARY CONTINENTAL 12/20

1126 Queens Hwy., Long Beach 90802
562-435-3511, *Lunch Mon.-Fri., Dinner Wed.-Sun., $$*

The closest you'll get to sailing on the Titanic in the Southland. We're glad that the gracious art-deco decor of this one-time queen of the seas has been preserved. Though the look is strictly '30s, there are a few up-to-date additions to the crab cocktail, paella and steak menu—sometimes exotic fish from the Amazon. After dinner, stop for a brandy in the picturesque Observation Bar, where there's live entertainment Wednesday through Saturday. If you fantasize, you might spot an iceberg off the starboard bow.

CHEZ MÉLANGE ECLECTIC 13/20

Palos Verdes Inn, 1716 P.C.H., Redondo Beach 90277
310-540-1222, *Breakfast & Lunch Mon.-Fri., Dinner nightly, Brunch Sun., $$*

At this innovative South Bay restaurant, they've always made their own sausage and served excellent sushi. Now they've added Cajun meatloaf to the menu, and hired a woman to make fresh soft tacos. We applaud the new Champagne-caviar-and-oyster bar, and their light-cooking selections such as lemon-rosemary salmon with steamed red potatoes, wilted romaine and chive vinaigrette. Chez Mélange remains not just one of the most adventurous restaurants in these parts, but also one of the most reliable.

CUCINA PARADISO ITALIAN 13/20

1611 S. Catalina Ave., Redondo Beach 90277
310-792-1972, *Lunch Mon.-Fri., Dinner nightly, $$*

A touch of Italy on the Southern California Riviera. Displayed in the glassed-in pasta drying room, red, green and white noodles hang on racks, to be transformed into amply portioned classic dishes, such as fettuccine with duck ragu. In addition to the pastas, we like the baked polenta with wild mushrooms, cheese fondue and truffles, the crabcakes on a bed of sautéed red onions and basil, the house-smoked Norwegian salmon, the rack of veal with pancetta and the rabbit braised in Barolo wine. The wine list includes many rare Italian labels. The wine "library" is a perfect spot for a private dinner.

DAVID'S CARIBBEAN/FUSION 13/20

531 N. Pacific Coast Hwy., Redondo Beach 90277
310 937-2677, *Lunch Fri., Dinner Tues.-Sun., $$$*

Stylish galvanized-steel cutouts of palm trees, jazz musicians and bubbles bursting from a Champagne bottle create a playful feel to this restaurant, a perfect setting for Chef David Slatkin's vibrantly flavored cuisine, which fuses Caribbean and Cuban flavors. From the open kitchen comes a parade of dazzling architecturally structured dishes (some of which are difficult to consume with grace). Among the standout dishes are Slatkin's crispy veal sweetbreads and the grilled Jamaican-jerk chicken. Between courses or after dinner, guests can retreat to the back patio, where the array of comfortable sofas and chairs invite one to light up a stogie.

DEPOT — NEW AMERICAN 13/20

1250 Cabrillo Ave., Torrance 90501
310-787-7501, *Lunch Mon.-Fri., Dinner Mon.-Sat., $$*

This popular restaurant is handsome and easy to settle into, and the chef's innovative cooking is multi-ethnic—you'll find evidence of Mexico, Japan, traditional American, England, Thailand, China, Italy, France and the Southwest. We've always found the appetizers the most intriguing: rock-shrimp-and-garlic sausage, mashed-potato pancakes topped with corn and oysters, crabcake flautas with avocado salsa. This is the sort of multi-cultural restaurant where a grilled-duck-and-fennel cassoulet sits comfortably next to "Thai-dyed" chicken served with black-bean "twists."

ENCOUNTER — INTERNATIONAL 12/20

209 World Way, L.A. Airport
310-215-5151, *Lunch & Dinner daily, $$*

When you land at LAX at night, you'll spot a building that looks like a flying saucer crouching between the runways, lit up by a changing rainbow of colored lights. You've just encountered Encounter. Inside, the futuristic decor looks like a cross between the club in *Star Wars* and the cave in *The Flintstones.* We love the bar, with its percolating lava lamps and soda dispensers that emit the sounds of ray guns. The menu features dishes from every cuisine under the sun—many of which are more complicated (and more expensive) than need be for a place this kitschy (i.e. grilled veal chop with a habañero chile sauce and vanilla-scented sweet potato for $29). Come for a "Jet Set" martini before or between flights, or to show an out-of-town friend a spot that's uniquely L.A.

555 EAST — STEAKHOUSE 13/20 

555 E. Ocean Blvd., Long Beach 90802
562-437-0626, *Lunch Mon.-Fri., Dinner nightly, $$$*

Since 1984, this clubby restaurant, with its traditional English decor, has been serving hand-cut prime steaks, which are broiled at over 1600 degrees to sear the outside and keep the inside juicy. You can also get fresh Maine lobsters and such specialties as baked goat cheese with roasted garlic and Colorado prime lamb with cassis sauce, garlic-mashed potatoes and spinach. The lively pub-style bar, where a pianist plays on weekends, features 18 single-malt Scotches.

GINA LEE'S BISTRO — PACIFIC RIM 12/20

211 Palos Verdes Dr., Redondo Beach 90277
310-375-GINA, *Lunch Mon.-Fri., Dinner Tues.-Sun., $$*

The staff here is as exuberant as a troupe of marionettes. The decor is that of a simple European bistro, with white linen-covered tables topped with pots of growing herbs, a few antique buffets and an exhibition kitchen. The weekly changing menu synthesizes various Asian flavors: spinach salad with shiitake mushrooms, oven-dried shallots and coconut vinaigrette, seafood potstickers with ponzu, ginger and cucumber relish, tamarind-marinated Chilean seabass—even a burger with mushrooms, Muenster cheese and herbed shoestring potatoes. Their chili jam adds zest to anything.

HABASH CAFÉ — MIDDLE EASTERN 12/20

233 Pacific Coast Hwy., Hermosa Beach 90254
310-376-6620, *Breakfast, Lunch & Dinner Mon.-Sat., $*

For more than twenty years, Mama Habash has been dishing up such delicious Middle-Eastern specialties as falafel, mjedara (lentil-and-rice salad) and ethereal lentil soup. Regulars also swear by her hummus, meltingly tender stewed squash and sweet pastries.

KING'S PINE AVENUE FISH HOUSE — SEAFOOD 13/20

100 W. Broadway, Long Beach 90802
310-432-7463, *Breakfast Sat.-Sun., Lunch & Dinner daily, $*

This is the place for a good selection of fresh oysters and clams, plenty of seafood dishes served over pasta, and fish from as far away as the South Pacific. If the alder-smoked- salmon sandwich is on the menu when you're there, definitely go for it. We like their impressive selection of American wines and microbrewery beers.

LANDREY'S — CALIFORNIAN/PAN-ASIAN 12/20

Sheraton Gateway Hotel, 6101 W. Century Blvd., L.A. 90045
310-274-6511, *Dinner Mon.-Sat., $$*

A soothing, contemporary setting for a relaxed meal between flights or before a long one. The service is friendly but can be slow, and the food is better than what you'd expect at an airport hotel. To start, you can get sushi, a Caesar salad, or such exotica as the smoked salmon rolled in a quinoa pancake with a chipotle-honey dressing. Entrées include grilled swordfish with a Yucatan-style citrus-herb paste, various pastas and a New York steak with smoked shallot sauce.

LE BEAUJOLAIS — FRENCH 11/20

522 Pacific Coast Highway, Redondo Beach 90277
310-543-5100, *Lunch & Dinner daily, Brunch Sat.-Sun., $$*

This intimate and elegant restaurant is ensconced in a small converted cottage. It provides not simply the ideal setting for a romantic meal, but also some very traditional—and very good—French cooking. If cholesterol isn't an issue and you've had it with the area's trendy California-French eateries, this is the spot to satisfy a sudden craving for such opulent Gallic traditions as filet mignon with melted brie and Roquefort-Cognac sauce, lobster bisque, foie gras and sweetbreads.

THE LIBRARY — AMERICAN 13/20

Los Angeles Renaissance Hotel, 9620 Airport Blvd., Inglewood 90045
310-337-2800, *Dinner nightly, $$$*

Just minutes from LAX, this hotel restaurant serves good fresh seafood, but basically it's a steakhouse, so plunge in and order the Delmonico cut, the porterhouse, rack of lamb or grilled veal chop. The wine list features more than a dozen

French and California hearty reds. You can linger comfortably over an after-dinner drink until it's time to catch your flight or just head home.

L'OPERA ITALIAN 13/20 

101 Pine Ave., Long Beach 90802
310-491-0066, *Lunch Mon.-Fri., Dinner nightly,* $$

Located in a former bank, L'Opera is one of the best-looking restaurants in Long Beach, and offers such Northern Italian delicacies as smoked goose prosciutto paired with mozzarella and olive oil infused with sun-dried tomatoes. There is a flavorful loin of grilled pork sautéed with grapes, brandy and balsamic vinegar served over polenta, and irresistible duck-and-Mascarpone ravioli in a satiny walnut sauce. The salads are tossed with a variety of zesty balsamic vinaigrettes and there are always rich special-occasion sweets. There are private dining rooms available.

McCORMICK & SCHMICK'S SEAFOOD 14/20 

2101 Rosecrans Ave., El Segundo 90245
310-416-1123, *Lunch Mon.-Fri., Dinner nightly,* $$

If the fish were any fresher, they'd jump onto your plate at this Pacific Northwest-based seafood restaurant decorated in dark woods, brass and leaded glass. The daily-changing menu features over 30 varieties of fresh fish, northwestern oysters and clams, and Dungeness crab. Try the cedar plank-baked British Columbian salmon with Pinot Noir sauce, the manila clams with white wine, garlic and herbs, and the flourless chocolate-truffle cake for dessert. The bar here is always lively, and the outdoor patio is appealing.

MICHI JAPANESE/MEDITERRANEAN 13/20 

903 Manhattan Ave., Manhattan Beach 90266
310 376-0613, *Lunch Mon.-Fri., Dinner Mon.-Sat.,* $$

Watch the beach town action through the French doors that span the main dining room—while sipping one of the 35 martinis they serve here. Michi Takahashi, the former chef at Chaya Brasserie, blends Asian ingredients with elements of French, Italian and Japanese cuisines. Most of the time it works. We've enjoyed the shrimp-and-eel-wrapped roasted asparagus, the tuna-and-avocado tartare in a dried shiitake mushroom broth, the grilled Dijon-mustard-glazed Chilean seabass with balsamic vinaigrette, the lamb chops with couscous and the hearty lobster ravioli. The fromage blanc with fruit and peach purée makes a refreshing finale. Original works of art by the chef's mother, a former Tokyo fashion designer, and Japanese artifacts provide intriguing wall decorations.

OLD TONY'S SEAFOOD 10/20

Redondo Pier, Redondo Beach 90277
310-374-1442, *Lunch Sat.-Sun., Dinner nightly,* $$

Serving a local following since 1952, this weathered landmark, with its circular bar perched above the restaurant, affords a birds-eye view of the marina and the ocean, and is good for dining with children. Start with the smoked salmon chowder or the oysters, followed by the lemon-garlic calamari steak or the signature baked halibut. Stop at Tony's Fish Market for fresh seafood to take home.

PAPADAKIS TAVERNA GREEK 12/20

301 W. Sixth St., San Pedro 90731
310-548-1186, *Dinner nightly, $$*

"Pleasure Palace for the Palate," trumpets the restaurant's brochure. Everyone comes here for enormous Greek dinners, Greek dancing and lots of fun. (Yes, they sometimes break plates here.) Starter choices are legion: octopus in lemony olive oil, flamed kasseri cheese, other Greek cheeses and olives, and a handful of phyllo-pastry triangles. Dinners come with salad and a bowl of traditional Greek lemon-and-rice soup, and feature such entrées as flavorful lamb or sea bass in phyllo pastry. Try the heavenly baklava if you have room for dessert.

PARKER'S LIGHTHOUSE SEAFOOD 12/20

435 Shoreline Dr., Long Beach 90802
562-432-6500, *Lunch & Dinner daily, Brunch Sun., $$*

A

A fanciful interpretation of a lighthouse located right on the water, Parker's offers views of the Queen Mary and the harbor. The emphasis is on fresh fish—usually mesquite-grilled and served with a choice of sauces on the side. You can also order prime rib, steaks and chicken dishes, and Mississippi mud pie or Key lime pie for dessert. The lively bar shakes up such specialty drinks as the Cadillac Margarita and Long Beach Ice Tea, and features a nice selection of regional and imported beers.

REED'S CALIFORNIAN/FRENCH 12/20

2640 N. Sepulveda Blvd., Manhattan Beach 90266
310-546-3299, *Lunch Mon.-Fri., Dinner nightly, $$*

A

This casual mini-mall restaurant has changed owners, but chef Al Casteneda is still supervising the kitchen. The changing specialties might include escargot with Brie, filet mignon in red wine, salmon with white-zinfandel sauce and crispy duck with raspberry sauce—most served with good garlic-mashed potatoes. Finish with the warm-apple tart .

RUSSELL'S NEW AMERICAN 12/20

5656 Second St., Long Beach 90803
310-434-0226, *Breakfast, Lunch & Dinner daily, $$*

Without a doubt one of the very best burger spots in Southern California. Their burgers are delicious, especially when topped with the great homemade chili. The other winners here are the crisp hash browns and the pies, from the sour cream to the banana to the peanut butter. The service is friendly, the atmosphere lively.

SHENANDOAH CAFÉ AMERICAN 13/20

4722 E. Second St., Long Beach 90803
310-434-3469, *Dinner nightly*, $$

Fans of true American cuisine will like the beer-batter shrimp, beef brisket in barbecue sauce and wonderful country sausages. The meat and the fish dishes are the best. Two in particular are worth a drive here: riverwalk steak, a thinly sliced flank steak in a mustard-caper sauce, and the very juicy blackened swordfish. Starters are unnecessary; dinners come with incredible warm apple fritters, a fine salad and homemade rolls.

SIMON'S SEAFOOD 11/20

Catalina Landing, 340 Golden Shore, Long Beach 90802
562-435-2333, *Lunch Mon.-Fri., Dinner nightly*, $$

A

Formerly Simon & Seaforth's, Simon's features a raucous bar where you'll probably end up when you're waiting for a table. There are appetizers available in the bar, but save your appetite for some of the good main dishes: fine New England clam chowder; Copper River salmon; Alaskan halibut with roasted-bell-pepper sauce and some mesquite-soaked Chilean swordfish with artichoke-and-vermouth garlic butter.

SIXTH STREET BISTRO MEDITERRANEAN 12/20

354 W. Sixth St., San Pedro 90731
310-521-8818, *Lunch Mon.-Fri., Dinner Tues.-Sun.*, $$

The dining room features a ceiling mural of a mythical grape harvest (there's a terrific sunflower mural in the ladies' room), woven-copper light fixtures and comfortable booths. The changing menu often includes recipes by chef/owner George Moussalli's Lebanese mother. Among our favorite dishes are spicy sizzling tiger prawns, paella, lamb osso buco, dilled lobster ravioli, polenta with rock shrimp and lobster sauce, rosemary grilled pork tenderloin, garlic chicken breasts with feta cheese and delectable fresh pastries. On a warm evening, sit out on the patio, sipping wine from the excellent by-the-glass list.

SPLASH! FRENCH/FUSION 14/20

350 N. Harbor Dr., Redondo Beach 90277
310 798-5348, Breakfast, *Lunch & Dinner daily*, $$$

A

At this colorful and lively new restaurant, chef Serge Burckel combines various ethnic ingredients and jazzy presentations to create his version of "fusion" cuisine. Excellent starters include the diced raw tuna topped with Japanese pickles and wasabi cream, and duck "firecrackers" with oyster sauce, bitter greens and mint. Compelling entrées include the salmon with a horseradish crust on purple Thai rice with vodka-orange dressing and salmon caviar, the steamed Chilean sea bass in a banana leaf with shiitake mushrooms, apple and asparagus purée and the roast lamb with polenta-zucchini-mushroom cake. Standout desserts include the twice-baked

crème brûlée topped with black pepper and the chocolate "dim sum." There is a good selection of wines by the glass on the extensive, fairly priced wine list. A party of six to ten can book the "chef's table" in the kitchen, where you can watch as Burckel prepares your special multi-course tasting menu.

TOSH II KOO FRENCH 13/20 

23863 Hawthorne Blvd., Torrance 90505
310-373-8187, *Lunch Tues.-Fri., Dinner Mon.-Sat., $$*

A

In this spare, high-tech setting, chef/owner Toshihiko Takahashi serves delicate interpretations of classic French dishes. The daily changing menu might include shrimp-and-smoked-cheese salad with lemon vinaigrette, seared Chilean sea bass with beet-butter sauce, sautéed foie gras with strawberry sauce, chicken spaghettini with soy-ginger cream sauce, pasta with clams, calamari and black mussels, salmon napoleon with crispy noodles, or baked venison loin with red wine-black pepper sauce. The Zen garden has a nifty frog fisherman.

VERSAILLES CUBAN 12/20

1000 N. Sepulveda Blvd, Manhattan Beach 90266
310-937-6829, *Lunch & Dinner daily, $*

See review in "L.A. Area—Dining."

WATERFRONT RESTAURANT & LOUNGE CALIFORNIAN 12/20

230 Portofino Way, Redondo Beach 90277
310-379-8363, *Lunch & Dinner daily, Brunch Sun., $$*

The interior's gray-blue sea tones blend softly with those of the shoreline, and every table commands an ocean view. We've enjoyed the spicy crabcakes, the penne with walnuts and asparagus and the garlicky rosemary-roasted lamb. On weekends, there's live music and dancing after dinner, and the Sunday buffet brunch is a lavish affair. We've enjoyed their special summer barbecue buffets on the deck, and we appreciate the complimentary appetizers from four to seven p.m. during the week all year round. Come on a sunny afternoon, order a bucket of the garlicky little neck clams, sit on the outdoor patio and watch the boats glide in and out of the marina.

WHALE & ALE ENGLISH PUB 12/20

327 W. Seventh St., San Pedro 90731
310-832-0363, *Lunch Mon.-Sat., Dinner nightly, Brunch Sun., $$*

The aroma of freshly roasted meat fills the dark oak-paneled dining rooms of this Victorian-style pub, where the bar is trimmed in brass, the sideboards are English antiques and a fire blazes in the hearth. You can get slow-roasted prime rib, turkey and sometimes lamb, served with creamed spinach, mashed potatoes and gravy, cranberry sauce and horseradish. In addition, there are daily fresh fish specials and traditional fish and chips. Pub-crawlers will appreciate the eight beers on tap, including several British and micro brews.

WOLFGANG PUCK CAFÉ CALIFORNIAN 13/20

2121 E. Rosecrans Ave., El Segundo 90245
310-607-9653, *Lunch & Dinner daily, $*

See review in "Dining—L.A. area."

ZAZOU CALIFORNIAN/PROVENÇAL 12/20

1810 S. Catalina St., Redondo Beach 90277
310-540-4884, *Lunch Tues.-Sat., Dinner nightly, $$*

Delight in sidewalk dining, tapas nights and garlic dinners at this casual eatery, where whimsical light fixtures cast the dining room in a golden glow and the tables are covered in rainbow-hued linens. Blending the tastes of the South of France with those of the South Bay, Zazou's serves such specialties as chopped tuna tartare with homemade potato chips and chile oil, carrot-jalapeño mashed potatoes, pappardelle with slow-cooked duck, sweet peppers, tomato sauce and fresh peas, and grilled rosemary-and-mustard infused pork tenderloin. Intriguing desserts include the chocolate-bourbon truffle torte.

AND ALSO...

THE BOTTLE INN ITALIAN

26 22nd St., Hermosa Beach 90254
310-376-9595, *Lunch & Dinner nightly, $$*

Hundreds of miniature liquor bottles decorate the walls of this cozy neighborhood spot that has been here forever. The service is friendly and the cuisine is traditional Italian: calamari, pastas and veal are among the specialties.

CAMACHOS GRILL CARIBBEAN/MEXICAN

655 N. Harbor Dr., Redondo Beach 90277
310-937-8812, *Lunch & Dinner daily, Brunch Sun., $$*

This spacious wood-planked hacienda looks out over the marina and boasts several patios. A trendy beach crowd comes for the killer margaritas and pitchers of beers, along with such dishes as jerk chicken, mango curried chicken, pork baked in a banana leaf and mango mousse. Their Tapas Bar serves everything from gazpacho to sushi, and it's easy to make a meal here.

CANTINA REAL MEXICAN

19 Pier Ave., Hermosa Beach 90254
310-372-3454, *Breakfast, Lunch & Dinner daily, $*

We like the Mexican-style wood floors, high ceilings, patio and plants cascading from the overhead beams. For breakfast try the eggs with chorizo or the crabmeat omelet, both served with fresh tortillas, rice, beans or fresh fruit. The steak or chicken picado is popular for dinner, along with fajitas. Do sample the flan with Kahlua or deep-fried ice cream for dessert.

CHARLEY BROWN'S AMERICAN

665 N. Harbor Dr., Redondo Beach 90277
310-318-3474, *Lunch & Dinner daily, Brunch Sun., $$*

This branch of a standard steak-and-seafood restaurant has the advantage of a terrific marina view, with many of its tables right over the boat slips. During "Happy Hour" in the sports bar, the TV is on and the appetizers are half-priced.

CHRISTINE ECLECTIC

Hillside Village, 24530 Hawthorne Blvd., Torrance 90505
310-373-1952, *Lunch daily, Dinner Wed.-Mon., $$*

In this light, contemporary spot that was formerly Fino's, chef Christine Brown serves sunny Mediterranean fare with Pacific overtones which she has dubbed "Christine Cuisine's." Tempting starters include the grilled tempura shrimp and the ahi-tuna roll, the seared ahi and the chilled shrimp with miso greens, crayfish and a mango-layered avocado tower. Brown's entrées range from a spicy cioppino to a thick-cut pork chop with goat cheese and porcini mushroom ravioli.

FONZ'S RESTAURANT NEW AMERICAN

1017 Manhattan Ave., Manhattan Beach 90266
310-376-1536, *Dinner nightly, Brunch Sat.-Sun., $$*

Russell Jackson had the eclectic Russell's on La Cienega for a number of years, then cooked for awhile at the Regent Beverly Wilshire Hotel. We're happy to have caught up with him again at this buzzing Manhattan Beach place, where he does a range of eclectic contemporary dishes and makes a killer chocolate brownie pie.

MARTHA'S 22ND ST. GRILL AMERICAN

25 22nd St, Hermosa Beach 90254
310-376-7786, *Breakfast & Lunch daily*

Within site of the ocean in this quaint beachy neighborhood, Martha's has long been serving up healthy fare to a local appreciative following. You can order everything from hot-spicy chicken wings to stir-fried vegetables and grilled teriyaki chicken. The wonderful breakfast menu draws crowds on the weekends and the wait can be hours, so sign in, take a walk on the beach, and look forward to eggs "Manhattan" with tomatoes, spinach and mushrooms or blueberry-cornmeal pancakes.

SCOTTY'S ON THE STRAND

1100 The Strand, Hermosa Beach 90254
310-318-7152, *Breakfast, Lunch & Dinner daily*

Right on the beach, this '50s diner has been serving solid, reasonably priced fare for over forty years. Locals fill the booths for such daily-changing specials as roast chicken with mashed potatoes, seafood pasta and fish-and-chips. A local piano player lends a nice touch to the roll of the ocean. Steps away, the volleyball nets attract serious team competitions that rage on the weekends throughout the summer.

THE SKY ROOM CONTINENTAL

The Breakers, 40 S. Locust Ave., Long Beach 90802
562-983-2707, *Dinner Wed.-Sun., Brunch Sun., $$$*

Back in the 1940s, The Breakers was a glamorous art deco hotel and one of the first Hiltons. In fact, Elizabeth Taylor honeymooned with Nicky Hilton here. Now a retirement residence, its 15th-floor rooftop dining room has been restored to its former grandeur, right down to the white, black and gold color scheme, the picture windows offering a 360-degree view of the harbor and the teak and ebony dance floor, where a seven-piece band plays. Capture the spirit of the good old days—or just dress up for a romantic evening—and dine on lobster bisque, salmon, rack of lamb or chateaubriand for two. There's even dancing during the Sunday brunch.

SPAGHETTINI ITALIAN

305 Old Ranch Pkwy., Seal Beach 90740
310-596-2199, *Lunch Mon.-Fri., Dinner nightly, $$*

Not surprisingly, there are quite a few pastas on this menu: tomato-basil pasta, grilled sausage pasta, various seafood pastas. Everything has a certain enthusiasm, especially the fine selection of crunchy, California-style pizzas topped variously with jumbo shrimps, artichokes, salami and other goodies. These make fine preludes to such entrées as chicken Marsala and grilled lamb chops.

SUNSET'S AMERICAN

117 Manhattan Beach Blvd., Manhattan Beach 90266
310-545-2523, *Lunch & Dinner nightly, Brunch Sat.-Sun., $*

Perched on a hill, this long-time favorite overlooks the promenade and pier and has a panoramic view of the coastline. Bright and airy, with snappy service and fresh seafood, it's popular with local professionals as well as beach-goers. At lunch, the Chinese chicken salad is a good bet. At dinner, try the blackened chicken pasta or the scallops with rice pilaf. Enjoy a beer and nachos while watching a glorious sunset.

THELEN'S MERMAID AMERICAN

11 Pier Ave., Hermosa Beach 90254
310-374-9344, *Breakfast, Lunch & Dinner daily, $*

The Mermaid has been here for over forty years, and has been a stage set in many movies. The darkly lit bar is an old-time classic and from the black vinyl booths, guests can look out at the ocean. Locals line up for the all-American home cooking, which includes prix-fixe daily specials such as Swiss steak, liver with bacon and onions, and roast turkey with all the trimmings. They serve quite a lavish "Happy Hour" buffet, and their homemade clam chowder is tops.

QUICK BITES

American/Coffee Shops/Cafés

BREADSTIX BAKERY & CAFÉ

1261 Cabrillo Ave., Torrance 90501
310-320-9500, *Lunch Mon.-Fri.*

This full-service bakery specializes in both traditional and trendy breads, everything from white to sun dried tomato-walnut and Kalamata olive. Buy a loaf to take home, then have lunch on the patio. They serve fresh pastas and salads, and sandwiches made with their fresh bread.

CHEESECAKE FACTORY

605 N. Harbor Dr., Redondo Beach 90277
310-376-0466, *Lunch & Dinner daily*

Like all the outlets of this chain, "factory" is the operative word, as they churn out bounteous salads, sandwiches and entrées from a menu that offers something for everyone. This particular Cheesecake Factory has a nice marina view—which means you'll have to wait even longer than at most. **Numerous other locations in the Southland.**

POLLY'S ON THE PIER

233 N. Harbor Dr., Redondo Beach 90277
310-318-3736, *Breakfast & Lunch daily*
No Cards

Out on the Redondo Pier, Polly's has a channel view, down-to-earth prices, and caters to the sports fishermen—they open at five a.m. Try huevos rancheros or eggs Benedict before trying your hand at fishing.

RUBY'S

245 N. Harbor Dr., Redondo Beach 90277
310-376-7829, *Breakfast, Lunch & Dinner daily*

Another in this campy and fun chain of retro-diners. See review in "ORANGE COUNTY—Quick Bites."

SHELLBACK TAVERN

116 Manhattan Beach Blvd., Manhattan Beach 90266
310-376-7857, *Lunch & Dinner daily, Breakfast Sat.-Sun.*

Just up from the pier, the Shellback has a view of the beach and the promenade, and serves a little bit of everything, from burgers to burritos. A fine spot for watching the beach volleyball games.

TOGO

616 89th St., Westchester 90045
310-338-0419, *Lunch & Dinner daily*

Take the family, get a lot of food for a little, and consider getting into the franchise food business yourself. Part of a chain, Togo meets its "fast service, not fast food" promise with a wide array of simple sandwich options: lean turkey or ham or roast beef with your choice of cheese and bread. Try the turkey and cranberry on rye, or cold roast beef and avocado. Hot sandwiches and salads are also available.

Bars & Pubs

CHILLERS BAR & GRILL

239 N. Harbor Dr., Redondo Beach 90277
310-798-3170, *Lunch & Dinner daily*

Tanned surfer dudes hang out on the breezy outdoor patios, or watch a game on the big TV screen inside. Order a beer and a burger or chili, try your hand at pinball or billiards and enjoy the local color. From Thursday through Saturday nights, Chillers becomes a hot nightclub, featuring a "battle of the bands" and terrific local talent.

HENNESSEY'S TAVERN

8 Pier Ave., Hermosa Beach 90254
310-372-5759, *Breakfast, Lunch & Dinner daily*

In this neighborhood meeting place, the house specialty is traditional corned beef and cabbage—in ample portions. There are also sandwiches, burgers, specialty fries and fresh salads to choose from. A big draw is the enticing selection of imported Irish beers, perfect for sipping while watching the sunset over the ocean.

Healthy

GOOD STUFF

1286 The Strand, Hermosa Beach 90254
310-374-2334, *Breakfast & Lunch*
No Cards

"You are what you eat...so eat Good Stuff" is their motto, and it's easy to do here. This beachside spot serves healthy burgers, vegetarian selections and fresh juices to the bikini-clad crowd. Try the albacore tuna wrap, the zucchini Parmesan and the garden omelet with whole-wheat pancakes. **Also in Manhattan Beach (1300 Highland Ave., 310-545-4775) and W.L.A. (11903 W. Olympic Blvd., 310-477-9011).**

THE SPOT

110 Second St., Hermosa Beach 90254
310-376-2355, *Lunch & Dinner daily*
No Cards

This homey restaurant serves "garden burritos" to the nature crowd. Some claim it's the best vegetarian around.

Mexican/Latin American

PANCHO'S

3615 Highland Ave., Manhattan Beach 90266
310-545-6670, *Lunch Mon.-Sat., Dinner nightly, Brunch Sun.*
A

Beach locals swear by this pretty two-tiered hacienda. We think the combo-plate Mexican food is generic, but you can't beat the beachy atmosphere and lively bar scene.

Pizza

BJ'S CHICAGO PIZZA & BREWERY

5258 E. Second St., Long Beach 90803
562-439-8181, *Lunch & Dinner daily*
A

See review in "ORANGE COUNTY—Quick Bites"

Seafood

CAPTAIN KIDD'S

209 N. Harbor Dr., Redondo Beach 90277
310-372-7703, *Breakfast, Lunch & Dinner daily*

Ask a local where to go for fresh seafood, and they'll probably send you here. Buy a piece of fish or a live crab from the fresh-fish market, and they'll prepare it for you char-broiled, grilled, Cajun-style or deep fried for only $3 extra—and that includes two side dishes. The deli-style service area is always busy, but the lines move quickly.

FUN FISH MARKET & RESTAURANT

121 International Boardwalk, Redondo Beach 90277
310-374-4277,
Lunch & Dinner daily

Located on the Redondo Pier next to the amusement center, Fun Fish serves fresh fish any way you like it, along with hearty side dishes. Choose your dinner form a live tank, or try the seafood cocktails, chowders, salads or sandwiches.

HERMOSA FISH MARKET CAFÉ

20 Pier Ave., Hermosa Beach 90254
310-372-1488, *Lunch & Dinner daily*

This little place specializes in fresh charbroiled fish, but it also serves pretty good seafood paella, cioppino and curry—even seafood tacos and teriyaki—all better tasting when you're sitting on the ocean-view patio.

SAN PEDRO FISH MARKET & RESTAURANT MEXICAN SEAFOOD

1190 Nagoya Way, San Pedro 90731
10-832-4251, *Breakfast & Lunch daily*
No cards

This rambling, bustling spot on the boardwalk adjacent to Ports O' Call Village, offers over 200 varieties of fresh seafood, including live lobsters and crabs in tanks. On weekends, the outdoor dining deck is filled with Hispanic families sharing trays heaped with shrimp, crab, and fish fajitas, while listening to the strolling Mariachi bands. If you didn't know better, you'd think you were in Mazatlan.

ORANGE COUNTY

ORANGE COUNTY

In just a couple of decades, Orange County has been transformed from a series of sleepy L.A. suburbs, to a vital sprawl of cities, housing developments, business parks and some of the state's biggest and best shopping centers, the whole crisscrossed by freeways and bounded on the west by miles of perfect ocean beaches. Residents swear by—and visitors marvel at—the easy-going lifestyle in Orange County. We're increasingly impressed by its selection of cafés, restaurants and fine-dining venues. Not surprisingly, many of them have outdoor seating and/or an enviable view of the Pacific Ocean.

Of course, we couldn't begin to cover all of the restaurants in Orange County here, so we're concentrating on the destinations that have the liveliest dining scenes: **Laguna Beach** and the **Newport Beach/Costa Mesa/Irvine** area, with occasional forays north, south and east. We wouldn't want to forget about theme park-adjacent **Anaheim**.

DINING

AEGEAN CAFÉ GREEK 11/20

540 S. Coast Hwy., Laguna Beach 92651
714-494-5001, *Lunch & Dinner daily, $$*

This is the liveliest—and perhaps most boisterous—restaurant in never-dull Laguna Beach. A team of new owners has revitalized the place and the food is quite good, from appetizers to desserts. Try the light zucchini fritters with the unpronounceable name (kolokothokeftedes), the juicy roast lamb leg and one of the honey-rich desserts. The waiters sing and dance until they—or you—drop. Literally.

AMELIA'S ITALIAN/SEAFOOD 11/20

311 Marine Ave., Balboa Island 92662
714-673-6580, *Lunch & Dinner daily, $*

A

This charming little neighborhood eatery has been around for nearly four decades. The menu is basic Italian during lunch, but at dinnertime, Hettie and chef Rudy Sanchez weave their magic with bouillabaisse and linguini with bay scallops and baby calamari. For those who have won the Lotto, there is a heady crab-stuffed abalone.

ANTONELLO ITALIAN 14/20 

S. Coast Plaza Village, 1611 Sunflower Ave., Santa Ana 92704
714-751-7153, *Lunch Mon.-Fri., Dinner Mon.-Sat., $$$*

A

Antonello remains a haven for O.C. business, political and social leaders. The decor is splashy and even romantic: a mock street from owner Antonio Cagnolo's hometown in Italy's Piedmont region. The kitchen produces a few Continental/Italian dishes that hark back to a more indulgent era of fine dining, such as the veal chop with porcini and truffles and richly sauced pastas. California and Italian selections dominate the wine list, but most of the heavy-hitters sip martinis, which are more in vogue than Chianti.

THE ARCHES CONTINENTAL 12/20

3334 W. Pacific Coast Hwy., Newport Beach 92663
949-645-7077, *Lunch Mon.-Fri., Dinner Mon.-Sat., $$$*

A

Plus ça change. The Arches, which opened in 1922 when Warren G. Harding was President, is the oldest restaurant in Orange County. The kitchen copes well with a huge menu that covers everything from abalone to sweetbreads, and puts the accent on steaks, seafood and tableside preparations. The hefty wine list has some of the best prices in town.

AUBERGINE FRENCH NO RATING

508 29th St., Newport Beach 92663
949-723-4150, *Dinner Tues.-Sat., $$$*

A

Owners Tim and Liza Goodell have been busy with their new Troquet, and at press time were in the process of remodeling this trend-setting restaurant, which is scheduled to reopen in the late summer of '98. The tables will be less crowded in this converted home, and there will be more seating. Goodell prepares some of the best dishes around, including a wonderful pear-and-Gorgonzola salad, grilled quail with smoked chicken and terrific smoked-and-grilled sturgeon with foie gras. For such fine quality, the prices are reasonable, the service relaxed and attentive.

BISTANGO CALIFORNIAN 14/20 

The Atrium, 19100 Von Karman Ave., Irvine 92715
949-752-5222, *Lunch Mon.-Fri., Dinner nightly,* $$

If the Atrium's atrium isn't enough to do it, the nightly jazz and the terrific revolving displays of art separate Bistango from the typical Orange County dining room. The fare changes regularly, but always includes pizzas, seared ahi with a vegetable-soy sauce, veal chops and some of the best desserts this side of Vienna, from the hand of Austrian-born executive chef Paul Gstein. The wine list offers about 200 labels, plus a wide choice of wines by the glass.

BLACK SHEEP BISTRO MEDITERRANEAN 12/20

303 El Camino Real, Tustin 92680
714-544-6060, *Lunch Fri., Dinner Wed.-Sun.,* $

At this airy spot in downtown Tustin, owner/chef Rick Bufford specializes in dishes from France, Italy and Spain. Top dishes include duck confit, one of the area's best paellas and intriguing pastas. Don't miss the fresh fish with Romesco sauce, and check out the eclectic wine list full of boutique producers from Provence, Languedoc and Tuscany. The Buffords also run a shop next door selling confit, sausages and other gourmet food items.

THE CAT & CUSTARD CUP CONTINENTAL 12/20

800 E. Whittier Blvd., La Habra 90631
714-992-6496, *Lunch Mon.-Fri., Dinner nightly,* $$

The Salisbury family, which built its reputation for Mexican food at L.A.'s El Cholo, owns this English Tudor-style restaurant with an American/Continental menu. Creed Salisbury and Chef George Avendano turn out excellent filet mignons and chateaubriands, a number of appealing veal dishes and seafood ranging from scampi to grilled ahi tuna. Sunday and Monday nights feature prime rib and Yorkshire pudding, and English trifle for dessert. Note the nice wine list and the entertainment in the bar.

THE CELLAR FRENCH 14/20 

305 N. Harbor Blvd., Fullerton 92632
714-525-5682, *Dinner Tues.-Sat.,* $$$

This has been one of Southern California's most romantic grottos since 1969, and it is truly a cellar—located downstairs in the Villa del Sol shopping center. Three dining rooms provide the proper atmosphere with their stone walls and pillars and beamed ceilings. We enjoy chef David Kessler's beef medallions with mustard sauce, roast breast of muscovy duck with sour cherries and rack of lamb with lavender and sweet garlic. Order the cloud-like Grand Marnier soufflé for dessert. The wine list is extensive.

CITRUS CITY GRILLE AMERICAN 12/20

122 N. Glassell St., Orange 92866
714-639-9600, *Lunch & Dinner Tues.-Sat., $$*

A

The hottest restaurant in Olde Towne Orange, this post-modern spot that works best when sticking to basic American cooking. Order what may be the county's best meatloaf, the broiled fish selections or a risotto, and a delectable pineapple upside-down cake for dessert. We applaud the earnest service and the good, fairly priced list of California wines.

CLAES SEAFOOD SEAFOOD 13/20 

Hotel Laguna, 425 S. Pac. Cst. Hwy., Laguna Beach 92651
949-494-1151, *Lunch & Dinner daily, $$*

A

An oceanfront fixture since 1888, the hotel and restaurant were recently remodeled, and so was the menu. Today you'll find such updated dishes as teriyaki halibut with jasmine and coconut rice, macadamia nut-crusted mahi-mahi in a pineapple beurre blanc sauce and Chilean seabass with wild mushrooms. Choose one of the 450 wines available, then relax and watch the ocean do its thing.

DAILY GRILL AMERICAN 12/20

957 Newport Ctr. Dr., Newport Beach 92660
949-644-2223, *Lunch & Dinner daily, $*

This is part of a stylish chain that features straightforward American food at reasonable prices. The menu is just what you'd expect, right down to such standards as meatloaf, chicken pot pie, calf's liver with bacon and onions, hamburgers, seafood, potatoes prepared in almost every way possible, and even tapioca pie. Great for families who like to eat well without a bank loan.

FIVE CROWNS AMERICAN 14/20 

3801 E. Pacific Coast Hwy., Corona del Mar 92625
714-760-0331, *Dinner nightly, $$*

A

Customers have been coming to the Five Crowns for prime rib, steaks and lamb for years, and they still pack the place nightly. The most charming dining area is upstairs, where the cross-beamed ceiling looks well suited to an English manner house. From the outside, the restaurant resembles a Tudor inn, so it is less shocking to see waitresses clad in wench-like uniforms. The best wines are found on the Captain's List, which must be requested.

FIVE FEET CHINESE 12/20

328 Glenneyre St., Laguna Beach 92651
949-497-4955, *Lunch Fri., Dinner Tues.-Sun., $$*

A

Five Feet is one of the hippest of all Orange County restaurants, and chef owner Michael Kang has been rewarded with a loyal, well heeled clientele. The art-filled, post-modern space has a sophisticated buzz, but we find the cooking inconsistent and some of the dishes overpriced. Appetizers like the potstickers are pleasant and the whole braised catfish is reasonably good, but we don't like paying $20 for a simple kung pao dish.

GOLDEN TRUFFLE FRENCH/CARIBBEAN 15/20

1767 Newport Blvd., Costa Mesa 92627
714-645-9858, *Lunch Tues.-Fri., Dinner Tues.-Sat., $$*

Alan Greeley cooks with a wild eye and a passion; one simply never knows what he will come up with. When he's in the mood, this restaurant can be brilliant. One day he'll make blue corn tortillas topped with spiced rock shrimp, followed by the best pan-seared lamb loin you've ever tasted. Another day he'll punch up sea urchin and free-range chicken with jerk spices and curries. The best strategy is to forget the regular menu, and ask Greeley to do his thing. The odds favor a great meal if he likes you.

GRANVILLE'S STEAKHOUSE 13/20

Disneyland Hotel, 1150 W. Cerritos Ave., Anaheim 92802
714-956-6755, *Dinner nightly, $$*

Granville's began life in 1981 as a gourmet hotel restaurant appealing mainly to Disneyland visitors. Then it was converted to a steakhouse, named after child star Bonita Granville, wife of Disney bigwig Jack Wrather. Today the clientele is heavily Japanese and the restaurant is always busy. Steaks, lamb chops and prime rib top the menu, along with swordfish and lobster—all rolled over to your table on a cart and dramatically presented. The wine list has plenty of California reds to go with all that red meat.

GUSTAF ANDERS CONTINENTAL 16/20 

South Coast Village, 1651 Sunflower Ave., Santa Ana 92704
714-668-1737, *Lunch Mon.-Sat., Dinner nightly, $$*

Owners William Gustaf Magnuson and Ulf Anders Strandberg are Swedish, and everything about this austere black, white and yellow restaurant reflects their highly evolved Scandinavian tastes. Strandberg runs the kitchen, and dazzles guests with gravlax and wild rice pancakes topped with smoked salmon, caviar and crème fraîche, filet of beef with Stilton cheese, delicious Swedish potted beef made with capers, pickles and beets and rack of venison with lingonberries. Add the rustic breads, aquavits, house-cured herrings, Swedish cheeses, the excellent wine list and a room filled with fine modern art, and you have what could be the best Scandinavian restaurant in the nation. A lower-priced menu is served in the rear dining room, *The Back Pocket.*

IL FORNAIO ITALIAN 12/20

18051 Von Karman Ave., Irvine 92715
949-261-1444, *Lunch Mon.-Fri., Dinner nightly, $$*

The open kitchen is a delight to watch, as is the bakery just beyond it, which produces the Italian-style breads served here and sold to go. The menu's best items are the roasted salmon with nuggets of potatoes, the rotisserie-roasted chicken, any of the ten or so pizzas and the fresh pastas. There's a good selection of Italian wines and a bar.

JW'S STEAKHOUSE STEAKHOUSE 13/20 

Anaheim Marriott, 700 W. Convention Way, Anaheim 92802
714-750-8000, *Dinner Mon.-Sat., $$$*

JW's high ceilings, 19th-century furniture, classic paintings and numerous connected rooms create an atmosphere of a private mansion. Formerly a fine-dining establishment, it recently converted to a steakhouse. The specialties include a great shrimp cocktail, excellent steaks and prime rib, and a few fresh seafood dishes. The excellent wine list is accompanied by some of the county's best selection of ports, Cognacs and sherries.

KAPPO SUI JAPANESE 13/20 

20070 Santa Ana Ave., Santa Ana Heights 92625
714-429-0141, *Dinner Mon.-Sat., $$*

O.C.'s best Japanese pub doesn't serve much sushi. Instead, the specialty is kappo, little dishes created as a complement for beer and sake. Master chef/owner Shirai-san keeps a small English menu, but the best dishes—grilled fish saikyoyaki, miso-marinated filet mignon and steamed dumplings—are scribbled in Japanese on a blackboard. There's a fine selection of boutique sakes and Japanese beer to mute the noise—which is considerable when the place is full of Japanese businessmen in a celebratory mood.

KITAYAMA JAPANESE 13/20 

101 Bay View Pl., Newport Beach 92660
949-725-0777, *Lunch Mon.-Fri., Dinner nightly, $$*

Kitayama's landscaping is marked by an immaculate garden just outside the ceiling-high glass walls, while inside, traditional Japanese flower arrangements and blond wood set off the Oriental decor. Cooked entrées arrive in a parade of platters, bowls, baskets and boxes, while the sashimi-quality fish is brought to the table in what can best be described as works of art. There is an excellent wine list as well as a full bar.

LA VIE EN ROSE FRENCH 13/20 

240 S. State College Blvd., Brea 92621
714-529-8333, *Lunch Mon.-Fri., Dinner Mon.-Sat., $$$*

This is about as close to a typical Perigord country farmhouse: the half-dozen picturesque dining rooms feature tapestry-covered booths, a bar is located in the turret and a huge stone fireplace dominates the lobby. There's even a small store with pastries and breads as well as some hard-to-get French food items. Hot rabbit pâté in puff pastry is one of the most popular appetizers, while the entrées are led by poached salmon in dill sauce, confit of duckling, and veal sweetbreads on a bed of arugula with a citrus beurre blanc sauce. The wine list offers California, French and Italian selections, many by the glass.

LAFAYETTE FRENCH 13/20 

12353 Garden Grove Blvd., Garden Grove 92843
714-537-7011, *Lunch Mon.-Fri., Dinner Mon.-Sat.,* **$$$**

A

Chef/owner Edmond Sarfati is a traditional French chef with an eternal twinkle in his eye and a mustache big enough to paint a bedroom with, but he is also one who's capable of greatness. His restaurant is a big, dimly lit establishment, where he prepares old chestnuts such as escargots, pâté maison, braised veal and pepper steak. The raison d'être is found in Sarfati's specials: navarin of lamb, confit of goose and classic beef á la bourguignon.

LAS BRISAS MEXICAN/SEAFOOD 11/20

361 Cliff Dr., Laguna Beach 92651
949-497-5434, *Breakfast, Lunch & Dinner daily,* **$**

A

A cliffside restaurant with a smashing view of the beach, Las Brisas has a rose garden and is adjacent to the Laguna Beach Art Museum. But it's the Mexican seafood and the margaritas that keep drawing customers. Best bets for dinner are the seafood brochettes and the pasta Las Brisas, fettuccini tossed with seafood in a tomato-saffron broth.

MAGGIANO'S LITTLE ITALY ITALIAN 12/20

3333 Bristol St., Costa Mesa 92626
714-444-4834, *Lunch & Dinner daily,* **$$**

This recreation of a New York City goombah palace called Guido's, serves huge portions of Southern Italian-inspired dishes in a grandiose dining room filled with red booths and enormous potted ferns. A few dishes, like grilled calamari and steak al forno, are outstanding. A few others, like starchy spaghetti crowned with two NBA-sized meatballs, strike the serious diner as mass-produced and distinctly lacking in Italian soul.

MANDARIN GOURMET CHINESE 11/20

1500 Adams St., Costa Mesa 92626
714-540-1937, *Lunch Mon.-Fri., Dinner nightly,* **$**

VISA MasterCard

Owner Michael Chiang has been preparing Mandarin Chinese delicacies at this location for over 20 years. The menu is huge, but the most popular dishes are the aromatic shrimp, and the Peking duck prepared in the traditional manner. There's a 60-label wine list plus wines by the glass.

MAYUR INDIAN 12/20

2931 E. Coast Hwy., Corona Del Mar 92625
949-675-6622, *Lunch Mon.-Fri., Dinner nightly,* **$$**

A

This is O.C.'s best Indian restaurant, mostly because owner Anju Kapoor serves food that tastes as if it were prepared for an Indian home supper. Ask for dahi wada, an off-menu snack composed of lentil balls in a cucumber-yogurt sauce, and the karahi lamb chops in a yogurt sauce spiked with coriander, ginger, garlic, cumin and cinnamon. The atmosphere is intimate and low key, in marked contrast to most of our Indian dining halls.

McCORMICK & SCHMICK'S SEAFOOD 13/20 

2000 Main St., Irvine 92714
949-756-0505, *Lunch Mon.-Fri., Dinner nightly, $$*

Wood paneling, high ceilings and leaded-glass windows make you feel you're in the Pacific Northwest at this branch of a Portland-based seafood restaurant chain. The fresh seafood choices are mind-boggling. We love the Dungeness crabcakes with spicy jalapeño sauce and, when it's in season, the Copper River salmon. The wine list is extensive, especially among the whites, and the service is friendly and knowledgeable.

MEMPHIS SOUTHERN/SOUL 13/20 

2920 Bristol St., Costa Mesa 92626
714-432-7685, *Lunch & Dinner daily, $$*

This tiny bastion of Cajun and soul-food cooking is located in the Lab, an alternative mall filled with odd shops and interesting places to eat. No one for miles around can match the chicken-and-sausage gumbo, the blackened fish specialties, the peerless fried chicken and the spiced pecan fried chicken salad. The desserts are gooey and rich, and there's always Dixie beer with which to wash it all down. The place is always packed, so plan ahead if you want to drop in.

MORTON'S OF CHICAGO STEAKHOUSE 14/20 

South Coast Plaza Village, 1661 Sunflower Ave., Santa Ana 92704
714-444-4834, *Dinner nightly, $$$*

Morton's bills itself as the great American steakhouse, and we are in no mood to argue. The beautifully marbled hunks of prime aged beef are broiled vertically at temperatures of up to 1500 degrees Fahrenheit, which locks in the natural juices. Terrific smoked salmon makes a great starter, and the hash-browned potatoes are the best anywhere. The service is polished and professional, and the house special dessert, a warm chocolate cake that oozes melted chocolate when cut open, is truly one for the books.

MR. STOX CALIFORNIAN 13/20 

1105 E. Katella Ave., Anaheim 92805
714-634-2994, *Lunch Mon.-Fri., Dinner nightly, $$$*

Unlike many of the hacienda-style restaurants in Orange County, Mr. Stox didn't start out as a ranch house. It was built to be a restaurant in 1968, and its innovative menu and 25,000-bottle wine cellar have been attracting diners ever since. Owners Ron and Chick Marshall are responsible for the wine cellar, but the cuisine comes from chef Scott Raczek, who prepares fine sauces and bakes a variety of colorful breads. Raczek also grows his own herbs. Dishes not to miss include fresh pastas, mesquite-grilled rack of lamb, braised rabbit in brandy-peppercorn sauce and seared ahi tuna.

NATRAJ OF INDIA INDIAN 12/20

2486I Alicia Pkwy., Laguna Beach 92653
949-58I-4200, *Lunch Mon.-Sat., Dinner nightly, Brunch Sun., $*

A

Owner Vijay Khosla provides good food and excellent service in this modest restaurant. We applaud the fresh seafood dishes added to the traditional lamb, chicken and vegetable items that most Northern Indian restaurants feature. Both lunch and Sunday brunch are lavish buffets, with anywhere from ten to fifteen dishes available.

ODESSA AMERICAN 12/20

680 S. Coast Hwy., Laguna Beach 9265I
949-376-8792, *Dinner nightly, $$$*

A

The American South meets classic French at this handsomely appointed restaurant partly owned by Norm Nixon, Debbie Allen and Denzel Washington. Chef Timothy Deab plies his customers with blue crab gumbo, fried chicken, and filet of beef with truffled mashed potatoes and foie gras. (Grandma never cooked this stuff, that's for sure.) Be prepared for a well heeled, elegantly dressed crowd and a sophisticated wine list.

P.F. CHANG'S CHINA BISTRO CHINESE 12/20

II45 Newport Center Dr., Newport Beach 92660
949-759-9007, *Lunch & Dinner daily, $$*

A

A 40-foot long Chinese mural is the first thing that catches the eye, but it's the food that keeps you coming back: good Chinese chicken salad, potstickers, spicy orange peel beef, lemon scallops or chicken in black bean sauce. They offer about 20 wines by the glass.

PASCAL FRENCH 16/20

Plaza Newport, I000 N. Bristol St., Newport Beach 92660
949-752-0I07, *Lunch Mon.-Fri., Dinner Mon.-Sat., $$$*

A

Year after year, this modest mall space wins plaudits from critics. Chef/owner Pascal Olhats hails from Normandy, but his restaurant has a breezy Provençal theme and serves cuisine that is often more than terrific. Sample exquisite Chilean seabass with a thyme crust, amazing rotisserie chicken and pork or grilled rack of lamb. There is also wonderful sautéed foie gras, superb duck confit and tempting lamb salad with apple-walnut dressing. For dessert, try the poached pear with chocolate sauce. Then stop in next door at **Pascal Epicerie**, where Olhats sells fine French cheeses, salads composées and Provençal wines.

THE PLEASANT PEASANT FRENCH 12/20

425I Martingale Way, Newport Beach 92660
949-955-2755, *Lunch Mon.-Fri., Dinner Mon.-Sat., $$*

A

This cheerful café serves top-notch French country dishes at bargain-basement prices. Laurent Ferre trained with the legendary Alain Chapel, and many of his rustic specialties have little touches of greatness: lamb shank Alain Chapel, cooked in a savory veal stock, a peerless goat cheese salad with mesclun greens and walnut dressing, salmon with sorrel sauce and perfect strawberries melba.

PREGO ITALIAN 13/20 

18420 Von Karman Ave., Irvine 92715
949-553-1333, *Lunch Mon.-Fri., Dinner nightly, $$*

An open kitchen with a wood-burning pizza oven is the main attraction at this spare, handsome Tuscan villa, and so is the food, which streams out of chef Alberto Morello's assembly line. Fortunately, it doesn't taste like assembly-line food. Try the superb homemade breadsticks and pizzas. Among the entrées, we're partial to the pork chops done with balsamic vinegar and rosemary, or the thin, squiggly Italian sausages served with spinach, polenta and roasted peppers.

RAMOS HOUSE CAFÉ NEW AMERICAN 12/20

31752 Los Rios St., San Juan Capistrano 92675
949-443-1342, *Breakfast & Lunch, Tues.-Sun., $*

Part of San Juan Capistrano's historic Rios district, this winsome cottage has an oak tree-shaded brick patio and a small weekly-changing menu. For breakfast, try the wonderful blueberry coffeecake or grits with dried cherries, raisins and brown sugar. Nifty lunch dishes include the smoked turkey, jack cheese and wild rice scramble, and basil-cured salmon in a light honey mustard sauce.

THE RITZ CONTINENTAL 13/20 

880 Newport Ctr. Dr., Newport Beach 92660
949-720-1800, *Lunch Mon.-Fri., Dinner Mon.-Sat., $$$*

This Newport Beach dining institution features an incredibly busy bar, three dining rooms including the Wine Cellar, equipped with a massive dining table, the Ritz Brothers Room, notable for cushy black leather booths and the Escoffier Room with its gleaming gold and copper rotisserie. Since 1977, The Ritz has been serving dishes like bouillabaisse, duck with red cabbage and spaetzle and outstanding seafoods. In recent years, owner Hans Prager has modernized the menu, adding rotisserie items and trendy entrées. Longtime chef Guadalupe Camarena, longtime maître d' Peter Jepsen and an experienced staff all make the right moves.

THE RITZ-CARLTON DINING ROOM FRENCH 16/20 

The Ritz-Carlton Laguna Niguel, 33533 Ritz.-Carlton Dr., Dana Pt. 92629
949-240-2000, *Dinner Tues.-Sun., $$$$*

The Dining Room may lack that spectacular ocean view found just steps away in the lobby bar, but then it doesn't really need one: the dining experience here is a world-class adventure all by itself. Alsatian-born chef Ivan Goetz has a way with foie gras, sturgeon, duck, lobster and other luxury comestibles, and his cooking matches that of starred chefs in his home province. In season, try the exquisite partridge with savoy cabbage and Riesling sauce, or any of Goetz' game specialties.

Service is impeccable, and the wine list contains several high-priced international gems. A variety of tasting menus is available with wines to match, for prices that border on stupefying. Still and all, if an elegant splurge appeals to you, The Dining Room is in a class by itself.

SCOTT'S SEAFOOD GRILL AND BAR SEAFOOD 14/20 

3300 Bristol St., Costa Mesa 92626
714-979-2400, *Lunch Mon.-Sat., Dinner nightly, Brunch Sun., $$*

The prices are a bit steep, but there are always seafood-eaters in this beautifully appointed branch of a San Francisco chain. Popular dishes include the baby calamari flash-fried with garlic butter and any number of daily fresh fish specials. There are also plenty of choices for red-meat eaters. Scott's offers a prix-fixe pre-theater menu for those holding tickets to the nearby Orange County Performing Arts Center or South Coast Repertory Theater.

SPLASHES CALIFORNIA/MEDITERRANEAN 11/20

Surf & Sand Hotel, 1555 S. Pacific Coast Hwy.,Laguna Beach 92651
949-497-4477, *Breakfast & Lunch Mon.-Sat., Din. nightly, Brunch Sun., $$*

Splashes is one the prettiest spots along the Laguna Beach coastline, thanks to the Mediterranean decor, the fireplace and the sounds of ocean waves crashing just outside. The menu offers a delightful granola and huevos rancheros at breakfast. Dinners include osso buco with basil fettuccine or salmon with a citrus vinaigrette.

THEE WHITE HOUSE ITALIAN 13/20 

887 S.Anaheim Blvd.,Anaheim 92805
714-772-1381, *Lunch Mon.-Fri., Dinner nightly, $$*

The pillars in front and the white color scheme qualify this ranch house-cum restaurant as a "white house," which may be why owner Bruno Serato chose the double "ee" to avoid confusion with the one in Washington D.C. The interior exudes elegance via the subdued wallpaper and wall lighting sconces. We've enjoyed the pork roast with apricot sauce, the black-and-white lobster ravioli and the grilled swordfish in citrus beurre blanc. The desserts are lavish, and the wine list includes many by the glass.

TROQUET FRENCH/AMERICAN 15/20 

3333 Bristol St., Costa Mesa 92626
714-708-6865, *Lunch & Dinner Mon.-Sat., $$$*

When Tim and Liza Goodell decided to open Troquet, there was much trepidation. Would it measure up to the high standards they'd set at Aubergine, their first restaurant? Now all the questions have been answered, and the result is Orange County's newest and brightest restaurant star, a casual but chic bistro where Tim's cooking is better than ever. Take one bite of his other-worldly lobster strudel, which he layers with country bacon, and you'll be suitably impressed. At lunch, the veal sweetbread club sandwich has to be one of the world's great sandwiches. The dishes that made Goodell successful at

Aubergine, such as veal cheeks, and pear-and-Roquefort salad are served here too. There are also fine homemade breads, appealing wines and cheeses, and highly polished service. This is a remarkable restaurant, one of the very best in the Southland.

TUTTO MARE ITALIAN/SEAFOOD 13/20 

Fashion Island, 545 Newport Ctr. Dr., Newport Beach 92660
949-640-6333, *Lunch Mon.-Sat., Dinner nightly, $$*

With its mahogany-and-glass decor and white tile floors, Tutto Mare looks like it belongs in New York. The menu changes every six months here, but a few dishes always remain, such as the angel hair pasta with prawns, crab and lobster, the grilled prawns with cannelini beans and the spinach-and-egg pasta with sun-dried tomatoes. Both California and Italian wines are available, many by the glass.

21 OCEAN FRONT SEAFOOD 14/20 

2100 W. Ocean Front, Newport Beach 92663
949-675-2566, *Dinner nightly, $$$*

This space has undergone various incarnations, but some things never change, including the black leather booths, the maroon color scheme, the long, mahogany bar and the marvelous ocean view. Chef Tracey Harter carries on the traditional menu in style. Specialties include bouillabaisse, soft shell crabs in season, an outrageously priced, Waverly wafer-crusted abalone and top-notch steaks. The list of boutique California and French wines is lengthy.

TWIN PALMS CALIFORNIAN 12/20

630 Newport Center Dr., Newport Beach 92660
949-721-8288, *Lunch & Dinner daily, Brunch Sun., $$*

This offshoot of the Twin Palms in Pasadena (Cindy Costner, Kevin's ex, is an owner) packs them in for the same reasons its sister restaurant does: a festive indoor-outdoor "town square" design with a floating canvas ceiling, two lively bars, regular live entertainment, and giant rotisseries where whole chickens, legs of lamb and loins of pork turn on the spit. You'll also find an array of pizzas and pastas, along with Asian-accented entrées.

WOLFGANG PUCK CAFÉ CALIFORNIAN 13/20 

3333 Bristol Ave., Costa Mesa 92626
714-546-9653, *Lunch & Dinner daily, $*

A colorful café where the celebrated superchef's pizzas, pastas and Asian-influenced dishes—and sometimes specialties from his native Austria—cost a lot less than at Puck's Spago Beverly Hills. We tend to stick with the egg rolls, the Chinese chicken salad, the rotisserie-roasted chicken and, yes, those famous designer pizzas. **Also in Newport Beach (841 Newport Center Dr., 949-720-9653) and Irvine (55 Fortune Dr., 949-453-9393).**

YAMABUKI JAPANESE 12/20

Disneyland Pacific Hotel, 1717 S.West St., Anaheim 92802
714-999-0990, *Lunch & dinner daily, $$$*

A

The menu is written in both English and Japanese, and features many combination dinners focusing on all the expected traditional Japanese dishes. Sit in a tatami room and order one of the cook-your-own specials, such as shabu shabu, sukiyaki and hibachi-grilled meats and vegetables.

YEN CHING CHINESE 12/20

574 S. Glassell St., Orange 92666
714-997-3300, *Lunch Mon.-Sat., Dinner nightly, $*

A

All the usual Szechwan and Mandarin dishes are here, but the best way to enjoy Yen Ching is to gather some friends, call ahead, give them a price and ask them to create a menu for your party. The Peking duck, a crisp-skinned masterpiece, is one of the best around.

ZOV'S BISTRO MEDITERRANEAN 13/20 

17440 17th St., Tustin 92680
714-838-8855, *Lunch Mon.-Sat., Dinner Wed.-Sat., $*

A

Juggling a busy restaurant and bakery with a popular catering business would be a trial for most mortals, but chef/owner Zov Karamardian makes it look easy. For lunch, we are partial to the golden lentil soup, the lamb sandwich, the chicken breast pita or the rolled roast beef sandwich, most of which deliver a pleasant garlic kick. At dinner, anything with lamb is outstanding, as are the pastas, the Middle Eastern appetizers and the homemade cookies.

AND ALSO...

CLAY OVEN INDIAN

15435 Jeffrey Rd., Irvine 92714
949-552-2851, *Lunch Mon.-Sat., Dinner nightly, Brunch Sun., $*

A

This shopping center restaurant produces some of the best tandoori and Mughlai cooking in the county. They also have outstanding Thanksgiving and Christmas dinners to go, which include tandoori turkey.

EL TORITO GRILL SOUTHWESTERN/MEXICAN

633 Anton Blvd., Costa Mesa 92626
714-662-2672, *Lunch Mon.-Fri., Dinner nightly, Brunch Sun., $*

The excellent Southwestern-Mexican food and service at this upscale spot raises the usual Mexican offerings by several notches. We love their juicy, flavorful carnitas.

McCHARLES HOUSE AMERICAN

335 C St., Tustin 92680
714-731-4063, *Lunch Mon.-Sat, Dinner Thurs.-Sat., $*

A quaint Victorian house sets the stage for this lovely family-run restaurant and tea house, which serves superb soups, salads and sandwiches for lunch. Owner Audrey Heredia uses family recipes for the dinners, which are best eaten on the outside patio under the eucalyptus trees.

PINOT PROVENCE FRENCH/CALIFORNIA

Westin South Coast Plaza Hotel
686 Anton Blvd., Costa Mesa 92626
714-444-5900, *Lunch Mon.-Fri., Dinner nightly, Brunch Sat.-Sun., $$*

As we went to press, Joachem and Christina Splichal were poised to open the latest in their succesful string of Pinot bistros, casual-chic bastions of California-French cuisine. Pinot Provence will feature two patios and three private dining rooms.

SFUZZI COSTA MESA ITALIAN

1870A Harbor Blvd., Costa Mesa 92627
714-548-9500, *Lunch & Dinner daily, $$*

A

This lively outpost of a national chain maintains a high level of cuisine. The flavors tend towards the robust and their strong suit is pizzas and pastas. Check out the daily fresh fish specials.

QUICK BITES

American & Delis

THE COTTAGE

308 N. Pacific Coast Hwy., Laguna Beach 92651
949-494-3023, *Lunch & Dinner daily*

It's a bit like visiting your grandmother's old California bungalow, which might explain why The Cottage has long been one of Laguna's most popular spots for breakfast, with numerous egg dishes, pancakes, French toast and our favorite, corned beef hash with a poached egg. Lunch leans toward burgers and pastas, but dinner can yield some good seafood, fish and chicken dishes.

JERRY'S FAMOUS DELI

3210 Park Center Dr., Costa Mesa 92626
714-662-3354, *Breakfast, Lunch & Dinner daily*

A

This is the closest thing Orange County has to a real New York deli. There are towering sandwiches on rye bread, and huge platters of smoked fish—some at prices which are a lot higher than you might expect. The menu offers 300-plus choices, but we advise avoiding anything too innovative or exotic, for deli's what they do best.

RUBY'S

1 Balboa Pier, Balboa 92661
949-675-7829, *Breakfast, Lunch & Dinner daily*

Ruby's has become a major success story since it began selling hamburgers, fries, cherry Cokes and a 1940s atmosphere from an old bait house on the end of the Balboa pier. The original spot is still going strong and the chain has grown. **Also in Huntington Beach (Huntington Pier, 949-969-7829), Costa Mesa (3333 Bear Ave., 714-662-7829) and Corona del Mar (2305 Pacific Coast Hwy. 949-673-7829).**

Asian

ASIAN DELI — INDONESIAN

320 E. Katella Ave., Orange 92667
714-532-4588, *Lunch & Dinner Tues.-Sun.*

Indonesian food hasn't been prominent in Orange County since a Corona del Mar restaurant shut its doors in the early 1970s, but Fred de Groot, a native of Jakarta, hopes to change that. Here you can try several versions of satay—meat grilled on bamboo skewers—along with Indonesian fried rice, rice noodles, vegetables in peanut sauce and rendang, meat stewed in spicy coconut milk and mashed into rice. There are also several excellent appetizers and many fish dishes.

HA NOI — VIETNAMESE

10528 McFadden Ave., Garden Grove 92643
714-775-1108, *Lunch & Dinner Tues.-Thurs.*
No Cards

Ha Noi specializes in the mild, faintly herbal cooking of northern Vietnam. Stunning barbecued catfish is served under a layer of fresh dill, and there's a delicious shrimp appetizer flavored with vinegar, lime juice and lemon grass. The menu's Vietnamese language section is filled with exotic delicacies.

HANA NO KI — JAPANESE

851 Baker St. B-15, Costa Mesa 92626
714-557-8715, *Lunch & Dinner Mon.-Sat.*

This tiny place doesn't serve sushi, but rather homey, rustic Japanese country-style dishes. Chef Tomohiko Munakato does a mean shime saba (seared white Norwegian mackerel in slices) and a blood-rare beef tenderloin. A list of premium sakes will help you wash everything down.

HUE RENDEZVOUS — VIETNAMESE

15562 Westminster Ave., Westminster 92683
714-775-7192, *Lunch & Dinner daily*
No Cards

This is one of the more unusual Vietnamese restaurants in Little Saigon—or elsewhere for that matter—because it specializes in food from the Hue area of what was Central South Vietnam. Try the Bun Bo Hue, a spicy soup made with thin rice noodles and beef, or the intriguingly named Ram It, a spicy, soft rice flour cake stuffed with both shredded and fried pork.

JAMILLAH GARDEN ISLAMIC CHINESE

2512 Walnut St., Tustin 92680
714-838-3522, *Lunch & Dinner daily*

A well scrubbed café belonging to the Ma family of Taiwan, this restaurant specializes in the Islamic cuisine of China. Any meal's centerpiece is sze ma da bing, a puffy, sesame-studded flatbread. Enjoy delicious lamb stew, terrific steamed dumplings and the seasonally available kan shim tsai, a hollow, reedy green.

Bakery-Cafés

CORNER BAKERY

3333 Bristol St., South Coast Plaza, Costa Mesa 92626
714-546-1555, *Breakfast, Lunch & Dinner daily*

A

A branch of a Chicago chain, this colorful bakery-café bakes 31 varieties of bread, and serves terrific sandwiches (ham on pretzel ficelle!), pizzas and focaccias, not to mention scores of fresh-baked pastries and coffee drinks to sip with them. **Also in Irvine (949-399-0999.)**

Cafés

CAFÉ ZINC

350 Ocean Ave., Laguna Beach 92651
949-494-6302, *Breakfast & Lunch daily*
No Cards

Not the biggest place in town, but that doesn't keep regulars from showing up for the café au lait or caffè latte, the muffins, scones or eggs for breakfast, or the small pizzas and healthy sandwiches for lunch. It's usually crowded but the food is worth the wait.

PLUMS CAFÉ & CATERING

369 E. 17th St., Costa Mesa 92627
714-548-PLUMS, *Breakfast & Lunch daily*

A

Portland native Kim Jorgenson stocks the shelves with goodies from the Pacific Northwest, everything from alder wood-smoked salmon to fudge made by monks in Amity, Oregon. Plums' breakfasts are sublime: hazelnut-honey pancakes with marionberry compote, shirred eggs with lusty pepper-bacon cured in Pendleton, Oregon. Lunches are good too, especially the confetti meatloaf. Take home some lemon bars and chocolate-dipped macaroons.

TOPAZ CAFÉ

Bowers Museum, 2002 N. Main St., Santa Ana 92701
714-835-2002, *Lunch Tues.-Sat., Dinner Thurs.*

A

This has become one of the best spots in Santa Ana for lunch, thanks to a revived and remodeled Bower's Museum, an excellent California-style menu and a Southwestern motif where the colors seem to change every hour as the sun passes over the skylights. Sweet corn tamales with grilled shrimp or chicken, salsa and sour cream are favorites.

Italian

RENATA'S CAFFÉ ITALIANO

227 E. Chapman Ave., Orange 92666
714-771-4740, *Lunch & Dinner daily*

A tiny place that draws a steady crowd of loyal customers eager to sample Renata Cerchiari's dishes, especially the rigatoni Renata, served in a cream sauce with sausage and sage, and the sea bass Italiano. In good weather, the best seats are on the patio.

ROMA D'ITALIA

611 El Camino Real, Tustin 92680
714-544-0273, *Lunch & Dinner daily*

This family-owned restaurant has been dishing out excellent pastas and pizzas for years at its Tustin home base. It's a fun place, especially for families with children, but that, of course, doesn't do much for the noise level. The food is worth it, especially the chicken-filled tortellini Gustavo served with creamy tomato sauce and diced mushrooms and chicken.

Mexican, Latin American & Southwestern

ANITA'S SOUTHWESTERN

600 S. Harbor Blvd., Fullerton 92632
714-525-0977, *Breakfast, Lunch & Dinner daily*

This is all-the-way New Mexican food. Lorie and Michael Tellez even import their chiles from Las Cruces, and their sopaipillas are the true, fluffy variety. Biggest sellers are the carne adobada with pork, marinated for 24 hours in a New Mexican chile sauce, or sopaipillas stuffed with pork and a green chile sauce.

EL MARIACHI MEXICAN

650 N. Tustin Ave., Orange 92667
714-532-4001, *Lunch & Dinner daily*

The Mariachi Nochistlan musicians play during the week with various Latin bands on hand for the weekends, when things really hum. The food's good too, especially the fajitas and the siete mares, a tomato-based soup with scampi-style shrimp. The deep booths and large tables are very popular with the customers, many of whom have celebrated anniversaries and weddings here for years.

FELIX CONTINENTAL CAFÉ CUBAN

36 Plaza Sq., Orange 92666
714-633-5842, *Breakfast, Lunch & Dinner daily*

Felix's serves Cuban dishes straight from the old days in Havana. Try the medianoche sandwich with roast pork, ham, Swiss cheese and mustard for lunch or the aporreado de Ternera, shredded veal in a Cuban sauce. But we like Felix best at breakfast with coffee, the morning paper and one of the menu's many omelets.

TACO LOCO MEXICAN

640 S. Pacific Coast Hwy., Laguna Beach 92651
949-497-1635, *Lunch & Dinner daily*

A

It might look like just a slightly extended taco stand, but the menu includes a selection of seafoods that rivals any Mexican restaurant in town. Try the blackened mushrooms and sautéed ahi tuna on blue corn tortillas, the fresh lobster, the mahi-mahi, or the mushroom-tofu burger that even meat eaters like. The tacos come with fresh guacamole.

TACO MESA MEXICAN

3533 E. Chapman Ave., Orange 92666
714-633-3922, *Lunch & Dinner daily*
No Cards

From the outside, this is a disarmingly simple storefront, but it serves Orange County's best low-priced Mexican food. Tortas come on yeasty homemade rolls. The steamed pork, blackened calamari tacos and burritos come with great Mexican rice, hearty whole beans and homemade tortillas. Amazingly, nothing is more than $6.

TORTILLA FLATS MEXICAN

1740 S. Pacific Coast Hwy., Laguna Beach 92651
949-494-6588, *Lunch & Dinner daily, Brunch Sun.*

This place has been a Laguna Beach institution since 1949, and the crowds are still coming—especially on Taco Tuesday when tacos are 50-cents each in the upstairs cantina. Big eaters might tackle the Tortilla Flats special with chicken, meat or green corn tamales, beef or chicken enchiladas, chile relleno, rice and beans. Sunday brunch can be a blast with margaritas like the ones served here. An outdoor patio offers a view of the ocean. **Also in Mission Viejo (27792 Vista del Lago, 714-830-9980).**

Pizza

BJ'S CHICAGO PIZZERIA

106 Main St., Newport Beach 92661
949-675-7560, *Lunch & Dinner daily*

Deep-dish pizza is the specialty of the house. Try BJ's Favorite, topped with just about everything. BJ's also features homemade pastas, sandwiches and salads. **Also in Laguna Beach (280 S. Coast Hwy, 714-494-0662) and Huntington Beach (200 Main St. 714-374-2224).**

CALIFORNIA PIZZA KITCHEN

2800 N. Main St., Santa Ana 92701
714-479-0604, *Lunch & Dinner daily*

A

The barbecue chicken pizza is still the most popular item at this chain of black- yellow- and white-tiled restaurants. Pastas and salads are served here too. **Also in Mission Viejo (25513 Marguerite Pkwy., 714-951-5026), Irvine (2957 Michaelson Dr.,**

714-975-1585), Laguna Hills (24155 Laguna Hills Mall, 714-458-9600) and Newport Beach (1151 Newport Center Dr., 714-759-5543).

CHICAGO PIZZA & PASTA

4533 Campus Dr., Irvine 92715
949-854-3000, *Lunch & Dinner daily*

Both deep-dish and crispy thin crust pizzas are served here, as well as pastas, Italian beef sandwiches and salads. Try the deep-dish special, featuring sausage, onions, mushrooms and green peppers.

Seafood

THE CRAB COOKER

2200 Newport Blvd., Newport Beach 92663
949-673-0100, *Lunch & Dinner daily*
No Cards

How good is a 46-year-old seafood restaurant that uses paper plates? Good enough to have lines of customers waiting to get in, and to have once told President Nixon he'd have to wait his turn like everyone else. OK, so it isn't fancy, but the fish is pretty good, the Manhattan chowder is legendary and the fish market is one of the best around. **Also in Tustin (17260 E. 17th St., 714-573-1077).**

Theme Restaurants

HARD ROCK CAFÉ ROCK 'N ROLL

451 Newport Center Dr., Newport Beach 92663
949-640-8844, *Lunch & Dinner daily*

See review in "L.A. AREA—Quick Bites"

PLANET HOLLYWOOD MOVIE'S

South Coast Plaza, 1641 Sunflower Ave., Costa Mesa 92626
714-668-7585, *Lunch & Dinner daily*

A

See review in "L.A. AREA—Quick Bites"

RAINFOREST CAFÉ JUNGLE

3333 Bristol St., Costa Mesa 92626
714-424-9200., *Lunch & Dinner daily, $$*

This theme restaurant goes Planet Hollywood one better through the use of animatronic jungle creatures, artificial mist and rain and the slickest decor this side of Disneyland's *Pirates of the Caribbean*. The food is beside the point. You'll nosh on enormous portions of kid-friendly fare: salads, sandwiches, pasta, entrées and gooey desserts, most of which have cutesy names that are supposed to make you think about your favorite jungle.

NAME ____________________

ADDRESS ____________________

CITY ____________________ STATE ________ ZIP ________

COUNTRY ____________________

PHONE ( ) – ____________________

The **Gayot/GaultMillau** series of guidebooks reflects your demand for insightful, incisive reporting on the best that the world's most exciting destinations have to offer. To help us make our books even better, please take a moment to fill out this anonymous (if you wish) questionnaire, and return it to:

GaultMillau, Inc.
P.O. Box 361144
Los Angeles, CA 90036;
Fax: (323) 936-2883.

1. How did you hear about the Gayot guides? Please specify: bookstore, newspaper, magazine, radio, friends or other. *(Please turn)*

2. Please list in order of preference the cities or countries which you would like to see Gayot cover.

3. Do you refer to the Gayot guides for your own city, or only when traveling?

A. ❐ Travels B. ❐ Own City C. ❐ Both

4. Please list by order of preference the three features you like best about the Gayot guides.

A. ....

B. ....

C. ....

5. What are the features, if any, you dislike about the Gayot guides?

6. Please list any features that you would like to see added to the Gayot guides.

7. If you use other guides besides Gayot, please list below.

8. Please list the features you like best about your favorite guidebook serie if it is not Gayot/GaultMillau.

A. ....

B. ....

C. ....

9. How many trips do you make per year, for either business or pleasure?

Business: International ....   Domestic ....

Pleasure: International ....   Domestic.........................

10. Please check the category that reflects your annual household income

❒ $20,000–$39,000   ❒ $40,000–$59,000

❒ $60,000–$79,000   ❒ $80,000–$99,000

❒ $100,000–$120,000   ❒ Other *(please specify)* ....

11. If you have any comments on the Gayot guides in general, please list them in the space below.

12. If you would like to recommend specific establishments, please don't hesitate to list them:

Name   ***City***   ***Phone***

13. Do you often/sometimes use the Internet to buy goods & services?

❒ Yes ❒ No   If so, what sorts of products?

We thank you for your interest in the Gayot guides, and we welcome your remarks and recommendations about restaurants, hotels, nightlife, shops, services and so on.

Palm Springs

PALM SPRINGS

For visitors, Palm Springs is a desert playground with clear skies, balmy weather and an endless variety of outdoor activities. When we refer to Palm Springs, we actually mean a good-sized chunk of the Coachella Valley, including the towns of **Cathedral City**, **Rancho Mirage**, **Palm Desert**, **Indian Wells**, **La Quinta** and **Desert Hot Springs**. We're happy to report, that the selection—and quality—of the restaurants in the area has improved greatly since the last edition of this book.

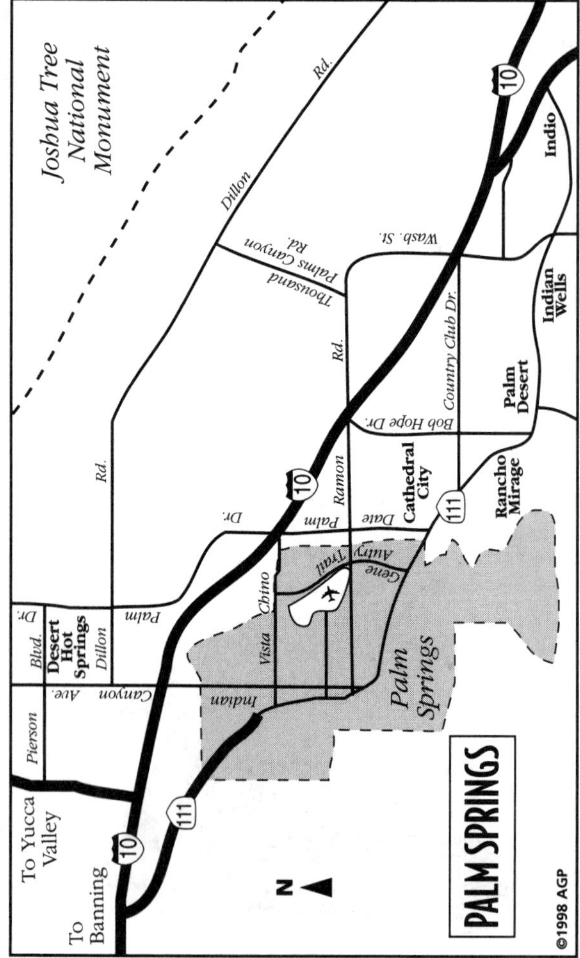

DINING

CUISTOT CALIFORNIAN/FRENCH 14/20 

73111 El Paseo, Palm Desert 92260
760-340-1000, *Lunch Tues.-Sat., Dinner Tues.-Sun., Closed Summer, $$$$*

Chef Bernard Dervieux creates consistently innovative dishes in an extended storefront, with a noisy dining room on one side and a quiet dining room on the other. By desert standards, the menu is downright audacious. The appetizers dash madly from tuna sashimi with a daikon and napa cabbage salad, to salmon cured with lemon, herbs and olive oil. Main courses are similarly eclectic: Chinese-style duck in a mango-Madeira-ginger sauce and roasted squab with asparagus tips in a white-wine-morel sauce.

THE DINING ROOM FRENCH/MEDITERRANEAN 15/20 

The Ritz-Carlton Hotel, 68900 Frank Sinatra Dr., Rancho Mirage 92270
760-321-8282, *Dinner Tues.-Sun., $$$*

Just as the name implies, the atmosphere is refined, and so is the service. A throwback to a time when impeccable manners were commonplace and dining out an event in and of itself, the Dining Room is sure to please those who appreciate tradition. The menu features classic dishes with creative touches. We've enjoyed the salad of upland watercress and goat cheese with figs, the grilled John Dory and the vegetable bouillabaisse provençal. There are always tasty low-fat spa-cuisine dishes. A string quartet often plays, further making dining here a special occasion.

JILLIAN'S CONTINENTAL 14/20 

74 155 El Paseo, Palm Desert 92260
760-776-8242, *Dinner nightly, $$$$*

In contrast to most desert restaurants, this is one where guests can dress to the nines and not feel out of place. Housed in an historic 1946 hacienda, Jillian's is richly decorated with old world art, tapestry-covered chairs and antiques. An outdoor courtyard, misted for comfort in summer and heated for cool evenings in winter, is a romantic spot for dining under the stars. Owner and chef Jay Trubee combines dishes from Northern Italy and Southern France with America's Southwest and eastern seaboard. The Lake Superior whitefish on a bed of spinach and mashed potatoes topped with a mustard sauce is a favorite. The wine list features all that's trendy now.

LAS CASUELAS NUEVAS MEXICAN 10/20

70050 Hwy. 111, Rancho Mirage 92270
760-328-8844, *Lunch Mon.-Sat., Dinner nightly, Brunch Sun., $*

Regulars call it Las Cas. And there are lots of regulars. In fact, on any weekend evening, expect to wait for a table in one of the dining rooms or flower-filled patios of this hacienda-style eatery. Not to worry. They'll keep you busy with muy grande margaritas and chips. Chef Narciso Dorado has made sure that all of the Mexican standards—from chimichangas to quesadillas—are well represented here. The atmosphere and food will satisfy any die-hard Mexican food fanatic.

LAS CASUELAS - THE ORIGINAL MEXICAN 10/20

368 N. Palm Canyon Dr., Palm Springs 92262
760-325-3213, *Breakfast, Lunch & Dinner daily, $*

Tourists may flock to the more glamorous Nuevas branch, but this is the original. It doesn't look like much, but the small kitchen turns out respectable Mexican home cooking with an emphasis on such Cal-Mex standards as enchiladas, burritos, tostadas and tacos. It's all as tasty and satisfying as it is simple and inexpensive—a Palm Springs institution undoubtedly worth a visit.

LE ST. GERMAIN FRENCH/CALIF. 12/20

74-985 Highway 111, Indian Wells 92210
760-773-6511, *Dinner nightly, $$*

A

An offshoot of Le Vallauris, one of the desert's first good French restaurants, this charming spot offers French bistro fare with California flair. Chef Francisco De La Torre painstakingly prepares each entrée with a perfectionist's attitude. We've found the sautéed Mexican seabass on a bed of spinach and mashed potatoes particularly flavorful. Even if you think you don't have room for dessert, try the chocolate-Grand Marnier soufflé.

LE VALLAURIS FRENCH 12/20

385 W. Tahquitz-McCallum Way, Palm Springs 92262
760-325-5059, *Lunch & Dinner daily, $$$*

A

A favorite with the retired set, this attractive and formal dining room features attentive, professional service and a daily-changing blackboard menu. Expect to find such French standards as onion soup, escargots and spinach salad. We applaud such contemporary dishes as the peppery beef filet with sesame sauce. The wine list is as impressive as the sumptuous setting.

THE NEST CONTINENTAL 11/20

75188 Hwy. 111, Indian Wells 92210
760-346-2314, *Dinner nightly, $$*

A

This high energy bistro offers an eclectic menu of Italian and French dishes with some Swiss specialties thrown in. The kitchen seems most comfortable with the Italian dishes, particularly the house specialty of cannelloni stuffed with veal and spinach. Fresh fish, generally prepared meunière, is also a good bet, and all the portions are ample. Watch for celebrities in the piano bar.

OTANI GARDEN RESTAURANT JAPANESE 13/20

266 Avenida Caballeros, Palm Springs 92262
760-327-6700, *Lunch Mon.-Fri., Dinner nightly, Brunch Sun., $$$*

A

You can pretend you're in a shogun's palace at this ornate Japanese restaurant. Order from both the yakitori and teppanyaki menus. Along with all the usual tempura items are tempura calamari, jumbo clams and a Japanese-style french fry. The yakitoris alone—grilled skewers of tiny quail eggs wrapped in bacon, chicken chunks interspersed with green onions, beef intertwined with asparagus—are worth a visit.

PALOMINO EURO-BISTRO MEDITERRANEAN 12/20

73-101 Hwy. 111, Palm Desert 92262
760-773-9091, *Dinner nightly, $$*

This trendy, upscale place has plenty of polished hardwood, hand-blown Italian glass and marble, and copies of Matisse paintings, but it doesn't charge upscale prices. Try the spit-roasted garlic chicken basted in extra-virgin olive oil with fresh rosemary, and the oak-grilled salmon with artichoke heart tartar sauce. The house sparkling wine is from Iron Horse with a Palomino label.

PATRICIA AT CUNARD'S FRENCH/CONTINENTAL 13/20 

78045 Calle Cadiz, La Quinta 92253
760-564-4443, *Dinner nightly, Closed Summer, $$$$*

Located in a courtly estate once belonging to photographer Margaret Mead Maddick, Patricia at Cunard's is a place from a bygone era. Dress for dinner and choose one of the five intimate dining areas complete with blazing fireplaces and the sound of the babbling brook outside. Chef Didier Tsirony prepares each entrée with the highest standards and the staff caters to all guests as if they were the only guests. Among our favorite dishes are the crab cakes with jicima salad, the grilled salmon cutlets with caviar, lemon-pepper fettuccini and the delicate peach ravioli dessert. This is cuisine with one foot in the past and one in the present; it's well prepared—and expensive.

RISTORANTE MAMMA GINA ITALIAN 11/20

73705 El Paseo, Palm Desert 92260
760-568-9898, *Lunch Mon.-Sat., Dinner nightly, $$*

Mamma Gina is a branch of a restaurant in Florence, Italy. No surprise, then, that the kitchen turns out authentic homemade pastas and such Tuscan specialties as deep-fried mozzarella, spinach sautéed in the Florentine manner (with lots of garlic), deep-fried artichokes, air-dried beef from the village of Valtellina, squid ink-blackened ravioli stuffed with lobster, marrow-filled osso buco in a rich meat sauce and, of course, bistecca alla fiorentina. The gelato, tiramisu and all the other desserts are made on the premises, and the wine list has more than 150 California and Italian labels. **Also in Newport Beach.**

RUTH'S CHRIS STEAK HOUSE STEAKHOUSE 13/20 

74040 Hwy. 111, Palm Desert 92260
760-779-1998, *Dinner nightly, $$$*

See entry in L.A. AREA—Dining.

SHAME ON THE MOON CONTINENTAL/CALIF. 12/20

69550 Frank Sinatra Dr., Cathedral City 92234
760-324-5515, *Dinner nightly, $*

A small, attractively decorated storefront in Cathedral City, Shame on the Moon serves California-tinged Continental cuisine to a hip and trendy crowd. The food is functional, simple and tasty, with such dishes as fettuccini carbonara, sauteed calf's liver with apple smoked bacon strips, pecan-crusted breast of chicken and fresh fish daily.

AND ALSO...

MARIO'S RISTORANTE ITALIANO ITALIAN

73-399 El Paseo, Palm Desert 92260
760-346-0584, *Dinner nightly, $$*

A little Tosca with your pasta? The staff sing operatic arias and foot-tapping show tunes while you dine on Northern Italian specialties. Mario and Edalyn Lalli recently moved their restaurant to this new location from its original site in La Quinta.

SCHATZI'S GRILL GERMAN

51-230 Eisenhower Dr., La Quinta 92253
760-564-0850, *Lunch & Dinner daily, $$*

At this family-friendly spot, Chef Monika Batzler whips up such hearty German standards as Bratwurstteller; a combination of three different charbroiled sausages served with warm potato salad and sauerkraut, and sauerbraten, pot roast marinated in red wine and vinegar.

QUICK BITES

American

DAILY GRILL

73061 El Paseo, Palm Desert
760-779-9911, *Lunch & Dinner daily, Brunch Sun.*

A branch of the L.A. chain that's a lower-priced spin-off of The Grill in Beverly Hills, this plain-and-simple (but *stylishly* plain-and-simple) spot serves good burgers and Caesar salad, grilled fish and chicken, and downhome apple pie and rice pudding for dessert.

Cafés

NAPA TAPAS

73-900 El Paseo, Palm Desert 92262
760-773-3436, *Lunch & Dinner daily*

This old-family European bar/bistro reeks of good times perhaps because they offer guests a complimentary drink. Take a sip of the Kruder family's barrel-select red wine or the sangría pamplona before digging into the spicy Spanish potato stew with sausages. The Hungarian gypsy goulash is also memorable. From 9 p.m. to 11 p.m., the food prices are 30% off.

Coffee Shops & Diners

BILLY REED'S

1800 N. Palm Canyon Dr., Palm Springs 92262
760-325-1946, Breakfast, Lunch & Dinner daily

In a town filled with American coffee shops, Billy Reed's may be the most upscale—and perhaps the most popular. There's always a wait for a table at this massive restaurant, where you'll find some of the most consistently good plates of roast chicken, meatloaf, baked fish and thick sandwiches in the desert. The cinnamon-pecan rolls are gargantuan and the Boston cream pie is served with hot fudge.

ELMER'S PANCAKE & STEAK HOUSE

1030 E. Palm Canyon Dr., Palm Springs 92262
760-327-8419, *Breakfast, Lunch & Dinner daily*

A

An old-fashioned spot for a generous and inexpensive home-cooked breakfasts. The specialty of the house is the German pancake, but fans agree that the date-nut pancakes, blueberry waffles, Oregon cheese blintzes and the specialty omelets are all worth the wait.

LOUISE'S PANTRY

124 S. Palm Canyon Dr., Palm Springs 92262
760-325-5124, *Breakfast, Lunch & Dinner daily*

This coffee shop dishes up good cooking like Mom used to make. As a matter of fact, there's a fleet of Moms serving you and making sure you clean your plate. You get reliable, simple food, all presented in an honest-but-uninspiring environment. Expect a long line in front on Saturday and Sunday mornings.

THE WHEEL INN

I-10, Main St. Exit, Cabazon 92262
909-849-7012, *Open daily 24 hours*

A

There's hardly a Palm Springs tourist who hasn't spotted the dinosaurs along Interstate 10 in Cabazon. They were built by Claude Bell, owner of this truck stop that stands slightly to the left of them. Inside, you'll find all the necessary amenities of truck-stop life: a tool section, a display of turquoise belt buckles, a great country-western jukebox, sassy waitresses and relentlessly filling food. The biscuits and gravy can't be beat on any interstate, and the fruit pies are awesome.

Italian & Pizza

DEVANE'S

80-755 Hwy. 111, Indio 92201
760-342-5009, *Lunch & Dinner Tues.-Sun.*

Owner/actor William Devane and his wife Eugenie refer to the menu selections as Jersey Italian. Hustling and bustling at all hours, this is a popular place for such casual dishes as pasta fagliola, calamari fritti, chopped salads and pizzas.

STRING CHEESE ITALIAN CAFÉ

44250 Town Center Way, Palm Desert 92260
760-773-3372, *Lunch and dinner daily*

For a relaxing lunch or dinner on a shoestring, this tiny pastaria tucked away in a shopping center serves authentic Northern Italian dishes with a healthy twist. Any dish can be made without oil or cheese. The soups, pastas and breads are made from scratch from the owner's personal family recipes. Dine outside on the patio—it's less cramped.

Our Pricing System

In our DINING and AND ALSO...reviews, we code restaurant prices using one to four dollar signs. **Prices reflect the average cost of dinner for one person including appetizer, entrée, dessert, coffee, tax and tip. Not included is wine or other beverages, which vary greatly in price.** Restaurants often change their menus—and their menu prices. Forgive us if a restaurant is more expensive when you visit it.

$ = under $20
$$ = under $35
$$$ = under $50
$$$$ = $50 & up

Symbols

All credit cards taken................................ A
Visa................................
MasterCard................................
American Express................................
Diners Club................................
Discover................................
Reservations suggested................................
Valet parking................................
Ties suggested................................
Romantic setting................................
Heart-healthy dishes................................
View................................
Outdoor dining................................

San Diego

SAN DIEGO

Despite the inevitable problems of urban sprawl, San Diego remains a breathtakingly beautiful spot, a spare, brush-dotted crust of broad beaches and grand coastal cliffs that give way to the wonderfully renewed downtown, the posh neighborhoods of La Jolla to the north, the mountains, which occasionally don ivory mantles of snow, to the east, and Tijuana and all of Mexico to the south. The beach and sky suffice for many, but cultural and sports activities abound. And increasingly, we're finding more and more good places to grab a quick bite, to savor exotic ethnic dishes or to dine in the grand manner.

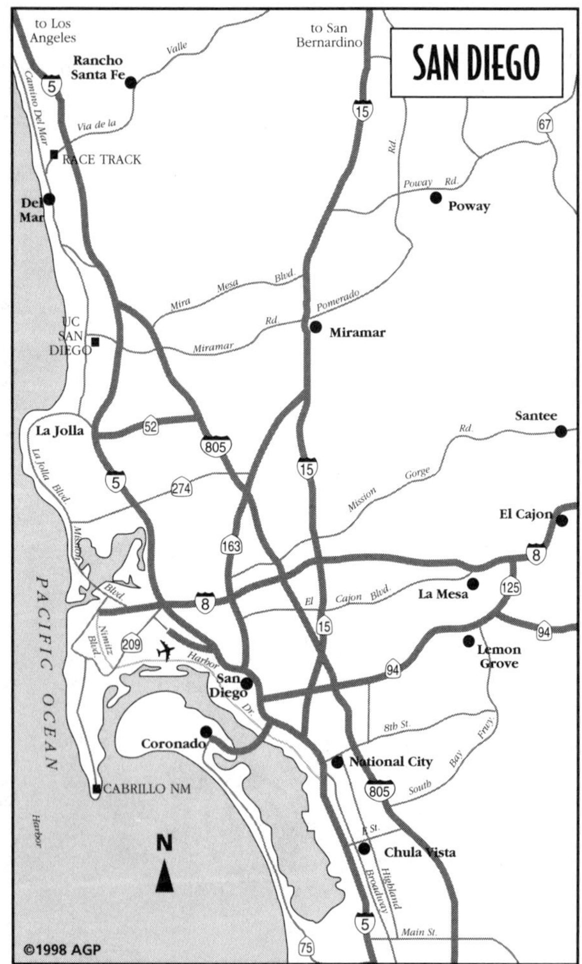

DINING

AZZURA POINT — NEW AMERICAN — 15/20 

Loews Coronado Bay Resort, Coronado 92118
619-424-6400, *Dinner nightly, $$$*

Newly remodeled with a post-modern decor that draws the eye up dramatic columns and down flowing draperies, this handsome room continues to dazzle with its unrivaled views of the San Diego Bay, the Coronado Bridge and the city skyline. Executive Chef James Boyce devises seasonal menus that use choice local produce, as well as seafood and meats produced around the globe. Our favorites include crab tortellini with sage and brown butter, delicate oysters in an iced sake-ginger sauce, and a wildly unusual pairing of veal tenderloin and skate wing with red wine risotto.

THE BELGIAN LION — FRENCH — 14/20 

2265 Bacon St., Ocean Beach 92106
619-223-2700, *Dinner Thurs.-Sat., $$$*

The Belgian Lion is a civilized dining destination in an otherwise funky beach neighborhood, and its loyal clientele regards itself as family. Patriarch Don Coulon and matriarch Arlene continue to wield the ladles and sauté pans in the kitchen, while their Paris-trained daughter, Michelle, prepares the pastries. The menu features both traditional French specialties and contemporary dishes, and is revered for such standing items as the salmon in sorrel sauce and the chicken Normande. The wine list features California vintages; there are frequent Sunday night wine dinners.

BELLEFLEUR — CALIFORNIAN/MEDITERRANEAN — 12/20

5610 Paseo Del Norte, Carlsbad 92008
Lunch & Dinner daily, $$

This dramatic new restaurant shares the premises of a Tuscan-style villa with a small working winery that already has won notice for its Sauvignon Blanc, Chardonnay and Pinot Noir. Chef Thomas Atkins fuses the cuisines of the Southwest, California and the Mediterranean into a hearty, wine-country-style menu. We recommend the shrimp tostadas, the grilled salmon in grape leaves and the pork chops sauced with Bellefleur's unique apple wine.

BLUE POINT — COASTAL CUISINE/SEAFOOD — 12/20

565 Fifth Ave., Gaslamp Quarter 92101
619-233-6623, *Lunch Mon.-Fri., Dinner nightly, $$*

Chef Darrell Henderlite has fun with a menu that ranges as far afield as a martini that marries two vodkas, salsa and an oyster, to pork tenderloin with Thai-inspired sweet-hot sauce, grilled ahi with ginger butter, nut-crusted calamari steak and lamb chops with a Cabernet Sauvignon sauce. The restaurant's classy setting takes advantage of a prime Gaslamp Quarter corner.

CAFÉ JAPENGO PACIFIC RIM 12/20

8960 University Centre Ln., La Jolla 92037
619-450-3355, *Lunch Mon.-Fri., Dinner nightly, $$*

The cuisine has Japanese overtones thanks to the kitchen wizardry of Chef Amiko Gubbins. Besides a hot bar scene and sushi turned out by an imaginative team of sushi pros, Japengo offers a wide-ranging menu. We're partial to the savory wok-toss of noodles with shellfish and peanut sauce, the roasted duck with tortillas, the fresh seafood dishes and the stir-fry of chicken with mushrooms.

CILANTROS SOUTHWESTERN 10/20

3702 Via de la Valle (near I-5), Del Mar 92014
619-259-8777, *Lunch and Dinner daily, Brunch Sun., $$*

Customers howled when this hip place experimented with a new menu. The old menu was revived in a hurry, which means you can still savor their seafood enchiladas smothered in a yellow tomato sauce, and their fire-roasted pork with sweet potato hash and apricot-chile sauce.

EL BIZCOCHO FRENCH 14/20

Rancho Bernardo Inn, 17550 Bernardo Oaks Dr., Rancho Bernardo 92128
619-487-1611, *Dinner nightly, Brunch Sun., $$$*

"El bizcocho" is a tough Spanish biscuit once carried by sailors on long journeys. It's an ironic name for a dining room as elegant as this one. Located in the posh Rancho Bernardo Inn resort, the restaurant offers dining in a French mood. The sautéed foie gras with pears makes us swoon, as does the wine list, which is comprehensive but pricey. Seasonal specialties might include pan-roasted pheasant breast stuffed with goat cheese and pine nuts, and grilled Norwegian salmon with portobello mushrooms, while you'll always find such El Bizcocho "classics" as chateaubriand for two, carved at tableside.

EMERALD SEAFOOD RESTAURANT CHINESE 12/20

3709 Convoy St., Kearny Mesa 92111
619-565-6888, *Lunch & Dinner daily, $$*

We love the cooking at this temple of Chinese haute cuisine, but we sure wish the place were better maintained. We're particularly partial to the dim sum, especially the shrimp pearl balls and the meat-stuffed tofu skins. In the evening, we enjoy the fresh seafood cooked in the manner of Canton, and the savory Peking Duck.

THE FISH MARKET SEAFOOD 12/20

750 N. Harbor Dr., Downtown 92101
619-232-3474, *Lunch & Dinner daily, $$-$$$*

People come here more for the spectacular view than for the food. But in the casual, less expensive downstairs restaurant, you can get a good honest piece of fish and sushi, or buy fresh fish to go. Upstairs, **Top of the Market** is more formal and more (sometimes too) expensive, but the Dungeness crab cocktail, briny oysters and grilled swordfish are delicious. Both floors offer great views of San Diego Bay.

FRENCH MARKET GRILLE FRENCH 12/20

15717 Bernardo Heights Pkwy., Rancho Bernardo 92128
619-485-8053, *Lunch & Dinner daily, Breakfast Sun., $$*

Veteran hotelier Patrick Halcewicz and Chef Herve Glin teamed to create one of the most delightful French restaurants in the North County region. We appreciate that the menu encompasses French classics such as boeuf bourguignon and coq au vin, along with updated dishes like lamb leg paired with artichoke ravioli, and halibut sauced with fennel essence. And while we enjoy the freshly baked specialty breads, we always save room for the crèpes Suzette.

GEORGE'S AT THE COVE CALIFORNIAN 14/20

1250 Prospect St.. La Jolla 92037
619-454-4244. *Lunch & Dinner daily, $$$*

A La Jolla mainstay, George's offers serious dining on the first floor, heavy flirting in the second floor bar, and on the rooftop terrace, inexpensive open-air dining in full view of glorious La Jolla Cove. Chef Scott Meskan presents ever-changing California cuisine epitomized by anise seed-dusted Arctic char, potato-encrusted whitefish and marinated rack of lamb with black olive-mashed potatoes.

HUMPHREY'S BY THE BAY CALIFORNIAN 12/20

2241 Shelter Island Dr., Shelter Island 92106
619-224-3577, *Breakfast, Lunch & Dinner daily, $$*

Chef Jim Hill, having honed his skills at various leading San Diego eateries, has created a new "coastal" menu for this once-dumpy, now beautifully redecorated establishment, which boasts a separate concert venue that hosts hot names in entertainment. The marinated seafood "margarita" arrives in an oversized cocktail glass and makes a good prelude to the baseball-cut sirloin in a Cabernet Sauvignon sauce, or the swordfish in an herby beurre blanc.

LA FONDA MEXICAN 12/20

5752 La Jolla Blvd., La Jolla 92037
619-456-7171, *Lunch and Dinner Tues.-Sun., $$*

Operated by the same family that for years has earned enthusiastic raves from Tijuanans at that city's La Fonda Roberto's, this cozy La Jolla restaurant avoids the clichés of Cal-Mex cuisine and serves instead a fine array of regional Mexican dishes. We could make a meal of the chalupitas poblanas, but this appetizer only opens a dinner that might include cactus salad, spiced lamb cooked in banana leaves and crêpes stuffed with squash blossoms.

LA VACHE & CO. FRENCH 12/20

420 Robinson Ave., Hillcrest 92103
619-295-0214, *Lunch & Dinner daily, $$*

Owner Phillipe Beltran has created a relaxed atmosphere in this quaint little restaurant decorated with homey knick-knacks and lush floral arrangements. Choose from an array of hearty bistro dishes: baked brie served over grilled bread or a shrimp and aïoli salad to start, followed by boeuf bourguignon or the fisherman's casserole, a melange of fresh salmon, seabass and shrimp.

LAUREL FRENCH/CONTEMPORARY 13/20 

505 Laurel St., Midtown 92103
619-239-2222, *Dinner nightly, $$$*

San Diego has seen few restaurant successes so enduring as this venture by Chef Douglas Organ and partner/wine expert Gary Parker, who also run the WineSellar & Brasserie. Located near the main entrance to Balboa Park, this sophisticated restaurant serves a daily-changing menu of imaginative starters, elegant entrées and whimsical desserts. We recommend the shellfish soup, the braised lamb shanks with olive purée, the Provençal-style clay-pot-roasted chicken, and the grilled New York steak with mustard sauce and parsley-leek fondue. They bake their own bread and offer pre- and post-theater dining.

THE MARINE ROOM FRENCH/CONTEMPORARY 15/20 

La Jolla Shores, 2000 Spindrift Dr., La Jolla 92037
619-459-7222, *Lunch Mon.-Sat., Dinner nightly, $$$*

So close to the ocean that the waves crash just under the windows, the Marine Room was reborn when it installed Bernard Guillas as chef. The new menu ventures in exotic directions, characterized by the appetizer of Lampong pepper-coated smoked venison loin "petals" with mache salad in truffled vinaigrette, the lobster tail in pomegranate-balsamic syrup, and the "trilogy" of muscovy duck, ostrich and squab with "beggars purses" constructed from mission figs. Come for one of their high-tide Sunday brunches.

MILLE FLEURS FRENCH 16/20 

6009 Paseo Delicias, Rancho Santa Fe 92067
619-756-3085, *Lunch Mon.-Fri., Dinner nightly, $$$$*

An elegant Moorish-style villa for the horsey set, where Chef Martin Woesle's daily menus move us. Sample such culinary triumphs as pan-roasted red snapper with fennel and pastis, squab breast in black truffle sauce, venison saddle medallions with juniper berry sauce and hazelnut spaetzle, and lobster soup with Maine sea scallops and a cauliflower flan. We're also intrigued with the rack of lamb with scarlet runner beans and saffron couscous, and the beef filet with Stilton cheese. The service and ambience are fine, and the wine list causes connoisseurs to swoon.

MORTON'S OF CHICAGO STEAKHOUSE 14/20 

285 J St., Suite J, Downtown 92101
619-696-3369, *Dinner nightly, $$$*

This upscale steakhouse chain has come to San Diego in the sensational surroundings of the soaring Harbor Club towers. Expect posh, clubby surroundings and the best beef in town, characterized by mammoth filet mignon, Porterhouse and New York strip steaks, along with crispy hash-browned potatoes and all-American desserts.

OSTERIA PANEVINO ITALIAN 12/20

722 Fifth Ave., Gaslamp Quarter 92101
619-595-7959, *Lunch & Dinner daily, $$*

One of the unusual dishes served here is the stuffed focaccia. Panevino also offers superb vegetarian antipasti, wonderful pastas and risotti, a number of great wines served by the glass, and quite wonderful osso buco. The terrace is popular with people-watchers and those who like to dine well, and the location in the heart of the Gaslamp Quarter entertainment district is unbeatable.

PACIFICA DEL MAR CALIFORNIA/PACIFIC RIM 12/20

Del Mar Plaza, 1555 Camino Del Mar, Ste. 321, Del Mar 92014
619-792-0476, *Lunch & Dinner daily, $$$*

Pacifica Del Mar boasts an ocean view and a menu tilting towards the Pacific Rim. Always innovative and frequently packed as a result, the restaurant offers a menu that ranges broadly from the plush kim chee "martini" fleshed out with Dungeness crab, the Caesar salad dressed with salmon jerky and the horseradish-crusted mahi mahi, to the sugar-spiced, barbecued king salmon.

PAMPLEMOUSSE GRILLE CALIFORNIAN 13/20 

514 Via de la Valle, Solana Beach 92075
619-792-9090, *Lunch Mon.-Fri., Dinner daily, $$$*

At this chic spot, chef Jeffrey Strauss amazes guests with a seasonal menu that utilizes San Diego's best produce and seafood in clever ways. We always start with his ravioli of the day, particularly when the paper-thin sheets of pasta encase Maine lobster in salmon-scallop mousse. The roasted tomato and fennel soup is a revelation of bright flavors. The lamb stew with oven-roasted vegetables captures the votes of traditionalists, while radicals opt for the buttery pork prime rib with mustard sauce or the grilled seafood stew.

PARIOLI ITALIAN BISTRO ITALIAN 11/20

647 S. Highway 101, Solana Beach 92075
619-755-2525, *Lunch Mon.-Fri., Dinner daily, $$*

The proprietors arrived recently from Italy and serve fare that is wonderfully authentic. Which means chewy, lightly sauced pasta, and squid marinated rather than fried, bathed with pesto and roasted garlic. A savory stew of porcini and shiitake mushrooms tops the grilled polenta, and, unusual for an Italian eatery, curry sauce finishes the sautéed scallops. Beware the pastry filled with pink watermelon jelly.

RAINWATER'S AMERICAN 13/20 

1202 Kettner Blvd., Downtown 92101
619-233-5757, *Lunch Mon.-Fri., Dinner nightly, $$$*

Rainwater's displays the belief that "more is better" every time it serves an immense Kansas City strip steak beneath a cargo of sautéed onions, mushrooms and bacon. Given the times, seafood now has equal billing on the menu, but we'll never give up our allegiance to the black bean soup and corn sticks. The power types who congregate here now have the option of choosing the new downstairs dining room which has a more contemporary menu, as evidenced by the herb-braised halibut with garlicky spinach, and wild Irish salmon and chervil-cream sauce.

RISTORANTE MICHELANGELO ITALIAN 12/20

2806 Shelter Island Dr., Shelter Island 92106
619-224-9478, *Lunch Mon.-Fri., Dinner nightly, $$*

This long-shuttered classic has been revivied not a moment too soon for fans of regional Italian cooking. Many dishes are unique to this establishment, including polenta with sautéed chard and loads of creamy cheese. The pastas are anything but commonplace, especially the Sardinian golosetti in red wine-enhanced tomato sauce, and there are several varieties of osso buco, including one that spikes the sauce with anchovy essence.

STAR OF THE SEA SEAFOOD 15/20 

1360 Harbor Dr., Downtown 92101
619-232-7408, *Dinner nightly, $$$*

What a world of difference the installation of Chef Jonathan Pflueger has meant to this formal "special occasion" restaurant. Pflueger has gradually honed his repertoire of specialties to include the most thoughtful and imaginative. A leek vinaigrette sauces a "charlotte" of asparagus and lump crab, langoustine tails take a whirl in the wok with arugula and citrus butter, and papaya, mint and garlic team to infuse poached halibut with novel, highly satisfying flavors. The major renovation slated for the fall of 1998 should usher this establishment quite nicely into the twenty-first century.

TOP O' THE COVE FRENCH 13/20 

1216 Prospect St., La Jolla 92037
619-454-7779, *Lunch & Dinner daily, Brunch. Sun., $$$*

A La Jolla culinary institution for more than four decades, this charming bungalow has returned to the top rank of local restaurants thanks to a menu that emphasizes not just quality, but luxury, an insistence that also characterizes the decor and service. The sautéed foie gras melts in the mouth, while light sauces dress the fresh salmon and delicate veal, and a breathy garlic-rosemary sauce gives memorable character to the ever-popular rack of lamb.

TRATTORIA PORTOBELLO ITALIAN 12/20

715 Fourth Ave., Gaslamp Quarter 92101
619-232-4440, *Lunch & Dinner daily, $$*

Combine the ambience of San Francisco with contemporary Italian cuisine and what you have is an upscale restaurant providing a swank dining experience in the historic Gaslamp Quarter. From the open kitchen come such dishes as the warm seafood salad, portobello mushroom risotto and grilled lamb with black olive reduction and garlic-mashed potatoes. The bar boasts a roster of 101 martinis.

VIVACE ITALIAN 12/20

Four Seasons Resort Aviara, 7100 Four Seasons Pt., Carlsbad 92009
760-603-6800, *Dinner nightly, $$*

Milan-born chef Marco Cavuoto designed a surprisingly easy-going menu for this exceptionally gorgeous, contemporary-styled—and almost over-staffed—hotel dining room. The wonder of it all is that you can dine on pizza in the principal restaurant of a luxury hotel. The food is quite good, especially the tagliolini with mushrooms and pancetta, the oregano-crusted lamb with caponata and the oven-roasted fish of the day. The double-espresso ricotta cheesecake is tops.

WINESELLAR & BRASSERIE NEW AMERICAN 16/20 

9550 Waples St., Sorrento Mesa 92121
619-450-9557, *Lunch Sat., Dinner Tues.-Sun., $$$*

Very much the tail that came to wag the dog, this popular room opened as an upstairs lunch spot for patrons of the ground-floor wine store. The shop has built one of the most impressive wine collections in the county, and all of it is available here at a reasonable mark-up. Patrons raise their glasses to chef Douglas Organ when he sends out such starters as roasted eggplant soup with olive croutons, wild rice pancakes with crisp sweetbreads and lobster, or leek-fava bean agnolotti with yellow pepper purée. His inspired entrées include Moroccan-spiced roasted rack of lamb, grilled sturgeon and honey-glazed pork loin.

WOLFGANG PUCK CAFÉ CALIFORNIAN 13/20 

1640 Caminio Del Rio N., Mission Valley 92108
619-295-9653, *Lunch & Dinner daily, $*

See review in "L.A. AREA—Dining."

AND ALSO...

BEEF EATERS OF CORONADO AMERICAN

155 Orange Ave., Coronado 92118
619-437-1717, *Lunch Mon.-Fri, Dinner daily, $*

You'll find whatever your carnivore's heart desires here, especially beef roasted, carved and tucked into sandwiches or piled on platters. We're partial to the Philly steak sandwich layered with mushrooms, peppers and sautéed onions under a sea of melted cheese, and the roast beef sandwich on a German caraway roll dripping with beefy juices.

EPAZOTE — SOUTHWESTERN

Del Mar Plaza, 1555 Camino Del Mar, Del Mar 92014
619-259-9966, *Lunch. & Dinner daily, Brunch Sun., $$*

This sister restaurant to Cilantros (see entry above) goes its own way with a menu that takes its cues from Mexico and the American Southwest. Try the intriguing salads, the shrimp with an unusually zesty sauce, and the braised carnitas with black beans, guacamole, tortillas and serrano chile salsa. The Mexican specialties are made without lard.

HOB NOB HILL — AMERICAN

2271 First Ave., Midtown 92101
619-239-8176, *Breakfast, Lunch & Dinner daily, $*

A

A temple to the American breakfast, Hob Nob is one of the oldest dining establishments in town. Nothing about the place ever seems to change, which is just fine with us. Notably attentive servers offer home-baked breads and pastries, lusty corned beef hash, and, at lunch and dinner, hearty fare such as turkey croquettes.

QUICK BITES

American & Deli

CORVETTE DINER BAR & GRILL

3946 Fifth Ave., Hillcrest 92103
619-542-1001, *Lunch and Dinner daily*

Crowds regularly form in front of this large, family-friendly eatery, which takes its mood, menu and decor from the 1950s. Burgers are the best bet, but the sandwiches, meatloaf and chicken-fried steak also are reliably good. Magicians and balloons artists sometimes entertain the kids while a disc jockey spins oldies but goodies.

D.Z. AKINS

6930 Alvarado Rd., San Diego 92120
619-265-0218, *Breakfast, Lunch & Dinner daily*

This cavernous deli serves good renditions of all the classics: chopped liver, matzo ball soup and mile-high corned beef sandwiches. The huge desert menu tempts with luscious pies and old-fashioned ice cream sundaes.

Barbecue

KANSAS CITY BARBECUE

610 W. Market St., Downtown 92101
619-231-9680, *Lunch & Dinner daily*

A sign advises that the "sleazy bar scene" in the movie *Top Gun* was filmed here, which is true. What matters more is that it's hard to find better barbecued meats anywhere in San Diego. To top things off, all the side dishes are excellent.

Chinese

MANDARIN GARDEN

8242 Mira Mesa Blvd., Mira Mesa 92126
619-566-4720, *Lunch & Dinner daily*

Long-adored for the sort of authentic Chinese cooking that makes few concessions to Western tastes, Mandarin Garden occupies a somewhat faded space in a somewhat faded shopping center, but it pleases us with its lengthy menu. We're partial to the hors d'oeuvre plate of Chinese cold cuts, jellyfish and the like, the boned pig's leg in brown sauce, "lion's head" meatballs and some nightly specials that sometimes take a bit of nerve to order.

Middle Eastern

ALADDIN MEDITERRANEAN CAFÉ

5420 Clairemont Mesa Blvd., Clairemont 92117
619-573-0000, *Lunch & Dinner daily*

Aladdin may have failed to request a fine cook when he summoned the genie from the bottle, but the proprietors of this comfortable, sometimes hectic and noisy establishment, did take the trouble to install a good chef in the kitchen. The result is a menu that veers from familiar snacks like hummus and baba ghanouj to exotic, lemon-flavored sausages and fanciful wood-fired pizzas topped with a sultan's ransom in herbs and seasonings.

Latin American

BERTA'S LATIN AMERICAN RESTAURANT

3928 Twiggs St., Old Town 92103
619-295-2343, *Lunch & Dinner Tues.-Sat.*

A

Putting two-thirds of the hemisphere's cuisine on one menu might seem futile, but the common features aid owner Berta Utreras in a cooking idiom that stretches from Tijuana to Tierra del Fuego. The Chilean pastel del choclo, the Peruvian lamb stew and the Brazilian pasta are tops.

Pizza

BJ'S CHICAGO PIZZERIA

8873 Villa La Jolla Dr., La Jolla 92037
619-455-0662, *Lunch & Dinner daily*

See review in "ORANGE COUNTY—Quick Bites"

Santa Barbara

SANTA BARBARA

Every weekend, countless Angelenos drive 90 miles north to fill up Santa Barbara's hotels and bed-and-breakfasts. Who can blame them? This sleepy beachside town has stunning Riviera-like views, lush Mediterranean foliage and authentic Spanish-Colonial architecture (it's a wonder what can result when a town saves historic buildings, and vetoes skyscrapers and billboards). Santa Barbara also offers infinite opportunities for outdoor activities—everything from beach volley ball and kayaking, to deep-sea diving and hang-gliding. Over the years, the number of good restaurants in Santa Barbara—and its tony suburb of Montecito—has gone through the roof. We happy to report that today, residents and visitors alike can take their pick of authentic ethnic spots, beachy hang-outs, lively bars and serious temples of gastronomy. Just be sure to make restaurant reservations well in advance for weekends—especially in the summer season.

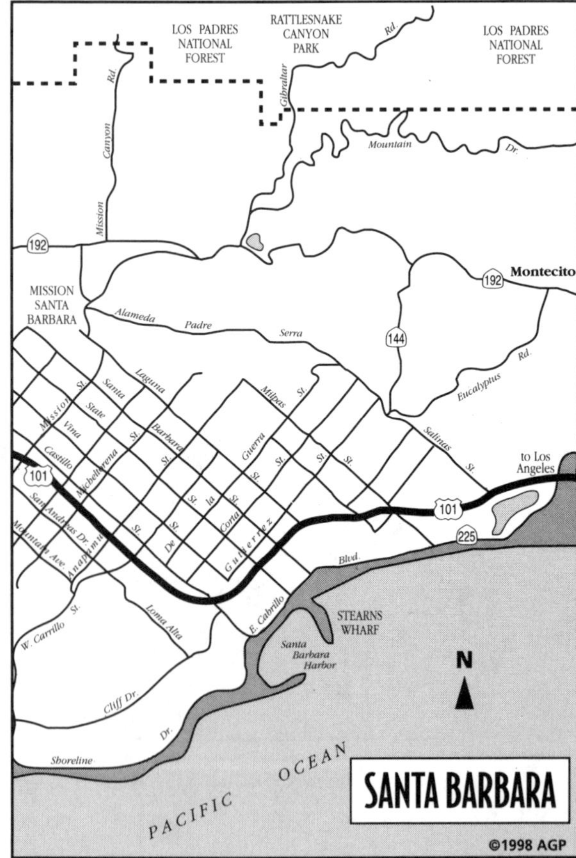

DINING

ARIGATO SUSHI JAPANESE 14/20 

11 W. Victoria St., Downtown 93101
805-965-6074, *Dinner nightly, $$*

Often hailed as "the Matsuhisa of Santa Barbara," Arigato is a small, lively restaurant and sushi bar with a smiling chef who is an artisan with 30 different special rolls and boatloads of innovative appetizers. Some of our offbeat favorites: sushi pizza, broiled spicy mussels, halibut carpaccio and shrimp ravioli. The menu features many daily specials and premium sakes, and the music on the stereo system blasts the latest sounds.

BACCIO ITALIAN 13/20 

905 State St., Downtown 93101
805-564-8280, *Lunch and Dinner daily, $*

We love the booths here, ideal for a tryst or a wheeling-and-dealing business lunch. The cooking draws from the sun-drenched flavors of the Mediterranean. The chef has a way with pizzas, pastas, chicken, seafood, steaks and lamb.

BAY CAFÉ & FISH MARKET SEAFOOD 13/20 

131 Anacapa St., Downtown 93101
805-963-2215, *Lunch daily, Dinner nightly, Brunch Sun., $$*

The Bay Café has been around for years and its durability is due to the fact that they serve super-fresh seafood in a romantic atmosphere. Lovers—and lovers of simply prepared good fish—flock to the jasmine-scented patio warmed with a fireplace. We like their seafood paella and prawns sautéed scampi-style with capers, though the steaks and pastas are popular. Within the restaurant is a busy seafood market, which peddles very fresh fish plucked from the nearby ocean.

THE BLUE SHARK BISTRO CALIFORNIAN 13/20 

21 W. Victoria St., Downtown 93109
805-564-7100, *Dinner nightly, $*

This Santa Barbara bistro caters to all tastes, from those in search of a quick burger or sandwich to those yearning for gourmet pastas and salads. The fish tacos have been hailed as the best thing to hit Santa Barbara since Jonathan Winters came to town. We like their moderate prices, lovely patio and impressive choice of local wines.

BRIGITTE'S CALIFORNIAN 13/20 

1327 State St., Downtown 93101
805-966-9676, *Lunch Mon.-Sat., Dinner nightly, $*

This busy neighborhood bistro is usually packed with regulars who find the light Californian cooking just right for their taste buds and pocketbooks. The gourmet pizzas cooked in a wood-burning oven, creative salads, pastas, grilled items and desserts are consistently good. Our favorites here are the fresh fish specials, the angel-hair pasta with rock shrimp, the lamb with a rosemary and red onion sauce and the venison. An adjacent deli and bakery offers cheeses, soups, salads and great sandwiches.

BROPHY BROTHERS SEAFOOD 13/20

119 Harbor Way, Downtown 93109
805-966-4418, *Lunch and Dinner daily, $*

This jumping second-floor walk-up is usually buzzing with a colorful mix of fishermen and Ralph Lauren-clad yuppies. Why not? The harbor and mountain views are compelling, and the chowder, calamari and oyster shooters are the best for miles. Daily fresh fish specials might include swordfish, roasted cashew-crusted albacore with lemon-tarragon sauce, or thresher shark marinated in olive oil and served with a citrus juice. Baked clams, steamers, scampi and cioppino are always available, along with a full bar selection.

BUCATINI NORTHERN ITALIAN 13/20

436 State St., Downtown 93101
805-957-4177, *Lunch and Dinner daily, $*

Bucatini has a friendly Italian atmosphere, a vest-pocket dining room and a large patio. In addition to the homemade soups and risottos, we favor the ravioli, and such fresh seafood dishes as the stuffed whole striped bass baked in a wood-burning oven. The reasonably priced wine list is a sight for sore eyes.

CA' DARIO ITALIAN 13/20

37 E. Victoria St., Downtown 93101
805-884-9419, *Lunch Mon.-Fri., Dinner nightly, $*

This busy little trattoria feels just like one in Italy. It helps that the staff is true Italian and that the cooking is as authentic as it gets. The Piedmontese chef prepares such classic Northern Italian dishes as spinach ravioli with butter-sage sauce, whole fresh striped bass and a veal chop that diners clamor for. The rotisserie dishes, including duck, chicken and rabbit, are remarkably succulent. A few tables line the sidewalk for those who like exhaust fumes with their pasta.

CAFÉ BUENOS AIRES ARGENTINE 13/20

1316 State St., Downtown 93101
805-963-0242, *Lunch daily, Dinner nightly, Brunch Sun., $*

Tangoing around the fountain is allowed at this authentic Argentine café. The interior evokes a stylish estancia with mahogany-framed paned windows, antique mirrors and a vintage bar imported from Eva Peron's mansion. From the cocina come tapas, empanadas, pastas and seafood dishes, including luscious roasted halibut with saffron-mashed potatoes. The beef sings of the pampas, especially the rib-eye steak cooked in wine and mushrooms. The live music on Wednesdays through Sundays makes this place even more fun.

CARLITOS CAFÉ Y CANTINA MEXICAN 13/20 

1324 State St., Downtown 93101
805-962-7117, *Lunch daily, Dinner nightly, Brunch Sat.-Sun., $*

Offering a taste of old Mexico with a new twist here and there, Carlitos features mesquite- grilled specialties and any flavored margarita you can dream up, including Carlitos' own Cuervo Gold. Enjoy the State Street scene from the heated patio while listening to live guitar music nightly. The salsas are prepared fresh daily, and the menu includes traditional favorites as well as Carlitos' versions of Southwestern cuisine.

CASA DE SEVILLA CONTINENTAL 13/20 

428 Chapala St., Downtown 93101
805-966-4370, *Lunch and Dinner Tues.-Sat., $$$*

Casa de Sevilla is as close to a dining institution as there is in Santa Barbara. A club-like refuge for old Montecito types, it's a welcome address for hungry tourists who favor a dark, Republican atmosphere and no-nonsense cooking. The margaritas are renowned and so are the chile rellenos. Beyond that, you'll find 17 fresh seafood items daily and beef dishes cooked on a barbecue. The dining area is divided into four quaint rooms, and a fireplace adds romantic ambience; we prefer the red room with the bullfight posters.

CAVA MEXICAN/SPANISH/SOUTHWESTERN 13/20 

1212 Coast Village Rd., Montecito 93108
805-969-8500, *Lunch daily, Dinner nightly, Brunch Sat.-Sun., $$*

The sister restaurant of downtown's Carlitos', Cava is one of Montecito's most beautiful dining spots, with soft yellow walls, fine art, beams and skylights. The chefs in the open kitchen are dedicated to blending authentic Spanish, Mexican and Southwest cuisine—and they're good at it. Their "gaucho" steak is a local favorite and their margaritas are powerful. Cava has a full bar and live music nightly.

CHAD'S NEW AMERICAN 13/20 

625 Chapala St., Downtown 93101
805-568-1876, *Dinner nightly, $$*

Chad's action takes place in a charming old Victorian house where Chad himself prepares unpretentious American regional creations, pastas, blackened seafood and such specials as caramelized Alaskan Halibut and stuffed Montana pork chop. The "sampler plate" allows guests to try a little bit of all the favorite entrées on the menu. The small outdoor patio seats twenty, and a cheery two-sided fireplace keeps guests warm inside on nippy days.

CITRONELLE FRENCH/CALIFORNIAN 15/20 

Santa Barbara Inn, 901 Cabrillo Blvd., E. Beach 93103
805-963-0111, *Breakfast, Lunch & Dinner daily, $$$*

Chef extraordinaire Michel Richard has split for Washington, D.C., but his legacy remains: a spectacular third-floor perch overlooking the Pacific. Many of Richard's original—and very creative—dishes are still served, but chef Felicien Cueff is flexing his innovative muscles and his is a talent to be reckoned with. Dishes that marry finesse and flavor include oven-roasted duck with couscous and cranberry-ginger sauce, grilled swordfish with shiitake risotto and smoked salmon terrine with cucumber-dill salad. The desserts at Citronelle—such as the fresh strawberry feuilletée—are sublime. It is a pity this restaurant feels a bit cold and impersonal and that service is often erratic.

COLD SPRING TAVERN AMERICAN 12/20

5995 Stagecoach Rd., San Marcos Pass 93105
805-967-0066, *Breakfast Sat.-Sun., Lunch & Dinner daily, $*

In this mountain-pass roadhouse from the 1800s, a favorite of motorcycle enthusiasts, the fire is always glowing in the hearth and the jukebox is tops. Standards include country biscuits with gravy, waffles and stuffed "Cold Springs chicken." The daily fresh fish selection lends the menu variety. Join the bikers for burgers, chili, ribs and live bluegrass on the weekends.

DOWNEY'S CALIFORNIAN 15/20

1305 State St., Downtown 93101
805-966-5006, *Dinner Tues.-Sun., $$$*

Chef John Downey is an institution in Santa Barbara, and his simple, contemporary restaurant has a dedicated clientele. Downey has always been devoted to Nouvelle California-French dishes which change with the seasons. Among the winners: grilled duck, gingered fresh foie gras, crisp striped bass floating in a shrimp broth brimming with tomatoes, fennel, potatoes and saffron, grilled local swordfish enhanced by a spicy papaya-cucumber salsa, and pork loin braised with fresh ginger and plums. This is a quiet, comfortable spot for serious and innovative cuisine, though we sometimes wish the atmosphere were a bit warmer.

EL ENCANTO DINING ROOM CALIFORNIAN 13/20

El Encanto Hotel, 1900 Lasuen Rd., The Riviera 93103
805-687-5000, *Breakfast, Lunch & Dinner daily, Brunch Sun., $$$*

A

This romantic country inn perched above the city, offers unequaled vistas of the city's red-tiled roofs and the cobalt ocean beyond. It is a shame its Dining Room has never excelled. The young staff tries hard and the manager is charming, but the kitchen pumps out mediocre hotel food that never achieves heights. Still and all, if one orders simply and carefully, and includes a good bottle of wine, a venture to El Encanto can be enchanting. Sunday brunch is a good bet.

EMILIO'S RISTORANTE AND BAR ITALIAN 13/20

324 W. Cabrillo Blvd., Downtown 93101
805-966-4426, *Dinner nightly, $$*

If you only went to Emilio's for the ocean view, it would be worth it. But the cooking is as stirring as the view: homemade pastas, fresh seafoods, and the best paella in town. The four-course chef's sampling menu is a good way to sample the best they offer, and the wine list has something for everyone.

INTERMEZZO CALIFORNIAN 13/20 

813 Anacapa St., Downtown 93101
805-966-9463, *Lunch and Dinner daily, Brunch Sun., $*

A new sibling of The Wine Cask, this cozy expansion in the historic El Paseo is where the after-work action is for thirsty downtown executives, male and female. The café and bar serve light bistro-style cuisine until late at night, and features indoor and outdoor seating, a crackling fireplace, comfy sofas and a very relaxed atmosphere. A fine selection of cigars is offered for smoking on the front patio.

JOE'S CAFÉ AMERICAN 10/20

536 State St., Downtown 93101
805-966-4638, *Lunch Mon.-Sat., Dinner nightly, $*

A colorful Santa Barbara hangout, ideal for studying the native language of the California beach scene. This is the joint for the stiffest drinks in town—no one here comes just for the food. As for the food, it runs the gamut from sandwiches to charbroiled steaks, and the portions are large, the prices low. Joe's will never win a culinary award, but legions of UCSB fraternity and sorority types pack in here nightly to imbibe and chow down.

LA MARINA CALIFORNIAN/PACIFIC RIM 15/20 

Four Seasons Biltmore Hotel, 1260 Channel Dr., Montecito 93108
805-969-2261, *Dinner Tues.-Sat., Brunch Sun., $$$*

The Four Seasons Biltmore recently overhauled their beautiful signature dining room. The result is a more casual room, but one that is still elegant and with a grand ocean view. Executive Chef Martin Frost hails from England but his cuisine tends towards the Pacific Rim, as exemplified by such dishes as rare ahi tuna in crispy phyllo with sesame relish and wasabi-whipped potatoes. The faithful still clamor for the hotel's signature roast rack of Colorado lamb with garlic gnocchi and New York steak with mushrooms. Sundays, La Marina is the setting for Santa Barbara's most lavish brunch.

LOUIE'S CALIFORNIAN/FRENCH 14/20 

Upham Hotel, 1404 De la Vina St., Downtown 93101
805-963-7003, *Lunch Mon.-Fri., Dinner nightly, $$*

Situated in the charming Upham Hotel (Santa Barbara's oldest hotel), this happy place has a wonderful veranda and features excellent Franco-Californian cuisine. No creams or butters are used, but look for their savory oils infused with cilantro and roasted red pepper. We're especially fond of the pork with sun-dried cherry sauce and the blackened salmon with papaya-mango-mint relish.

MA DOLCE VITA MEDITERRANEAN 13/20 

700 State St., Downtown 93101
805-965-3535, *Breakfast, Lunch, & Dinner daily, $$*

The aromas of fresh roasted coffee and homemade bread always draw us into Ma Dolce Vita, where the cuisine is inspired by the flavors of Chile, Spain, North Africa, Southern France and the Mediterranean. At breakfast, we favor such dishes as the seared wheat polenta and grilled duck sausage, or the Via Veneto chicken sausage frittata with fresh fruit. We love their gelato any time of the day.

MERITAGE ECLECTIC 13/20 

920 De la Vina, Downtown 93109
805-882-1200, *Dinner nightly, $$*

Meritage appeals with its intimate setting—a cozy house with fireplaces, flowers, candles, hardwood floors and a marble bar. Chef Lydia Gaitan creates dishes that blend the spices of Latin America and the exotic flair of the Pacific Rim with the comforts of America. She succeeds most of the time. We recommend the ceviche in a corn tostada with mango salsa, the cioppino and the seared duck breast with yam pancakes. A terrific wine list features the best from Santa Barbara County vines. A small patio awaits al fresco diners.n

MIMOSA FRENCH 14/20 

2700 De La Vina, Downtown 93101
805-682-2272, *Lunch Mon.-Fri., Dinner nightly, $*

Chef/Owner Camille Schwartz never disappoints with his imaginative renditions of casual French cuisine. This modest restaurant has a comfy south-of-France ambience. Loyal regulars return again and again for the salads, pastas and such house specialties as bouillabaisse, osso bucco, fresh fish, venison, lamb and ostrich. Homemade pastries and an excellent selection of French and California wines complete the rosy picture.

THE MONTECITO CAFÉ CALIFORNIAN 13/20

1295 Coast Village Rd., Montecito 93108
805-969-3392, *Lunch and Dinner daily, $$*

A steady hand is at work in the kitchen and the front of the house; that's why this pleasant café has endured for so many years. A favorite of Montecito matrons and rich nabobs, the café recently added a full bar and a pianist for those who want to stay up late and do cocktails. But the real appeal here is the good, simple and well-priced cuisine. Such dishes as the goat cheese pancakes with gravlax and salmon caviar, the Emmenthaler cheese-filled pork chops, the leg of lamb, veal scaloppini and various pastas, are why we consider this a must stop.

THE PALACE CAFÉ CAJUN/CREOLE 13/20

8 E. Cota St., Downtown 93101
805-966-3133, *Dinner nightly, $$*

This friendly and busy restaurant features Cajun and Creole dishes of distinction, plates heaped with blackened filet mignon stuffed with Cajun-spiced Louisiana crawfish, etoufée, jambalaya, soft-shell crabs, blackened redfish and rich gumbos. The kitchen also turns out tasty Caribbean-style dishes, Italian pastas and wonderful key lime and potato-pecan pies. The service is the best in town and operates on a unique team system. The good times roll here, especially after a few potent Cajun martinis.

PANE E VINO ITALIAN 14/20

1482 E.Valley Rd., Montecito 93108
805-969-9274, *Lunch Mon.-Sat., Dinner nightly, $$*

Michael Douglas and Dennis Miller are regulars at this inviting little trattoria, with its open kitchen, counter heaped with crusty Tuscan bread, tile-and-woodwork bistro decor and outdoor patio. Tear into the marinated shrimps and then go for the herby tomato-bread soup, the heavenly seafood risotto, the savory tortelloni with butter and sage or the succulent grilled veal chop with rosemary. Owner Pietro Bernardi deserves all the credit for this gem.

PARADISE CAFÉ AMERICAN 13/20

702 Anacapa St., Downtown 93101
805-962-4416, *Lunch & Dinner daily, Breakfast Sun, $$.*

A funky Spanish building with a simple '40s decor, the Paradise has a straightforward bar with interesting old murals, a split-level dining room and a sunny patio. A young crowd gathers here to laugh and talk while eating pastas, omelets and egg dishes (try the tortilla-wrapped combo of scrambled eggs, black beans, salsa and cheese), terrific hamburgers, sandwiches, seafood, and good oak-grilled steaks, chops and fish. The bar scene jumps when the sun sets.

THE PATIO CALIFORNIAN 13/20

Four Seasons Biltmore Hotel, 1260 Channel Dr., Montecito 93108
805-969-2261, *Breakfast, Lunch & Dinner daily, $$*

The Four Seasons Biltmore Hotel's casual garden-like Patio allows guests to dine on pleasant California-Continental fare—with a focus on seafood and robust salads—either outside overlooking the sea or indoors under a retractable roof. Thursdays through Sundays, elaborate themed buffet dinners tempt with seasonally and ethnically changing dishes.

PIATTI ITALIAN 13/20

516 San Ysidro Rd., Montecito 93108
805-969-7520, *Lunch & Dinner daily, $*

Most of Montecito flocks to this upbeat, noisy and casual Italian restaurant. Sip Chianti and sample the cannelloni, spit-roasted chicken with rosemary, spinach lasagna and other delights in the inviting dining room with its vegetable murals and fireplace, or outside on the patio beside the sycamore-shaded creek.

STELLA MARE'S CALIFORNIAN 13/20 

50 Los Patos Way, Montecito 93108
805-969-6705, *Lunch Tues.-Sat., Dinner Tues.-Sun., Brunch Sun., $$*

This handsome and romantic restaurant overlooks the shimmering Santa Barbara Bird Refuge. The casual, French provincial interior is irresistible: a glass greenhouse, sofas by the fire, pine furniture and bright fabrics. We just wish the contemporary cuisine—New York steak or pork tenderloin from the wood-burning grill, roasted halibut with couscous—were more consistently good. Still, there is an excellent wine list and live music on Wednesday, Friday and Saturday evenings.

STONEHOUSE NEW AMERICAN 15/20 

San Ysidro Ranch, 900 San Ysidro Ln., Montecito 93108
805-969-5046
Breakfast, Lunch & Dinner daily, Brunch Sun., $$$

Set in a 150-year-old ranch house, the Stonehouse's rough white stone walls contrast with the fine linens and silver, and the latticed patio provides a lovely setting for al fresco weekend brunches, complete with spectacular ocean and mountain vistas. The chef, David Adjey keeps adding excitement to the menu, with such dishes as lamb chops served with goulash-stuffed acorn squash. This hideaway in the hills has a rustic charm that's hard to beat.

TRATTORIA MOLLIE'S ITALIAN 13/20 

1250 Coast Village Rd., Santa Barbara 93108
805-565-9381, *Lunch & Dinner Tues.-Sun., $$*

The cuisines of Tuscany, Rome and Umbria are the specialty of the charming chef-owner, Mollie, who hails from Ethiopia and formerly cooked in some of Italy's finest eateries. Molly also baked bread for the Pope, and her pizza is one of the best in town. Fresh pastas include spaghetti with mussels and shrimp, and mezzelune stuffed with eggplant and zucchini. Molly makes everything by hand, just as she was taught in Padua. The homemade gelato is sublime.

WINE CASK CALIFORNIAN 16/20 

813 Anacapa St., Downtown 93101
805-966-9463 *Lunch Mon.- Fri., Dinner nightly, Brunch Sat. & Sun., $$$*

Owner Doug Margerum has emerged as Santa Barbara's premier restaurateur. Located in the historic El Paseo downtown, this majestic flower-filled eatery sports a vintage-1926 hand-painted ceiling, a baronial fireplace and a luxurious maple bar, all bathed in discreet Italian halogen lighting. The adjoining flagstone courtyard seduces with blossoming trees and a babbling fountain. Choose your wine from over 2000 bottles priced a mere $10 over retail and available for purchase in the adjacent wine store. Chef David Cecchini combines tradition and innovation, to create dishes that are cutting edge. We've enjoyed the foie gras and the lobster risotto, the peppercorn-encrusted ahi tuna and the lamb sirloin. For dessert, we tend towards the the pear napoleon. Finish things off with a digestif and a cigar next door.

YOUR PLACE THAI 13/20 

22 N. Milpas St., Downtown
805-966-5151, *Lunch Tues.-Sun., $*

The oldest Thai restaurant in Santa Barbara, Your Place features fresh seafood and vegetarian dishes zested with exotic spices. Such specialties as the heady Thai-barbecued chicken or juicy cashew nut chicken, the rich curries, bell pepper beef, tangy spareribs and fragrant ginger vegetables, recall satisfying feasts we have enjoyed in Bangkok.

THE ZIA CAFÉ MEXICAN 13/20 

532 State St., Downtown 93101
805-962-5391, *Lunch & Dinner daily, Breakfast Sun., $*

An attractive little space done up in Santa Fe-style, the Zia serves Southwestern food with Indian and Mexican influences. We recommend the blue corn tortillas, chile rellenos stuffed with cheese and piñon nuts, sopaipillas and blue corn pancakes. They cook vegetarian dishes as well. Hip hedonists gravitate to the balcony for strong drinks and the splendid view of the action on State Street.

QUICK BITES

American

EAST BEACH GRILL

1118 E. Cabrillo Blvd., Downtown 93109
805-965-8805, *Breakfast and Lunch daily, Dinner during summer*

You can't get any closer to dining on the beach without a picnic basket. Literally steps from the water, this grill features a patio where you can enjoy hamburgers, burritos and sandwiches for lunch, or banana-wheat pancakes for breakfast, while watching for dolphins swimming by. The Santa Barbara omelet, made with a variety of cheeses and homemade salsa, is a favorite of the local surfers, along with the Californian sandwich with avocado and cream cheese.

Cafés

ARTS & LETTERS CAFÉ

7 E. Anapamu, Downtown 93101
805-730-1463, *Lunch Mon.-Fri., Dinner Tues.-Sun., Brunch Sat.-Sun.*

This petite café serves light bistro fare in a setting surrounded by fine art, and is a favorite among Santa Barbarans for pre-theatre dining. The pumpkin soup is a winner, as are the zesty salads and hearty sandwiches. Experience the privacy of a walled garden and patio or indoor gallery seating, behind the highly regarded Sullivan Goss Books & Prints.

BARCLIFF & BAIR

1112 State St., Downtown 93101
805-965-5742, *Breakfast and Lunch daily*

Homemade sandwiches and soups, daily specials, and afternoon tea are on the menu at this very European café set at La Arcada Court. Sit outside and watch the pedestrian parade on State Street. The Lilliputian dining room has an old-world feel, with its vaulted ceiling, fine botanical prints, mahogany paneling and massive wrought-iron chandelier.

BISTRO MED

1129 State St., Downtown 93101
805-965-1500, *Lunch & Dinner daily*

This handsome courtyard bistro draws on the Mediterranean's unique history of hospitality, and the kitchen is committed to culinary traditions from the Danube to the Jordan River. On the menu are grilled lamb, chicken, hummus and stuffed grape leaves plus a selection of vegetarian options. A fountain gurgles day and night.

MONTECITO WINE BISTRO

1280 Coast Village Rd., Montecito 93108
805-969-3955, *Lunch daily, Dinner Tues.-Sun.*

This vest pocket café keeps getting better and better. The wine shop has a sophisticated and extensive selection of wines, most of which you can sample before buying. Cigar aficionados will find a humidor stocked with interesting international buys. Bask in the sun by day, savor jazz by night, while the kitchen serves up good salads, crisp pizzas, yummy sandwiches and scores of wines by the glass.

MUSEUM CAFÉ

1130 State St., Downtown 93101
805-963-4364 ext 287, *Lunch daily*

Located in the Santa Barbara Museum of Art, this petite café is a charmer serving salads, sandwiches and soups of the day. A fine wine list of half bottles (bravo!) provides good choices to accompany your meal, and there are excellent coffees and desserts. A local favorite is the mango-chicken curry salad with almonds, currents and toasted coconut. This café is run by the Wine Cask, so we know it is dependable.

NAPOLEON CAFÉ

808 State St., Downtown 93101
805-899-1183, *Breakfast, Lunch & Dinner daily*

This jewel-like French bakery prides itself on homemade pastries, breads, quiches, sandwiches and soups. The beau monde usually packs the small terrace area munching on such delights as quiche Lorraine or baguettes heaped with turkey, guacamole, prosciutto, lettuce and Brie. For breakfast, the chocolate eclairs are calculated to raise your blood sugar.

Healthy

MAIN SQUEEZE CAFÉ

138 E. Canon Perdido, Downtown 93101
805-966-5365, *Breakfast, Lunch & Dinner daily*

A hangout for the trim and beautiful who are after natural, healthy, non-dairy food and juices. The fare includes fresh fish, chicken, innovative pastas and breads from Our Daily Bread bakery.

THE NATURAL CAFÉ

508 State St., Downtown 93101
805-962-9494, *Lunch & Dinner daily*
No cards 

Fit food for the fit. The Natural Café is packed with those in search of great food, friendly service and true value. The menu features homemade soups, fresh salads, sumptuous sandwiches, vegetarian entrées, pasta, chicken and seafood dishes, as well as a complete juice bar, microbrewed beers and local wines. The sunny patio is perfect for sipping wheat-grass juice and watching the social parade on State Street. The shop next door carries a large selection of vitamins, herbs, candles, incense and other spiritual goods.

SOJOURNER CAFÉ

134 E. Canon Perdido, Downtown 93101
805-965-7922, *Lunch & Dinner daily*

Located in the historical center of town, this has been a favorite for wholesome natural foods since 1978. Renowned for its friendly, nurturing and energetic atmosphere, the Sojourner serves a variety of creative, internationally influenced vegetarian, chicken and seafood dishes, such as the vegetable stir-fry and the polenta cake royale. The popular espresso bar serves some of the best home-baked desserts in town, and is a good spot to start or end your day.

Italian

TUTTI'S

1209 Coast Village Rd., Montecito 93108
805-969-5809, *Breakfast, Lunch & Dinner daily*

Every time we visit Santa Barbara, we make a pit stop at Tutti's: for French toast and eggs at breakfast, a dynamite Caesar salad at lunch, citrus-stuffed rotisserie-roasted game hens and chicken at dinner, or gourmet picnic items all day long. Mix-and-match the fresh pastas with a variety of sauces; choose a reasonably priced bottle of wine from the deli fridge; chomp on the fresh breadsticks and focaccia; sample one of the homemade Italian pastries. The service is always friendly.

VIA VAI

1483 E.Valley Rd. #20, Montecito 93108
805-565-9393

This culinary cousin of Pane e Vino bakes savory, thin-crust pizzas in their authentic woodburning oven, creating an aroma which can be inhaled for blocks. Sit on the patio for a grand view of the mountains. The faithful return for Via Vai's spaghetti al coccio, with clams, prawns, mussels, scallops, and fish in a clay pot and covered with pizza crust, then baked in the wood oven.

Mexican

LA SUPER-RICA

622 N. Milpas St., Downtown 93101
805-963-4940, *Lunch & Dinner daily*

No Cards

Regulars (and Julia Child) swear that this tiny stand-in-line-and-wait joint serves the best soft tacos you'll ever have: fresh, hot homemade corn tortillas sandwiching grilled chicken, pork, beef or chorizo. You must also try the frijoles, an addictive dish of beans, sausage, bacon and chiles.

Central Coast

CENTRAL COAST

Located between San Francisco to the north and Los Angeles to the south, the Central Coast is not one of California's primary tourist attractions. But in recent years, with the growth of its award-winning vineyards—and visitors' appreciation of its oak-studded valleys, wide-open spaces and sweeping coastline—the area that includes the **Santa Ynez Valley**, **Santa Maria**, **San Luis Obispo**, **Templeton/Paso Robles** and such beach towns as **Morro Bay**, **Pismo Beach** and **Cambria**, is becoming more popular as a vacation destination. As a result, our list of favorite Central Coast-area restaurants has grown. Some of the dining spots below are quite new, run, in a few cases, by chefs who fled L.A. for greener (literally) pastures. Others have been local hangouts for decades, and are bound to give out-of-towners an authentic taste of what we call "Northern Southern California."

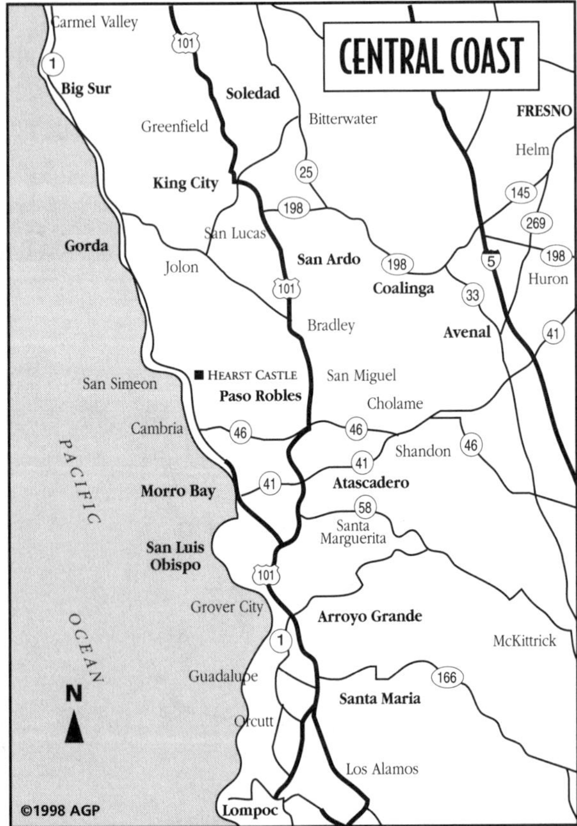

DINING

BALLARD STORE — CALIFORNIAN/CONTINENTAL — 11/20

2449 Baseline Ave., Ballard 93463
805-688-5319, *Dinner Wed.-Sun., Brunch Sun., $$*

Just outside Solvang, past horse farms and orchards, you'll come across the Ballard School, a little red schoolhouse dating back to 1883 with a steeple and framed by a pair of black walnut trees. Next to the school, you'll find the former general store for the area in the '20s and '30s. Today it houses this charming restaurant run by a former chef from New York's 21 Club, who serves quite good Californian/Continental dishes such as fresh fish, filet mignon, duck, lamb, scampi and lobster.

BISTRO LAURENT — FRENCH — 14/20 

1202 Pine St., Paso Robles 93446
805-226-8191, *Dinner Mon.-Sat., $$*

French chef Laurent Grangien (late of the Inn on Morro Bay) found a cozy, corner location on a Paso Robles side street in which to open his own restaurant. Grangien, who was once Michel Rostang's partner in a series of French bistros, certainly knows his way around the kitchen. Start with the warm potato-goat cheese salad with roasted pine nuts, or the crab risotto with tomato coulis and tarragon. Among the entrées, the roasted salmon with asparagus and red wine sauce is smashing, as is the rabbit fricassee. Even classics like rack of lamb Provençal and roasted chicken seem refreshed in Grangien's hands. The four-course prix-fixe dinner changes nightly and is a good bargain.

BRAMBLES — AMERICAN — 11/20

4005 Burton Dr., Cambria 93428
805-97-4716, *Dinner nightly, Brunch Sun., $$$*

Before Cambria became a popular vacation spot, Brambles was THE destination restaurant in the area. Part of the attraction is the building itself, a quaint nineteenth-century English-style home that makes you feel like you're visiting your great-grandmother's house for Sunday dinner. The menu has kept up with the times: oakwood-fired steaks, grilled salmon, fresh salads and pastas are offered, as well as the traditional olde-English prime rib with Yorkshire pudding. The wine list features local selections.

BROTHERS — CALIFORNIAN — 14/20 

The Storybook Inn B & B, 409 First St., Solvang 93463
805-688-9934, *Dinner Wed.-Sun., $$*

Matt and Jeff Nichols honed their culinary craft at three of L.A.'s finest eateries: Spago, Trumps and Ocean Avenue Seafood. Their seasonally changing menu brings a breath of fresh air to cutesy Solvang, and centers on the wood-burning mesquite grill. Our favorite selections: spring rolls filled with shrimp, shiitake mushrooms and cilantro; risotto with earthy white truffles; a surreally large veal chop; and pork chops with fried potatoes and homemade applesauce. Fish is a top choice too, especially the grilled swordfish with Thai coconut sauce and mango salsa, and the salmon with niçoise olive-tomato vinaigrette and parsley potatoes.

BUONA TAVOLA ITALIAN 12/20

1037 Monterey St., San Luis Obispo 93401
805-545-8000, *Lunch & Dinner Mon.-Sat., $$*

Buona Tavola would be perfectly at home in Italian restaurant-crazed Los Angeles. In fact, chef-owner Antonio Varia came to SLO after a stint in L.A.'s Locanda Veneta. Starters include artichoke hearts with Parmesan or a house salad of arugula, radicchio and earthy mushrooms. Pastas, like "angry" penne with dried chili pepper in a tomato sauce spiked with toasted garlic, are exemplary. Entrées range from a T-bone steak seasoned with garlic, thyme and rosemary, to chicken in a garlic-mustard sauce, to fresh fish.

CAFÉ CHARDONNAY CALIFORNIAN 12/20

2436 Baseline Ave., Ballard 93463
800-638-2466, *Dinner Wed.-Sun., $$*

Located in the Ballard Inn, a fifteen room Victorian-style farmhouse, this intimate dining room is a good choice for travelers seeking fine food to equal the wines of the surrounding Santa Ynez Valley. Fresh organic greens, soups, pastas and grilled meats are featured on the short menu. Among our favorites are the half-roasted chicken with garlic-mashed potatoes, the grilled pork chops with potato pancakes and the marinated grilled leg of lamb. On warm evenings, the front porch is a delightful spot for dinner.

CAFÉ ROMA ITALIAN 13/20

1819 Osos St., San Luis Obispo 93401
805-541-6800, *Lunch Mon.-Fri., Dinner Mon.-Sat., $$$*

Since 1980, Mama Maria Rosa Rizzo has been serving up stylish trattoria fare in the renovated bottom floor of the 1910-vintage former Reidy Hotel. With tables cozily arranged, there's no room for stuffiness here as diners trade menu suggestions and wine tips. Freshly baked bread comes hot to the table for dipping in basil-scented olive oil. The pastas are always good and the broiled Tuscan-style chicken and osso buco are the top entrée choices. The wine list offers Central Coast and Italian selections.

CHEF RICK'S ULTIMATELY FINE FOODS CALIFORNIAN 13/20

4869 S. Bradley Rd., Santa Maria 93454
805-937-9512, *Lunch & Dinner Mon.-Sat., $*

Don't let the shopping center location fool you. Ultimately fine food is served. Chef Rick Manson is THE caterer at many winery events in Santa Barbara County, but you can get a taste of his spicy amalgamation of New Orleans/Southwestern/Mexican cuisine here. There's often Yucatan chicken soup with lime and tortillas or beer-battered coconut shrimp with tangy sweet-hot dipping sauce. The jambalaya concoction of shrimp, chicken and andouille over pasta is well spiced, while the grilled Mexican sea bass with roasted tortilla sauce, black beans and salsa ranchera is terrific. We appreciate the selection of local wines at reasonable prices.

GARDENS OF AVILA CALIFORNIAN 12/20

1215 Avila Beach Dr., Avila Beach 93424
805-595-7365, *Lunch Tues.-Sat, Dinner Tues.-Sun., Brunch Sun., $$$*

In the last few years, Sycamore Mineral Springs, known for its mineral springs hot tubs, has been renovated so that old timers would barely recognize it. The sprucing up extends to this attractive dining room, where experienced chef Michael Albright adds Southwestern, Provençal and Asian accents to his contemporary cuisine. Baked halibut is encrusted with garlic and herbed bread crumbs; Dungeness crab gets wrapped in spring rolls to dunk in a spicy peanut dipping sauce. Seafood kebabs deliver a subtle punch from a chipotle chile-orange juice glaze.

GIUSEPPE'S ITALIAN 11/20

891 Price St., Pismo Beach 93449
805-773-2870, *Lunch Mon.-Fri., Dinner nightly, $$*

Here's an old-style Southern Italian pizza and pasta place that serves up hearty portions of both food and fun. The funky interior, with burnished woods and big windows, reminds us of a more civilized Hussong's Cantina. There are bountiful pizzas and pastas in the traditional style—no designer flourishes here. Fresh fish is always spotlighted, as well chicken, veal, scampi and lamb.

THE HITCHING POST AMERICAN 12/20

3225 Point Sal Rd., Casmalia 93429
805-937-6151, *Dinner nightly*

In Santa Ynez, barbecuing means grilling over an oakwood fire, in this case behind a glassed-in cooking area. Prime beef is king here, where the preferred cuts are filet mignon, New York and top sirloin, accompanied by such old-fashioned items as shrimp cocktail, green salad, garlic bread, a baked potato or french fries, a relish tray (remember those?) and, this being California, a bowl of tasty salsa. The newer location in **Buellton (406 E. Highway 246, 805-688-0676)** also features items like fresh fish, smoked duck and seasonal game, as well as a grilled artichoke for dipping in roasted ancho pepper mayo. Ask for one of the chef's own special handcrafted bottles of Pinot Noir to accompany dinner.

HOPPE'S AT 901 CALIFORNIAN 14/20 

901 Embarcadero, Morro Bay 93442
805-772-9012, *Lunch Fri.-Sun, Dinner Wed.-Mon., Brunch Sun., $$$*

If chef Wilhelm Hoppe had opened his restaurant in Los Angeles, he would have the reputation of a Michel Richard by now. Instead he chose to stay out of the media limelight and landed in Morro Bay. From his restaurant's big bay windows, guests can see Morro Rock, an imposing five-hundred-foot volcanic boulder that juts majestically from the sea. Fortunately, Hoppe's food is equal to the view. Among his inventive dishes: a "tiramisu" mousse of smoked salmon and lobster, sea bass in a black pepper-peanut sauce, Peking duck with a fig-red onion compote and a hefty chipotle-spiced rib-eye steak for two. The four-course prix-fixe menu is a bargain. In fact, the quality/price ratio doesn't get much better than this.

IAN'S — CALIFORNIAN — 13/20

2150 Center St., Cambria 93428
805-927-8649, *Lunch Fri. & Sat., Dinner nightly, Brunch Sun.*, $$

Ian's is named after chef Ian McPhee, even though he's no longer cooking at this airy, comfortable restaurant in Cambria. The menu features top-quality meat, poultry and fish, embellished with fresh seasonal greens and vegetables. Starters might include a salad of grilled asparagus and goat cheese in a sun-dried tomato vinaigrette. Entrées, like filet mignon with a sauce of smoked tomato and cider vinegar, are inspired. Crême brûée and "chocolate decadence" bring dinner here to a luxurious finish. The wine list features local labels.

MATTEI'S TAVERN — AMERICAN — 10/20

Hwy. 154, Los Olivos 93441
805-688-4820, *Lunch Thurs.-Sun., Dinner nightly*, $$

This restaurant dates back to 1886, when Felix Mattei established the Central Hotel for weary stagecoach travelers. In the '30s and '40s, Clark Gable stayed here while on hunting trips. Today, Mattei's in no longer a hotel, but a weathered saloon and restaurant that has aged gracefully. Steak, prime rib, pork chops, chicken and rainbow trout top the menu, all served with green salads and warm bread.

McPHEE'S GRILL — CALIFORNIAN — 13/20 

416 Main St., Templeton 93465
805-434-3204, *Lunch Fri., Dinner nightly*, $$

Chef Ian McPhee shows the same obsession with quality ingredients that made his former restaurant (Ian's in Cambria) famous. The cooking reveals more cross-cultural influences, with such appetizers as Thai-inspired shrimp tempura with peanut dipping sauce and duck-and-cheese quesadillas with salsa fresca. Chinese-style, crispy-skinned duck with "secret kung fu sauce," and pizza with duck, Asiago cheese, red onions and ancho chile sauce, bursts with flavor. McPhee's charges only a few dollars per bottle over retail to encourage customers to discover the new vintners in this burgeoning wine-growing region.

OLDE PORT INN — SEAFOOD — 12/20

Port San Luis Pier 3, Avila Beach 93424
805-595-2515, *Lunch & Dinner daily*, $$

Local fishermen deliver their fresh catch right to the front door. The restaurant itself is just what you might expect at the end of a working fishing pier: a rough-hewn sea shanty with dark timbers overhead and big bay windows looking out to sea.

The downstairs dining room has been remodeled to provide an additional view of the ocean—through the floor. The specials here include a lusty cioppino, stuffed shrimp, red snapper, sole, halibut and salmon.

RODNEY'S CALIFORNIAN 12/20

1315 Second St., Baywood Park 93402
805-528-0459, *Dinner Wed.-Mon., $$*

On the other side of Morro Bay (the side without the rock) in Baywood Park, Rodney's looks like a beach shack that's weathered one too many storms. Don't be frightened off by the façade, though. This waterfront dive is the province of chef Rodney Aanerud, who offers inspired interpretations of California cuisine. You might find chicken breast stuffed with Stilton cheese and chopped walnuts served over a port wine sauce, or lime-marinated prawns served over linguine with avocado. The wine list is decent, and bargain dinners are offered nightly before six p.m.

TRATTORIA GRAPPOLO ITALIAN 12/20

3687-C Sagunto St., Santa Ynez 93460
805-688-6899, *Dinner Wed.- Mon., $$*

Grappolo rose from the ashes of the former Cicada, and it's the standard-bearer of contemporary Italian cuisine for miles around. The wood-burning oven cranks out zesty pizzas, and the Caesar salad, carpaccio and various pastas are first-rate. Our favorites: the falling-off-the-bone osso buco and the roasted half chicken.

VINTNERS' BAR AND GRILL CALIFORNIAN 13/20 

Hilton Hotel, 3455 Skyway Dr., Santa Maria 93454
805-928-3183, *Dinner nightly, $$*

Paul Kwong brings Italian, Mexican and Pacific Rim influences to California comfort food. Pork riblets with Asian black bean sauce or grilled crab cakes with a roasted chipotle mayo are good starters. We recommend the New York steak, cut into thin thirds, quickly grilled and served with fried onions and a twice-baked potato, and the albacore tuna with a Tuscan-style salad of grilled sqaush and white beans. The wine list is strictly local and all 200 selections are available by the glass.

AND ALSO...

ATARI YA JAPANESE

1551 Stowell Plaza, Santa Maria 93454
805-922-0025, *Lunch and Dinner daily, $$*

It's the yin-yang of West meets East when you stumble upon a restaurant in the middle of a Santa Maria shopping center that serves up raw fish rather than well-done chunks of beef with pinquito beans. It's not a mirage though, as this cozy little place serves sushi, sashimi and tempura with relish. The "soy cowboys" usually found dining here are local winemakers or recent immigrants from L.A., who come here to get their sushi fix. The quality is good, though the service is sometimes problematic. **Also in San Luis Obispo (1350 Madonna Rd., 805-541-2754).**

CAFÉ ANGELICA — CALIFORNIAN

490 First St., Solvang 93463
805-686-9970, *Lunch and Dinner daily*, $$

With the proliferation of Danish-style restaurants in Solvang, Café Angelica offers a refreshing alternative with its salads and sandwiches at lunch. On the dinner menu, you might find a gingered-carrot or a cold cucumber soup as well as a seafood chowder that's an entire meal. Crabcakes in aïoli sauce, spicy grilled prawns and the fresh catch of the day are flavorfully presented. Good pastas and even quesadillas show the diverse talent of the kitchen, though it's best to stick with the simpler dishes. The wine list features local labels.

DORN'S — AMERICAN

801 Market St., Morro Bay 93442
805-772-4415, Breakfast, *Lunch & Dinner daily*, $$

Get an eye-popping piece of the rock (Morro Rock, that is) from the bay-view windows of Dorn's, perched above the embarcadero. Breakfast is the big deal here, with lots of retro anachronisms like pigs-in-a-blanket. If you order blueberry pancakes, you get the blueberries hidden inside the flapjacks. At lunch and dinner, you'll find salads, pastas, clam chowder and fresh fish.

F. McLINTOCK'S — AMERICAN

750 Mattie Rd., Shell Beach 93449
805-773-1892, *Lunch & Dinner daily, Brunch Sun.*, $$

If you're looking for a cowboy saloon and roadhouse that cranks up the country-and-western music along with the cowboy steaks, McLintock's is the place. Serious beefeaters can tear into two pounds of meat, while those who are beef-adverse can opt for chicken or seafood. The place really jumps on the weekends but expect a wait—so many people get herded though the doors that McLintock's is one of the top grossing restaurants in America.

MUSTACHE PETE'S — ITALIAN

4090 Burton Dr., Cambria 93428
805-927-8589, *Lunch & Dinner daily, Brunch Sun.*, $

Here's a cozy Italian restaurant that masquerades as a bustling sports bar and is a local hangout. The Italian menu is nothing earth shaking, but pizza, pasta and seafood are the popular choices and the portions are huge.

OLD HARMONY PASTA FACTORY — ITALIAN

2 Old Creamery Rd. & Hwy. 1, Harmony 93435
805-927-5882, *Lunch & Dinner daily, Brunch Sun.*, $$

Harmony was once promoted as the smallest town in California and, in fact, it's just one lane of rustic buildings right off Hwy.1. Only a short drive from Cambria and Hearst's Castle, it's fun to dine in what was once an old creamery that has been artfully renovated. Salads, pizzas and pastas top the menu, but there are also shrimp, pork and chicken, all done in an Italian way.

QUICK BITES

American & Delis

APPLE FARM

2015 Monterey St., San Luis Obispo 93401
805-544-6100, *Breakfast, Lunch & Dinner daily*

The cutesy faux-Victorian architecture is a bit over the top for some. But there's no denying that this is a best bet for breakfast, with apple pancakes and waffles topped with real maple syrup and honey. At lunch and dinner, there are homey offerings like pot pie, barbecued ribs and meatloaf that are a notch above coffee shop fare.

JOCKO'S

Tefft St. & Thomas Rd., Nipomo 93444
805-929-3686, *Breakfast, Lunch & Dinner daily*

Here's a true American roadhouse circa 1950, with paper placemats, folding chairs, hanging plants and cattle brands burned into the woodwork. Local farmers and ranchers patronize this place and it's easy to see why. Their "farm boy" breakfasts are the real thing; you won't go away hungry when you order the slab of ham steak with fried potatoes, biscuits and gravy with salsa on the side. At dinnertime, beef is king and the steaks include fries, salsa and pinquito beans.

LINN'S BIN

2277 Main St., Cambria 93428
805-927-0371, *Breakfast, Lunch & Dinner daily, Brunch Sun.*

Sooner or later, everyone who browses through Cambria's shops, will end up at Linn's. It's like an old general store that serves as a local meeting place, with something for everybody. The café serves American food—salads, sandwiches and pot pies—while the bakery turns out a variety of breads. The gift shop has a large selection of local wines as well as their own line of jams, jellies and preserves.

OLD COUNTRY DELI

600 Marsh St., San Luis Obispo 93401
805-541-2968, *Lunch daily, Dinner Thurs.*

One of the best stocked full-service delis in town, Old Country Deli has a cornucopia of meats, pasta salads, cheeses and breads as well as a full compliment of beers and local wines. An obvious place to stock up before heading out for a day of winery touring. It also features its award-winning barbecued ribs Thursdays to Sundays only.

OLD CUSTOM HOUSE

324 Front St., Avila Beach 93424
805-595-7555, *Breakfast, Lunch & Dinner daily*

Earlier in this century, this quaint waterfront restaurant actually was the government customs facility for the Port of San Luis. A hangout for locals, it's especially popular for breakfast, when it serves a variety of egg dishes. Lunch and dinner feature grilled beef, pork and fresh fish.

PAULA'S PANCAKE HOUSE

1531 Mission Dr., Solvang 93463
805-688-2867, *Breakfast & Lunch daily*

There's always a line for breakfast at Paula's, but it moves quickly and the wait is worth it. The extensive menu features thin Danish pancakes, old-fashioned buttermilk pancakes, waffles (with or without fresh fruit and whipped cream!) as well as sausages, eggs and omelets. Service is brisk and the coffeepot is bottomless.

Brew Pub

SLO BREWING CO.

1119 Garden St., San Luis Obispo 93401
805-543-1843, *Lunch & Dinner daily*

The first brewpub on the Central Coast is wildly successful, principally because the students from nearby Cal-Poly hang out here. Most nights there's live music in the upstairs dining room, so eat early if you like quiet conversation with the above-average burgers, chicken wings, nachos and other bar food munchies. We like to sample the Brickhouse Pale Ale and Cole Porter in the first-floor pool hall, while shooting a few games of eight ball.

Creole

BON TEMPS CREOLE CAFÉ

1000 Olive St., San Luis Obispo 93401
805-544-2100, *Lunch and Dinner daily*

A made-over motel coffee shop that still retains its funky, Formica feel, Bon Temps serves Creole food at near coffee-shop prices. The Cajun popcorn (shrimp) is exemplary, as is the bowl of gumbo ya-ya with chunks of chicken and andouille sausage. The fried catfish with hush puppies is of the melt-in-your-mouth variety, and a number of etoufées are offered nightly, including alligator! Don't forget the sides of red beans and rice, and a couple of Dixie beers to wash it down with.

Ice Cream

SLO MAID ICE CREAM FACTORY

728 Higuera St., San Luis Obispo 93401
805-541-3117, *Open daily*
No Cards

Forget Thirty-One flavors. These folks go way beyond that. They crank out a panoply of flavors of ice creams, sherbets, sorbets and frozen yogurts. Popular with the locals (who support their own), this shop is a hub of activity in downtown San Luis.

Mexican

LA SIMPATIA

827 Main St., Guadalupe 93434
8052-343-9284, *Breakfast, Lunch & Dinner Tues.-Sun.*

It's a journey back in time to visit this restaurant in Guadalupe, about ten miles west of Santa Maria. Main Street is right out of the '30s, and La Simpatica itself looks like the old diner that it is, preserved with a patina of age. The Mexican fare is standard: combo plates, enchiladas, chile verde, Corona and magaritas. But you don't come here for the food. This place has authentic—and hard to find—regional character.

PETE'S SOUTHSIDE CAFÉ

1815 Los Osos St., San Luis Obispo 93401
805-549-8133, *Lunch & Dinner daily*

Pete's is a way casual, Formica top-tabled place that sits next to (and in contrast to) the tonier Café Roma. It's likely that owner/chef Pete Kelley himself will be manning the stoves and serving up the tasty Mexican fare: shrimp tacos, beef enchiladas and black bean burritos that are a notch above. The locals go for a touch of the islands—Caribbean, that is—with dishes like grilled snapper with plantains.

SALSITAS

0703 El Camino Real, Atascadero 93466
805-461-5500, *Lunch & Dinner daily*

A real find just off Hwy. 101 in Atascadero, Salsitas is the type of Mexican seafood restaurant we'd expect to find in Mazatlan. Deliciously fresh fish and chicken are smothered in your choice of a garlic-butter sauce, a spicy red chile sauce or the house special Veracruzano. The beef-and pork-based caldillos (stews) are well flavored. Homemade tortilla chips, as well as four distinctly different homemade salsas, are complimentary.

Seafood

SAN LUIS FISH & BARBEQUE

574 Marsh St., San Luis Obispo 93401
805-541-4191, *Open daily*
No Cards

This fresh fish market gets its daily catch from local fishermen. You can buy the raw fish to take home, but why bother when the proprietors prepare great grilled fish to go with their piquant sauces and side dishes. Halibut with mustard sauce or salmon in Champagne sauce, as well as a light and fluffy fish and chips, are just a few of the dozen menu offerings.

Thai

THAI-RRIFIC

208 Higuera St., San Luis Obispo 93401
805-541-THAI, *Lunch Mon.-Fri., Dinner nightly*

This small Bangkok-style Thai restaurant dishes up excellent renditions of classics like pad Thai noodles, chicken satay with peanut sauce and hot-and-sour seafood soup. They use liberal amounts of fresh garlic, serrano chiles, mint, lime, cilantro and lemon grass in many of their (spicy) dishes.

Wine-Tasting

Since the Central Coast is home to some of Southern California's best new wineries, we've included some spots where you can sample their bounty.

LOS OLIVOS TASTING ROOM & WINE SHOP

2905 Grand Ave., Los Olivos 93441
805-688-7406, *Open daily*

Located in one of the oldest buildings in town dating back to 1887, this wine shop and tasting room is devoted to quality local wineries that are closed to the public. For $3, you can taste any of the ten or so wines opened daily. You'll recognize some of the cult wineries, such as Au Bon Climat and Qupe, and you'll discover the newest from smaller family wineries like J. Kerr, Lane Tanner and Clairborne and Churchill. Along with the wines, there is often a small selection of olive oils and other condiments for sale.

LOS OLIVOS WINE & SPIRITS EMPORIUM

2531 Grand Ave., Los Olivos 93441
805-688-4409, *Open daily*

Located in the historic Los Olivos Market, this wine-tasting room features local wines that are not widely available, including Alban, Chimere, Makor and Whitcraft. It's one of the few places we've ever seen the lush Pinot Noir and Sauvignon Blanc from Kathy Joseph's tiny Fiddlehead Cellars. While the spirits—brandies, grappas, grape infusions, ports, liqueurs and small-batch bourbons—are not available for sampling, ten wines are available to taste for a $4 tariff. Check on their monthly winemaker dinners.

POPOLO'S

1255 Monterey St., San Luis Obispo 93401
805-543-9543, *Open Mon-Sat.*
No Cards

This small take-out shop will put together a wonderful picnic for winery touring, or you can select from the bountiful menu. Delicious Italian and French breads, along with cold pastas and salads, compliment the house dish: rotisserie chicken infused with fresh herbs and garlic.

Mountain Resorts

MOUNTAIN RESORTS

In the San Bernardino Mountains, just under a three-hour drive east of Los Angeles, are Southern California's most popular four-season recreational resort towns: **Big Bear** and **Lake Arrowhead**. With some peaks as high as 11,000 feet, it's no surprise that on snowy winter weekends, the mountains are overrun with skiers headed for the slopes. Summer is just as busy, when city people come here to fish, hike, water-ski, mountain bike and relax in the open spaces. As the dress code in these parts is pretty much jeans and athletic shoes, don't expect fancy coat-and-tie restaurants. Do expect homespun places, many with a rustic mountain decor and good home cooking. Many restaurants change their days and hours of operation according to the season, so call ahead if you're planning to stop in.

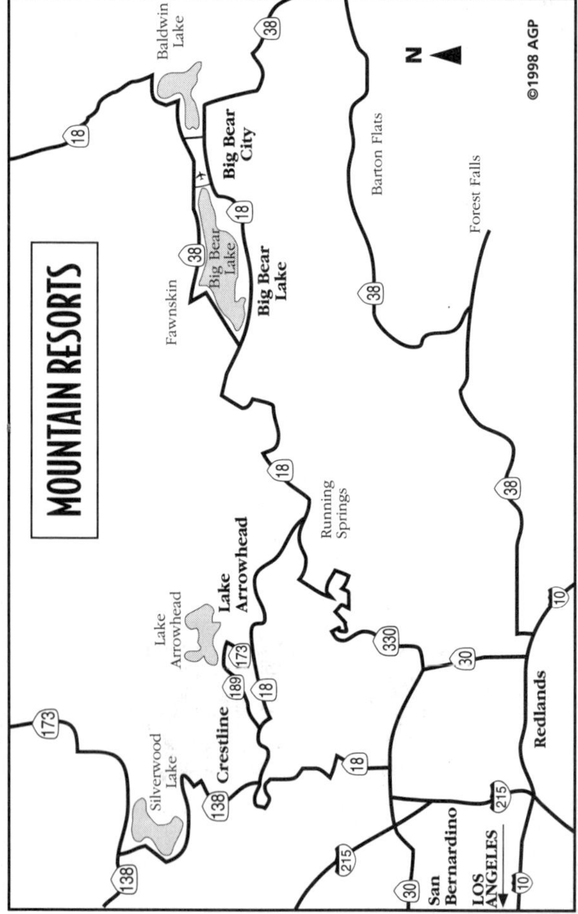

BIG BEAR

DINING

THE BLUE WHALE & TAIL OF THE WHALE AMERICAN 11/20

350 Alden Rd., Big Bear Lake 92315
909-866-5771, *Dinner nightly, Brunch Sun., Lunch in summer, $$*

Perched right over the lake, this Big Bear old-standby has a rustic decor—beamed ceiling, stone fireplace—and friendly service. Expect everything from pastas to roast duck to steaks and fresh fish, plus a salad bar. The adjoining Tail of the Whale bar is a bit more casual and often a lot livelier, especially on summer weekends when boaters moor at the dock and pop in for cocktails and the live music.

THE IRON SQUIRREL FRENCH/CALIFORNIAN 11/20

646 Pine Knot Blvd., Big Bear Lake 92315
909-866-9121, *Lunch Wed.-Sat., Dinner nightly, $*

A friendly family-run place that's been serving good French-country cooking for over 17 years. Entreés come with soup and salad, and include the comfort-food likes of veal Normande with apples, roast chicken and lamb shanks. Try the house pâté or one of the hearty pastas. The California-leaning wine list changes with the seasons.

MADLON'S AMERICAN 12/20

829 W. Big Bear Blvd. Big Bear City 92314
909-585-3762, *Breakfast & Lunch Sat. & Sun., Dinner nightly, $$*

Where Big Bear locals stop for their weekly omelet fix—often filled with ham, avocado, cheese and onions. Lunch features burgers, sandwiches, salads and south-of-the-border dishes. Dinners usually begin with cream of jalapeño soup and move on to fresh fish entrées or steaks, accompanied by fine wines.

AND ALSO...

THE BLUE OX BAR AND GRILL AMERICAN

441 W. Big Bear Blvd., Big Bear City 92314
909-585-7886, *Dinner nightly, $*

Peanut shells litter the floor of this informal, rowdy place. Catering to all food types from vegetarian dishes to Paul Bunyan-sized portions of steaks, ribs and chicken, this is a good spot for family dining.

MAGGIO'S PIZZA PIZZA

42160 Big Bear Blvd., Big Bear Lake 92315
909-866-8815, *Lunch & Dinner daily, $*

Year-rounders claim this the best pizza joint in Big Bear. The generous pizzas are made with fresh ingredients; the atmosphere is friendly, the prices low.

STILLWELL'S — AMERICAN

Northwoods Resort, 40650 Village Dr., Big Bear Lake 92315
909-866-3121, *Breakfast, Lunch & Dinner daily, Brunch Sun., $$*

Named after Big Bear's oldest family, Stillwell's has a rustic mountain lodge ambience, with Adirondack-style furniture crafted by a local artisan of raw birch, alder, pine and willow. The menu selections have cutesy names—"Papoose," "The Saloon Keeper's Daughter"—but they translate into eclectic American dishes, from ribs, spinach fettuccini and steaks to a raspberry margarita cheesecake.

LAKE ARROWHEAD

DINING

CASUAL ELEGANCE — AMERICAN/CONTINENTAL — 12/20

26848 Highway 189, Agua Fria 92317
909-337-8932, *Dinner Wed.-Sat., Brunch Sun., $$*

A cozy dinnerhouse with a big fireplace and a warm ambience. Entrées change with the seasons and include the likes of New York steak with béarnaise sauce, pork tenderloin with dried cherries and Atlantic salmon with raspberry sauce or chicken Marsala.

CHEF'S INN & TAVERN — AMERICAN/CONTINENTAL — 11/20

29020 Oak Terrace, Cedar Glen 92321
909-336-4487, *Lunch & Dinner daily, Brunch Sun., $$*

At this gingerbready inn (said to have been at one time a brothel) two miles from Lake Arrowhead Village, you'll find steaks, fish and pasta, along with excellent German sauerbraten, potato pancakes and Bavarian cabbage. Wednesday is $10.95 prime-rib night. The Inn has a modest wine list, and serves cocktails made in the first floor Tavern.

HISTORIC ANTLERS INN — AMERICAN — 10/20

26125 Highway 189, Twin Peaks 92391
909-337-4020, *Lunch Sat., Dinner daily, Brunch Sun., $*

This historic inn, built in the '20s, has an immense stone fireplace and is surrounded by forest. The menu is big on buffalo: buffalo steak, buffalo roast, buffalo hamburgers—even buffalo chili. Skillet-herb bread accompanies the entrées and the black-bean soup is savory. Behind the Antlers is Strawberry Peak, a local hangout for the California Spotted Owl. Entertainment on some weekends.

THE MULBERRY TREE — CONTINENTAL — 11/20

23794 Lake Dr., Crestline 92325
909-338-2793, *Breakfast Sat., Lunch & Dinner Wed.-Sun, Brunch Sun., $$*

This antique-filled restaurant features such eclectic offerings as mulberry-marinated steak, shark, quiches and gourmet pizzas. It's also one of the few mountain places with a lox-and-cream cheese bagel lunch. There are over 50 varieties of beer available. Yes, the antiques are authentic—the Wenzels own the antique shop next door.

THE ROYAL OAK CONTINENTAL 12/20

27187 Hwy. 189, Blue Jay 92317
909-337-6018, *Lunch Tues.-Sat., Dinner nightly, $$*

With its dark-paneled Irish/English/Scottish look, The Royal Oak has been doing what it does best for over twenty years: offering such classic dishes as veal Oscar, French-cut lamb chops, chateaubriand, chicken dishes and steaks. The place is a madhouse on St. Patrick's Day. Adjoining—but out of earshot—is a rowdy sports bar.

WR'S EATERY AT SNOW VALLEY CONTINENTAL 11/20

The Snow Valley Resort
909- 867-4160, *Lunch & dinner daily, $*

When snow is on the ground, skiers roar down the hill to the end of the run in front of WR's, a picturesque Alpine restaurant serving such hearty winter dishes as cheese fondue and beef bourguignon. Catch some rays and enjoy the view on the balcony.

AND ALSO...

EL PAPAGAYO'S MEXICAN

26824 Highway 189, Agua Fria 92317
909-337-9529, *Lunch & Dinner daily, $*

This is as good as it gets for Mexican food in the mountains, and the margaritas are served by the bucket. Super flautas.

SEASONS CONTINENTAL

Lake Arrowhead Resort
27984 Highway 189, Lake Arrowhead Village 92352
909-336-1511, *Dinner Thurs.-Sun., Brunch Sun. (open more often in summer), $$$*

This handsome wood-paneled, chandeliered dining room in the Lake Arrowhead Resort, has a wall of windows overlooking the lake. All the old-fashioned Continental favorites: veal, seafood, steaks and chicken dishes, served in elegant (for the mountains) surroundings.

Italcheese: Following Tradition To Bring Back Flavor and Nutrition

It's night and day. It's the difference between a wax coated or a vine ripened tomatoe. It's the difference that patience makes. The integrity to time proven traditions. And now Italcheese is proud to offer authentic Mozzarella di Bufala—or as the Italians like to say, "real Mozzarella." Carefully crafted and naturally fermented from the milk of actual water buffaloes, this wonderfully complex cheese is the only one of its kind produced in the United States. Its natural fermentation process allows its flavor to fully develop and, rather than creating lactose, this method creates lactic acid which aids the body in digestion. So for a healthy culinary treat, try Italcheese's Mozzarella di Bufala or any of their fine gourmet cheeses.

ITALCHEESE, INC.

400 E. Alondra Blvd.
Gardena, CA 90248
Tel:(310) 515-1481 Fax:(310) 515-1094
Email:italchees@aol.com
www.italcheese.com

CATALINA

CATALINA

Just 26 miles across the ocean is the island of Catalina, known for its aura of romance and California history and its pristine, rugged terrain—but not for its restaurants. Since many visitors come here to hike, bike, snorkel, dive, fish and swim—and enjoy Catalina's unique island environment, however, we'd like to point out the best places to eat. As some restaurants are open less frequently when the summer rush is over, check ahead on days and hours of operation. And if you're planning to go for a summer weekend, make dinner reservations well before you hit the beach. If you're lucky, you'll dine in a restaurant with great views, a festive vacation ambience and terrific fresh-caught seafood.

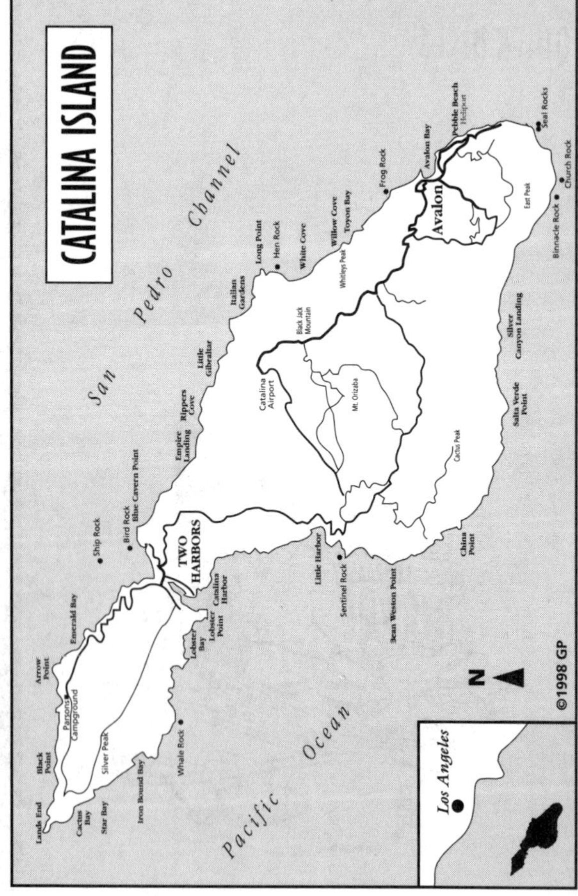

DINING

ARMSTRONG'S SEAFOOD 12/20

306 Crescent Ave., Avalon 90704
310-510-0113, *Lunch & Dinner Tues.-Sun., $$$*

With its cheery deck and blue awnings overlooking the water, Armstrong's is the quintessential Catalina restaurant. The fresh fish dinners are reasonably priced (swordfish, local red snapper and sometimes sand dabs for under $20), and the cooking is done on a mesquite grill.

CAFÉ PREGO ITALIAN 11/20

603 Crescent Ave., Avalon 90704
310-510-1218, *Summer Lunch & Dinner daily, Winter Dinner nightly, $*

An intimate spot on the waterfront with homey service, great views and decent food. The fresh fish entrées—swordfish, calamari—are good, as are such pastas as the rigatoni with broccoli, the cheesy lasagne and the linguine.

CATALINA COUNTRY CLUBHOUSE AMERICAN 12/20

1 Country Club Dr., Avalon 90704
310-510-7400, *Lunch & Dinner daily, Brunch Sun., $$*

Set in the historic (circa-1928) Catalina Island Country Club, this newly restored restaurant is filled with Chicago Cubs memorabilia (the team practiced here in the 1930s) and serves perhaps the most adventurous cuisine on the island. In the high-ceilinged dining room overlooking the golf course and the ocean, sample dishes that range from a hot crab-and-artichoke sandwich or onion-and-green-apple soup for lunch, to pad Thai, smoked mango baby back ribs or smoked prime rib and sweet-pepper pizzettes for dinner.

THE CHANNEL HOUSE CONTINENTAL 10/20

205 Crescent Ave., Avalon 90704
310-510-1617, *Lunch & Dinner, Tues.-Sun., $$*

Many tourists go from the ferry straight to the Channel House for an al fresco lunch on the terrace overlooking the harbor. Lunch is mostly salads and sandwiches, but the German platter of bratwurst, smoked pork loin, schnitzel and home fries, often accompanied by an exotic drink, is popular. Dinner is more formal, with tableside preparation of Caesar salads and flambéed desserts.

DOUG'S HARBOR REEF AMERICAN 11/20

Two Harbors
310-510-7265, *Lunch & Dinner daily in season, $$*

In remote Two Harbors, this is THE restaurant where boaters, campers and the lucky few able to get into the Banning House B&B nearby, come to drink and dine (it's also the only restaurant here). Stick with the fresh catch of the day and imbibe the local specialty drink, "Buffalo Milk,"an intoxicating brew of crème de cacao, crème de banana, vodka, milk, whipped cream and nutmeg. After a couple, you may end up dancing to the Golden Oldies that a disc jockey spins on weekend evenings.

RISTORANTE VILLA PORTOFINO ITALIAN 11/20

101 Crescent Ave., Avalon 90704
310-510-0508, *Dinner nightly, closed Jan., $$*

Adjacent to the Hotel Villa Portofino, this romantic restaurant offers ocean views and classic Italian cuisine. The result is a crowd, so be sure to make reservations for weekends. All the Italian basics: carpaccio, lobster ravioli, veal with lemon and white wine and large grilled shrimp. By Catalina standards, they are admirably prepared.

AND ALSO...

ANTONIO'S PIZZERIA ITALIAN/AMERICAN

230 Crescent Ave., Avalon 90704
310-510-0008, *Breakfast, Lunch & Dinner daily, $$*

Decorated with stuffed buffalo heads, 1950s-style bubblegum machines and jukeboxes, this waterfront eatery and bar is a good bet for everything from a hearty breakfast to a late supper. In addition to pizzas, expect meatball heroes and pastas. The live entertainment continues until late on weekends, and often includes rowdy talent contests.

BLUE PARROT AMERICAN

Metropole Market Place, Avalon 90704
310-510-2465, *Lunch & Dinner daily, $*

This casual and inviting spot is on a second-floor perch above the Metropole Market Place, and commands a terrific view of Avalon Bay. Stop in for a cocktail or one of their terrific burgers.

BUFFALO SPRINGS STATION AMERICAN

Catalina Airport, 1 Airport Rd., Avalon 90704
310-510-2196, *Breakfast & Lunch daily, $*

Named after the natural spring located at the base of the runway where the infamous Catalina bison used to gather, this casual spot specializes in—what else?—buffalo burgers, buffalo chili and buffalo tacos. L.A. business people in their small planes often hop over here for a quick lunch. A shuttle bus transports tourists from Avalon for a small fee.

QUICK BITES

CATALINA COOKIE COMPANY

205 Crescent Ave., Avalon 90704
310-510-2447, *Open daily, $*

This is where to get your chocolate-chip-cookie fix and a good cup of coffee. Among their repertoire of fresh-baked cookies are peanut-butter, oatmeal-raisin, fabulous piña colada macaroons and the "Eclipse," a fudge cookie dipped in white chocolate.

Outlying Areas

OUTLYING AREAS

On your way to Santa Barbara, Bakersfield, Palm Springs or Las Vegas? Here are some restaurants that are too far awa to be included in our Los Angeles, San Fernando Valley or San Gabriel Valley chapters, but ones we don't want to overlook. Where to eat if you're in **Upland, Claremont, Valencia, Saugus, Westlake Village, Simi Valley and Thousand Oaks.**

INLAND EMPIRE

DINING

CAFÉ PROVENÇAL FRENCH 13/20

967 W. Foothill Blvd., Upland 91786
909-608-7100, *Lunch & Dinner Mon.-Sat., $$*

If you think the Inland Empire and south of France hav nothing in common, you owe yourself a meal at this café where Ange and Nicole Lamonica turn out wonderful bouillabaisse and other regional specialties. Not unlike a countr French inn, the café features a roaring fireplace, sturdy wooden tables, dried flowers and hanging copper pots. We recommend the pâtés, French onion soup, coq au vin, veal flambée with Calvados, ostrich in a port wine reduction and file mignon in Roquefort sauce.

EL TANGO ARGENTINE 12/20

1077 W. Foothill Blvd., Claremont 91711
909-624-0334, *Dinner Tues.-Sun., $*

This family-owned eatery is adorned with travel poster gaucho gear and Argentine soccer-team pennants. In one corner, a pair of elderly men are often found hunched over chess board, glasses of Argentine wine in hand. The parillad an assortment of grilled meats, is a house specialty. So are th terrific empanadas, tender milanesas and the postre Borracho a dessert made of lady fingers soaked in sweet wine and layere with vanilla and chocolate puddings.

TUTTI MANGIA ITALIAN GRILL ITALIAN 12/20

102 Harvard Ave., Claremont 91711
909-625-4669, *Lunch Mon.-Fri., Dinner nightly, $$*

Sporting black awnings, a sleek glass facade, exposed bric and-sponge-painted walls and gallery artwork, Tutti Mang looks as if it should be in West Hollywood. It is more imbue however, with the friendly spirit of owner Eddie Inglese's other restaurant, the family-style Spaghetti Eddie's in Glendora. Recommended dishes include polenta with sautéed mushrooms, fried calamari, orecchiette with chicken, mushrooms and spinach in creamy garlic sauce, mushroom risotto and chicken in Gorgonzola sauce.

NORTH SAN FERNANDO VALLEY

DINING

CLAIM JUMPER — AMERICAN — 11/20

25740 The Old Road, Valencia 91831
805-254-2628, *Lunch & Dinner daily, $*

The size of the portions here are so huge, they'd satisfy both Paul Bunyan and Babe his Blue ox. The size of this eatery could easily accommodate them too, and we're sure they'd feel right at home with the hunting-lodge decor dripping in Western kitsch. Go for the earthy black-bean soup, ribs, pork-and-beef meatloaf and the spicy Tex-Mex egg rolls. Lots of micro-brews to go with. **Numerous other locations, including Torrance, Monrovia, Irvine, Long Beach, Rancho Cucamonga and Northridge.**

LE CHÊNE — FRENCH — 12/20

12625 Sierra Hwy., Saugus 91350
805-251-4315, *Dinner daily, Brunch Sun., $$*

Le Chene is located just this side of nowhere, but it's worth a drive to the far reaches of the Valley for its genuine French food and homey atmosphere. The menu is on a chalkboard, but your heart's desire is up there: escargots, tongue vinaigrette, shrimp Escoffier, veal forestière, roast quail Veronique. Classics like the thick-and-savory onion soup and the filet mignon au poivre are good, and you're sure to find something among the 700 wines on the house list.

SISLEY ITALIAN KITCHEN — ITALIAN

24201 W. Valencia Blvd., Valencia 91831
805-287-4444
See review in "SAN FERNANDO VALLEY—Dining."

WEST SAN FERNANDO VALLEY

DINING

BISTROT BY THE WATER — CALIF./PACIFIC RIM — 13/20 

860 Hampshire Rd., Suite Z, Westlake Village 91361
805-381-0094, *Lunch Tues.-Sat., Dinner Mon.-Sat., $$*

Chef Masao Itakura performs culinary magic in his little jewel box of a restaurant, hidden away downstairs in a business complex. It may take some looking to find it, but do. You'll enjoy the likes of crabcakes with a halo of yellow bell pepper sauce, shrimp and enoki mushrooms with a subtle sherry vinaigrette, roasted monkfish with caramelized shallots and green lentils. Even mundane-sounding entrées like rib-eye steak and pan-roasted chicken turn to gold in chef Itakura's capable hands.

DAKOTA'S BARBECUE/STEAKHOUSE 12/20

2525 Stow St., Simi Valley 93063
805-582-1700, *Dinner nightly $*

Formerly Tony Roma's, this large hilltop restaurant features some of the best mesquite barbecue around. It's so busy, that management passes out pagers to waiting customers. Wait it out for crispy fried onions, crunchy ribs, grilled chicken or any of the combo barbecue plates.

FINS SEAFOOD GRILL SEAFOOD 12/20

982 S. Westlake Blvd. #8, Westlake Village 91361
805-494-6494, *Lunch Mon.-Sat., Dinner nightly, $$*

Fins is a happenin' spot (at least for Westlake Village), especially if you drop in on a weekend night, when a jazz combo keeps the party going until late. As the name implies, Fins serves all manner of seafood—grilled, broiled, sautéed or deep-fried to your specifications—with potatoes, rice or pasta and seasonal vegetables. Starters range from Cajun seafood gumbo to sashimi-grade ahi tuna. Macadamia nut-crusted halibut and grilled salmon over cranberries and leeks in a citrus sauce show the kitchen can get creative.

GALETTO CAFFÈ AND GRILL BRAZILIAN/ITALIAN 12/20

982-2 Westlake Blvd., Westlake Village 91361
805-449-4300, *Lunch Mon.-Sat., Dinner nightly, $*

A rare outpost of Brazilian food in suburbia, Galetto offers Italian fare for less adventuresome eaters. But you owe it to yourself to try the "misto Brasileiro" of fried yucca, polenta and spicy sausage, the luscious empanadas and the marinated and grilled brochettes of shrimp or sausage with chunks of tomato, onion and green chile. You'll also find shrimp, skirt steak and pork chops, all given the Brazilian treatment, served with plenty of black beans, rice, plantains and the highly addicting chimichurri (garlic with cilantro, in place of the usual parsley) sauce.

MANDEVILLA ITALIAN/CALIF. 12/20

951 S. Westlake Blvd., Westlake Village 91361
805-497-8482, *Lunch Mon.-Fri., Dinner Mon.-Sat., $$*

Tom Sweet, one of the partners at L.A.'s trendy Ca'Brea, and that restaurant's former sous chef, Nick Blinoff, have upped the ante for fine dining in the West San Fernando Valley at this attractive restaurant. Though the majority of entrées are Italian-themed—we recommend the risotto-crusted

·hitefish—you'll also find crabcakes with spicy chipotle chili ream and a green apple tart for dessert. Except for one parkling wine, the small, but well selected and reasonably ·riced list features all California vintages.

:ITROVO ITALIAN 13/20

125 Lindero Canyon Rd., Westlake Village 91362
18-889-0191, *Lunch Mon.-Sat., dinner nightly, $$*

At this not-very-well-kept Westlake Village secret, Italian-orn chef Ambrogio Taramelli is whipping up virtuoso concoc-ıons like risotto pescatore, a blend of oysters and rice in :hampagne-and-white-truffle sauce, savory sage-rubbed lamb nd veal chops, grilled vegetables and wonderfully garlicky aby clams.

USCANY IL RISTORANTE ITALIAN 11/20

68 S. Westlake Blvd. #4, Westlake Village 91361
05-495-2768, *Lunch Mon.-Fri., Dinner Mon.-Sat., $$*

Neighborhood trattorias are virtually a fact of life in urban reas, but in Westlake Village, Tuscany is the only contender. Ve like the complimentary bruschetta, the over-the-top apoleon of grappa-cured salmon and Mascarpone or the sim-ler grilled portobello mushroom salad studded with garlic nd goat cheese. We've found some of the pastas have been isappointing, but the garlic-roasted filet mignon with mustard auce and green peppercorns is tasty as is the stuffed chicken reast in thyme sauce. Tuscany has one of the better wine lists n this part of the Valley.

087-AN AMERICAN BISTRO CALIFORNIAN 13/20 

087 E. Thousand Oaks Blvd, Thousand Oaks 91362
05-374-2087, *Lunch Tues.- Fri., Dinner Tues.-Sun., Brunch Sun., $$*

In the shadow of the new Thousand Oaks Civic Center, 087 has a light and airy bistro ambience. The contemporary ıenu includes such starters as a green salad with Gorgonzola, ears and roasted walnuts and another that features warm oat cheese with a sherry-shallot vinaigrette. Crispy whitefish is ppropriately crusty, with a splash of olive oil, lemon and apers, and grilled swordfish is topped with mango-avocado ılsa and accompanied by a wild mushroom tamale. The wine st is all Californian, well chosen and reasonably priced.

Northern Baja

NORTHERN BAJA

Due mainly to the influence of U.S.-bound travelers who wound up stuck in Baja, the peninsula's cuisine is a riot of flavors and styles. The Caesar salad was invented in Tijuana in the 1920s by an Italian dishwasher, who was homesick for his mother's. Mexican fishermen developed fish tacos. Baja-style lobster cooking, was dreamed up by the wives of Pacific coast fishermen. In fact, the influx of Chinese laborers, French miners, Russian farmers, Italian tradesmen and Spanish merchants created a unique crossroads cuisine in Baja.

A word about eating in Baja: The old warning "Don't drink the water" still applies, so always order bottled water in a restaurant. By law, ice is supposed to be potable, but you never know. If a restaurant looks reasonably clean and is doing a brisk business, you can feel reasonably confident about eating there. One thing is certain: it's hard to spend more than $20 per person on a meal, even at the best restaurants.

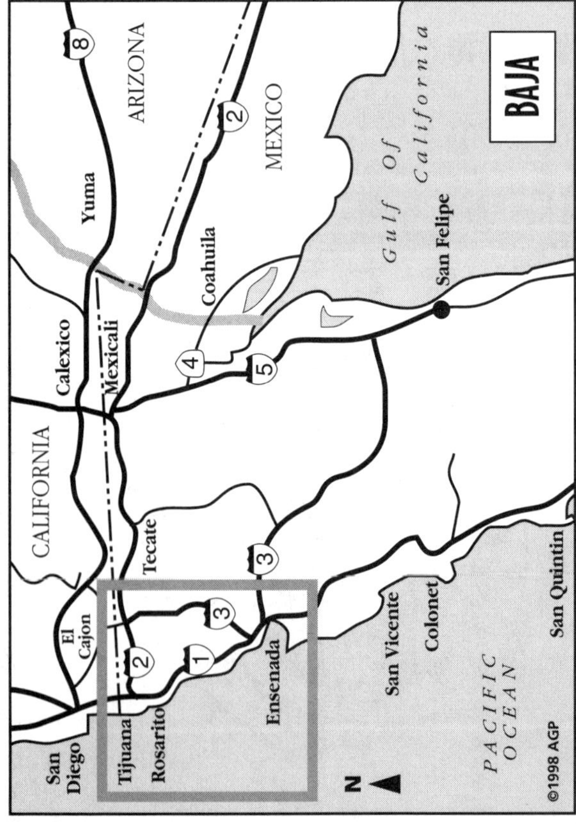

TIJUANA

DINING

BOCCACCIO'S NUEVO MARIANNA ITALIAN 11/20

2500 Agua Caliente Blvd.
01152-66-86-2266, *Lunch & Dinner daily, $*

This has been the most respected Italian restaurant in Tijuana for four decades. It may also be the most romantic, with rose-marble floors, softly glowing chandeliers, comfy booths and excellent service. Livio Santini, the inventor of the Caesar salad, who died in 1995, said this was the place with the most authentic Caesar. The homemade pastas come with distinctive sauces, and there are also many seafood dishes, along with some unusually well-prepared Mexican standards. *(Directions: Cross the border at San Ysidro and follow the signs to Centro. Turn left at Avenida Francisco Madero and stay on it for about half a mile until it ends at Agua Caliente Blvd. Turn left. About a mile down you'll pass the twin towers of the Grand Hotel de Tijuana. Just past them, you'll see the restaurant on the left with its own parking lot.)*

CIEN AÑOS MEXICAN NUEVO 11/20

1407 Jose Maria Velazco, Rio District
01151 66 34 30 39, *Lunch Mon.-Sat., Dinner nightly, $*

The Mexican "haute cuisine" served here is upscale but not snooty. The high-backed chairs and cushy booths are lit just brightly enough to read the all-Baja wine list. For a thrill, try the fried worms fresh from the agave (used to make tequila), served with blue corn tortillas and three salsas. The shrimp-stuffed chiles in lobster sauce, and a pungent rose petal sauce that graces a couple of dishes, are helping to define a new class of Mexican food. *(Directions: Follow the signs to the Rio District, go out past four traffic circles until you see the amusement park Mundo Divertido on your left. The restaurant is on the side street facing the amusement park.)*

GYPSYS SPANISH TAPAS 11/20

Pueblo Amigo
01152 66-83-6006, *Lunch & Dinner Tues.-Sun., $*

Dali reproductions abound in this art deco-style Spanish tapas bar and restaurant. The owner hails from Barcelona, and his Catalan-style menu carries not only the classic tapas (potato omelet, Mallorca dry sausage, shrimp croquettes, fried calamari), but also some powerhouse entrées, such as lusty paellas and baked halibut in anchovy sauce. The house sangria has a lovely cinnamon edge. *(Directions: At the border, follow the signs to Pueblo Amigo, a shopping center about 1/4 mile below the border. Look for the multi-story Holiday Inn, and follow the well-marked roadway leading to it. Located across a small plaza from a sports-betting parlor, the restaurant has a portrait of Salvador Dali outside.)*

THE RITZ PUB-CAFÉ — CONTINENTAL — 10/20

Plaza Sta. Maria, Local 6 Otay Constituyentes
01152-66-23-7011, *Breakfast, Lunch & Dinner daily, $*

The Ritz is a favorite of the plant managers and executives from Tijuana's thriving maquiladora industries, who can be heard discussing business in four or five different languages. The food is up to the challenge of worldly palates. Fresh spinach salad, tossed with a balsamic vinaigrette and brown sugar, is a house specialty, as are mushrooms sautéed at your table. Pato a la Naranja (duck a l'orange) is sensational, and for an indigenous Baja specialty, try the bacon-wrapped griddled quail. Italian dishes and pastas have recently been added to the menu. *(Directions: Take highway 905 east off I-5 or 805 to the Otay Mesa border crossing. Go straight on Industrial Blvd. six-tenths of a mile and take the right fork, following the signs: Aeropuerto/Centro. In less than a mile this road dead-ends at the Tijuana airport. Turn left. At the first signal, bear left around the traffic circle and look for the restaurant's sign on your right.)*

QUICK BITES

ORTEGA'S BUFFET — MEXICAN BUFFET

Rio District
01152-66-34-3655, *Breakfast, Lunch & Dinner daily*
No Cards

All-you-can-eat buffets caught on in Baja a few years ago, and continue to grow in popularity. At this mini-chain (there's another branch in Tijuana and one in Rosarito), guests sample from lavish spreads for $8 to $10 per person. Expect luscious tropical fruits, customized omelets (at breakfast), and grilled meats including lamb, beef and baby goat. Locals far outnumber tourists at these places, with large families attracted to the good value. *(Directions: Cross the border at San Ysidro and follow the signs to the Rio district. Ortega's is on the right about a mile south of the border.)*

ROSARITO BEACH

DINING

EL NIDO — MEXICAN — 10/20

67 Ave. Juarez
01152-66-12-1430, *Breakfast, Lunch & Dinner daily, $*
No cards

Mexican beef is lean, with that resonant range-fed flavor, and El Nido's mesquite grilling brings it out best. The brick and cactus-wood motif is particularly inviting. The house specialty is a fist-sized filet mignon, served with a small mountain of fresh guacamole on the side. The whole grilled quail here are also well prepared and farm-fresh—the owner has his own quail farm fifty miles south. *(Directions: El Nido is on the west side of the main road, about three blocks north of the Rosarito Beach Hotel.)*

QUICK BITES

CARNITAS LA FLOR DE MICHOACAN MEXICAN

291 Ave. Juarez
01152-66-13-0278, *Breakfast, Lunch & Dinner daily, $*
No cards

Surfers, campers, retirees and whole generations of local families grew up on the carnitas served here: thin-sliced deep-fried pork loin and steaming homemade corn tortillas for roll-your-own tacos. The condiments—salsas, guacamole, pickled carrots, chopped cilantro and onion—are consistently fresh and the refried beans are masterfully subtle. *(Directions: From the border, follow the signs to the Ensenada toll road. Rosarito is a fifteen-minute drive south of Tijuana. Take the first Rosarito exit onto the main drag. After the fifth stop sign, you'll see the restaurant on the right, marked by a sign depicting two nuzzling pigs.)*

ORTEGA'S BUFFET ROSARITO MEXICAN BARBECUE/BUFFET

See review in "TIJUANA"

PALMIRA PACIFIC RIM 10/20

Kilometer 46, Cantamar
01152-66-14-1203, *Breakfast Fri.-Sun., Lunch & Dinner daily, $*

About 12 miles south of Rosarito, this attractive thatched-roof roadhouse comes into view, with a menu you'll need a margarita to negotiate. For breakfast, try the menudo and Mexican omelets; at lunch, the Baja Bouillabaisse, the baked garlic cloves, the Caesar salad and the Crepes St. Jacques; at dinner, the lobster bisque under a cloud of puff pastry, the salmon in lemon-caper sauce and either the rack of lamb or the porterhouse steak. The tables on the rear porch overlook a grove of trees and are usually bathed in warm sun. *(Directions: Exit the toll road at Cantamar. The restaurant is right at the exit.)*

PUERTO NUEVO SEAFOOD 11/20

Kilometer 106, 10 miles south of Rosarito
Breakfast, Lunch & Dinner daily, $
No cards

This festive cluster of about 30 restaurants exists for one purpose: to serve Pacific lobster the way Neptune would want to eat it: split, shallow-fried in vegetable oil, and served with fresh flour tortillas, beans, rice and melted margarine. If you want a view, pick a place that appeals to your funkiness quotient. The place with the best reputation is farthest from the water: Puerto Nuevo #1 is its name; just look for the people waiting outside, while there are plenty of empty seats at other restaurants. The price per lobster varies with size, but you should be able to get a legally sized one for under $15. *(Directions: Take the Puerto Nuevo exit off the toll road, about ten minutes south of Rosarito.)*

ENSENADA

DINING

EL REY SOL — FRENCH — 13/20 

1000 Ave. Lopez Mateos
01152-61-78-1733, *Breakfast, Lunch & Dinner daily,* $

El Rey Sol has been around since 1947 and is much loved by Baja regulars. Offering French food and pastries, and attentive, professional service in an elegant but tourist-friendly setting, it is hard to beat on either side of the border. Chicken, duck, quail, fish, lobster, shrimp, beef and lamb are all well prepared, along with fresh vegetables from the restaurant's own garden. The abalone chorizo breakfast is a one-of-a-kind. Bring in some fish you caught and they'll cook it for you. *(Directions: Located on the east side of the main tourist street, Lopez Mateos, at the corner of Blancarte, toward the south end of town.)*

LA EMBOTELLADORA VIEJA — FRENCH/ITALIAN — 11/20

Ave. Miramar at Seventh St.
01152-61-74-0807, *Lunch & Dinner Mon.-Sat., Lunch Sun.,* $

Part of the Santo Tomas winery, the dark dining room is decorated with huge wine casks. Wine sauces are featured on a variety of seafood, meats and pastas. Only fresh local seafood is offered, so don't expect to find shrimp. Lobster is available in the spring. There are specials every day, and the pastas are all made in-house. Stand-out items include the cream of garlic soup and duck in Chardonnay sauce. We like the good selection of Baja wines. *(Directions: Enter Ensenada along the waterfront onto Lazaro Cardenas Blvd. Turn left onto Macheros Ave., which becomes Miramar. Follow it to Seventh St.)*

PUNTA MORRO — NEW AMERICAN — 12/20

Kilometer 106, Tijuana-Ensenada Hwy.
01152-61-78-3507, *Breakfast Sat.-Sun., Lunch & Dinner daily,* $

Perched on pilings above a rocky cove, Punta Morro is the place to be at sunset with your enamorata. The homemade bread comes with the house pâté and herbed butter. Among the most memorable dishes: a simple tomato salad with capers and sliced onions, and plump shrimp rolled in shredded coconut and fried golden-brown, resting on mango sauce. *(Directions: Punta Morro is a hotel and restaurant about five minutes north of Ensenada. There's a large sign directing the way from the toll road.)*

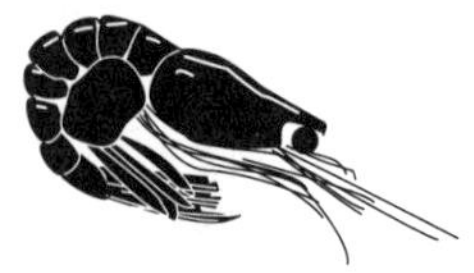

Las Vegas

LAS VEGAS

Since it is only a five to six-hour drive from Los Angeles, and discount airplane tickets and special hotel packages are readily available, Las Vegas is a popular weekend destination for Southern Californians. In the past few years, the opening of bigger and grander—and more grandiose—hotels & casinos have added to Las Vegas' luster as the capital of glitzy entertainment and high-living in the country, if not the world. People don't just come to visit this oasis in the desert. In fact, Las Vegas is one of the fastest growing cities in the nation. With the influx of more people, more venues and more money, the possibilities for fine dining have expanded as well.

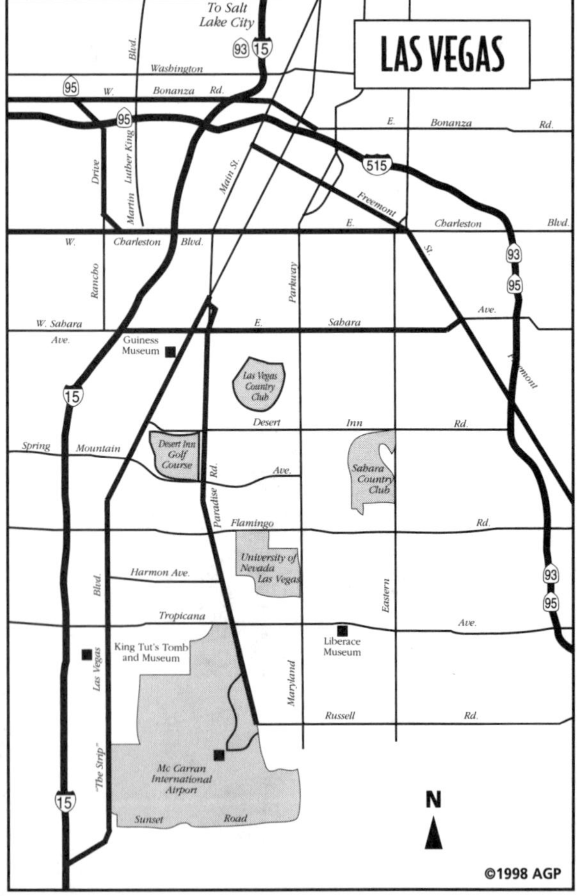

DINING

ANTONIO'S ITALIAN 12/20

Rio Hotel & Casino, 3700 W. Flamingo Ave., L.V. 89103
702-252-7737, *Dinner nightly, $$*

Often when you dine in a casino, the food is at best only okay—and very expensive. Antonio's is an exception. The antipasti bar offers luscious grilled eggplant, smoked shrimp, roasted red peppers and home-cured olives, and the bakery provides tasty Italian bread. Entrées include chicken or veal Marsala, fresh fish, made-to-order pasta dishes and much more. The wine list offers a nice selection, and the dessert cart carries a complimentary glass of Frangelica, Sambucca or Amaretto.

BAMBOO GARDENS CHINESE 12/20

4850 W. Flamingo Ave., L.V. 89103
702-871-3262, *Lunch & Dinner daily, $$*

In a warm, intimate and surprisingly English atmosphere, the owners do Chinese their own way, and it works. Freshly prepared spring rolls make exceptionally tasty appetizers, and the entrée selection offers a number of dishes unique to Las Vegas, including pineapple duck, grandfather chicken and firecracker beef. If you like it spicy, ask. The wine list falls short, but there are a couple of selections by the glass.

BERTOLINI'S ITALIAN 12/20

Caesar's Forum Shops, 3500 Las Vegas Blvd. South, L.V. 89109
702-735-4663, *Lunch & Dinner daily, $$*

A good reason to visit the colorful Caesar's Forum, Bertolini's offers patio or indoor seating and a delightful menu. We've enjoyed the pizza with roasted potatoes, rosemary and three cheeses, and the pasta tossed with wild mushrooms and a zesty red wine sauce. The wine list is limited. Still, this is a lively spot for people-watching.

BUCCANEER BAY CLUB CONTINENTAL 13/20

Treasure Island Hotel, 3300 Las Vegas Blvd. South, L.V. 89109
702-894-7350, *Dinner nightly, $$$*

Several small, nautically themed rooms with galleon windows form this "sea"-side restaurant. Beware: if you get a window table, you'll have half the restaurant clambering to peek over your shoulders at the hourly fight to the finish "sea battle" raging on the waves outside. Between the fiery cannons and sinking ships, enjoy starters of smoked salmon napoleon, silken lobster ravioli, and a buttery brioche filled with escargots. Entrées include spicy lobster Fra Diavalo and garlic chicken. Although some of the super-rich desserts could sink the proverbial ship, we like the Jack Daniels cake with fresh berries. If you linger over coffee, you're likely to see yet another sea battle between the pirates and the good guys. This being Las Vegas, the buccaneers always win.

BUZIO'S SEAFOOD 12/20

Rio Hotel & Casino, 3700 W. Flamingo Ave., L.V. 89103
702-252-7777, *Lunch & Dinner daily, $$*

A great find for those who love fresh seafood, which is flown in daily. We especially like the New Zealand mussels in garlic butter, the cioppino and the bouillabaisse. Fresh-baked crackers and bread complement your meal in this unpretentious dining room, where the background jazz provides a welcome change from the clang of slot machines.

CHINOIS CHINESE/PAN-ASIAN 15/20 

The Forum Shops, 3500 Las Vegas Blvd., L.V. 89109
702-737-9700, *Lunch and Dinner daily, $$$*

The latest Wolfgang Puck creation to be cloned in Las Vegas, this dazzling eatery features the cuisine that Puck created at his Santa Monica original, an inspired mix of Asian/French ingredients and styles. Puck-trained chef Munehiro Mori delights diners with such dishes as the chicken spring rolls with sweet-and-sour sauce, the pad-Thai noodles in a light peanut sauce, the duck-fried rice and wok-charred salmon. Chinois also features a terrific sushi-bar menu and exotic desserts, including fresh ginger cheesecake in a spicy gingersnap crust.

COYOTE CAFÉ DINING ROOM SOUTHWESTERN 14/20 

MGM Grand Hotel & Casino, 3805 Las Vegas Blvd. South, L.V. 89109
702-891-7349, *Dinner nightly, $$$*

In the middle of the glitzy MGM Grand Hotel is this New Mexican adobe building with high ceilings, traditional wooden vigas and terra-cotta walls. Owner Mark Miller has duplicated his Santa Fe restaurant and its signature modern Southwestern cuisine, implementing the distinct flavors of blue corn and hot-and-sweet peppers. Try the barbecued duck quesadillas and black bean soup laced with smoked cheddar cheese, the venison with corn-and-pecan succotash and the chicken with tomatillo-chayote salsa. Some of the dishes are tongue-numbing, but you can cool off with a tequila from their vast collection.

DRAI'S FRENCH/CALIFORNIAN 14/20 

Barbary Coast Hotel, 3595 Las Vegas Blvd. South, L.V. 89109
702-737-7111, *Dinner nightly, $$$*

It's L.A. in L.V.—a recreation of Victor Drai's Hollywood celebrity haunt in the desert. Old books line the shelves of the lounge, where, only if you have a dinner reservation, you can have cocktail drinks or listen to jazz until late. We suggest the pizza-like tarts, the whitefish-and-onion-marmalade on filo dough, and all of the fresh fish entrées, which are served with silken garlic-kissed mashed potatoes. The velvety crème brûlée, served in a china gratin dish, is sublime.

EMERIL'S SOUTHERN/SEAFOOD 14/20 

MGM Grand Hotel, 3799 Las Vegas Blvd., L.V. 89103
702-891-7374, *Lunch & Dinner daily, $$$*

Culinary legend Emeril Lagasse brings a taste of his native New Orleans to the desert. Decorated in nouveaux-French Quarter—louvered shutters, stone floors and a jungle of plants—Emeril's serves Louisiana crabcakes, turtle soup and lobster cheesecake with Creole-spiced tomato coulis—sometimes prepared by Emeril himself. Save room for a hefty slice of banana-cream pie.

ISIS CONTINENTAL 13/20 

Luxor Hotel & Casino, 3900 Las Vegas Blvd. South, L.V. 89119
702-262-4773, *Dinner nightly, $$$*

After wandering with craned necks through the world's largest hotel atrium, ride the private elevator to this small second-floor restaurant. The circular room, with large booths around its perimeter, displays glass cases of Egyptian tomb-treasure replicas, almost making us feel as if we're in the Egyptian wing of the Metropolitan Museum of Art. We've enjoyed the juicy breast of pheasant with foie gras, the crisp sliced duck in a cassis-and-ginger sauce, and a tender lobster tail with seafood mousse in buttery puff pastry. Desserts bring such favorites as strawberries Romanoff, chocolate soufflé, and our favorite, baked Egypt, which is slightly more exotic than baked Alaska.

LA SCALA ITALIAN 13/20 

MGM Grand Hotel, 3805 Las Vegas Blvd. South, L.V. 89109
702-891-7220, *Dinner nightly, $$$*

An elegant new eatery open for dinner only, La Scala offers both Northern and Southern Italian dishes on a nightly changing menu. Adjoining it is the casual Tre Visi, which serves three meals a day and features a wide selection of pizzas, pastas, chicken, veal and meat entrées.

MORTON'S OF CHICAGO STEAKHOUSE 14/20

Fashion Show Mall, 3200 Las Vegas Blvd., L.V. 89109
702-893-0703, *Dinner nightly, $$$*

As in all the other outlets of this upscale national steakhouse chain, the surroundings are clubby, the fare revolves around hefty and tender prime steaks, big baked potatoes and expensive wines to consume your winnings. See full review in "L.A. AREA—Dining."

NAPA NEW AMERICAN/FRENCH 15/20 

Rio Suites Hotel & Casino, I-15 & Flamingo Rd., L.V. 89103
702-252-7777, *Dinner nightly, $$$$*

Jean-Louis Palladin previously cooked for the high-and-mighty of Washington at his venerable Watergate restaurant. Now he's dishing up his sophisticated contemporary cuisine for high rollers of another kind. Among Palladin's specialties: caramelized endive tart with Maine lobster and lobster emulsion, wild salmon steak with ragout of cocoa beans and rack of veal with cardamon juice, spaghetti squash and foie gras. Amazingly, the wine list includes more than 600 selections, 240 of which you can order by the glass. Note the modern art on the walls, and the bronze sculpture that appears to climb, almost organically, from the floor to the ceiling in the middle of the room.

P.F. CHANG'S CHINESE 13/20 

4165 S. Paradise Rd., L.V. 89104
702-792-2207, *Lunch & Dinner daily, $$*

While P.F. Chang's offers culinary creations from the major regions of China, the light and airy eatery also creates specialties that draw on a multitude of traditions. On the menu, go right to the "Chang's Recommends" for such dishes as the lemon-pepper shrimp, spicy chicken, vegetables in soothing lettuce wraps and dumplings.

PALACE COURT FRENCH 13/20 

Caesar's Palace Hotel, 3570 Las Vegas Blvd. South, L.V. 89119
702-731-7731, *Dinner nightly, $$$$*

Tucked away in Caesar's Palace, this opulent spot was one of this city's first serious dining rooms and firmly maintains that tradition. The circular room has well-spaced tables among the trees and solemn statues of Roman dignitaries, and there's a dramatic domed stained-glass ceiling. The well-trained servers treat everyone like VIP high-rollers. The fancy food is for high-rollers too: a salad of grilled foie gras, tasty shrimp or lobster ravioli, garlicky rack of lamb with perfect pommes soufflés, a gigantic veal chop with mustard sauce and moist salmon in a potato crust.

PIERO'S ITALIAN/SEAFOOD 13/20 

366 Convention Center Dr., L.V. 89109
702-369-2305, *Dinner nightly, $$$*

This huge (345-seat) restaurant manages to be warm and welcoming in spite of its size, perhaps because there are various alcoves that insure privacy and owner Freddi Guzzman usually plays host. All the usual Italian dishes, with an emphasis on seafood; we've never enjoyed swordfish steak as thick and tender as it's done here.

RUTH'S CHRIS STEAK HOUSE STEAKHOUSE 13/20 

4561 W. Flamingo Ave., L.V. 89103
702-248-7011, *Dinner nightly, $$$*

Another pricey-and first-rate steakhouse chain. Here, the steaks are served dripping in butter, New Orleans style. See full review in "L.A. AREA—Dining."

SPAGO CALIFORNIAN 15/20 

Caesar's Forum Shops, 3500 Las Vegas Blvd. South, L.V. 89119
702-369-6300, *Lunch & Dinner daily, $$$*

One of the best—and most festive—restaurants in Vegas. Sample the brilliant culinary talents of America's number-one celebrity chef, who, when he's in town, can't stay out of the kitchen. The delicate foie gras with blackberries may make you think of France, but other dishes will remind you of the Great Wall of China: the lobster spring rolls, mu-shu beef and chicken potstickers. We always like Puck's pastas, such as duck breast with wild mushroom ravioli, along with such entrées as calf's liver with bacon marmalade and grilled chicken with double-blanched garlic. A more casual café fronts the restaurant.

TERRAZA ITALIAN 14/20 

Caesars Palace Hotel, 3570 Las Vegas Blvd. South, L.V. 89109
702-731-7731, *Lunch Wed.-Sat., Dinner nightly, Brunch Sun., $$$*

Set in an ornate rotunda overlooking the hotel's swimming pools and gardens, Terraza is casual by day, more elegant by night. And it's one of the few upscale hotel restaurants with outdoor seating. The menu includes all the Italian classics and such innovations as grilled herb-infused mahi mahi and, for brunch, cheese-potato pancakes. In the adjoining **Trattoria Lounge**, which boasts comfortable sofas, you can order pizzas and pastas.

WOLFGANG PUCK CAFÉ CALIFORNIAN 13/20 

MGM Grand Hotel & Casino, 3805 Las Vegas Blvd. South, L.V. 89119
702-895-9653, *Lunch & Dinner daily, $*

A knock-off of Spago, this is the place for zesty pastas and pizza while on a break from the tables—which are right at your elbow here. For something less Italian, count on the Chinese chicken salad or the rotisserie-roasted chicken with garlic-mashed potatoes.

AND ALSO...

COZYMEL'S MEXICAN

355 Hughes Center Dr., Las Vegas 89109
702-732-4833, *Lunch & Dinner daily, $$*

This coastal-themed Mexican eatery serves the standard tacos, enchiladas and tamales, along with an array of fresh Mexican seafood specialties. Try the grilled salmon marinated in ancho pepper and spices with a rich white wine-cream sauce, or ask for your fish grilled plain.

FRANCESCO'S ITALIAN

Treasure Island Hotel & Casino, 3300 Las Vegas Blvd., L.V. 89109
702-894-7111, *Dinner nightly, $$*

Francesco's handsome setting offers guests a glimpse into the excitement of the kitchen as chefs prepare Italian specialties. The dining experience is further complemented by celebrity artwork, including pieces by Tony Bennett, Phyllis Diller and Tony Curtis. The extensive menu includes fresh pastas, antipasti, Mediterranean-style seafood and fresh-baked breads. Among the classic entrées, are veal Parmigiano, veal Marsala and sautéed chicken with asparagus and mushrooms in a white wine sauce over grilled polenta.

SFUZZI

Fashion Show Mall, 3200 South Las Vegas Blvd, L.V. 89102
702-699-5777, *Lunch & Dinner daily, $$*

Sfuzzi (slang for fun food) is a tastefully done Italian bistro serving American-ized Italian food. Choose from pizzas and pastas, fresh salads, seafood and steaks.

QUICK BITES

Buffets

CARNIVAL WORLD BUFFET

Rio Suites & Casino, 3700 W. Flamingo Ave., L.V. 89103
702-252-7777, *Lunch & Dinner daily*

A

Every hotel in Vegas has a buffet, but this one stands out—many locals swear it is hands-down the best. Nearly 500 people come through here every half hour, filling their plates at stations representing ethnic cuisines from around the world.

GOLDEN NUGGET BUFFET

Golden Nugget Hotel & Casino, 129 E. Fremont, L.V. 89101
702-385-7111, *Lunch & Dinner daily*

A

This is one of the most popular buffets in Las Vegas, perhaps because it offers a huge array of traditional fare: roast beef, pastas, salad, soups, and fresh seafood including crab legs, oysters on the half-shell and peel-and-eat shrimp. Prepare to wait in line.

Delis

STAGE DELI

Forum Shops at Caesar's, 3570 Las Vegas Blvd. South, L.V. 89119
702-893-4045, *Breakfast, Lunch & Dinner daily*

A

A descendant of one of New York's finest delis, and a lot roomier, this flashy spot serves all the deli classics, from matzoh ball soup to thick corned-beef sandwiches.

Theme Restaurants

HARD ROCK CAFÉ ROCK 'N ROLL

4475 Paradise Rd., L.V. 89104
702-733-8400, *Lunch & Dinner daily*

A

In most cases, hotel-casinos open restaurants. In this case, however, the rock-and-roll-themed Hard Rock Café built a hotel-casino to go with it. After chowing down on burgers and a good Caesar salad, guests can stop in **The Joint**, a concert hall with live music—or hit the tables.

PLANET HOLLYWOOD MOVIES

3500 Las Vegas Blvd. South, L.V. 89109
702-791-7827, *Lunch & Dinner daily*

A

See review in "L.A. AREA—Quick Bites"

Glossaries & Indexes

BEACH EATS

In Los Angeles County, over forty-two miles of Pacific Ocean beach stretch from north of **Zuma Beach** just below the Ventura County line, to **Redondo Beach** in the south, near the Orange County line. Even if you dined out every day for a year, it would be nearly impossible to explore the myriad restaurants, cafés and take-out stands spread along this Los Angeles County coastal route. While in the past, perhaps some of these coastal restaurants drew customers more for the view than the food (and often *in spite* of the food), today that's no longer the case. The restaurants on or near the ocean cater to some of the most sophisticated people in L.A.—who can afford to *live* near the beach. When they go out to eat, they expect not only a great view—but great food as well. We're happy to have discovered ocean-view restaurants with food so enticing, we'd go there even if they weren't perched over the sea.

Because waterfront restaurants are in demand by residents and tourists alike, we warn you: reserve well in advance, and expect to wait for a table at those that don't take reservations—especially in perfect California weather. Though each beach-adjacent eatery has its own personality, ambience and type of cuisine, they all have one thing in common—an air of casual, fun-in-the-sun festivity, where you can experience the *California Dreamin'* lifestyle all year long.

For those who enjoy eating within sight or sound of the ocean—or seek a place to dine en route to or from the beach—we've devised this **Beach Eats** tour. Here we briefly describe our favorite beachside—and beach-adjacent—eateries from **Zuma** to **Redondo**. If you find one that piques your interest or meets your needs, turn to the page number indicated in parenthesis to locate the complete review, address and phone number.

We start our BEACH EATS tour in northern L.A. County and head south…

ZUMA BEACH

At the southern end of this windswept stretch of sand, the friendly, family-run **Monroe's Restaurant** (p.65) is snuggled under the cliffs. With its unimpeded view of the ocean, and its warm, personal service, Monroe's is a cozy hideaway for a romantic dinner or Sunday brunch. Try the halibut in a macadamia-nut crust or the Cajun catfish with pecan-artichoke sauce.

Just around the bend of **Pacific Coast Highway** that curves south from Zuma Beach, the tree-shaded **Coral Beach Cantina** (p.121)serves moderately priced Mexican fare and its own micro-brew. Celebrities who have houses in Malibu often bring their kids here. Sharing the Cantina's patio is **Zooma Sushi** (p.91), a popular dinner-only eatery where reservations are a must. In addition to good sushi, Zooma features excellent steamed clams and fried calamari.

SOUTH OF ZUMA

Perched high on a hillside looking south, **Geoffrey's/Malibu** (p.41) enjoys a most spectacular view of the coastline—perhaps the best of any coastal restaurant. The garden terrace is perfect for romantic dinners and for Sunday brunch, when eggs with caviar are among the offerings.

CORAL BEACH

Further down the coast, **Beau Rivage** (p.92) may be across PCH from the beach, but it offers a fine ocean view from the second floor dining room. Beau Rivage's flower-filled patio and fountain—and Continental menu—lend a Mediterranean flavor. **The Malibu Fish & Seafood Café** (p.128) sits on a windswept hillside above the ocean, where, from the tiered outdoor patio, all diners have a panoramic view of the cove. The place is usually packed with bikers and surfers enjoying the modestly priced fresh seafood.

THE MALIBU COLONY

The "Colony" is famous for its million-dollar beach houses, where Hollywood's rich and famous spend their weekends. When they go out to eat, they often choose Wolfgang Puck's **Granita** (p.43), a colorful undersea-fantasy of a restaurant serving Mediterranean cuisine along with Puck's famous pizzas. They also venture across the bridge to the restaurants in the **Malibu Country Mart**. There, **Malibu Mutts** (p.99) makes good burgers and hot dogs; the casual-chic **Fins** (p.38) serves fresh fish and sushi, and is popular for its weekend jazz evenings and its Sunday brunch; the family-run **Tra Di Noi** (p.96) trattoria features fat-free pastas; and **Taverna Tony** (p.84) serves authentic Greek food in a casual setting.

MALIBU

In California's most famous beach town, two local hang-outs are not on the beach at all, but across the street: **Allegria** (p.19) has a delightful garden patio and serves crisp-crusted pizzas, homemade pastas and, on weekends, features a special seafood grill; the **Malibu Inn** (p.99) is decorated with nearly 200 photos of its celebrity customers, and is popular for burgers and sandwiches, and breakfast all day long.

Perched over the ocean, the deck of the **Pier View Café and Cantina** (p.73) is always crowded. If you can get in (and do try—the view is worth it), enjoy the blackened chicken with tequila-lime sauce followed by the decadently rich Snickers cake. Further south, the upbeat **Dukes at Malibu** (p.35) typifies the California beach lifestyle. The sprawling surfing-themed restaurant has open-air seating, long narrow dining rooms where every table has a view, and a sand-floored patio bar. Two additional right-over-the-crashing-waves restaurants are **Moonshadows Bar and Grill** (p.95), a romantic setting for fresh seafood, and the wood-paneled **Chart House** (p.93), known for its steaks and seafood.

On the "land" side of PCH, beach-goers stop for sushi and tempura at the very casual **Something's Fishy** (p.96). Next door, sawdust covers the floor of the **Reel Inn** (p.76), known for fresh, reasonably priced seafood. **Hannah's Cantina** (p.122)serves healthy no-lard, low-oil Mexican dishes on its funky open-air deck, and has the ambience of a beachside café in Baja.

WHERE SUNSET MEETS PCH

There's always a crowd at **Gladstone's 4 Fish** (p.43), a huge restaurant that does a bigger business than just about any other restaurant in Southern California. If you have to wait for a table (which you undoubtedly will), grab a handful of peanuts from the barrel on the deck, order a beer and a bucket of clams, and sit back and watch the seagulls. Once inside, hold out for a window table, and dine on huge portions of fresh crab, lobster and "mile-high" chocolate cake.

SANTA MONICA

Ocean Avenue is where Santa Monica's commercial district dead-ends at the palm-tree-lined bluffs overlooking the sea. In most of the restaurants here, you'll get a ocean view from one of the window or patio tables. We urge diners to come at sunset. On a clear day, everyone stops what they're doing to watch the sun sink over the horizon, tinting the sea and the clouds day-glo hues of pink, orange and violet.

On Ocean Avenue, the best spot for fresh seafood is the modern, sleek-lined **Ocean Avenue Sea Food** (p.68), where the oyster bar is busy all day long. Nearby, **I Cugini** (p.45) is an airy—and sometimes boisterous—Italian trattoria with an open kitchen and a sunny sidewalk patio. A favorite with celebrities is the **Ivy at the Shore** (p.48), the sister restaurant to the tony Ivy in West Hollywood. Yes, it's pricey, but the upscale-beach-shack interior, bar scene, and such dishes as crabcakes and Cajun prime rib are hard to beat. Two neighboring spots are less expensive: **Il Fornaio** (p.46) of the venerable Italian bakery/café chain, and **Red** (p.75) where the staff is hip, the food is contemporary (we love the portobello mushroom sandwich) and the interior is all done in..what else?...*red.*

THE SANTA MONICA PIER

From **Ocean Avenue**, take the overpass to this legendary landmark, where visitors can ride the old-fashioned carousel or the new roller coaster. There are penny arcades and take-out joints selling everything from corn-dogs and burgers to fish 'n chips. A terrific place for breakfast and lunch *right on the beach* is **Back On The Beach** (p.106). Wiggle your toes in the sand while enjoying a feta-spinach omelet or a barbecued chicken pizza.

SOUTH OF THE SANTA MONICA PIER

Loews Santa Monica Beach Hotel has a stunning new restaurant, **Lavande** (p.55), which has a sublime view and serves upscale French Provençal cuisine with a Californian twist. We especially recommend the garlic-scented fish soup, and the lavender-scented ice cream for dessert. Where Pico Blvd meets the beach is **Shutters Hotel,** a swank reproduction of a '40s beach cottage right out of *Martha Stewart Living.* The hotel's signature restaurant, **One Pico** (p.69) serves fine New American cuisine—it's where celebrities dine when they hope the people sitting nearby will be staring at the ocean view, *not* at them. Downstairs, just a few feet from the bike path, the hotel's sunny **Pedals Café** (p.72) is popular for Sunday brunch, when Belgian waffles with strawberries are the popular choice.

THE VENICE BEACH PROMENADE

South of Shutters, this colorful and chaotic stretch of ocean boardwalk has been an L.A. landmark since the '60s—and still retains much of its "Hippie" look and feel. Among the tattoo parlors, T-shirt shops, pizza joints and ice-cream stands, there are some pretty good places to eat: Sit on the crowded patio of the **Venice Bistro** (p.110) and try a chicken burrito or pizza while watching the frenetic boardwalk parade. Grab a wonderfully spicy-and-sloppy sausage sandwich at the original **Jody Maroni's** (p.98). **The Figtree** (p.116) serves (very slowly) such lusty dishes as grilled polenta with pure maple syrup and latkes with herbed chicken sausage and apple butter. **The Sidewalk Café** (p.109) is set in one of the few remaining original Venice buildings, which dates back to 1904. Along with a full menu, they serve breakfast all day long on the sidewalk patio.

VENICE

Several popular restaurants are within a block or so of the beach: **James' Beach** (p.49) draws an artsy neighborhood crowd (and remember, this is a neighborhood full of famous artists). They come to hang out at the bar, listen to jazz and dine on such contemporary dishes as the "Venice pu-pu plate" and the seared ahi tuna. On the casual patio of **26 Beach Café** (p.110), diners chow down on burgers and a variety of hearty pastas. **C&O Trattoria** (p.117) serves enormous portions of low-priced Italian food, killer garlic rolls, but is most famous for its sing-a-longs.

MARINA DEL REY

South of Venice, Marina del Rey is famous for its yacht harbor, sailboat races—and singles' scene. Marina restaurants tend to be huge sprawling affairs, with great harbor views, lively bars and popular Sunday brunches. Many are part of national chains: **The Chart House** (p.93), features steaks and a mega-salad bar; **The Cheesecake Factory** (p.107) draws big crowds with its something-for-everyone menu and reasonable prices; the over fifty-year-old **Casa Escobar** (p.92) features Mexican food, a lively sports bar and dancing on the weekends. **Teaser's** (p.106) is a Yuppie haven with a wall of big screens above the bar showing all the games of the season. At **Waikiki Willie's Rock & Roll Seafood** (p.97) there is always a party—featuring flaming cocktails, sing-a-longs and dinner 'til midnight.

For upscale, more elegant dining in the Marina, there are two options. **The Dining Room of the The Ritz-Carlton Hotel Marina del Rey** (p.77) offers distinctive Californian/French fare in a dark-and-quiet wood-paneled dining room. The sleekly-modern **Café Del Rey** (p.25) features dramatic presentations of inventive Pan-Asian food. Both restaurants have superb service and offer lovely marina views.

If you wish to dine not just facing the Marina but *on* it, sign up for a weekend dinner or brunch cruise on a **Hornblower Cruises** yacht (p.44). The cruises leave from **Fisherman's**

Village, and are especially good for special occasions. Where the Marina meets the sea at the breakwater is **Shanghai Reds** (p.80). Almost every table has a view of the sailboats, their sails billowing like Chinese lanterns. We love dipping their fresh-baked focaccia rolls into the buttery-lemon steamed clam broth.

SOUTH OF MARINA DEL REY AND LAX

The **Beach Cities** flow down the coast, merging nightly into a ribbon of lights. Yet each of them—**Manhattan Beach, Hermosa Beach and Redondo Beach**—retains its own unique charm and distinct flavor.

MANHATTAN BEACH

Pancho's (p.199), a colorful two-tiered hacienda-style restaurant, is a local favorite for Mexican food and partying. **Sunset's** (p.196) overlooks the promenade and the **Manhattan Beach Pier**, and offers a panoramic view of the coastline through its second-floor picture windows. Bright and airy, with snappy service and fresh seafood, Sunset's is a perfect place to grab a beer and nachos in the afternoon, and watch the volleyball games on the beach below. Across the street, the **Shellback Tavern** (p.197) serves everything from burritos to spaghetti, and has good perches for watching the surfing.

You'll find more serious restaurants in Manhattan Beach too: **Café Pierre** (p.186) serves California-French fare—expect everything from steak to duck-sausage cassoulet. At the new, high-tech and very hip **Michi** (p.190), everyone comes for the myriad martinis and inventive Californian-Euro-Asian food.

HERMOSA BEACH

The Bottle Inn (p.194) is named for the collection of tiny bottles that cover the walls, the windows—the whole restaurant. It's been here forever, and serves old-fashioned Italian food in friendly surroundings. A bit out of the way, but well-known by beach-city locals, is **Martha's 22nd St. Grill** (p.195). Its breezy ocean-view patio is usually packed on weekends, where breakfast is served all day long. Try their eggs "Manhattan" with tomato, spinach and mushrooms.

Old Town Hermosa is the lively area near the **Hermosa Beach Pier,** where you'll find places for coffee, comedy, billiards, and every food imaginable, all within a few blocks of the beach. Directly on the beach, **Good Stuff** (p.198) serves healthy burgers and wrap sandwiches, and draws bikini-clad beach-goers who opt for the whole-wheat pancakes.

Pier Avenue is lined with restaurants and shops. Among them, **Thelen's Mermaid Restaurant** (196) is a local landmark—its dark bar and wooden booths have been seen in many a movie. Locals line up for such all-American favorites as roast turkey with all the trimmings. Nearby, **Cantina Real** (p.194) serves Mexican food with California accents, both on the sunny patio and in the inviting sky-lit interior. **Hennessey's Tavern** (p.198) serves a large selection of imported Irish beers and specializes in corned beef and cabbage. Sit on the ocean-view patio and try the mini "gourmet burger sampler." Next door is the **Hermosa Fish Market Café** (p.199), where you'll find at least eight varieties of fresh char-broiled fish daily, along with fish curry, fish tacos and fish teriyaki. Again, there's a pleasant patio for dining in the ocean breeze.

Facing the beach, **Scotty's on the Strand** (p.195) is a genuine '50s diner that's been serving solid, reasonably-priced fare for over 40 years, and is a favorite with the volleyballers who hit the nets nearby. **The Spot** (p.198) serves healthy vegetarian lunches and dinners to a loyal local following.

REDONDO BEACH

The **King Harbor Marina** is a sprawling restaurant-and-shopping complex flanking the yacht harbor, and offers many good dining choices. The **Chart House** (p.186)—the first Southern California outlet of what over thirty years has become a national chain—is right here, and commands a 180° view of the coastline. Some say that it's the best of the chain, especially with such additions as caviar to its salad bar. Another chain restaurant, **Charley Brown's** (p.195), also offers a view along with steak, seafood—and a rollicking "Happy Hour."

The hacienda-style **Camachos Grill** (p.194) is known for its killer margaritas, Caribbean-spiced dishes, and spicy salsa music on Saturday nights. Next door, **The Cheesecake Factory** (p.197) has a marina view. At the **Waterfront Restaurant** (p.193), expansive windows take in the view of the channel. On a sunny afternoon, share a bucket of clams on the patio; on Saturday nights, stay after dinner for live music and dancing. The Sunday buffet brunch is one of the most elaborate on the coast.

Splash! (p.192) is perhaps the most exciting new restaurant on the coast. Located next to the Crowne Plaza Hotel, Splash! features a spectacular contemporary decor, lovely ocean views and innovative Euro-Cal-Asian dishes created by chef Serge Burckel.

There are a number of casual spots—with patios—where you can grab a bite: **Ruby's** (p.197), a red-white-and-hip '50s-style diner; **Chillers Bar and Grill** (p.198), a favorite with surfers by day and with music-lovers on weekend evenings when it hosts a "battle of the bands"; and **Polly's on the Pier** (p.197), which caters to sports fishermen—they open at 5 a.m. **The Blue Moon** (p.185) features panoramic views of the channel from its several intimate dining rooms. For fresh seafood, stop at **Captain Kidd's** (p.199), where you can pick your fish from the tank and they'll cook it to order.

THE REDONDO PIER

At the **International Boardwalk**, among the shops and amusement rides, are a few restaurants and cafés. Try the **Fun Fish Market and Restaurant** (p.199) for fresh fish and a variety of seafood cocktails, chowders, salads and sandwiches. Across the breakwater on **Redondo Pier** is **Old Tony's** (p.190), which has survived high tides and storms since 1952. We like the circular bar perched above the restaurant, where you get a birds-eye view of the marina and the ocean.

Fun & Unusual Ways to Dine

Tired of going to the same old restaurants? Need some excitement in your life? Here are some ideas to add zip to your everyday dining experiences in the Southland. All the restaurants mentioned below are reviewed in the book. Check the index for the page number where you can find a complete description, address and phone number.

- Watch Kavee, the Thai Elvis impersonator, sing *Blue Suede Shoes*, while eating pad Thai at the **Thai Food Court** in **Hollywood**.
- Go whale-watching in **Morro Bay**, then dine with a view of the rock at **Hoppe's at 901**, one of the best restaurants in the **Central Coast** area.
- Grab a corned-beef sandwich at four in the morning at **Jerry's Deli** in **Westwood**—they're open all night.
- Only in **Las Vegas**: Watch the faux sunset every hour on the hour while dining at **Bertolini's** in the **Caesar's Forum Shops**.
- Do like Homer Simpson and pig out at **Todai's** all-you-can-eat sushi buffet in the **Beverly Center**.
- Down a "Drunk Ivan" vodka drink with the Russians who spend their Saturday nights at **Ubekestan** in **Hollywood**, where there's good chicken Kiev and a wild one-man band.
- Pick up a bag of warm bagels, cream cheese and lox at **Goldstein's** in Arcadia, on your way to **Santa Anita Race Track**. Your horse may not come in, but you'll be well-fed—Goldstein's bagels are the best in the Southland.
- Take the train to **Santa Barbara**, spend the day on the beach, then dine and watch the State Street scene from the balcony of the **Zia Café,** before hopping back on the train for the trip home.
- Be a part of the casual-chic crowd dining al fresco at glamorous **Sunset Plaza** on Sunset Strip. Among our favorite spots: **Chin Chin** and **Pasta, Etc**.
- Gallop through the hills of **Griffith Park** at sunset, then enjoy enchiladas and margaritas at a Mexican restaurant in

the valley before the night ride back. (**Sunset Stables**, 3400 N. Beachwood Dr., Hollywood; 213-464-9612)

- You'll think you're in Mazatlan: Share a tray of fresh shrimp fajitas while listening to the strolling Mariachis at the **San Pedro Fish Market**, adjacent to **Ports O' Call Village** in **San Pedro**.
- Clap your hands and sway to the music at the Sunday Gospel brunch at Sunset Strip's **House of Blues.**
- Practice your Spanish while sitting at one of the communal tables and eating empanadas at **Guelaguetza**, L.A.'s best Oaxacan restaurant.
- No lifeboats necessary. Dress up and pretend you're dining on the *Titanic* at **Chelsea**, aboard the *Queen Mary* in **Long Beach**.
- Take the train to **San Juan Capistrano**, watch the swallows at the Mission, then dine on the oak tree-shaded patio of the historic **Ramos House Café**.
- See *Blue Boy* and other famous English paintings at the **Huntington Library & Gardens**, then stop for afternoon tea in their tea salon. Afterwards, stroll through their exquisite gardens.
- Go salsa dancing on Thursday nights at **La Bamba** in **Pasadena**, where the Caribbean-accented food is as spicy as the music.
- Take a soaring helicopter ride over the city skyline, then dine at **Typhoon**, overlooking the **Santa Monica Airport** (800-998-4354).
- Check out Chinatown, then stop for dim sum at one of the many Chinese restaurants that do dumplings, such as **Ocean Star** or **Empress Pavilion**.
- Go rollerblading on the Santa Monica beach bikepath, then dine with your toes in the sand at **Back on the Beach.**
- Rent a boat on **Big Bear Lake**, then moor it at **The Blue Whale** for Sunday brunch and live music.
- Break some plates at the lively Greek taverna, **Papadakis**, in **San Pedro**.
- Take swing-dancing lessons in between courses at the '40s-style **Moonlight** in Sherman Oaks.
- In **Palm Springs**, pick up lunch to-go at **Louise's Pantry**, then take it up to the top of the **Palm Springs Aerial Tramway** for a hike and a picnic.
- Luxuriate in the "Japanese Experience" at **Little Tokyo's New Otani Hotel**, which includes an overnight stay in a Japanese-style suite, a Japanese massage, and a Japanese dinner in the hotel's **A Thousand Cranes** restaurant.
- Get a ringside seat for the sea battle of the pirates and the good guys at the **Buccaneer Bay Club** in **Las Vegas' Treasure Island Hotel**. This being Vegas, the pirates always win.
- Watch your sushi chef break into a tap-dancing routine at the lively **Sushi on Tap** in **Studio City**—make sure he's not holding his knife!

- Tour the **Santa Barbara Mission**, then have brunch in the **El Encanto Hotel Dining Room,** enjoying the magnificent view of the Pacific coastline.
- Take the trolley car from **San Diego** to **Tijuana** for shopping, then dine at **Boccacco's Nuevo Marianna**, where, they say, the Caesar salad was invented.
- Lift weights with Arnold Schwarzenegger at World Gym in **Venice**, then carbo-load at his restaurant, **Schatzi on Main**.
- Tour **The Hearst Castle** in **San Simeon,** then dine at **Ian's** in **Cambria**, a quaint town set among pine trees that still has a '60s feel.
- Stand in line behind Julia Child for the soft tacos at **La Super-Rica** in **Santa Barbara**—Julia says they're the best north of Mexico.
- Steel yourself for an overnight flight to Europe—or pretend that you are—while dining among the lava lamps at **LAX's** zany futuristic restaurant **Encounter**.
- Make a meal of little tapas, washed down with Sangria, at **Allegria** in **Long Beach**. Tapas are also big at **Cava** in **West Hollywood**, where there's live music upstairs on the weekend.
- Pamper yourself in the **Ojai Valley Inn's Spa**, then dine in the cozy comfort of **Suzanne's** in **Ojai.**
- Go mountain biking in the **Santa Ynez Mountains** to a destination where a picnic lunch prepared by the **San Ysidro Ranch's Stonehouse Restaurant** awaits you.
- Take the fast boat to **Catalina's Two Harbors**, go for a hike, then cool off with a "Buffalo Milk" drink at **Doug's Harbor Reef Restaurant.**
- Go hiking in **Topanga State Park**, then dine al fresco at **Inn of the Seventh Ray**, where the Sixties never ended.
- Have a Moroccan feast in a billowing Bedouin tent on the beach, catered by **Koutoubia** of **Westwood.**
- Go on a fishing cruise from the **Malibu Pier**, then dine with the stars at Wolfgang Puck's **Granita** in **Malibu.**
- Get centered at the **Self-Realization Fellowship Lake Shrine**, then chow down on super pizza at **Vittorio!, Pacific Palisades'** favorite pizza parlor.
- Take a taste of Tuscany to the beach, by picking up a picnic first at **Rösti** in **Brentwood.**

MENU SAVVY

A GUIDE TO INTERNATIONAL FOOD TERMS

FRENCH

Agneau: lamb

Aïoli: garlicky mayonnaise

Américaine: sauce of white wine, Cognac, tomatoes and butter

Andouille: smoked tripe sausage, usually served cold

Anglaise: boiled meats or vegetables

Béarnaise: sauce made of shallots, tarragon, vinegar and egg yolks, thickened with butter

Béchamel: sauce made of flour, butter and milk

Beurre blanc: sauce of wine and vinegar boiled down with minced shallots, then thickened with butter

Beurre noisette: lightly browned butter

Bisque: rich, velvety soup, usually made with crustaceans, flavored with white wine and Cognac

Blinis: small, thick crêpes made with eggs, milk and yeast

Boeuf bourguignon: beef stew with red wine, onions and lardons (Lardoon; larding fat cut into long strips and threaded through lean cuts of meat by a special larding needle in order to moisten the meat as it cooks).

Bombe glacée: molded ice cream dessert

Bordelaise: fairly thin brown sauce of shallots, red wine and tarragon

Borscht: thick Eastern European soup of beets and boiled beef, often garnished with a dollop of sour cream

Boudin noir: blood sausage

Bouillabaisse: various fish cooked in a soup of olive oil, tomatoes, garlic and saffron

Bourride: sort of bouillabaisse, usually made with large white fish, thickened with aïoli; served over slices of bread

Brie: cow's milk cheese with a soft, creamy inside and a thick crust, made in the shape of a disk and sliced like a pie

Brioche: a soft loaf or roll, often sweetened and used for pastries

Brochette: on a skewer

Canapé: small piece of bread topped with savory food

Canard: duck

Carbonnade: pieces of lean beef, first sautéed then stewed with onions and beer

Carré d'agneau: rack of lamb

Cèpes: prized wild mushroom, same family as the Italian porcini

Chanterelles: prized wild mushroom, trumpet-shaped

Charcutière: sauce of onions, white wine, beef stock and gherkins

Charlotte: dessert of flavored creams and/or fruit molded in a cylindrical dish lined with ladyfingers (if served cold) or strips of buttered bread (if served hot)

Chèvre: goat cheese

Choucroute: sauerkraut; often served with sausages, smoked bacon, pork loin and potatoes

Clafoutis: a dessert of fruit (usu. cherries) baked in an eggy batter

Confit: pork, goose, duck, turkey or other meat and sealed in its own fat

Coquilles St-Jacques: sea scallops

Coulis: thick sauce or purée, often of vegetables or fruit

Court-bouillon: stock in which fish, meat and poultry are cooked

Crème chantilly: sweetened whipped cream

Crêpe Suzette: crêpe stuffed with sweetened mixture of butter, Curaçao, tangerine juice and peel

Croque-monsieur: grilled ham and cheese sandwich

Croûte (en): in pastry crust

Crudités: raw vegetables

Daube: beef braised in red wine

Ecrevisses: crayfish

Entrecôte: "between the ribs"; steak cut from between the ribs

Epinards: spinach

Escalope: slice of meat or fish, flattened slightly and sautéed

Escargots (la bourguignonne): snails (with herbed garlic butter)

Financière: Madeira sauce enhanced with truffle juice

Florentine: with spinach

Foie gras: liver of a specially fattened goose or duck

Fondue: a bubbling pot of liquid into which which pieces of food are dipped—most commonly cheese and bread; can also be chocolate and fruit or various savory sauces and cubes of beef. Also, vegetables cooked at length in butter and thus reduced to pulp

Forestière: garnish of sautéed mushrooms and lardons (Lardon; larding fat cut into long strips and threaded through lean cuts of meat as it cooks).

Galantine: boned poultry or meat, stuffed and pressed into a symmetrical form, cooked in broth and coated with aspic

Galettes and crêpes (Brittany): galettes are thin pancakes made of buckwheat flour and are usually savory. Crêpes are made of wheat flour and are usually sweet

Gâteau: cake

Gelée (en): in aspic (gelatin usually flavored with meat, poultry or fish stock)

Génoise: sponge cake

Granité: lightly sweetened fruit ice

Gratin dauphinois: sliced

potatoes baked in milk, sometimes with cream and/or grated Gruyère

Grenouille: frog (frogs' legs: cuisses de grenouilles)

Hollandaise: egg-based sauce thickened with butter and flavored with lemon

Jambon: ham

Julienne: vegetable soup made from a clear consommé, or any shredded food

Langoustine: saltwater crayfish

Lapin: rabbit

Limon: lime (also, citron vert)

Lotte: monkfish or anglerfish; sometimes called "poor man's lobster"

Madrilène (la): garnished with raw, peeled tomatoes

Magret (Maigret): breast of fattened duck, cooked with the skin on; usually grilled

Médaillon: food, usually meat, fish or foie gras, cut into small, round pieces

Moules marinière: mussels cooked in the shell with white wine, shallots and parsley

Noisettes: hazelnuts; also, small, round pieces of meat (especially lamb or veal)

Nougat: sweet made with roasted almonds, egg whites, honey and sugar

Oeufs: eggs

Pain: bread

Parfait: sweet or savory mousse; also a layered ice cream dessert

Parisienne: garnish of fried potato balls

Paupiettes: thin slices of meat stuffed with forcemeat and shaped into rolls

Pissaladière: tart with onions, black olives and anchovy filets

Pommes: apples

Pommes de terre: potatoes

Poulet: chicken

Profiteroles: small puffs of choux paste often filled with whipped cream of crème patissiere and piled high in a dish with chocolate sauce poured over

Provençale (' la): with garlic or tomato and garlic

Quiche: tart of eggs, cream and various fillings (such as ham, spinach or bacon)

Ratatouille: stew of eggplant, tomatoes, bell peppers, zucchini, onion and garlic, all sautéed in oil

Rémoulade: mayonnaise with capers, onions, parsley, gherkins and herbs

Rouille: sort of mayonnaise with pepper, garlic bread soaked in bouillon, olive oil and possibly saffron

Sabayon: fluffy, whipped egg yolks, sweetened and flavored with wine or liqueur; served warm

Saint-Pierre: John Dory, a white-fleshed fish

Salade niçoise: salad of tomatoes, hard-boiled egg, anchovy filets, tuna, sweet peppers, celery and olives (also can include green beans, potatoes, basil, onions and/or broad beans)

Sole meunière: sole dipped in flour and sautéed in butter with parsley and lemon

Sorbet: sherbet

Spätzle: round noodles, often made from eggs

Steak au poivre: pepper steak; steak covered in crushed peppercorns, browned in a frying pan, flambéed with

Cognac; also sauce deglazed with cream
Tapenade: a paste of olives, capers and anchovies, crushed in a mortar with lemon juice and pepper
Tartare: cold sauce for meat or fish; mayonnaise with hard-boiled egg yolks, onions and chopped olives
Tarte: tart, round cake or flan; can be sweet or savory
Tarte tatin: upside-down apple tart
Truffe: truffle; highly esteemed subterranean fungus, esp. from Périgord

ITALIAN

Acciughe: anchovies
Aceto: vinegar
Aglio: garlic
Agnello: lamb
Agnolotti: crescent-shaped, meat-filled pasta
Amaretti: crunchy almond macaroons
Anguilla: eel
Aragosta: spiny lobster
Arrosto: roasted meat
Baccalo: dried salt cod
Bagna cauda: hot, savory dip for raw vegetables
Bierra: beer
Biscotti: cookies
Bistecca (alla fiorentina): charcoal-grilled T-bone steak (seasoned with pepper and olive oil)
Bolognese: pasta sauce with tomatoes and meat
Bresaola: air-dried spiced beef; usually thinly sliced, served with olive oil and lemon juice
Bruschetta: toasted garlic bread topped with tomatoes
Bucatini: hollow spaghetti
Calamari (calamaretti): (baby) squid
Calzone: stuffed pizza-dough turnover
Cannellini: white beans
Carbonara: pasta sauce with ham, eggs, cream and grated cheese
Carciofi (alla giudia): (flattened and deep-fried baby) artichokes
Carpaccio: paper thin, raw beef (or other meats)
Cassata: ice-cream bombe
Cipolla: onion
Conchiglie: shell-shaped pasta
Coniglio: rabbit
Costoletta (alla milanese): (breaded) veal chop
Cozze: mussels
Crespelle: crêpes
Crostata: tart
Fagioli: beans
Fagiolini: string beans
Farfalle: bow-tie pasta
Fegato alla veneziana: calf's liver sautéed with onions
Focaccia: crusty flat bread
Formaggio: cheese
Frittata: Italian omelet
Fritto misto: mixed fry of meats or fish
Frutti di mare: seafood (esp. shellfish)
Funghi (trifolati): mushrooms (sautéed with garlic and parsley)
Fusilli: spiral-shaped pasta
Gamberi: shrimp
Gamberoni: prawns
Gelato: ice cream
Gnocchi: dumplings made of cheese (di ricotta), potatoes (di patate), cheese and spinach (verdi) or semolina (alla romana)
Grana: hard grating cheese
Granita: sweetened, flavored grated ice
Griglia: grilled
Insalata: salad
Involtini: stuffed meat or fish rolls
Maccheroni: macaroni pasta
Manzo: beef
Mela: apple
Melanzana: eggplant

Minestra: soup; pasta course
Minestrone: vegetable soup
Mortadella: large, mild Bolognese pork sausage
Mozzarella di bufala: fresh cheese made from water-buffalo milk
Noce: walnut
Orecchiette: ear-shaped pasta
Osso buco: braised veal shanks
Ostriche: oysters
Pane: bread
Panettone: brioche-like sweet bread
Panna: heavy cream
Pancetta: Italian bacon
Pappardelle: wide, flat pasta noodles
Pasticceria: pastry; pastry shop
Patate: potatoes
Pecorino: hard sheep's-milk cheese
Penne: hollow, ribbed pasta
Peperoncini: tiny, hot peppers
Pepperoni: green, red or yellow sweet peppers
Pesca: peach
Pesce: fish
Pesce spada: swordfish
Pesto: cold pasta sauce of crushed basil, garlic, pine nuts, parmesan cheese and olive oil
Piccata: thinly-sliced meat with a lemon or Marsala sauce
Pignoli: pine nuts
Polenta: cornmeal porridge
Pollo: chicken
Polipo: octopus
Pomodoro: tomato
Porcini: prized wild mushrooms, known also as boletus
Prosciutto: air-dried ham
Ragu: meat sauce
Ricotta: fresh sheep's-milk cheese
Rigatoni: large, hollow ribbed pasta
Risotto: braised rice with various savory items
Rucola: arugula
Salsa (verde): sauce (of parsley, capers, anchovies and lemon juice or vinegar
Saltimbocca: veal scallop with prosciutto and sage
Semifreddo: frozen dessert, usually ice cream, with or without cake
Spiedino: brochette; grilled on a skewer
Spumone: light, foamy ice cream
Tartufi: truffles
Tiramisu: creamy dessert of rum-spiked cake and triple-crème Mascarpone cheese
Tonno: tuna
Tortellini: ring-shaped dumplings stuffed with meat or cheese
Uovo (sodo): egg (hard-boiled)
Verdura: greens, vegetables
Vitello (Tonatto): veal (in a tuna and anchovy sauce)
Vongole: clams
Zabaglione: warm whipped egg yolks flavored with Marsala
Zucchero: sugar
Zucchine: zucchini
Zuppa: soup
Zuppa inglese: cake steeped in a rum-flavored custard sauce

SPANISH & LATIN AMERICAN

Because there are so many regional dialects in Spain and Latin America, the term for one food product might easily have four or five variations. We've chosen those ingredients and dishes most often found in Southern California restaurants.

Aceite: oil
Ajo: garlic
All-i-oli: aïoli; garlicky mayonnaise
Arroz: rice
Bacalao: dried, salted codfish

Burrito: soft, wheat-flour tortilla rolled and stuffed with meats, refried beans, cheese and vegetables
Caldo: broth
Camarones: shrimp
Carne: meat
Cerveza: beer
Ceviche: raw fish marinated in citrus juice
Chalupa: a small, thick corn tortilla folded into a boat shape, fried and filled with a mixture of shredded meat, cheese and/or vegetables
Chilequile: flat tortilla layered with beans, meat, cheese and tomato sauce
Chile relleno: large, mild chile pepper, stuffed with cheese and fried in an egg batter
Chorizo: spicy pork sausage flavored with garlic and spices
Empanada: pie or tart filled variously with meat, seafood or vegetables
Enchilada: a tortilla, fried and stuffed variously with meat, cheese and/or chiles
Entremeses: appetizers
Flan: a baked custard with a caramel coating (also crema caramela)
Frito (frita): fried
Gambas: shrimp
Garbanzo: chick pea
Gazpacho: Andalusian; a cold soup of fresh tomatoes, peppers, onions, cucumbers, olive oil, vinegar and garlic (also celery, breadcrumbs)
Guacamole: an avocado dip or filling, with mashed tomatoes, onions, chiles and citrus juice
Higado: liver
Huachinango: red snapper
Huevos: eggs
Huevos rancheros: tortillas topped with eggs and a hot, spicy salsa
Jalapeño: very common hot chile pepper, medium size
Jamón: ham
Licuado: fruit milkshake
Lima: lime
Limón: lemon
Mariscos: shellfish
Masa: cornmeal dough; essential for making tortillas
Menudo: a stew featuring tripe
Mole: sauce; most often a thick, dark sauce made with mild chiles and chocolate
Nachos: a snack dish of tortilla chips topped with melted cheese and chiles
Nopales: leaves of the prickly pear cactus; simmered and used in various dishes
Paella: a dish of saffron-flavored rice studded with meat (chicken, ham, sausages, pork), shellfish and vegetables
Papas: potatoes (also, patatas)
Papas fritas: literally "fried potatoes "; french fries
Parrillada: grilled
Pescado: fish
Pez espada: swordfish
Pimiento: red chile pepper; can be sweet or hot
Plátano: plantain; a starchy, mild-tasting variety of banana popular in Latin American; usu. cooked and served as a side dish
Pollo: chicken
Poblano: large, mild, dark green chile pepper; used for chile rellenos
Puerco: pig
Quesadilla: a soft, folded tortilla filled with cheese (and/or other savory stuffings) and toasted or fried

Queso: cheese
Salchicha: sausage
Salsa: sauce; also, an uncooked condiment employing fresh tomatoes, onions and chiles
Sangría: Spanish drink made with red wine, soda water, chopped fresh fruits and sugar, often with a touch of brandy; served on ice
Sopa: soup
Taco: a folded, fried tortilla filled with ground beef (or other meats or fish), refried beans, shredded lettuce, tomatoes, onion, cheese and salsa
Tamale: Corn dough made with lard, filled with a savory stuffing, wrapped up in a piece of corn husk, and steamed
Tapa: appetizer, Spanish in origin; usu. enjoyed with an apéritif such as dry sherry
Tortilla: a flat, unleavened bread made with cornmeal flour (masa) or wheat flour
Tostada: a fried tortilla topped with a saladlike mix of ground beef or chicken, beans, lettuce, tomato, guacamole

ASIAN

Chinese

Bao bun: dim sum item; small, steamed buns, white in color, stuffed with a variety of minced fillings (often chicken, shrimp, pork or lotus beans)
Bird's-nest soup: soup that has been thickened and flavored with the gelatinous product derived from soaking and cooking the nests of cliff-dwelling birds
Bok choy: Chinese white cabbage
Chop suey: strictly a Chinese American dish; meat or shrimp and vegetables (mushrooms, water chestnuts, bamboo shoots, bean sprouts) stir-fried together and served over rice
Chow mein: strictly a Chinese American dish; meat or shrimp and vegetables (mushrooms, water chestnuts, bamboo shoots, bean sprouts) stir-fried and served over crispy egg noodles
Dim sum: figuratively, "heart's delight"; a traditional meal featuring a variety of small dumplings, buns, rolls, balls, pastries and finger food, served with tea in the late morning or afternoon
Egg roll: thin wrapper stuffed with pork, cabbage or other vegetables, rolled up, and deep-fried or steamed
Fried rice: cooked, dried rice quickly fried in a wok with hot oil, various meats or vegetables and often an egg
Hoisin: a sweet, rich, dark brown sauce made from fermented soy beans; used as a base for other sauces
Lo mein: steamed wheat-flour noodles stir-fried with bean sprouts and scallions and either shrimp, pork, beef or vegetables
Lychee: small, round, fleshy fruit; used fresh, canned, preserved and dried
Mu shu: a delicate dish of stir-fried shredded pork

and eggs rolled up in thin pancakes

Oyster sauce: a thick, dark sauce of oysters, soy and brine

Peking duck: an elaborate dish featuring duck that has been specially prepared, coated with honey and cooked until the skin is crisp and golden; served in pieces with thin pancakes or steamed buns, and hoisin

Pot sticker: dim sum item; dumpling stuffed with meat, seafood or vegetables, fried and then steamed

Shark's fin soup: soup thickened and flavored with the cartilage of shark's fins, which provides a protein-rich gelatin

Shu mai: dim sum item; delicate dumpling usu. filled minced pork and vegetables

Spring roll: a lighter version of the egg roll, with fillings such as shrimp or black mushrooms

Szechuan: cuisine in the style of the Szechuan province, often using the peppercorn-like black Chinese pepper to make hot, spicy dishes

Thousand-year-old eggs: chicken, duck or goose eggs preserved for 100 days in ashes, lime and salt (also, 100-year-old eggs)

Wonton: paper-thin, glutinous dough wrapper; also refers to the dumpling made with this wrapper, stuffed with minced meat, seafood or vegetables

Wonton soup: a clear broth in which wontons are cooked and served

Japanese

Amaebi: sweet shrimp

Awabi: abalone

Azuki: dried bean; azuki flour is often used for confections

Ebi: shrimp

Edamame: soy beans, served boiled and salted as an appetizer

Enoki (Enokitake): delicate mushrooms with long stems and small caps

Hamachi: yellowtail

Hibachi: small, open charcoal grill

Ikura: salmon roe

Kaiseki: Multicourse menu of luxury dishes reflecting the seasons with the use of seasonal foods and artistic dinnerware and presentation

Kappa: cucumber

Kobe beef: cattle raised in exclusive conditions (frequent massages and a diet featuring large quantities of beer), which results in an extraordinarily tender, very expensive beef

Konbu: dried kelp; used in soup stock, for sushi and as a condiment

Maguro: tuna

Maki: rolled

Mako: shark

Mirugai: giant clam

Miso (soup): soybean paste from which a savory broth is made, usu. served with cubes of tofu or strips of seaweed

Ono: wahoo fish; a relative of the mackerel often compared in taste to albacore

Ramen: soup noodles

Saba: mackerel

Sake: salmon

Saké: traditional rice wine served hot or cold

Sashimi: thinly sliced raw fish on rice, usually served with soy sauce

and wasabi
Shabu shabu: similar to sukiyaki; beef and vegetables cooked tableside in a broth
Shiitake: Prized cultivated mushroom, dark brown with a large cap
Shoya: soy sauce
Soba: buckwheat noodles
Sukiyaki: braised beef and vegetable dish with broth added after cooking
Sushi: Rounds of vinegared rice wrapped in dried seaweed with a center of raw rish or vegetables, served with wasabi and soy
Tako: octopus
Tamago: egg
Tamari: dark sauce similar in composition and taste to soy; often used for dipping
Tempura: deep-fried, batter-dipped fish or vegetables
Teriyaki: A marinade of soy and sweet sake, used on meats, fish and poultry
Tofu: bean curd, processed into a liquid and then molded into large cubes
Toro: fatty belly cut of tuna
Udon: wheat noodles
Uni: sea-urchin roe
Wasabi: a hot, spicy condiment made from the roots of Japanese horseradish, chartreuse in color
Yakitori: a dish of pieces of chicken and vegetables, marinated in a spicy sauce, skewered and grilled

Thai

Kaeng (or Gaeng): large and diverse category of dishes; loosely translates as "curry"
Kaeng massaman: a variety of coconut-milk curry
Kaeng phed: a red, coconut-cream curry
Kaeng som: a hot-sour curry
Khao: rice
Khao suai: white rice
Khao phad: fried rice
King: ginger
Kung: prawns
Lab (or Larb): dish of minced meat with chilies and lime juice
Mu: pork
Nam: sauce
Nam pla: fish sauce
Nam phrik: a hot chili sauce
Nuea: beef
Ped: duck
Phad: fried
Phad king: fried with ginger
Phad phed: fried hot and spicy
Phad Thai: pan-fried rice noodles with chicken, shrimp, eggs, peanuts and bean sprouts
Phrik: chili pepper
Si racha (or Sri racha): spicy chili condiment
Tom kha kai: chicken coconut-cream soup flavored with lemongrass and chilies
Tom yam kung: hot-sour shrimp soup flavored with lemon grass, lime and chilies
Yam: flavored primarily with lime juice and chilies, resulting in a hot-sour taste; usually "salads" but can also be noodle dishes or soup
Yam pla: raw fish spiked with lime juice, chili, lemongrass, mint and fish sauce

COFFEE SAVVY

THE ORIGINS OF THE COFFEE CRAZE

Nearly every culture in the world has a passion for coffee, and there are various stories about how it all started. One of our favorites has to do with a goat herder in ancient Abyssinia (Ethiopia) who one morning discovered his goats gleefully cavorting around a shiny, dark-leafed shrub with red berries. After nibbling a few of the red berries himself, the goat herder joined his goats in their spirited romp. Another story attributes the discovery to an Arabian dervish who, when exiled by enemies to the wildnerness, survived by making a broth from water and the berries he plucked from coffee trees.

Regardless of which story is true, botanical evidence indicates that coffea arabica actually originated on the high plateaus of what is now Ethiopia in Africa. Traders undoubtedly brought it across the Red Sea to what is now Yemen, where it was cultivated from the sixth century on. Though at first coffee was used as a medicine—and by dervishes readying for a spin—it soon became a popular social beverage, resulting in coffeehouses where men exchanged ideas and gossip while sipping cups of hot brew in cities from Cairo to Mecca.

Though the Arabs jealously guarded their discovery, a few sneaky coffee fanatics managed to smuggle seeds from Arabia into India and Java, where it was cultivated with great success. By the seventeenth century, the coffee culture had spread to Europe. Coffeehouses attracted politicians, seafarers, merchants, authors and scholars, who often used the premises for discussions, reading, musical performances and even duels. At a time when Europeans wealthy enough to afford exotic luxuries were enjoying their two, three or four cups a day, the greatest French lover of luxury, King Louis XIV, supposedly built the first greenhouse to house a coffee tree given him by the mayor of Amsterdam. It's said that from the Sun King's royal coffee tree, sprang billions of arabica trees, including those growing today in Central and South America.

THE COFFEEHOUSE FOR THE NINETIES

Cut, as they say in Hollywood, to Seattle, in the rainy Pacific Northwest. Here, the current coffee craze was born just over a decade ago with a—then tiny—coffee company named **Starbucks** (after the first mate in the classic novel, *Moby Dick*). Starbucks re-invented the coffeehouse for modern times, creating attractive, relaxed and congenial meeting places where men and women exchange ideas and gossip—or read, work or simply think—while enjoying a cup of coffee. And we're not just talking about *a cup of coffee.* The choices of specialty coffee drinks made with "specialty" coffee beans—those of the highest quality—are endless, which is why we've put together this brief primer on the vocabulary of specialty coffees:

THE WORLD OF COFFEE

Like wine grapes, specialty coffee beans get much of their distinctive flavor from the growing conditions and preparation methods of the regions in which they're produced. We can classify coffee flavor and aroma according to geographic origin:

CENTRAL & SOUTH AMERICAN COFFEES

The most popular origins in the U.S. market, these are usually light-to-medium bodied, with clean lively flavors. Their balance and consistency make them the foundation of good coffee blending as well. Among these are beans from Colombia, Costa Rica, Guatemala and Mexico. Kona, though geographically a product of the Pacific islands, falls within this Latin American range of taste and aroma.

EAST AFRICAN COFFEES

These unique beans—from Kenya, Ethiopia, Tanzania and Zimbabwe—often combine the sparkling acidity of the best Central Americans with unique floral or winy notes, and typically are medium-to-full bodied.

INDONESIAN COFFEES

Usually full-bodied and smooth, low in acidity, and often possessing earthy and exotic taste elements, coffee beans from Java, Sumatra, Papua New Guinea and Sulawesi are an important "anchor" component of choice blends.

DARK ROASTS

Coffees from varying geographic origins are dark-roasted to provide a specific range of flavors, from the caramel spice of Espresso, to the smoky tang of Italian Roast, to the pungent French Roast.

BLENDS

Typically, a blend might play off Central American acidity with Indonesian smoothness, or spice up a delicate origin with the tang of a dark roast. At its best, blending coffee is high art, offering a balance or diversity which few straight coffees can match.

DECAFFEINATED

Some coffee-drinkers find the effects of too much caffeine unpleasant; others are looking for a hot cup to enjoy before bedtime. For that reason, coffee beans from many geographic origins are put through a decaffeinating process.

GLOSSARY OF COFFEE TASTING TERMS

THE BASICS:

Flavor: the total impression of aroma, acidity and body.

Acidity: the sharp, lively quality characteristic of many high-grown coffees. Acid is not the same as bitter or sour. Acidity is the brisk, snappy, spicy quality which makes coffee refreshing and palate-cleansing.

Body: the tactile impression of the weight of the brewed beverage in the mouth. It may range from watery and thin, through light, medium and full, to buttery or even syrupy in the case of some Indonesian varieties.

OTHER USEFUL TERMS:

Aroma: the fragrance of brewed coffee. Terms used to describe aroma include: caramelly (candy or syrup-like), carbony (for dark roasts), chocolaty, fruity, floral, herbal, malty (cereal-like), rich (over-used), rounded, spicy.

Bitter: a basic taste perceived primarily at the back of the tongue. Dark roasts are intentionally bitter, but bitterness is more commonly caused by over extraction (too little coffee at too fine a grind).

Bland: the pale, insipid flavor often found in low-grown coffees. Under-extracted coffee (made with too little coffee or too coarse a grind) is also bland.

Briny: a salty sensation caused by application of excessive heat after brewing. (The familiar smell of "truck stop" coffee.)

Earthy: the spicy, "of the earth" taste of Indonesian coffees.

Exotic: coffee with unusual aromatic and flavor notes, such as floral, berry, and sweet spice-like qualities. Coffees from East Africa and Indonesia often have such characteristics.

Mellow: the term for well-balanced coffee of low-to-medium acidity.

Mild: a coffee with harmonious, delicate flavor. Fine, high-grown Latin American coffee is often described as mild.

Soft: low-acid coffees such as Indonesians, that may also be called mellow or sweet.

Sour: a primary taste perceived mainly on the posterior sides of the tongue, characteristic of light-roasted coffees.

Spicy: an aroma or flavor reminiscent of a particular spice. Some Indonesian arabicas, especially aged coffees, evoke an association with sweet spices like cardomom. Others, such as Guatemala Antiqua, are almost peppery.

Strong: technically the relative proportion of coffee solubles to water in a given brew.

Sweet: a general term for smooth, palatable coffee, free from defects and harsh flavors

Tangy: a darting sourness, almost fruit-like in nature, related to wininess. A fine high-grown Costa Rican coffee is frequently tangy.

Wild: a coffee with extreme flavor characteristics; it can be a defect or a positive attribute, and denotes odd, racy nuances of flavor and aroma. Arabian Mocha Sanani nearly always exhibits such flavors.

Winy: a desirable flavor reminiscent of fine red wine; the contrast between fruit-like acidity and smooth body creates flavor interest. Kenyan coffees are examples of winy coffee flavor.

GLOSSARY OF SPECIALTY COFFEE DRINKS

made by a **Barista**, an expert at preparing espresso drinks

Espresso: A small but intense shot of coffee produced by forcing hot water under pressure through tightly packed coffee, one cup at a time.

Espresso Con Panna: A shot of espresso with a dollop of whipped cream.

Espresso Macchiato: Espresso lightly "marked" with foamed milk.

Caffè Americano: A shot of espresso diluted with hot, purified water, to produce a full-flavored but still mild cup of coffee.

Caffè Latte: A shot of espresso plus steamed milk, topped off with foamed milk.

Caffè Mocha: A squirt of chocolate syrup on the bottom of the cup, then espresso topped by steamed milk, a crown of whipped cream and a sprinkle of cocoa powder.

Cappuccino: Espresso topped with steamed milk and a generous cap of foamed milk.

Frappuccino: A cold and creamy low-fat blend of fresh-brewed Starbucks Italian roast coffee, milk and ice. Variations: with a shot of espresso (**Espresso Frappuccino**), with dark chocolate syrup (**Mocha Frappuccino**), or with a protein and vitamin supplement (**Power Frappuccino**).

*The Glossary of Coffee Tasting Terms and Specialty Coffee Drinks was provided courtesy of **Starbucks Coffee Company**, which has retail stores in the U.S. and abroad. Starbucks coffee and coffee products can also be found on major airlines, in fine hotels and restaurants, and in grocery stores (in addition to coffee beans, Starbucks produces wonderfully rich and delicious coffee ice creams).*

WINE SAVVY

THE EMERGENCE OF CALIFORNIA WINES

Though immigrant families started it in the late nineteenth century, California's wine industry did not flourish until the 1970s, when it fostered a new American interest in wine and a healthy increase in per capita consumption. California wine was thought to come of age at a blind tasting in Paris, where eminent French judges chose several California wines over those produced in France. The American media seized on this with a vengeance, much to the delight of the California wine industry. .

Meanwhile, others trends took hold in the popular segment of the wine market, including the seemingly unquenchable thirst for "a glass of **Chardonnay**, please." By the early 1980s, there was an influx of new talent into the California winemaking industry. Many of these new winemakers had been educated in viticulture and enology at UC-Davis, while others were cellar rats who learned through on-the-job training. These young winemakers were committed to producing quality wine through better viticulture practices, proper utilization of soil and climate and better winemaking techniques.

A number of these winemakers struck out on their own, experimenting with different types of grapes while challenging the "varietal imperialism" of **Cabernet** and **Chardonnay**. Wines made from **Rhone Valley varietals**, like **Syrah, Grenache** and **Mourvedre**, became increasingly popular and offered different flavors than the previous spectrum of California red wines. Plantings of **Italian varietals**, such as **Nebbiolo**, **Sangiovese** and **Malvasia** sprang up in order to take advantage of the Mediterranean-like growing climate of California.

The winemaking business fractured into many segments. While giant corporate wineries gained their market share, smaller artisan wineries also found their niche. Given the time and money, dreamers could build winery empires based on individual winemaking philosophies, whereas thirty years before, the rules of the game had seemed far more proscribed.

Today, California winemakers now understand that certain climates and soils that are good for, say, Cabernet, are not good for Pinot Noir. As more acreage is planted or grafted over, the most appropriate varietals are planted in the most appropriate environment. This not only increases the quality of the wines, but also furthers the movement of specialty wineries to the forefront. In essence, wineries no longer sell half a dozen different wines, but concentrate on only two or three—the best grapes from the best varieties that the region has to offer.

TODAY: MORE WINE, BETTER VINTAGES, AND LOWER PRICES

In the late '90s, we are quite possibly entering the "Golden Age" of California winemaking. A new generation of vintners is fashioning wines with an intensity of flavor that is California's birthright, owing to its sunny climate and rich soils. They are refining their techniques to preserve the innate characteristics of the fruit, while at the same time building in more structure and complexity to enhance drinkability and longevity. Through their meticulous attention to detail, they are eliminating distracting elements from the wine in favor of creating a harmonious variety of complex aromas and flavors.

Today, in the best vintages, the wines are still powerful but now tempered with suppleness, finesse and depth. The most recent California grape harvest was a windfall for California winemakers. The 1997 crush was 2.87 millions tons, far outstripping the previous record set in 1993. For consumers, this translates as not only more wine but better wine (weather and growing conditions were near ideal) at lower prices, particularly for premium wines in the $10-$20 range. True, there will always be high-ticket "trophy" wines, like **Opus One**, **Dominus** and **Cardinale**. Good, solid, lower-priced wines that meet the needs of the everyday dining table, however, are also plentiful, due to both the bounty of the harvest and the recent influx of inexpensive imports.

In red wines, **Cabernet Sauvignon** is still king, though vintners are trying to catch up to the demand for **Merlot** by feverishly planting hundreds of new acres yearly. More interestingly, **Pinot Noir**—made in a smooth and silky style—has come of age, with excellent examples produced now in Santa Barbara, Carneros and the Russian River Valley (and Oregon's Willamette Valley). After a string of great vintages, **Zinfandel** is on the comeback trail, and is now being made in a more food-friendly style. Upstart red varietals, which have a long heritage in France and Italy, have taken their rightful place beside old standbys on wine lists: look to **Sangiovese, Nebbiolo, Syrah, Mourvedre** and **Cabernet Franc** for intriguing flavors.

In white wines, the thirst for **Chardonnay** is seemingly unquenchable; it's far and away the white wine of choice. However, **Sauvignon Blanc**, at half the price, partners better with a wide variety of dishes, including many featuring seafood and chicken. A host of **Rhone**-style varietals, such as **Viognier, Marsanne** and **Roussanne,** are beginning to penetrate the marketplace, as consumers discover there is life beyond Chardonnay. The floral aromas of these wines are beguiling, and their flavors follow through with bright, refreshing fruitiness. Likewise, Italian varietals in California—like **Pinot Grigio** and **Tocai Friulano**, also offer unique flavor profiles, with a crispness and high acidity that cleanses the palate.

Guide to California Regions

It's been said that there are no climatic differences in California wine growing regions, as there are in Europe, and thus "every year is a vintage year" in California. Nothing could be further from the truth. For proof, merely contrast a 1989 Napa Valley Chardonnay (where it rained at harvest) and a 1989 Central Coast Chardonnay (where it didn't). The myth of statewide sunny weather also needs dispelling. There are certain pockets of land in California (usually associated with mountain ranges) that have vastly different weather and climatic conditions than the rest of the state. And from a viticultural standpoint, certain grape varieties that do well in one environment do not perform well in another. Check out a Pinot Noir from the Sanford and Benedict Vineyards in the (very cool) Santa Ynez Valley versus one from the (hot) Calistoga area of Napa Valley. Where the wine comes from *does* make a difference—the difference between a balanced, complex wine and a harsh, unpleasant one.

ALEXANDER VALLEY

A largely unpopulated area of northern Sonoma County, the Alexander Valley is warmer than the rest of the county. There has been success here with Cabernets as well as Bordeaux style blends (white and red). The Chardonnays can be interesting.

AMADOR/SIERRA FOOTHILLS

Just east of Sacramento, Amador County is home to some of the oldest continuously producing vineyards in the state. The principal wine is Zinfandel and its ubiquitous offspring, White Zinfandel. There is also Cabernet and Barbera, along with experimental acreage planted for Rhône varietals like Syrah, Mourvedre and Grenache.

CALIFORNIA

The use of this geographical term indicates only that all the grapes came from within the confines of the state.

CARNEROS

At the southernmost end of Napa and Sonoma Counties, this recently developed area borders on the cool San Pablo Bay. Perhaps the coolest area in either county, the climate is perfect for Pinot Noir and Chardonnay.

CENTRAL COAST

This is a very broadly defined area that covers coastal wine-growing regions from Santa Cruz on the north to Santa Barbara on the south. An entire spectrum of grape varieties is grown here, depending on which particular varietal is suitable for the individual microclimate.

CENTRAL VALLEY

Another broad area that covers the inland wine growing area from Sacramento to Bakersfield. This is the hottest, driest grape-growing region in the state. A wide variety of wines are made, most of them passable but few of them distinctive.

DRY CREEK VALLEY

Parallel to and west of the Alexander Valley in Sonoma County, its relatively warm climate has produced good red wines, particularly Zinfandel and Cabernet. Chardonnay is a drawing card, too.

MENDOCINO/LAKE COUNTIES

The northernmost grape growing counties share a fairly cool growing season. Chardonnay, Pinot Noir, Gewürztraminer and Riesling can be particularly impressive.

MONTEREY

The cooling influence of the Monterey Bay has created a great environment for Chardonnay, while Pinot Noir has been less successful. Further inland, individual pockets of land have produced good Cabernets.

NAPA VALLEY

The most famous wine-growing region in California and a top tourist attraction. The name "Napa" is synonymous with quality. Its long-lived Cabernets have achieved worldwide notoriety. Chardonnay, Pinot Noir, Sauvignon Blanc and sparkling wines have also proven themselves here.

RUSSIAN RIVER VALLEY

A district of widely varying soils and climate in western Sonoma County; the cooler regions enjoy a reputation for Chardonnay, Pinot Noir and sparkling wine.

SANTA BARBARA COUNTY

Home to the Santa Ynez and the Santa Maria Valleys, it is the only region in California that has an east-west mountain range funneling cool ocean fog and breezes to the vineyards. That fact belies its southern California heritage that says it's too warm for grape growing. Pinot Noir, Chardonnay, Riesling and Syrah are prominent.

SONOMA COUNTY

Encompassing several different valleys with varying microclimates, it is probably the most versatile grape-growing region in California. Cabernet, Merlot, Pinot Noir, Chardonnay, Sauvignon Blanc and sparkling wine do well here.

TEMECULA

This southernmost grape-growing region, halfway between L.A. and San Diego, is also the most recently planted. Thus far its best efforts have been with Chardonnay and sparkling wine, while the red wines are on the rustic side.

WINE TOURING

Visiting the wineries of Southern California can provide a pleasant day or two's break from the excitement of the city. The selected wineries below have tasting rooms and are open to the public on a regular basis. Nevertheless, you'll do well to phone ahead before setting out on your wine touring adventure. For comprehensive information on the wineries of California and Mexico, see Gayot/Gault Millau/AAA's **The Best Wineries of North America**. (Order form in the back of this book).

Babcock Vineyards
5175 Highway 246
Lompoc 93436
805-736-1455

Cambria Winery & Vineyard
5475 Chardonnay Lane
Santa Maria 93454
888-339-9463
(Sat & Sun only)

Eberle Winery
Highway 46 East
PO Box 2459
Paso Robles 93447
805-238-9607

Fess Parker Winery
6200 Foxen Canyon Road
Los Olivos 93441
800-841-1104

Firestone Vineyard
PO Box 244
Los Olivos 93441
805-688-3940

Maison Deutz
453 Deutz Dr.
Arroyo Grande 93420
805-481-1763

Meridian Vineyards
7000 Highway 46 East,
PO Box 3289
Paso Robles 93447
805-237-6000

Qupé
PO Box 440
Los Olivos 93441
805-688-2477

Santa Barbara Winery
202 Anacapa St.
Santa Barbara 93101
805-963-3646

Zaca Mesa Winery
6905 Foxen Canyon Road
Los Olivos 93441
800-350-7972 x308

Santa Ynez Valley Wine Trail
Comprised of 11 premium wineries in the heart of Santa Barbara wine country (**Arthur Earl**; **Beckmen Vineyards**; **Brander Vineyard**; **Buttonwood Farm Winery**; **Foley Estates**; **Gainey Vineyard**; **Lincourt Vineyards**; **Longoria Winery**; **Los Olivos Vintners**; **Rusack Vineyards**; **Sunstone Vineyards & Winery**). For more information, call **800-563-3183.**

GLOSSARY OF TASTING TERMS

Acidity: a principal component of wine that shows up as a sharpness or tartness, giving it snap.

Aroma: the smell the wine acquires from the grapes themselves and fermentation process.

Astringency: the mouth-puckering quality found in many young red wines.

Austere: a wine unusually high in acidity; lacking roundness or wholeness.

Balanced: no individual component of the wine stands out; all the elements contribute to a harmonious whole.

Berry: taste characteristic found in many red wines, it resembles the taste of fruit like blackberry, blueberry and cherry.

Body: the weight of the wine in the mouth; usually manifested by a richness, fullness or viscosity.

Bouquet: the smell that develops from the process of aging wine in the bottle.

Buttery: a component that gives white wines a rich, roundness that resembles the taste of butter.

Chewy: a rich red wine with big body and dense flavor.

Clarity: the appearance of a young wine should be clear, not cloudy.

Complex: a wine that displays many levels of flavor.

Dry: a wine with no apparent residual sugar. Novice wine drinkers may describe this as "sour."

Earthy: positive characteristics of loamy topsoil, mushrooms or truffles sometimes found in red wines. In French, "goût de terroir."

Fat: a wine with good fullness and length, although it may lack finesse.

Floral: flowery aromas and tastes, usually associated with white wines.

Fruity: the taste of the fruit of the grapes themselves; it often manifests itself as other fruit flavors, such as apples, strawberries or black currants.

Grassy: an herbaceous flavor, like new-mown grass, common to Sauvignon Blanc; negative if extreme.

Hard: a wine that does not have generous flavors; applied to red wines that have excessive tannins.

Herbaceous: a general term descriptive of various herbal flavors in wine, recognized by aroma and taste.

Hot: a wine in which the high level of alcohol is out of balance with the other elements.

Intense: powerful, dense, and rich in flavor

Jammy: in red wines, intense fruitiness combined with berry-like flavors.

Nose: all the elements detected by the sense of smell, including both the aroma and bouquet.

Oaky: flavors of the oak in which the wine is fermented and/or aged.

Smoky: a roasted aroma or taste characteristic attributable to aging in oak barrels.

Spicy: descriptive of the spice-like flavor elements found in wine such as pepper, cardamon, clove and cinnamon.

Supple: a wine that tastes soft and smooth; easy to drink.

Tannic: a mouth puckering astringency found in young red wines.

GLOSSARY OF GRAPES

Red Wine Varietals

CABERNET SAUVIGNON

The king of red wines in California, Cabernet's reputation was established by wineries in the Napa Valley, although it has proved distinctive in other regions as well. While sometimes a bit harsh in its youth, it has the ability to mature into a most complex and full-bodied wine, much like the great wines of Bordeaux. Its flavors are comfortable with simple grilled meats as well as more complex dishes like venison in mushroom sauce. Great and consistent producers of Cabernet can be found in the Napa and Sonoma Valley, as well as Australia, Chile, Argentina and, of course, the châteaux of Bordeaux which produce the true benchmark of this varietal.

MERLOT

This variety was once relegated to blending into other lots of red wine. But in the last twenty years it has taken on an identity of its own. Merlot has herbal and fruity flavors similar to Cabernet, but it has a smooth and supple character in the mouth without the bite of tannins. It complements the same type of foods that Cabernet does, albeit less distinctively. Top producers hail from Bordeaux (where the wine is mostly blended, but sometimes bottled separately, depending on the region) Chile, Argentina, Napa, Sonoma and Washington State.

PINOT NOIR

Pinot Noir has the potential to be the most seductive, beguiling red wine in existence. Unfortunately past examples from California left a lot to be desired. In the past decade or so, however, Pinot Noir has shown the greatest increase in quality of any varietal. The perseverance of younger winemakers and traditional winemaking methodology is resulting in Pinots that can stand side by side with the wines of Burgundy. Lighter than Cabernet, Pinots have a richness and intensity of fruit that is unparalleled. The best of them drink like velvet and accompany a wide variety of foods. Top French Burgundies are bottled under a variety of different names and labels, depending on region, vineyard and producer. In America, considerable success with this Burgundian varietal has been from Napa, Sonoma (Carneros), Santa Barbara and Oregon.

SYRAH

The great grape of the Rhône Valley has become more widely planted in California in the last ten years. Highly aromatic wines with meaty, smoky, spicy flavors are the trademark of the Syrah grape. When made in a lighter style, it's a good quaffing wine to pair with simple bistro type food. When made in a richer style, it's a good accompaniment to lamb and all manner of wild game. Syrah is the grape found in French Côte Rotie, St. Joseph and Cornas, and plays a major role in the spicy Châteauneuf-du-Papes of the southern Rhône too. In California, the Syrah grape is being cultivated in such diverse regions as Santa Barbara, Sonoma, Monterey, the Amador Foothills and Yolo County.

ZINFANDEL

Real Zinfandel is red, a fact many wine drinkers are rediscovering now that the trend for "white" zinfandel has stabilized. "Peppery," "briary," "brawny" and "chewy" are only a few of the adjectives used to describe this mouth-filling wine. It has a real zest for matching up with tomato-based pasta dishes and other highly herbalized preparations. There is no European counterpart for this variety; it is one that the first Italian winemakers propagated and cultivated when they came to California. Its origins are obviously European, but today it's a grape variety that is unique to California. Vintners in Napa, Sonoma and Amador seem to do the best job with it.

White Wine Varietals

CHARDONNAY

In the '80s it became de rigeur to ask for "a glass of Chardonnay" in a restaurant and passé to simply request "a glass of white wine." Chardonnay is the most popular wine in California for a reason: it's cold, fruity and easy to drink. It's pleasant with just about any dish involving cheese, eggs, fish or fowl. Winemakers have divided into two camps over the style of Chardonnay; one school of thought emphasizes the high-toned, steely, fruit-like qualities of the wine through little or no use of oak, while the other school emphasizes barrel and malolactic fermentation in addition to the fruit characteristic, which lends the wine a rounder, buttery taste. Benchmarks for Chardonnay are (rich and extracted) white Burgundies and (steely and crisp) Chablis. In California, there are fine Chardonnays from just about every region, including Napa, Sonoma, Mendocino, Monterey and Santa Barbara.

GEWÜRZTRAMINER

This so-called "aromatic" varietal is making a minor comeback in California. "Gewürz" translates as "spice" and it's immediately detectable when poured into a glass. The flavors echo the fragrant and flowery nose echoes, while providing an additional punch from a piquant, spicy component. Made with some residual sweetness, the wine seems to be a good counterpoint for spicy Chinese and Thai dishes. The Alsatian region of France has about four centuries of experience in producing these wines in the traditional style. In California, the cooler growing regions, like Sonoma, Mendocino and Santa Barbara, do well with this grape.

RIESLING

Another "aromatic" that is finding a home in California again, Riesling can be a particularly refreshing alternative to the Chardonnay/Sauvignon Blanc white wine tandem. Unlike its cousin, Gewürztraminer, this varietal has little spice and instead relies on its delicate aromas and subtle flavors for its special niche. Usually lighter in style and sometimes with residual sweetness, it's better paired with lighter fare. The Riesling is a mainstay of German winemaking and also ripens to full maturity in Alsace. The top California producers have generally been those who have also had success with Gewürztraminer.

SAUVIGNON BLANC

This variety is often considered the poor man's Chardonnay; it can be vinified similarly but costs only half as much. But Sauvignon Blanc has a number of identities ranging from a clean, slight grassy white wine to a herbaceous, full-bodied wine backed up with oak aging. It does its best service at the table when paired with strong, forceful, herbal flavors like goat cheese and raddichio salad. Unheralded but excellent examples come from Sancerre and Pouilly-Fumé in the Loire Valley. In California, just about every region produces a Sauvignon Blanc, although the North Coast counties seem to have a real knack for it.

SPARKLING WINES

Domaine Chandon (owned by Moet & Chandon) set up shop in Napa Valley around twenty years ago, and after its initial success, almost every French Champagne house has come to California to establish its foothold. The main reason for their interest in the New World is that Champagne is a geographically limited area which is almost fully planted, and California was almost virgin territory for sparkling wine. While the legacy of Champagne seems to be tiny pinpoint bubbles that reveal delicate and subtle flavors, their California counterparts are more often bold, upfront and fruity with their flavors. The prevailing wisdom is that the delicate nuances of the wine (in particular, Champagne) get lost when paired up with hearty, complex or highly seasoned dishes. It's certainly the perfect aperitif wine. All the California sparklers are of high quality so it seems to be a matter of house style as to what is preferred. Names to remember are Domaine Carneros, Domaine Chandon, Gloria Ferrer, Mumm-Napa, Piper-Sonoma, Mirassou, Roederer Estates, Scharffenberger, Schramsberg, Iron Horse, Handley, Cordonui, J, and Maison Deutz.

VINTAGE WINE CHART

VINTAGE CHART: The World's Wines																			
	FRANCE											GER.	ITALY		CALIFORNIA			
	Red Bordeaux	White Bordeaux	Sauterne	Red Burgundy	White Burgundy	Beaujolais	Côtes du Rhône	Provence	Alsace	Loire: Anjou, Muscadet	Pouilly, Sancere	Champagne	Rhine, Moselle, Nahe	Piedmonte	Chianti	Cabernet Sauvignon	Chardonnay	Pinot Noir	Zinfandel
1995	5	4	3	3	4	4	5	4	5	4	4	—	4	4	3	5	5	4	*Ex*
1994	4	3	2	2	4	3	3	4	5	3	3	—	4	2	3	*Ex*	5	5	*Ex*
1993	4	3	3	3	3	4	3	4	4	4	4	—	5	4	2	5	5	4	5
1992	3	3	3	3	5	2	3	3	3	3	3	—	5	3	2	5	5	4	5
1991	3	3	2	4	4	*Ex*	4	3	3	1	3	1	4	2	2	4	5	4	5
1990	5	4	5	Ex	4	4	5	5	5	5	5	*Ex*	5	5	5	5	5	4	5
1989	5	4	*Ex*	5	5	*Ex*	5	5	*Ex*	5	5	5	5	5	2	4	3	4	4
1988	4	4	*Ex*	5	5	4	4	4	5	4	4	5	5	5	5	3	5	4	4
1987	3	4	1	4	3	2	1	2	3	3	2	3	4	4	2	4	3	4	5
1986	5	5	5	3	3	3	3	3	4	4	4	3	4	3	4	5	5	4	4
1985	5	5	2	*Ex*	5	5	5	3	5	5	5	5	4	5	5	*Ex*	4	4	5
1983	5	5	*Ex*	3	5	—	5	4	*Ex*	4	4	5	5	2	3	3	4	4	3
1982	*Ex*	4	3	2	4	—	4	—	2	5	5	5	3	5	4	4	3	4	3
1981	4	5	4	—	—	—	3	—	3	5	5	5	4	3	3	4	4	4	4
1979	4	4	3	3	5	—	4	—	—	—	—	5	4	4	2	4	4	3	4
1978	4	5	—	*Ex*	5	—	*Ex*	—	—	—	—	4	2	5	4	5	4	4	4

EX: EXCEPTIONAL
5: VERY GREAT
4: GREAT
3: GOOD

2: MEDIUM
1: PASSABLE
—: SMALL YEAR

* This is only meant to be a general guide. Start by learning which regions and years are better than others; once you develop a good knowledge, buy according to your preferences.

The European wines are categorized by the region in which the grapes were grown. This is their "appellation," displayed on the label along with the phrase *Appéllation controlée or Denominazione di origine contrallata* to guarantee the wine's authenticity. The California wines are categorized by grape name, as they are throughout the United States.

California Food & Wine Events
& Seasonal Food Tips

(Dates vary with the year)

JANUARY

- Oysters are fresh now—eat them with Champagne to ring in the New Year. Also, this is the month for wild mushrooms, tangerines, oranges, red apples, Camembert and blue cheeses.
- Chinese New Year (late January to mid-February), Chinatown, L.A. Various activities including a street carnival and the colorful Golden Dragon Parade.
- Japanese New Year (December 17 to end of January), Little Tokyo, L.A. The New Year's activities are highlighted by the Line Dance, a form of blessing, which winds its way through the shops of Little Tokyo.

FEBRUARY

- Artichokes are best this time of year.
- National Date Festival, Indio. Going strong since the '40s, this festival celebrates Indio's prized fruit with entertainers and food booths.
- Masters of Food and Wine, Highlands Inn, Carmel (408-624-3801). A prestigious annual gathering of international chefs and winemakers celebrating great cuisine and wine.
- Santa Barbara Method Champenoise Festival. A three-day festival dedicated to the bubblies of the world. Anchored at the Santa Barbara Biltmore Hotel during Valentine's Day celebration (805-969-2261).
- American Wine Appreciation Week. The last week of February has been proclaimed "American Wine Appreciation Week" by a resolution of the U.S. Congress. Look for corresponding celebrations, wine tastings and other activities to be sponsored by wineries and wine retailers across the country.

MARCH

- Spring lamb comes fresh to markets this month. So does asparagus.

APRIL

- Strawberries debut this month.
- Monterey Wine Festival, Monterey (408-656-WINE.) The largest celebration of California wines in the U.S.
- Santa Cruz Spring Passport. A self-guided tour of 22 wineries in the Santa Cruz Mountains. Some of these wineries are not normally open to the public (408-479-9463).
- Sweet Onion Festival, California Mid-Winter Fairgrounds, Imperial. Onion-eating and onion ring contests, food booths, entertainment, games and crafts, sponsored by the Imperial Vegetable Growers Association.

- L.A. Opera International Wine Auction. An elegant affair to benefit Los Angeles Music Center Opera, featuring an auction of wine, and gourmet dining and travel packages (213-972-7621).

MAY

- This is the month for strawberries, red onions, haricots verts, mangoes and goat cheese.
- Paso Robles Wine Festival (805-239-8463). An annual event featuring wine from local Central Coast wineries.
- California Strawberry Festival, Oxnard (805-385-7578). The "Strawberry Capital of the World" celebrates Oxnard's heritage as the backyard vegetable garden to Los Angeles. Food and wine samplings, food and beverage booths, children's area and entertainment, sponsored by local non-profit organizations.
- Bouillabaisse Festival, Brander Vineyard (off Highway 154 at Roblar), Los Olivos (805-688-2455). This winery-sponsored event, typically held the third weekend of May, features a bouillabaisse competition among Central Coast restaurants, as well as food and wine samplings. Proceeds benefit local hospital facilities.
- L.A. Culinary Evening with the California Winemasters. This benefits the Cystic Fibrosis Foundation, and showcases celebrated chefs, restaurateurs and winemasters (310-479-8585).
- National Orange Show, N.O.S. Event Center, San Bernardino (909-888-6788.) Annual citrus fair.
- Los Angeles County Fair Wine of the Americas Competition, L.A. County Fairgrounds, Pomona (909-623-3111). Over four hundred wineries place entries of wines grown in the Americas.

JUNE

- Peaches ripen this month. So do nectarines, cherries, boysenberries and melons.
- Beaumont Cherry Festival, Beaumont (909-845-9541). An annual celebration for nearly 80 years of the local cherry industry, with cherry-picking and cherry eating.
- "Summerday," Pacific Design Center, (310-450-5183). An elegant food-and-wine tasting benefit sponsored by KCRW (89.9 FM). Includes a rare-wine auction.
- Napa Valley Wine Auction (707-942-9783). Serious wine connoisseurs flock to St. Helena annually to participate in an elegant series of dinners, tastings, auctions and more.
- L.A. Taste of the Nation (800-955-TASTE). This nationwide event's incarnation in L.A. includes food stations, live entertainment and a silent auction. Proceeds benefit the hunger-fighting organization "Share Our Strength."
- Taste of Orange County, Irvine (714-753-1551). A weekend-long food-and-music fest offering local food tastes, chef demos and numerous live music stages.

JULY

- Corn is at its peak. So are tomatoes, avocados and garlic.
- Central Coast Wine Classic, San Luis Obispo (805-781-3026). Winery dinners, an auction of California sparkling wines and much more.
- Gilroy Garlic Festival, Gilroy (408-842-1625). In the "Garlic Capital of the World," this annual festival will take your

breath away: live music, tennis and golf tournaments, and tastings of garlic in every food variation imaginable, from pizza to ice cream.

AUGUST

- Bordeaux wines arrive in the U.S. This is the last good month for corn and summer fruits.
- Santa Barbara Annual Wine Festival (805-682-4711). This benefit for the S.B. Museum of Natural History includes a gala dinner, auctions, wine tastings and tours of Santa Ynez wineries.

SEPTEMBER

- Wine-grape harvesting begins this month, which means tastings and celebrations in California's wine-growing areas.
- Central Coast Wine Festival, San Luis Obispo (805-541-1721). A benefit for the Arthritis Foundation, with wine tasting, live wine auction, gourmet food and live music.
- American Wine & Food Festival, Los Angeles (310-476-4786). A food-and-wine-tasting extravaganza hosted by Wolfgang Puck and Barbara Lazaroff, to benefit "Meals-On-Wheels."
- Big Bear Lake Oktoberfest (September and October), Big Bear (909-866-4607). A boisterous celebration of the Bavarian holiday, with wurst feasts and beer-drinking contests.
- Oak Glen Apple Harvest Festival (each weekend through December), Oak Glen (909-797-6833) For over 100 years, this event has celebrated apple-picking season with thousands of gallons of cider, and other apple products.

OCTOBER

- Truffles and chanterelles are unearthed this month. Also pears and Dungeness crab are good.
- Pismo Beach Clam Festival (805-773-4382). Jazz festival, parade, fair and clams galore.
- L.A. Wine & Spirits Focus (888-34-FOCUS). *Bon Appetit* sponsors a serious wine tasting accompanied by foods from local chefs, at the Pacific Design Center.
- The Ritz-Carlton World of Food and Wine, Laguna Niguel (714-489-5897). This lavish weekend-long event, at the elegant Ritz-Carlton, is for both professional and amateur food and wine enthusiasts.

NOVEMBER

- Beaujolais Nouveau is released, with celebrations everywhere.
- Napa Valley Wine Festival (707-253-3511). Vintners celebrate the harvest with informal tastings of wines from about 50 wineries.
- Santa Barbara Wine Auction Weekend (805-969-WINE). This even to benefit the Music Academy of the West includes a grand outdoor wine-tasting, food and wine demos, dinners and a fine-wine auction.

DECEMBER

- It's black truffle month!

FOOD & WINE PAIRINGS

Consider the myriad foods available at our grocers and food preparations that can be enjoyed in our restaurants. Then consider the number of varietal wines available and all their styles. It quickly becomes clear that the enterprise of pairing food and wine can be as complicated as you wish to make it. If you'd like some rules of thumb to help you sort out the possibilities, here are two that have stood the test of time. Rule One: Drink red wine with meat, and white wine with fish and poultry. Rule Two: Forget about Rule One and marry any food with any wine you wish; when it comes to personal preferences, there are no rights and wrongs.

There are, of course, some classic food and wine matches that satisfy again and again. And there are exciting new standards being discovered daily as the range of foods and wines available continues to expand. Based on our experience, the following matches of widely available dishes and cuisines with the wines of North America are worthy of special consideration. One caveat: Sauces can change everything, so ask the cook or a waiter for a flavor forecast.

APPETIZERS & FIRST COURSES

ANTIPASTO

Pinot Gris, (Dry) Chenin Blanc, Sauvignon Blanc, Pinot Blanc, Gamay Beaujolais, Barbera

ASPARAGUS

Sauvignon (Fumé) Blanc, (Dry) Riesling, Vidal Blanc

CARPACCIO (BEEF)

Barbera, Cabernet Rosé, Rhône Blends

CARPACCIO (TUNA)

Sauvignon (Fumé) Blanc, Vin Gris

CAVIAR

Brut Sparkling Wine

CLAMS (RAW OR CASINO)

Sauvignon (Fumé) Blanc, Brut Sparkling Wine, (Dry) Chenin Blanc, Pinot Blanc, Seyval Blanc

COLD MEATS

Vin Gris, Riesling, Gamay Beaujolais, Barbera, Seyval Blanc, (Dry) Vignoles, Chambourcin Rosé

CRUDITÉS

Pinot Blanc, Chenin Blanc, Chardonnay, Gamay Beaujolais

FOIE GRAS

Brut Sparkling Wine; Late-Harvest Riesling, Sauvignon Blanc, or Gewürztraminer, Muscat, Pinot Noir

NIÇOISE SALAD
Sauvignon (Fumé) Blanc

NUTS AND/OR OLIVES
Brut Sparkling Wine

OYSTERS (RAW)
Sauvignon (Fumé) Blanc, Brut Sparkling Wine, Pinot Gris, Chardonnay, (Dry) Riesling, Pinot Blanc, Chenin Blanc

PASTA SALAD
Sémillon, Sauvignon (Fumé) Blanc, (Dry) Chenin Blanc, (Dry) Riesling

PASTA WITH CREAM SAUCE
Chardonnay, Pinot Blanc

PASTA WITH SHELLFISH
Sauvignon (Fumé) Blanc, Chardonnay

PASTA WITH TOMATO SAUCE
Barbera, Sangiovese, Zinfandel, Rhône Blends

PASTA WITH VEGETABLES
Pinot Blanc, Dry Riesling, Sauvignon Blanc, Viognier, Gamay Beaujolais, Barbera

PATÉS
Gewürztraminer, Seyval Blanc, Gamay Beaujolais, Riesling, Brut Sparkling Wine, Cabernet Franc, Vin Gris

PROSCIUTTO AND MELON
Pinot Blanc, Riesling, Late Harvest Riesling or Gewürztraminer, Muscat

QUICHE
Riesling, Chenin Blanc, Chardonnay, Viognier, Gamay Beaujolais

SCALLOPS
Sauvignon (Fumé) Blanc, Chardonnay, Brut Sparkling Wine, Pinot Noir, Sémillon

SMOKED FISH (TROUT, HERRING)
Riesling, Gewürztraminer, Pinot Blanc, Brut Sparkling Wine

SOUPS
Usually none, or (Solera) Sherry

Fish & Shellfish

CRAB
Sauvignon (Fumé) Blanc, Brut Sparkling Wine, Chardonnay

LOBSTER
Brut Sparkling Wine, Chardonnay

MUSSELS
Chenin Blanc, Pinot Blanc, Pinot Gris, Sauvignon (Fumé) Blanc

RED SNAPPER
Chardonnay, Sauvignon (Fumé) Blanc

SALMON
Pinot Noir, Sauvignon Blanc, Pinot Gris, Sémillon, Vin Gris

SALMON TARTARE
Brut Sparkling Wine, Pinot Gris

SASHIMI, SUSHI
Brut Sparkling Wine, Semi-Dry Riesling

SCALLOPS, OYSTERS, CLAMS
See appetizers

SHRIMP
Pinot Blanc, Chenin

Blanc, Sauvignon (Fumé) Blanc, Chardonnay, Colombard, Vidal Blanc

STRIPED BASS

Chardonnay, Pinot Blanc, Viognier, (Dry) Vignoles

SWORDFISH

Sauvignon (Fumé) Blanc, Brut Sparkling Wine, Vin Gris, Pinot Noir

TUNA

Sauvignon (Fumé) Blanc, Pinor Noir, Merlot, Vin Gris, Chardonnay

OTHER WHITE FISH

Chardonnay, Viognier, Dry Riesling, Semillon

MEAT & POULTRY

CHICKEN

Chardonnay, Vin Gris, Riesling, Merlot, Gamay Beaujolais, Chenin Blanc, Pinot Noir, (Lighter) Cabernet Sauvignon

CHICKEN SALAD

Riesling, Chenin Blanc, Gewürztraminer, Pinot Blanc

CHICKEN (SMOKED)

Vin Gris, Pinot Noir, Zinfandel

DUCK

Pinot Noir, Merlot, Rosé Sparkling Wine, Cabernet Sauvignon, Zinfandel

FRANKFURTER

Riesling, (Chilled) Gamay Beaujolais

HAM

Vin Gris, Gamay Beaujolais, Merlot

HAMBURGER

Cabernet Sauvignon, Gamay, Syrah, Chancellor, Barbera, Zinfandel, Rhône Blends

LAMB (GRILLED, BROILED)

Meritage, Cabernet Sauvignon, Merlot, Pinot Noir, Marechal Foch, Chancellor, Zinfandel

PHEASANT

Pinot Noir, Syrah

QUAIL

Pinot Noir

RABBIT

Riesling, Pinot Noir, Barbera, Merlot, Zinfandel

SAUSAGE

Riesling, Brut or Rosé Sparkling Wine, Barbera, Gamay Beaujolais, Norton or Cynthiana, Syrah, Zinfandel

STEAK (GRILLED, BROILED)

Cabernet Sauvignon, Merlot, Rhône Blends, Zinfandel, Meritage, Norton or Cynthiana, Brut Sparkling Wine

TURKEY

Zinfandel, Merlot, Chardonnay, Gamay Beaujolais

VEAL

Chardonnay, Barbera, Merlot, Cynthiana

VENISON

Syrah, Rhône Blends, Petite Sirah, Zinfandel, Pinot Noir, Norton, Chancellor, Cabernet Sauvignon

Other Main Courses

COUSCOUS

Cabernet Franc, Merlot, Petite Sirah, Rosé Sparkling Wine, Syrah, Vin Gris

CURRY, FISH OR CHICKEN

Riesling, (Chilled) Gamay Beaujolais, Sauvignon (Fumé) Blanc, Zinfandel

MOUSSAKA

Merlot, Sangiovese, Barbera, Zinfandel

PIZZA

Barbera, Zinfandel, Sangiovese, Brut or Rosé Sparkling Wine, Cabernet Rosé

SPICY CHINESE

Dry (and off-dry) Riesling, Pinot Gris, Pinot Blanc, Brut or Rosé Sparkling Wine, Merlot

SPICY MEXICAN

Dry (and off-dry) Riesling, Vin Gris, Chenin Blanc, (Chilled) Gamay Beaujolais

THAI

Chenin Blanc, Pinot Blanc, Riesling, Gewürztraminer, Brut or Rosé Sparkling Wine

Cheeses

GOAT

soft: Brut or Rosé Sparkling Wine, Sauvignon (Fumé) Blanc, Cabernet Sauvignon, Merlot, Pinot Noir

hard: Pinot Noir, Merlot, Syrah, Cabernet Sauvignon

COW & SHEEP

medium: Pinot Noir, Petite Sirah

hard: Cabernet Sauvignon, Petite Sirah, Zinfandel, Port Blue, Late-Harvest Riesling, Chenin Blanc, Gewürtraminer, Muscat, Zinfandel

Desserts

APPLE PIE, TART & BAKED

Late-Harvest Riesling, Various Ice Wines, Muscat, Demi-sec Sparkling Wines, Blueberry Wine

BERRIES

Brut Sparkling Wines, Demi-sec Sparkling Wines, Late-Harvest Riesling, Muscat, Zinfandel

CHOCOLATE

Late-Harvest Riesling, Raspberry Wine, Black Muscat, Cabernet Sauvignon

CAKES

Demi-sec Sparkling Wines, Late-Harvest Riesling, Muscat, Various Ice Wines

CREAMS, CUSTARDS, PUDDINGS

Demi-sec Sparkling Wines, Late-Harvest Riesling, Muscat, Various Ice Wines

FRESH FRUIT

Late-Harvest Chenin Blanc, Riesling, Gewürztraminer, Muscat

ICE CREAMS, SORBETS

Usually none, perhaps fruit wine or fruit liqueurs

NUTS

Port, Brut Sparkling Wine, Angelica

TIRAMISU

Angelica

RESTAURANT INDEXES

Los Angeles Area (LA), **San Fernando Valley** (SFV), **Pasadena & San Gabriel Valley** (SGV), **South Bay** (SoB), **Orange County** (OC), **Palm Springs** (PS), **San Diego** (SD), **Santa Barbara** (SB), **Central Coast** (CC), **Catalina Island** (Cat.), **Mountain Resorts** (Mts.), **Northern Baja, Mexico** (MX), **Outlying Areas** (OA) , **Las Vegas** (LV)

RESTAURANTS BY CUISINE

AMERICAN

Apple Farm (CC)
Beef Eaters of Coronado (SD)
Blue Ox Restaurant (Mts.)
Blue Parrot (Cat.)
Blue Whale & Tail of the Whale, The (Mts.)
Brambles (CC)
Broadway Bar & Grill (LA)
Buffalo Springs Station (Cat.)
Cadillac Café, The (LA)
Catalina Country Clubhouse Bar & Grille (Cat.)
Charley Brown's (SoB)
Chart House (SoB, LA)
Citrus City Grill (OC)
Claim Jumper (OA)
Cold Spring Tavern (SB)
Cottage, The (OC)
Daily Grill, The (SFV,LA,OC,PS)
Delacey's Club 41 (SGV)
Dickenson West (SGV)
Dorn's (CC)
Doug's Harbor Reef (CI)
East Beach Grill (SB)
Engine Co. No. 28 (LA)
F. McLintock's (CC)
Five Crowns (OC)
Grill on the Alley, The (LA)
Historic Antlers Inn (Mts.)
Hitching Post, The (CC)
Hob Nob Hill (SD)
Ivy, The (LA)
Ivy at the Shore, The (LA)
Jake & Annie's (LA)
Jocko's (CC)
Joe's Café (SB)
Kate Mantilini (LA)
Kathleen's (SGV)
Lawry's The Prime Rib (LA)
Library, The (SoB)
Lola (LA)
Marston's (SGV)
Martha's 22nd St. Grill (SoB)
Mattei's Tavern (CC)
McCharles House (OC)
Miss Gregory's (LA)
Moody's (LA)
Morton's (LA)
Odessa (OC)
Pacific Dining Car (LA)
Paradise Café (SB)
Rainforest Café (OC)
Rainwater's (SD)
Raymond, The (SGV)
Ruby's (OC)
Saddle Peak Lodge (SFV)
Scotty's on the Strand (SoB)
Shenandoah Café (SoB)
Smokehouse, The (SFV)
Stillwell's (Mts.)
Sunset's (SoB)
Taylor's Steakhousc (SGV)
Thelen's Mermaid (SoB)
Tulsa (LA)
Washington Street Bar and Grill (LA)

AMERICAN/CONTINENTAL

Casual Elegance (Mts.)
Chasen's (LA)
Chef's Inn & Tavern (Mts.)
Gypsy Grill, The (SFV)
Moonlight Tango Café (SFV)
Pacific Dining Car (LA)

CALIFORNIAN

CALIFORNIAN/ASIAN

CALIFORNIAN/CONTINENTAL

CALIFORNIAN/ECLECTIC

CALIFORNIAN/FRENCH

CALIFORNIAN/HAWAIIAN

CALIFORNIAN/IRISH

CALIFORNIAN/MEDITER-RANEAN

Maple Drive (LA)
Splashes (OC)

CALIFORNIAN/ MEXICAN

Cobalt Cantina (LA)

CALIFORNIAN/PACIFIC RIM

Bistrot by the Water (OA)
La Marina at Four Seasons Biltmore Hotel (SB)
Pacifica Del Mar (SD)
Landrey's (SoB)

CARIBBEAN/JAMAICAN

Cha Cha Cha (SFV,LA)
Coley's Place (LA)
Kingston Café (SGV)
La Bamba (SGV)
Limbo Restaurant (LA)
Montego Bay (LA)

CARIBBEAN/FUSION

David's (SoB)
Camachos Grill (SoB)

CHICKEN

Koo Koo Roo (LA)
Rotisserie Chicken of California (SGV)
Zankou Chicken (LA,SGV)

CHILEAN

Rincon Chileno (LA)

CHINESE

ABC Seafood (LA)
Bamboo Gardens (LV)
Bamboo Inn (SFV)
Chin Chin (SFV,LA)
Dumpling Master (SGV)
Emerald Seafood Restaurant (SD)
Feast From The East (LA)
Five Feet (OC)
Fung Lum (SFV)
G.C. River (SGV)
Genghis Cohen (LA)
Gourmet 88 (SGV)
Harvest Inn Chinese Restaurant (SGV)
Hong Kong Paradise Seafood Bistro (SFV)
Hu's Szechwan Restaurant (LA)
J.R. Seafood Restaurant (LA)
Joss (LA)
Lake Spring Cuisine (SGV)
Mandarette (LA)
Mandarin, The (LA)
Mandarin Deli (LA)
Mandarin Garden (SD)
Mandarin Gourmet (OC)
Manhattan Wonton Company (LA)
Ocean Star Seafood (SGV)
Oriental Seafood Inn (LA)
P.F. Chang's (LV)
P.F. Chang's China Bistro (OC)
Quanjude Beijing Duck Restaurant (SGV)
Taipan (LA)
Xi-an (LA)
Yang Chow (SFV)
Yen Ching (OC)
Yujean Kang's (LA)
Yujean Kang's Gourmet Chinese Cuisine (SGV)

CHINESE/DIM SUM

Charming Garden (SGV)
China Star (SFV)
Empress Pavilion (LA)
Harbor Village (SGV)
NBC Seafood (SGV)
Ocean Seafood (LA)
Sea Star (SGV)

CHINESE/ISLAMIC

Jamillah Garden (OC)

CHINESE/PAN-ASIAN

Chinois (LV)

CHINESE/SEAFOOD

Dragon Regency Seafood Restaurant (SGV)
J.R. Seafood Restaurant (LA)
Mon Kee (LA)
Royal Star Seafood (LA)
V.I.P. Harbor Seafood Restaurant (LA)

CHINESE/SOUTHEAST ASIAN

Le Chine Wok (LA)

COASTAL CUISINE/SEAFOOD

Blue Point Coastal Cuisine (SD)

COFFEE SHOP

Billy Reed's (PS)
John O'Groats (LA)
Louise's Pantry (PS)
Malibu Inn, The (LA)
Old Custom House (CC)
Original Pantry (LA)
Picnik (LA)
Silver Spoon Restaurant (LA)
Wheel Inn, The (PS)

COFFEEHOUSE

Caffé Latte (LA)
Coffee Bean and Tea Leaf (LA)
Prebica Coffee (LA)

Seattle's Best Coffee (S.B.C.) (LA)
Starbucks (LA)

CONTEMPORARY/CONTINENTAL

456 Caretta (LA)

CONTINENTAL

Arches, The (OC)
Bistro Garden at Coldwater, The (SFV)
Brae, The (SGV)
Brandywine Café, The (SFV)
Buccaneer Bay Club (LV)
California Canteen (SFV)
Casa de Sevilla (SB)
Cat and Custard Cup, The (OC)
Channel House, The (CI)
Chelsea on the Queen Mary (SoB)
Chez Jay (LA)
Grill, The (SGV)
Gustaf Anders (OC)
Isis (LV)
Jillian's (PS)
Mulberry Tree, The (Mts.)
Musso & Frank's Grill (LA)
Nest, The (PS)
Oaks on the Plaza (SGV)
Ritz, The (OC)
Ritz Pub Café, The (MX)
Royal Oak, The (Mts.)
Season's (Mts.)
Sky Room, The (SoB)
Spencer's Restaurant & Patio (SGV)
Stoney Point Bar & Grill (SGV)
Tower, The (LA)
WR's Eatery at Snow Valley (Mts.)
Hollywood Canteen (LA)

CONTINENTAL/CALIFORNIAN

Shame on the Moon (PS)

COOKIES

Catalina Cookie Co. (CI)

CUBAN

El Floridita (LA)
Felix Continental Café (OC)
Havana on Sunset (LA)
Versailles (LA,SFV,SoB)

DELI

Bagel Nosh (LA)
Barney Greengrass (LA)
Canter's (LA)
D.Z. Akins (SD)
Greenblatt's Delicatessen (LA)
Jerry's Famous Deli (OC,LA)
Langer's (LA)
Nate 'n' Al's Delicatessen (LA)
New York Bagel (LA)
Old Country Deli (CC)
Stage Deli (LV,LA)

DELI/ECLECTIC

Broadway Deli (LA)

DINER

Corvette Diner, Bar & Grill (SD)
Fred 62 (LA)
Mel's Drive In (LA)
Millie's (LA)Rae's (LA)
Ruby's (OC,SoB)
Snug Harbor (LA)

ECLECTIC

Beach City Grill (SoB)
Blue Pyramid (SGV)
Chez Mélange (SoB)
Christine (SoB)
Farmers' Market, The (LA)
410 Boyd (LA)
Gerlach's Grill (SGV)
Holly Street Bar & Grill (SGV)
Lumpy Gravy (LA)
Mamagaya (LA)
Meritage (SB)
Nic's and the Martini Lounge (LA)
Out Take Café (SFV)
Rix (LA)
Stepps on the Court (LA)
Tahiti (LA)
2424 Pico (LA)
Victor Hodd's (LA)Vida (LA)

ETHIOPIAN

Ibex (SGV)
Rosalind's (LA)

FRENCH

Aubergine (OC)
Belgian Lion, The (SD)
Bistro K (LA)
Bistro Laurent (CC)
Bistro of Lunada Bay (SoB)
Bistrot Provençal (LA)
Bizcocho at Rancho Bernardo Inn, El (SD)
Café Beaujolais (SGV)
Café Bizou (SFV)
Café des Artistes (LA)
Café Maurice (LA)
Café Pinot (LA)
Café Provençal (OA)
Cellar, The (OC)
Chez Mimi (LA)

Citrus (LA)
Dining Room, The (OC)
Drai's (LA)
El Rey Sol (MX)
French Market Grille (SD)
Gigi (LA)
L'Orangerie (LA)
La Frite Café (SFV)
La Parisienne (SGV)
La Vache & Co. (SD)
La Vie en Rose (OC)
Lafayette (OC)
Le Beaujolais (SoB)
Le Chardonnay (LA)
Le Chéne (OA)
Le Dôme (LA)
Le Petit Bistro (SFV, LA)
Le Vallauris (PS)
Les Deux Cafés (LA)
Les Frères Taix (LA)
Louis XIV (LA)
Mille Fleurs (SD)
Mimosa (SB, LA)
Mistral Brasserie (SFV)
Moustache Café (LA)
Palace Court (LV)
Pascal (OC)
Pastis (LA)
Pinot Bistro (SFV)
Pinot Hollywood (LA)
Pleasant Peasant Country Bistrot, The (OC)
Ritz-Carlton Dining Room, The (LA)
Rive Gauche Café (SFV)
Riverside Café (SFV)
Top O' The Cove (SD)
Tosh ii Koo (SoB)
Wine Bistro, The (SFV)

FRENCH/ASIAN

Papashon (SGV)

FRENCH/CALIFORNIAN

Bistro 45 (SGV)
Café Pierre (SoB)
Chez Sateau (SGV)
Citronelle at Santa Barbara Inn (SB)
Drai's (LV)
Iron Squirrel, The (Mts.)
La Cachette (LA)
Lavande (LA)
Le St. Germain (PS)
Lunaria (LA)
Patina (LA)
Pinot at the Chronicle (SGV)
Troquet (OC)

FRENCH/CARIBBEAN

Golden Truffle, The (OC)

FRENCH/CHINESE

Chinois on Main (LA)

FRENCH/CONTINENTAL

Patricia at Cunard's (PS)

FRENCH/CONTEMPORARY

Laurel (SD)
Marine Room, The (SD)
Chalet de France (SoB)

FRENCH/FUSION

Splash! (SoB)

FRENCH/ITALIAN

La Embotelladora Vieja (MX)

FRENCH/JAPANESE

Nouveau Café Blanc (LA)
Shiro (SGV)

FRENCH/MEDITERRANEAN

Aimee's (SoB)
Dining Room, The (PS)

FRENCH/PACIFIC RIM

Cinnabar (SGV)
Sesame Grill (SGV)

GERMAN

Knoll's Black Forest Inn (LA)
Schatzi's Grill (PS)

GREEK

Aegean Café (OC)
Great Greek, The (SFV)
Nikos (SGV)
Papadakis Taverna (SoB)
Sofi (LA)

HAMBURGERS

Apple Pan, The (LA)
Cassell's Hamburgers (LA)
Hampton's (LA)
Malibu Mutts (LA)
Tommy's (LA)

HEALTHY

Figtree's Café (LA)
Good Stuff (SoB, LA)
Inn of the Seventh Ray (LA)
Jamba Juice (all)
Main Squeeze Café (SB)
Natural Café and Juice Bar, The (SB)
Newsroom Café, The (LA)
Real Food Daily (LA)
Soujourner (SB)
Spot, The (SoB)

HOT DOGS

Jody Maroni's Sausage Kingdom (LA)

Pink's Hot Dogs (LA)
Tail O'the Pup (LA)

HUNGARIAN

Hortobagy (SFV)

ICE CREAM

Al Gelato (LA)
Bigg Chill, The (LA)
Charly Temmel (LA)
Coldstone Creamery (LA)
Double Rainbow (LA)
Eiger (LA)
Fair Oaks Pharmacy and Soda Fountain (LA)
SLO Maid Ice Cream Factory (CC)
Soda Jerks (SGV)

INDIAN

All India Café (SGV)
Anarbagh (SFV)
Bombay Café (LA)
Bombay Palace (LA)
Chamika Catering (LA)
Clay Oven (OC)
Clay Pit, The (LA)
East India Grill (LA)
Gaylord (LA)
Mayur (OC)
Natraj of India (OC)
Nawab of India (LA)
Chameli (SGV)

INDONESIAN

Asian Deli (OC)

INTERNATIONAL

Encounter (SoB)

ITALIAN

Ago (LA)
Allegria (LA)
Alto Palato (LA)
Amelia's (OC)
Angeli Caffè (LA)
Antonello Ristorante (OC)
Antonio's (LV)
Antonio's Pizzeria & Cabaret (CI)
Baccio (SB)
Bertolini's (LV)
Boccaccio's Nuevo Marianna (MX)
Bona Corso's (SGV)
Bottle Inn Ristorante, The (SoB)
Buca di Beppo (SGV)
Bucatini (SB)Buona Tavola (CC)
C & O Trattoria (LA)
Ca' del Sole (SFV)
Ca'Brea (LA)
Ca'Dario (SB)
Café Dell 'Opera (LA)
Café Piccolo Trattoria (SoB)
Café Prego (CI)
Café Roma (CC)
Café Solé (SGV)
Celestino (SGV)
Charlie's Trio (LA,SGV)
Chianti (LA)
Chianti Cucina (LA)
Chicago-Chicago Pizza & Pasta (OC)
Ciao Trattoria (LA)
Cicada (LA)
Coco Pazzo (LA)
Cucina Paradiso (SoB)
Da Pasquale (LA)
Dan Tana's (LA)
Devane's (PS)
Dino's Italian Inn (SGV)
Divino (LA)
Drago (LA)
Emi Ristorante (LA)
Emilio's (SB)
Fabiolus Café No.1 (LA)
Fabiolus Café No.2 (LA)
Fabiolus Café No.3 (LA)
Far Niente (SGV)
Fontana de Trevi (SFV)
Francesco's (LV)
Franco's Sunny Italy, The (SGV)
Fresco Ristorante (SGV)
Fritto Misto (LA)
Gennaro's Ristorante (SGV)
Giovanni's Trattoria (LA)
Girasole (LA)
Giuseppe's (CC)
Hugo's (LA)
I Cugini (LA)
Il Cielo (LA)
Il Fornaio (OC, LA)
Il Forno (LA, SFV)
Il Grano (LA)
Il Moro (LA)
Il Nido (LA)
Il Pastaio (LA)
Il Piccolino (LA)
Il Sole (LA)
Il Tiramisu (SFV)
Il Tramezzino (LA)
Intermezza (LA)
L'Arancini (LA)
L'Opera (SoB)
La Bruschetta (LA)
La Finestra (SFV)
La Fornaretta (SGV)
La Loggia (SFV)
La Luna Ristorante (LA)
La Scala (LV)
Locanda del Lago (LA)
Locanda Veneta (LA)
Madeo (LA)
Maggiano's Little Italy (OC)
Maito (LA)

JAPANESE

JAPANESE/MEDITERRANEAN

JAPANESE/NOODLES

JAPANESE/SUSHI

KOREAN

KOSHER

Milky Way (LA)
Nessim's (LA)
Pico Kosher Deli (LA)

LATIN AMERICAN

Berta's Latin American Restaurant (SD)

LATIN AMERICAN/SOUTHERN

Sabor (LA)

LEBANESE

Al Amir (LA)

MALAYSIAN

Kuala Lumpur (SGV)

MEDITERRANEAN

Abiento (SGV)
Aïoli Restaurant & Tapas Bar (SoB)
Araz (SFV)
Auberge, The (SoB)
Barsac Brasserie (SFV)
Black Sheep Bistro (OC)
Café Santorini (SGV)
La Ve Lee (SFV)
Little Door, The (LA)
Ma Dolce Vita (SB)
Palomino Euro-Bistro (PS)
Sixth Street Bistro (SoB)
Terrace, The (SGV)
Zov's Bistro (OC)

MEXICAN

Antonio's (LA)
Border Grill (LA)
Cantina Real (SoB)
Carlitos Café Y Cantina (SB)
Carnitas La Flor de Michoacan (MX)
Casa Escobar (LA)
Casablanca (LA)
Casita del Campo (LA)
Cava (SB)
Cien Años Mexican Nuevo (MX)
Coral Beach Cantina (LA)
Cozymel's (LV)
El Chavo (LA)
El Cholo (LA)
El Coyote (LA)
El Emperador Maya (SGV)
El Mariachi (OC)
El Nido (MX)
El Papagayo's (Mts.)
El Tepayac Café (LA)
El Torito Grill (OC)
Guelaguetza (LA)
Hannah's Cantina (LA)
La Cabana Restaurant (LA)
La Fonda (SD)
La Parilla (SFV, LA)
La Salsa (LA)
La Serenata (LA)
La Serenata de Garibaldi (LA)
La Simpatia (CC)
La Super-Rica (SB)
Las Brisas (OC)
Las Casuelas Nuevas (PS)
Las Casuelas – The Original (PS)
Lucy's El Adobe Café (LA)
Lula Cucina Mexicana (LA)
Marix Tex Mex Café (LA)
Merida (SGV)
Mexica (LA)
Mexico City (LA)
Mi Familia (LA)
Monte Alban (LA)
Ortega's Buffet (MX)
Pancho's (SoB)
Pete's Southside Café (CC)
Poquito Mas (LA)
Rebecca's (LA)
Salsitas (CC)
San Pedro Fish Market & Restaurant (LA)
Señor Fish (LA, SGV)
Taco Loco (OC)
Taco Mesa (OC)
Tamayo (LA)
Tortilla Flats (OC)
Tortilla Grill (LA)
Viva (SFV)
Yuca's Hut (LA)
Zia Café, The (SB)
Zumaya's (LA)

MIDDLE EASTERN

Aladdin Gourmet Foods and Deli Café (SD)
Burger Continental (SGV)
Habash Café (SoB)
Marouch (LA)
Sunnin (LA)
Tempo (SFV)
Wahib's Middle Eastern (SGV)

MOROCCAN

Dar Maghreb (LA)
Koutoubia (LA)

NEW AMERICAN

Azzura Point, Loews Coronado Bay Resort (SD)
Bernard's (LA)
Buffalo Club, The (LA)
Chad's (SB)
Depot (SoB)
Dynasty Room (LA)
Fonz's Restaurant (SoB)
Hal's Bar & Grill (LA)
James' Beach (LA)

NICARAGUAN/SALVADORAN

NUEVO LATINO

PACIFIC RIM

PAN-ASIAN

PANCAKES

PERSIAN

PERUVIAN

PIZZA

POLISH

POLYNESIAN

RUSSIAN

SANDWICHES

SCOTTISH

SEAFOOD

SOUTHERN/SOUL FOOD

SOUTHWESTERN

SPANISH

STEAKHOUSE

TEA ROOM

TEX-MEX/CALIFORNIAN

THAI

THEME RESTAURANTS

VIETNAMESE

VEGETARIAN (SEE HEALTHY)

WINE TASTING

Restaurants By Notable Features

We've included only the BEST in each category.

BEST BREAKFAST

A Thousand Cranes (LA)
Aunt Gussie's Place (SGV)
Baccio (SB)
Back on the Beach (LA)
Bagel Nosh (LA)
Barcliff & Bair (SB)
Barney Greengrass (LA)
Barney's Beanery (LA)
The Belvédère (LA)
Blueberry (LA)
Broadway Deli (LA)
The Cadillac Café (LA)
Café Rodeo (LA)
Café Zinc (OC)
Caffé Luna (LA)
California Canteen (LA)
Campanile (LA)
Canter's (LA)
Checkers Restaurant (LA)
Chez Mélange (LA)
Citronelle (SB)
Dinah's (LA)
East Beach Grill (SB)
Elmer's Pancake & Steak House (PS)
Fair Oaks Pharmacy (SGV)
The Farm of Beverly Hills (LA)
The Farmer's Market (LA)
Figtree Café (LA)
Fred 62 (LA)
Gardens (LA)
Gladstone's 4 Fish (LA)
Good Stuff (So.B.)
Greenblatt's (LA)
Hob Nob Hill (SD)
The Hotel Bel-Air Dining Room (LA)
Hugo's (LA)
Il Fornaio (LA & others)
Jerry's Famous Deli (LA & others)
John O'Groats (LA)
Julienne (SGV)
Kate Mantilini (LA)
Kathleen's (SGV)
Kings Road Café (LA)
La Cajole (LA)
Langer's (LA)
Lipton Tea House (SGV)

Louise's Pantry (PS)
Ma Dolce Vita (SB)
Madlon's Landings...The Café (Mts)
Main Squeeze Café (SB)
The Malibu Inn (LA)
Mel's Drive In (LA&others)
Millie's (LA)
Napoleon's Cafe (SB)
Nate 'n' Al's Delicatessen (LA)
New York Bagel Company (LA)
The Newsroom Café (LA)
Old Town Bakery (SGV)
Original Pantry (LA)
Pacific Dining Car (LA)
Pangaea (LA)
Pasadena Baking Co. (SGV)
The Patio (SB)
Pedals Café (LA)
Picnik (LA)
Pier View Café (LA)
Polly's on the Pier (SoB)
Polo Lounge (LA)
Q Bakery (LA)
Rae's (LA)
The Regent Dining Room (LA)
Riverside Café (SFV)
Roscoe's House of Chicken 'n' Waffles (LA&others)
The Rose Café (LA)
Ruby's (SoB&others)
Russell's (SoB)
Sidewalk Café (LA)
Silver Spoon (LA)
Soda Jerks (SGV)
Snug Harbor (LA)
Splash! (SoB)
Stage Deli (LA,LV)
Sweet Lady Jane (LA)
Tulsa (LA)
Tutti's (SB)
Vienna Café (LA)
The Wheel Inn (PS)

BEST BRUNCH

17th Street Café (LA)
A Thousand Cranes (LA)
Abiento (SGV)
Asian Deli (OC)
Aunt Kizzy's Back Porch (LA)
Ballard Store (CC)
Barcliff & Bair (SB)
Bay Café & Fish Market (SB)
The Belvédère (LA)
Bizcocho at Rancho Bernardo Inn, El (SD)
The Blue Whale & Tail of the Whale (Mts.)
The Brae (SGV)
Brambles (CC)
Café Bizou (SFV)
Café Del Rey (LA)
Carnival World Buffet (LV)
Chaya Venice (LA)
Chez Mélange (LA)
Chez Mimi
Cilantros (SD)
Claes Seafood (OC)
Clearwater Seafood (SGV)
Cobalt Cantina (LA)
Coco Pazzo (LA)
Coley's Place (LA)
Duke's at Malibu (LA)
El Encanto (SB)
Five Crowns (OC)
The Fish Market and Top O' The Market (SD)
Four Oaks Restaurant (LA)
Granita (LA)
Hal's Bar & Grill (LA)
Historic Antlers (Mts.)
Holly Street Bar & Grill (SGV)
Hoppe's (CC)
Hornblower Yacht Cruises (LA)
The Hotel Bel-Air Dining Room (LA)
House of Blues (LA)
Ian's (CC)
Inn of the Seventh Ray (LA)
Intermezzo (SB)
Itana Bahia (LA)
The Ivy (LA)
The Ivy at the Shore (LA)
James' Beach (LA)
Joe's (LA)
Kathleen's (SGV)
La Luna Negra (SGV)
La Marina at Four Seasons Biltmore Hotel (SB)
Las Brisas (OC)
Las Casuelas Nuevas (PS)
Lavande (LA)
Le Chêne (OA)
Lyon (SGV)
The Marine Room (SD)
Mon Kee (LA)
Monroe's (LA)
The Mulberry Tree (Mts)
Mustache Pete's (CC)
Oaks on the Plaza (SGV)
Ocean Avenue Seafood (LA)
Old Harmony Pasta Factory (CC)
Otani Garden (PS)

BEST BUSINESS DINING

La Parisienne (SGV)
Landrey's (SoB)
Lavande (LA)
Lawry's The Prime Rib (LA)
Le Beaujolais (LA)
Le Chardonnay (LA)
Le Chêne (OA)
Le Dôme (LA)
The Library (SoB)
Lunaria (LA)
Madeo (LA)
The Mandarin (LA)
Maple Drive (LA)
McCharles House (OC)
McCormick & Schmick's (LA & others)
Michael's (LA)
Michi (LA)
Mille Fleurs (SD)
Mimosa (SB)
Mimosa (LA)
Mistral Brasserie (SFV)
Montecito Café (SB)
Morton's (LA)
Morton's Of Chicago (SD&others)
Musso & Frank's Grill (LA)
Napa (LV)
Nic's and the Martini Lounge (LA)
Nicola (LA)
Oaks on the Plaza (SGV)
Ocean Avenue Seafood (LA)
Off Vine (LA)
One Pico (LA)
Osteria Nonni (LA)
P.F. Chang's China Bistro (OC)
Pacific Dining Car (LA)
The Palace Café (SB)
Palace Court (LV)
The Palm (LA)
Pane e Vino (LA&SB)
Pangaea (LA)
Papashon (SGV)
Paradise Café (SB)
Pascal (OC)
Patina (LA)
Piatti (SB)
Piero's Seafood House (SFV)
Pinot Bistro (SFV)
Pinot Hollywood (LA)
Pinot Restaurant (SGV)
Polo Lounge (LA)
Posto (SFV)
Prego (LA)
Primi (LA)
Reed's (LA)
The Regent Beverly Wilshire Dining Room (LA)
Remi (LA)
Renata's Caffé Italiano (OC)
Restaurant Devon (SGV)
The Ritz-Carlton Dining Room (LA,SGV,OC)
Ruth's Chris Steak House (LA&others)
Seoul Jung (LA)
72 Market Street Oyster Bar & Grill (LA)
Sfuzzi Costa Mesa (OC)
Shiro (SGV)
Simon's (LA)
Spago (LA&LV)
Spago Beverly Hills (LA)
Spencer's Restaurant & Patio (SGV)
Splash! (LA)
Stepps on the Court (LA)
The Stonehouse (SB)
Stoney Point Bar & Grill (SGV)
Taylor's Steakhouse (SGV)
Tesoro Trattoria (LA)
The Tower (LA)
Trader Vic's (LA)
Troquet (OC)
Tuscany (OA)
2424 Pico (LA)
Valentino (LA)
Vincenti Ristorante (LA)
Water Grill (LA)
The Wine Bistro (SFV)
The Wine Cask (SB)
Xiomara (SGV)
Yujean Kang's Gourmet Chinese Cuisine (LA&SGV)

HOTEL DINING ROOMS

A Thousand Cranes (LA)
Antonio's (LV)
The Auberge (SoB)
The Belvédère (LA)
Bernard's (LA)
The Brae (SGV)
Brasserie (LA)
Brothers (CC)
Buccaneer Bay Club (LV)
Buzio's (LV)

Café Chardonnay (CC)
Carnival World Buffet (LV)
Cava (LA)
Checkers (LA)
Chelsea on the Queen Mary (SoB)
Citronelle (SB)
Claes Seafood (OC)
Coco Pazzo (LA)
Coyote Café Dining Room (LV)
Diaghilev (LA)
Drai's (LV)
Dynasty Room (LA)
El Encanto Dining Room (SB)
Emeril's (LV)
Epicentre (LA)
Fenix (LA)
Francesco's (LV)
The Garden Room (LA)
Gardens (LA)
Gardens of Avila (CC)
Golden Nugget (LV)
Granville's (OC)
The Grill (SGV)
Hotel Bel-Air Dining Room (LA)
Isis (LV)
JW's Steakhouse (OC)
La Cajole (LA)
La Marina, Four Seasons Santa Barbara (SB)
La Scala (LV)
Landry's (SoB)
Lavande (LA)
The Library (SoB)
Louie's (SB)
Napa (LV)
Oaks on the Plaza (SGV)
One Pico (LA)
Palace Court (LV)
Pangaea (LA)
The Patio (SB)
Pedals (LA)
Polo Lounge (LA)
The Regent Beverly Wilshire Hotel Dining Room (LA)
Ristorante Villa Portofino (Cat.)
The Ritz-Carlton Dining Room (OC, SGV, LA)
Seasons (Mts.)
Splash! (SoB)
Splashes (OC)
Stillwell's (Mts.)
The Stonehouse (SB)
The Terrace (SGV)
Terraza (LV)
Top of Five
Trader Vic's (LA)
Yamabuki (OC)
Wolfgang Puck Café (LV)

BEST SPOTS TO MEET FOR A DRINK

Allegria (SoB)
Alto Palato (LA)
Antonello (OC)
Arnie Morton's (LA)
Barfly (LA)
Barney's Beanery (LA)
Bel-Air Bar & Grill (LA)
Bellefleur (SD)
The Bistro Garden at Coldwater (SFV)
The Blue Ox (Mts.)
Blue Parrot (Cat.)
The Blue Whale & Tail of the Whale (Mts.)
Bluepoint (SD)
Café del Rey (LA)
Café Pinot (LA)
Chaya Brasserie (LA)
Chaya Venice (LA)
Cicada (LA)
Cilantro's (SD)
Crustacean (LA)
DC 3 (LA)
El Torito Grill (OC)
Encounter (SoB)
Engine Company #28 (LA)
Fenix (LA)
Fins Seafood Grill (OA)
The Fish Market (SD)
Five Crowns (OC)
George's at the Cove (SD)
The Gypsy Grill (SFV)
Gypsys (MX)
Hennessay's Tavern (SoB)
Hollywood Canteen (LA)
Humphrey's By the Bay (SD)
Ivy at the Shore (LA)
James' Beach (LA)
Jillian's (PS)
Jimmy's (LA)
John Bull (SGV)
Kass Bah (LA)
Las Brisas (OC)
Las Casuelas Nuevas (PS)
Las Casuelas The Original (PS)
Laurel (SD)
Le Colonial (LA)
Le Dôme (LA)
Les Deux Cafés (LA)
Limbo (LA)
Lola (LA)
Lunaria (LA)
Maple Drive (LA)

The Marine Room (SD)
Mattei's Tavern (CC)
McCormick & Schmick's (LA & others)
Michi (SoB)
Mille Fleurs (SD)
Monsoon Café (LA)
Montecito Wine Bistro (SB)
Morton's of Chicago (PS & others)
Mr. Stox (OC)
Nic's & The Martini Lounge (LA)
ObaChine (LA)
O'Brien's Pub (LA)
Ocean Avenue Seafood (LA)
P.F. Chang's China Bistro (OC)
Pacifica del Mar (SD)
Pamplemousse Grille (SD)
Paradise Café (SB)
Parker's Lighthouse (SoB)
Pinot Bistro (SFV)
Pinot Hollywood (LA)
Pinot Restaurant & Martini Lounge (SGV)
Polo Lounge (LA)
Prezzo (SFV)
Punta Morro (MX)
Rebecca's (LA)
Red Rock (LA)
The Ritz (OC)
Rix (LA)
Shanghai Red's (LA)
Simon's (SoB)
The Sky Room (SoB)
SLO Brewing Company (CC)
Spago Beverly Hills (LA)
Splash! (SoB)
Stillwell's (Mts.)
Stoney Point Bar & Grill (SGV)
Tahiti (LA)
Teasers (LA)
Thelan's Mermaid (SoB)
Top O' The Cove (SD)
360
Trader Vic's
Tutto Mare (OC)
21 Ocean Front (OC)
Twin Palms (SGV & OC)
Typhoon (LA)
Vintner's Bar & Grill (CC)
Waikiki Willie's Rock & Roll Seafood (LA)
Water Grill (LA)
Waterfront Restaurant & Lounge (SoB)
Whale & Ale (SoB)
The Wine Cask (SB)
The Zia Café (SB)

BEST LATE-NIGHT DINING

Ago (LA)
Allegria (SoB)
Alto Palato (LA)
Atlantic (LA)
B.B. King's Blues Club (SFV)
Barfly (LA)
Barney's Beanery (LA)
Bertolini's (LV)
Bistrot Provençal (LA)
Bourbon Street Shrimp (LA)
Brasserie (LA)
Buccaneer Bay Club (LV)
Ca' del Sole (SFV)
The Cadillac Café (LA)
Café La Boheme (L.A)
Café Maurice (LA)
Caffé Luna (LA)
California Canteen (SFV)
Canter's (LA)
Cava (LA)
Cha Cha Cha (LA & SFV)
Chasen's (LA)
Chaya Brasserie (LA)
Chaya Venice (LA)
Chez Jay (LA)
Chianti Cucina (LA)
Chinois (LV)
Cilantros (SD)
Fred 62 (LA)
Genghis Cohen (LA)
The Gypsy Grill (SFV)
Gypsys (MX)
Hal's Bar & Grill (LA)
Havana on Sunset (LA)
House of Blues (LA)
Indochine (LA)
The Ivy at the Shore (LA)
James' Beach (LA)
Jerry's Famous Deli (LA & SFV)
Jimmy's (LA)
Joe's Café (SB)
Kass Bah (LA)
Kate Mantilini (LA)
La Bamba (SGV)
La Frite Café (SFV)
La Loggia (SFV)
La Luna Negra (SGV)
La Parrilla (LA)
La Poubelle (LA)
La Ve Lee (SFV)
Le Chêne (OA)
Le Colonial (LA)

Le Dôme (LA)
Les Deux Cafés (LA)
Limbo (LA)
The Little Door (LA)
Locanda Veneta (LA)
Lola (LA)
Louis XIV (LA)
Lunaria (LA)
Mel's Drive In (LA)
Monsoon Café (LA)
Moonlight (SFV)
Moustache Café (LA)
Nic's & The Martini Lounge (LA)
Original Pantry (LA)
P.F. Chang's China Bistro (OC)
Pacific Dining Car (LA)
Pane e Vino (SB & LA)
Paradise Café (SB)
Parkway Grill (SGV)
Pasion Supper Club (SFV)
Pink's Hot Dogs (LA)
Prego (OC)
Prezzo (SFV)
Rainwater's (SD)
Rebecca's (LA)
Rix (LA)
Roscoe's House of Chicken 'n' Waffles (LA)
Ruth's Chris Steak House (LV)
72 Market Street Oyster Bar & Grill (LA)
The Shark Bar (LA)
Shibucho (LA)
Spago (LA & LV)
Spencer's Restaurant & Patio (SGV)
Tempo (SFV)
Trader Vic's (LA)
Twin Palms (SGV & OC)
Typhoon (LA)
The Wine Bistro (SFV)

BEST LIGHT & HEALTHY FARE

Allegria (LA)
Barsac Brasserie (SFV)
The Belvédère (LA)
The Bistro Garden at Coldwater (SFV)
Bistrot Provençal (LA)
Brasserie Restaurant & Bar (LA)
Café Del Rey (LA)
Café Rodeo (LA)
Checkers Restaurant (LA)
Chin Chin (LA & others)
Cicada (LA)
DC3 (LA)
Dynasty Room (LA)
El Encanto Dining Room (SB)
Fenix (LA)
Figtree's Café (LA)
Four Oaks Restaurant (LA)
Gardens at the Four Seasons Hotel (LA)
Gardens on Glendon (LA)
Koo Koo Roo (LA & others)
Lavande (LA)
Main Squeeze Café (SB)
The Natural Café and Juice Bar (SB)
The Newsroom Café (LA)
Real Food Daily (LA)
Rotisserie Chicken of California (SGV)
Señor Fish (SGV & others)
Stage Deli (LA)
The Spot (LA)
Togo (LA)
Tra Di Noi (LA)
Xi-an (LA)

BEST LIVE MUSIC/ ENTERTAINMENT

Antonio's Pizzeria & Cabaret (Cat.)
B.B. King's Blues Club (SFV)
Beckham Place (SGV)
Bernard's (LA)
The Blue Whale & Tail of the Whale (Mts.)
Boccaccio's Nuevo Marianna (MX)
Brasserie (LA)
Buccaneer Bay Club (LV)
Café Dell 'Opera (LA)
Canter's (LA)
Carlitos Café Y Cantina (SB)
Cava (LA)
Cha Cha Cha (SFV)
Chad's (SB)
The Channel House (Cat.)
Cicada (LA)
Claes Seafood (OC)
Clancy's Crab Broiler (SGV)
Corvette Diner, Bar & Grill (SD)
Dar Maghreb (LA)
DC3 (LA)
Diaghilev (LA)

Ed Debevic's (LA)
Far Niente (SGV)
Fins Seafood Grill (OA)
Genghis Cohen (LA)
The Great Greek (SFV)
Gypsy Grill (SFV)
Havana on Sunset (LA)
Holoworld (SGV)
House of Blues (LA)
James' Beach (LA)
Jimmy's (LA)
JW's (OC)
L.A. Food Court (LA)
La Bamba (SGV)
La Luna Negra (SGV)
La Ve Lee (SFV)
Limbo (LA)
Lola (LA)
Lumpy Gravy (LA)
Lunaria (LA)
Mamagaya (LA)
Maple Drive (LA)
Montego Bay (LA)
Moonlight (SFV)
Palace Court (LV)
Palmira (MX)
Papadakis Taverna (SoB)
Parkway Grill (SGV)
Pasion Supper Club (SFV)
Prezzo (SFV)
Punta Morro (MX)
The Regent Beverly Wilshire Hotel Dining Room (LA)
72 Market Street (LA)
The Sky Room (SoB)
Stoney Point Bar & Grill (SGV)
Sushi on Tap (SFV)
Tempo (SFV)
Tutto Mare (OC)
21 Ocean Front (OC)
Twin Palms (SGV & OC)
Uzbekistan (LA)

OPEN 24 HOURS

Canter's (LA)
Fred 62 (LA)
Jerry's Famous Deli (LA, SFV)
Mel's Drive In (LA, SFV)
Original Pantry (LA)
Pacific Dining Car (LA)

BEST OUTDOOR DINING

26 Beach Café (LA)
Aïoli Restaurant & Tapas Bar (LA)
Allegria (LA)
Alto Palato (LA)
Armstrong's Fish Market & Seafood Restaurant (Cat.)
Back on the Beach (LA)
Barney Greengrass (LA)
Bay Café & Fish Market (SB)
Bel-Air Bar & Grill (LA)
Bellefleur (SD)
Bistro K (LA)
Bistro Laurent (CC)
Bistro Med (SB)
Bistro of Lunada Bay (LA)
Bistrot Provençal (LA)
Blue Point Coastal Cuisine (SD)
The Blue Whale & Tail of the Whale (Mts.)
Brophy Bros. Clam Bar & Restaurant (SB)
Brothers (CC)
Ca' Del Sole (SFV)
Café Buenos Aires (SB)
Café Chardonnay (CC)
Café Del Rey (LA)
Café Pinot (LA)
Café Provençal (OA)
Café Rodeo (LA)
Café Solé (SGV)
Café Zinc (OC)
Caffé Luna (LA)
Captain Kidd's (SoB)
Cha Cha Cha (LA & other locations)
Chad's (SB)
Chez Mimi (LA)
Citrus (LA)
Clearwater Seafood (SGV)
Cobalt Cantina (LA)
Coco Pazzo (LA)
The Coffee Table (LA)
Coley's Place (LA)
Doug's Harbor Reef (Cat.)
Duke's at Malibu (LA)
El Encanto Dining Room (SB)
The Farmers' Market (LA)
The Figtree (LA)
Fins of Malibu (LA)
Fins Seafood Grill (OA)

Wolfgang Puck Café (LA & other locations)
WR's Eatery at Snow Valley (Mt.)
Zazou (LA)
The Zia Café (SB)
Zooma Sushi (LA)
Zov's Bistro (OC)

BEST VIEW RESTAURANTS

A Thousand Cranes (LA)
The Admiral Risty (SoB)
Armstrong's (Cat.)
Azzura Point (SD)
Back on the Beach (LA)
Barney Greengrass (LA)
Beau Rivage (LA)
The Blue Moon (SoB)
Blue Parrot (Cat.)
Blue Point (SD)
The Blue Whale (Mts.)
The Bottle Inn (SoB)
The Brae (SGV)
Brasserie (LA)
Brophy Brothers (SB)
Buccaneer Bay Club (LV)
Buffalo Springs Station (Cat.)
Café del Rey (LA)
Café Pinot (LA)
Café Prego (Cat.)
Café Santorini (SGV)
Camacho's Grill (SoB)
Captain Kidd's (SoB)
The Channel House (Cat.)
The Chart House (LA & SoB)
Chelsea on the Queen Mary (SoB)
Citronelle (SB)
Claes Seafood (OC)
Coco Pazzo (LA)
DC 3 (LA)
Dorn's (CC)
Doug's Harbor Reef (Cat.)
Duke's at Malibu (LA)
El Bizcocho (SD)
El Encanto Dining Room (SB)
Emilio's (SB)
Encounter (SoB)
Epazote (SD)
Fenix (LA)
The Figtree (LA)
The Fish Market (SD)
Fung Lum (SFV)
The Getty Center Restaurant (LA)
Gladstone's 4 Fish (LA)
Geoffrey's (LA)
George's at the Cove (SD)
Good Stuff (SoB)
The Grill at The Ritz-Carlton Hotel (SGV)
Hoppe's at 901 (CC)
Hornblower Yacht Cruises (LA)
Hotel Bel-Air Dining Room (LA)
I Cugini (LA)
Il Fornaio (LA)
Inn of the Seventh Ray (LA)
Ivy at the Shore (LA)
Kitayama (OC)
La Marina (SB)
Las Brisas (OC)
Lavande (LA)
Le Dôme (LA)
L'Opera (SoB)
Malibu Inn (LA)
Malibu Seafood (LA)
Martha's 22nd Street Grill (SoB)
The Marine Room (SD)
Mayur (OC)
Monroe's (LA)
Moonshadows (LA)
Ocean Avenue Seafood (LA)
Old Tony's (SoB)
Olde Port Inn (CC)
One Pico (LA)
Osteria Panevino (SD)
Pacifica del Mar (SD)
Parker's Lighthouse (SoB)
Pedals Café (LA)
The Patio (SB)
Pier View Café (LA)
Polly's on the Pier (SoB)
Punta Morro (MX)
Red (LA)
Ristorante Villa Portofino (Cat.)
The Ritz-Carlton Dining Room, Marina del Rey (LA)
Ruby's (SoB, OC)
Saddlepeak Lodge (SFV)
San Pedro Fish Market (SoB)
Scotty's on the Strand (SoB)
Seasons (Mts.)
Shanghai Red's (LA)
Shellback Tavern (SoB)
Sidewalk Café (LA)
The Sky Room (SoB)
Spago Hollywood (LA)
Splash! (SoB)
Splashes (OC)
Star of the Sea (SD)
Stella Mare (SB)

The Stonehouse Restaurant (SB)
Sunset's (SoB)
Thelen's Mermaid (SoB)
Top O' the Cove (SD)
The Tower (LA)
360 (LA)
Troquet (OC)
21 Ocean Front (OC)
Typhoon (LA)
Venice Bistro (LA)
Via Vai (SB)
Vivace (SD)
Waikiki Willie's (LA)
Waterfront Restaurant (SoB)
WR's Eatery at Snow Valley (Mts.)
Zenzero (LA)

BEST ROMANTIC RESTAURANTS

Al Amir (LA)
Atlantic (LA)
The Bel-Air Hotel Dining Room (LA)
Bellefleur (SD)
The Belvédère (LA)
Bernard's (LA)
Bertolini's (LV)
Bistro 45 (SGV)
The Bistro Garden at Coldwater (SFV)
Bistro Med (SB)
Bistrot Provençal (LA)
Black Sheep Bistro (OC)
Boccaccio's Nuevo Marianna (MX)
Café Chardonnay (CC)
Café Del Rey (LA)
Café La Boheme (LA)
Café Prego (CI.)
Cava (LA)
Chad's (SB)
Checkers Restaurant (LA)
The Cellar (OC)
Chelsea on the Queen Mary (LA)
Chez Mimi (LA)
Chianti (LA)
Cicada (LA)
Cien Años Mexican Nuevo (MX)
Crustacean (LA)
Dar Maghreb (LA)
David's (LA)
Delacey's Club 41 (SGV)
Diaghilev (LA)
The Dining Room of the Ritz-Carlton Hotel (LA,OC,PS)
Dynasty Room (LA)
El Encanto Dining Room (SB)
El Rey Sol (MX)
Fontana de Trevi (SFV)
Four Oaks Restaurant (LA)
Francesco's (LV)
French Market Grille (SD)
Fresco Ristorante (SGV)
Gardens at the Four Seasons Hotel (LA)
Gennaro's Ristorante (SGV)
Gypsys (MX)
Hoppe's at 901 (CC)
Humphrey's By The Bay (SD)
Il Cielo (LA)
Inn of the Seventh Ray (LA)
Isis (LV)
The Ivy (LA)
L'Opera (LA)
L'Orangerie (LA)
La Cachette (LA)
La Embotelladora Vieja (MX)
La Luna Ristorante (LA)
La Marina at Four Seasons Biltmore Hotel (SB)
La Scala (LV)
Laurel (SD)
Lavande (LA)
Le Beaujolais (LA)
Le Chardonnay (LA)
Le Chêne (OA)
Le Vallauris (PS)
Les Deux Cafés (LA)
The Little Door (LA)
Louie's at Upham Hotel (SB)
McCharles House (OC)
Meritage (SB)
Michael's (LA)
Mille Fleurs (SD)
Monsoon Café (LA)
Moonlight (SFV)
Napa (LV)
One Pico (LA)
Palmira (MX)
Patina (LA)
Piatti (SB)
Polo Lounge (LA)
Punta Morro (MX)
The Raymond (SGV)
The Regent Beverly Wilshire Hotel Dining Room (LA)
Restaurant Devon (SGV)
Ristorante Villa Portofino (Cat.)
Saddle Peak Lodge (SFV)
Shiro (SGV)
Sky Room
Sofi (LA)
Star of the Sea (SD)
Stella Mare's (SB)
The Stonehouse (SB)
Tango D'Amore (SFV)
Terraza (LV)
The Sky Room (LA)

The Tower (LA)
Top O' The Cove (SD)
Top of Five
Tra Di Noi (LA)
Trader Vic's (LA)
Tuscany (OA)
Valentino (LA)
Vintners' Bar & Grill (CC)
The Wine Bistro (SFV)
The Wine Cask (SB)
Xiomara (SGV)
Zenzero (LA)

THE YOUNG & THE RESTLESS

(Good for Kids & Teens)
ABC Seafood (LA)
Antonio's (LA)
Antonio's Pizzeria & Cabaret (Cat.)
The Apple Pan (LA)
Arirang (SGV)
Armstrong's Fish Market & Seafood Restaurant (Cat.)
Asahi Ramen (LA)
Aunt Kizzy's Back Porch (LA)
Barcliff & Bair (SB)
Beadle's Cafeteria (SGV)
Blue Ox Restaurant (Mts.)
The Blue Whale & Tail of the Whale (Mts.)
Broadway Deli (LA)
Buca di Beppo (SGV)
Burger Continental (SGV)
C & O Trattoria (LA)
Cadillac Café (LA)
California Pizza Kitchen (LA & others)
Canter's Deli (LA)
The Channel House (Cat.)
Clancy's Crab Broiler (SGV)
Cobalt Cantina (LA)
Cold Spring Tavern (SB)
Coley's Place (LA)
Corvette Diner, Bar & Grill (SD)
The Crab Cooker (OC)
Crocodile Café (SGV)
D.Z. Akins (SD)
The Daily Grill (LA & others)
DC3 (LA)
Devane's (PS)
Dinah's (LA)
Dive! (LA)
Don Felix (LA)
Double Rainbow (LA)
Dumpling Master (SGV)
Ed Debevic's (LA)
El Chavo (LA)
El Cholo (LA)
El Coyote (LA)
El Morfi (SGV)
El Nido (MX)
El Tango (OA)
El Tepayac (LA)
Elmer's (PS)
Empress Pavilion (LA)
Fair Oaks Pharmacy and Soda Fountain (SGV)
Figtree's Café (LA)
Fins Seafood Grill (OA)
The Franco's Sunny Italy (SGV)
Fred 62 (LA)
Gardens on Glendon (LA)
Genghis Cohen (LA)
George Petrelli's Steakhouse (LA)
Gerlach's Grill (SGV)
Gladstone's 4 Fish Malibu (LA)
Golden Nugget (LV)
Gourmet 88 (SGV)
Granita (LA)
Guelaguetza (LA)
Hard Rock Café (LA, SFV & LV)
Harold & Belle's (LA)
Hu's Szechwan Restaurant (LA)
Hugo's (LA)
Il Fornaio (LA)
Il Forno (LA)
The Iron Squirrel (Mts.)
Jacopo's (LA)
Jake & Annie's (LA)
Jamba Juice (LA)
Jerry's Famous Deli (LA)
Jitlada (LA)
Jody Maroni's Sausage Kingdom (LA)
John O'Groats (LA)
Kate Mantilini (LA)
Kathleen's (SGV)
Knoll's Black Forest Inn (LA)
Koutoubia (LA)
La Bamba (SGV)
La Embotelladora Vieja (MX)
La Finestra (SFV)
La Parrilla (LA)
La Plancha (LA)
La Salsa (LA)
La Serenata de Garibaldi (LA)
La Super-Rica (SB)
Langer's (LA)
Louise's Pantry (PS)
Malibu Seafood (LA)
Mel's Drive In (LA)

Merida (SGV)
Mon Kee (LA)
Nate 'n' Al's Delicatessen (LA)
The Natural Café and Juice Bar (SB)
Pancho's (LA)
Papadakis Taverna (LA)
Philippe's Original Sandwich Shop (LA)
Pink's Hot Dogs (LA)
Planet Hollywood (LA & others)
The Reel Inn (LA)
Rotisserie Chicken of California (SGV)
Saladang (SGV)
Señor Fish (SGV & others)
Soda Jerks (SGV)
Stage Deli (LA & LV)
Tail O' the Pup (LA)
Tarantino's Pizzeria (SGV)
Tempo (SFV)
The Philadelphia Connection (SGV)
Tommy's (LA)
Tortilla Flats (OC)
Tutti's (SB)
Tutti Mangia Italian Grill (OA)
Uzbekistan (LA)
Versailles (LA)
Viva (SFV)
Wolfgang Puck Café (LA & others)

BEST WINE LISTS

Ago (LA)
Antonello's (OC)
The Arches (OC)
Arroyo Chop House (SGV)
Azzura Point (SD)
The Belgian Lion (SD)
The Belvédère (LA)
Bellefleur (SD)
Bernard's (LA)
Bistango (OC)
Bistro 45 (LA)
Café del Rey (LA)
Campanile (LA)
The Cellar (OC)
Chianti (LA)
Chinois Las Vegas (LV)
Chinois on Main (LA)
Citronelle (SB)
Citrus (LA)
Claes Seafood Etc. (OC)
Devon (SBV)
The Dining Room Ritz-Carlton Hotel (OC, PS, LA)
Drago (LA)
El Bizcocho (SD)
Fenix (LA)
The Fish Market & Top of the Market (SD)
Five Crowns (OC)
George's at the Cove (SD)
Granita (LA)
Hotel Bel Air Dining Room (LA)
Jillian's (PS)
Jiraffe (LA)
Joss (LA)
Jozu (LA)
JW's Steakhouse (OC)
La Cachette (LA)
La Marina (SB)
Laurel (SD)
Le Chardonnay (LA)
Le Chêne (OA)
Le Vallauris (PS)
L'Orangerie (LA)
McPhee's Grill (CC)
Michael's (LA)
Montecito Wine Bar (SB)
Morton's (LA)
Mr. Stox (OC)
Napa (LV)
Pacifica del Mar (SD)
Pamplemousse Grille (SD)
Parkway Grill (SGV)
Patina (LA)
Pinot Bistro (SFV)
Pinot Café (LA)
Pinot Hollywood
Pinot Restaurant & Martini Bar (SGV)
Posto (SFV)
Primi (LA)
The Regent Beverly Wilshire Hotel Dining Room (LA)
The Ritz (OC)
72 Market Street (LA)
Spago (LA & LV)
Splash!
The Stonehouse (SB)
Top O' the Cove (SD)
Troquet (OC)
2087 Bistro (OA)
2424 Pico (LA)
21 Ocean Front (OC)
Valentino (LA)
Vintner's Bar & Grill (CC)
Water Grill (LA)
Wine Cask (SB)
Winesellar & Brasserie (SD0

Restaurants By Area

LOS ANGELES AREA

BEL AIR
Bel-Air Bar & Grill
Four Oaks Restaurant
The Getty Center Restaurant
The Hotel Bel Air Dining Room
Le Chine Wok
Sushi-Ko
Starbucks
Terrazza of Bel Air

BEVERLY HILLS
Al Gelato
Barney Greengrass
The Belvédère
Bistro K
Bombay Palace
Café Rodeo
California Pizza Kitchen
Chasen's
Cheesecake Factory
Chin Chin
Coffee Bean and Tea Leaf
Crazy Fish
Crustacean
The Curry House
Da Pasquale
The Farm of Beverly Hills
456 Caretta
Gardens at the Four Seasons Hotel
Ginza Sushi-Ko
The Grill on the Alley
Il Buco
Il Cielo
Il Fornaio
Il Pastaio
Il Tramezzino
Kate Mantilini
Jacopo's
Jamba Juice
The King & I
Koo Koo Roo
La Provence
La Salsa
Maito
The Mandarin
Maple Drive
Matsuhisa
McCormick & Schmick's
Mulberry Street Pizzeria
Nate n' Al's
Nic's and the Martini Lounge
Nouveau Café Blanc
ObaChine
On Canon
Paddington's Tea Room
Papa Jake's
Pangaea
Piazza Rodeo
Planet Hollywood
Polo Lounge
Porta Via
Prego
Rösti
The Regent Beverly Wilshire Hotel Dining Room
Ruth's Chris Steakhouse
Seattle's Best Coffee (S.B.C.)
Spago Beverly Hills
Starbucks
Trader Vic's
Trattoria Amici
Xi-an

BRENTWOOD
California Pizza Kitchen
Cheesecake Factory
Chin Chin
Coffee Bean and Tea Leaf
The Daily Grill
Divino
Eiger
Jamba Juice
Koo Koo Roo
Mon Kee
New York Bagel Company
Pizzicotto
Porter's
Rösti
Starbucks
Taiko
Takao
Toscana
Vincenti Ristorante
Woodside

CENTURY CITY
Dive!
Jimmy's
La Cachette
Lunaria
Stage Deli

CULVER CITY/PALMS
Dinah's
George Petrelli's Steakhouse
Giovanni's Trattoria
Guelaguetza
Versailles

DOWNTOWN
A Thousand Cranes
ABC Seafood
Bernard's
Café Pinot
Checkers
Ciao Trattoria
Cicada
Empress Pavilion
Engine Co. No. 28
Epicentre
410 Boyd
Guelaguetza
Kachina Grill
Kyoto
La Plancha
Langer's
Mandarin Deli
McCormick & Schmick's
Mon Kee
Moody's
Nicola
Ocean Seafood
Oomasa
Oriental Seafood Inn
Original Pantry
Philippe's Original Sandwich Shop
R-23
Señor Fish
Seoul Jung
Shibucho
Starbucks
Stepps on the Court
Tesoro Trattoria
The Tower
Traxx
Umemura
V.I.P. Harbor Seafood
Water Grill

EAST L.A.
Charlie's Trio
El Tepayac Café
La Parrilla
La Serenata de Garibaldi

HANCOCK PARK/LARCHMONT
Chan Dara
Girasole
La Luna Ristorante

HOLLYWOOD
Café des Artistes
Café Pinot
Chamika Catering
Chan Dara
Chao Praya
Dar Maghreb
Don Felix
El Chavo
El Floridita
Fabiolus Café
Hamptons Hollywood Café
Havana on Sunset
Hollywood Canteen
Itana Bahia
Jitlada
L.A. Food Court
La Poubelle
Les Deux Cafés
Musso & Frank's Grill
Off Vine
Palermo
Pink Pepper
Pinot Hollywood
Robert's Cuisine & Grille
Roscoe's House of Chicken Ôn' Waffles
Shabu Hana
Taipan
Thai Beer
Thai Seafood
360
Uzbekestan
Zankou Chicken

LOS FELIZ/ ATWATER VILLAGE/ E. HOLLYWOOD
Café Dell 'Opera
Cha Cha Cha
Chan Dara
Fred 62
Katsu
Les Frères Taix
Marouch
Mexico City
Osteria Nonni
Restaurant Spain
Tam O'Shanter Inn
Tommy's
Trattoria Farfalla
Vida
Yuca's Hut

MALIBU
Allegria
Beau Rivage
The Chart House
The Coral Beach Cantina
Dukes at Malibu
Fins of Malibu
Froggy's Topanga Fresh Fish Market
Geoffrey's
Granita
Hannah's Cantina
The Malibu Inn
Malibu Mutts
Malibu Seafood
Monroe's
MoonShadow Bar & Grill
Pier View Café & Cantina
The Reel Inn
Something's Fishy
Tra Di Noi
Zooma Sushi

MARINA DEL REY
Aunt Kizzy's Back Porch

SAN FERNANDO VALLEY

Moonlight
Posto
Prezzo
Rasputin
Rive Gauche Café
Sharkey's
Shihoya
Sisley Italian Kitchen
Skewers
Sumiya
The Wiener Factory

STUDIO CITY
Araz
Asenebo
Art's Deli
The Bistro Garden at Coldwater
DuPar's Coffee Shop
The Gaucho Grill
Hortobagy
Iroha Sushi
Jerry's Famous Deli
La Loggia
La Ve Lee
Mani's Bakery
Out Take Café
Pasion Supper Club
Perroche
Pinot Bistro
Sompun
Spumante
Sushi Nozawa
Sushi on Tap
Talesai
Teru Sushi
Todai
The Wine Bistro

TARZANA
Kushiyu
La Finestra
Tabu Bistro

TOLUCA LAKE
Prosecco
Yamakawa

UNIVERSAL CITY
B.B. King's Blues Club
California Canteen
Fung Lum
The Hard Rock Café
Mallory's
Wolfgang Puck Café

VAN NUYS
Dr. Hogly Wogly's Tyler, Texas Barbecue
El Criollo
Mom's Bar-B-Q House
Restaurante Morazan
Zankou Chicken

WEST HILLS
Andaluz

WOODLAND HILLS
Anarbagh
Big Daddy's Kitchen
The Brandywine
Brother's Sushi
Fontana de Trevi
Maria's Italian Kitchen
Paoli's Pizzeria
Yang Chow

SAN GABRIEL VALLEY

ARCADIA
Chez Sateau
Goldstein's Bagel Bakery
Sesame Grill

ALHAMBRA
Charlie's Trio
Sea Star
Senor Fish
Wahib's

CITY OF INDUSTRY
The Brae

EAGLE ROCK
Café Beaujolais
Senor Fish

GLENDALE
A Bientot
Blue Pyramid
Cinnabar
Clancy's Crab Broiler
Crocodile Café
El Morfi
Far Niente
Fresco Ristorante
Gennaro's Ristorante
Gourmet 88
Harvest Inn
Mamita
Noodles
Todai
Zankou Chicken

LA CANADA-FLINTRIDGE
Café Solé
Goldstein's Bagel Bakery
Min's Kitchen
Taylor's Steakhouse

MONROVIA
La Parisienne
Restaurant Devon

MONTEREY PARK
Charming Garden
Dragon Regency
Dumpling Master
Harbor Village
Lake Spring Cuisine
NBC Seafood
Ocean Star Seafood

PASADENA
Abiento
All India Café
Arirang
Arroyo Chop House
Aunt Gussie's Place
Beadle's Cafeteria
Beckham Place
Bistro 45
Bona Corso's
Buca di Beppo
Burger Continental
Café Santorini
California Pizza Kitchen
Cameron's Seafood
Celestino
Clearwater Seafood
Crocodile Café
De Lacey's Club 41
Dickenson West
Dino's Italian Inn
The Francos' Sunny Italy
Gerlach's Grill
Goldstein's Bagel Bakery
Gordon Biersch
The Grill
Holly Street Bar & Grill
Holoworld
Hugo Molina Restaurant
Ibex
Jasmine Terrace
John Bull English Pub
Kathleen's
Kingston Café
Kuala Lumpur
La Bamba
La Fornaretta
La Luna Negra
The Lipton Tea House
Lyon
Market City Caffè
Marston's
McCormick & Schmick's
Merida
Mi Piace
Nikos
Oaks on the Plaza
Old Town Bakery
Papashon
Parkway Grill
Pasadena Baking Co.
The Philadelphia Connection
Pinot Restaurant & Martini Bar
The Raymond
Rotisserie Chicken of California
Saladang
Senor Fish
Soda Jerks
Spencers
Stoney Point Bar & Grill
Sushi of Naples
Sushi Polo
Tarantino's Pizzeria
The Terrace
Tommy Tang's
Twin Palms
Xiomara
Yujean Kang's

ROSEMEAD
Chameli
Quanjude Beijing Duck Restaurant

SAN GABRIEL
El Emperador Maya
G.C. River
Sam Woo Seafood

SAN MARINO
Chelsea
Huntington Library & Gardens Tea Room
Julienne
Rose Tree Cottage

SIERRA MADRE
Restaurant Lozano

SOUTH PASADENA
Fair Oaks Pharmacy and Soda Fountain
Nick's
Shiro

THE SOUTH BAY

EL SEGUNDO
McCormick & Schmick's
Wolfgang Puck Café

HERMOSA BEACH
The Bottle Inn
Cantina Real
Good Stuff
Habash Café
Hennessay's Tavern
Hermosa Fish Market Café
Martha's 22nd St. Grill
Scotty's on the Strand
The Spot
Thelen's Mermaid

LAX-ADJACENT
Encounter
Landrey's
The Library

LONG BEACH
Allegria
BJ's Chicago Pizza & Brewery
Chelsea on the Queen Mary
555 East
King's Pine Avenue Fish House
L'Opera
Parker's Lighthouse
Russell's

DOWNTOWN
The Fish Market
Kansas City Barbecue
Morton's of Chicago
Rainwater's
Star of the Sea

GASLAMP QUARTER
Blue Point
Osteria Panevino
Trattoria Portobello

HILLCREST
Corvette Diner
La Vache & Co.

KEARNY MESA
Emerald Seafood Restaurant

LA JOLLA
BJ's Chicago Pizzeria
Café Japengo
George's at the Cove
La Fonda
The Marine Room
Top O' The Cove

MIDTOWN
Hob Nob Hill
Laurel

MIRA MESA
Mandarin Garden

MISSION VALLEY
Wolfgang Puck Café

OCEAN BEACH
The Belgian Lion

OLD TOWN
Berta's Latin American

RANCHO BERNARDO
El Bizcocho
French Market Grille

RANCHO SANTA FE
Mille Fleurs

SAN DIEGO
D.Z. Akins

SHELTER ISLAND
Humphrey's By The Bay
Ristorante Michelangelo

SOLANA BEACH
Pamplemousse Grille
Parioli Italian Bistro

SORRENTO MESA
Winesellar & Brasserie

SANTA BARBARA

DOWNTOWN
Arigato Sushi
Arts & Letters Café
Baccio
Barcliff & Bair
Bay Café & Fish Market
Bistro Med
The Blue Shark Bistro
Brigitte's
Brophy Brothers
Bucatini
Ca'Dario
Café Buenos Aires
Carlitos Café & Cantina
Casa de Sevilla
Chad's
Downey's
East Beach Grill
Emilio's Ristorante & Bar
Intermezzo
Joe's Café
La Super-Rica
Louie's
Ma Dolce Vita
Main Squeeze Café
Meritage
Mimosa
Museum Café
Napoleon Café
The Natural Café
The Palace Café
Paradise Café
Sojorner Café
Wine Cask
Your Place
The Zia Café

EAST BEACH
Citronelle

MONTECITO
Cava
La Marina
The Montecito Café
Montecito Wine Bistro
Pane e Vino
The Patio
Piatti
Stella Mare's
Stonehouse
Trattoria Mollie's
Tutti's
Via Vai

THE RIVIERA
El Encanto Dining Room

SAN MARCOS PASS
Cold Spring Tavern

CENTRAL COAST

ATASCADERO
Salsitas

AVILA BEACH
Gardens of Avila
Old Custom House
Olde Port Inn

BALLARD
Ballard Store
Café Chardonnay

BAYWOOD PARK
Rodney's

CAMBRIA
Brambles
Ian's
Linn's Bin
Mustache Pete's

CASMALIA
The Hitching Post

GUADALUPE
La Simpatia

HARMONY
Old Harmony Pasta Factory

LOS OLIVOS
Los Olivos Tasting Room
Los Olivos Wine & Spirits Emporium
Mattei's Tavern
Popolo's

MORRO BAY
Dorn's
Hoppe's at 901

NIPOMO
Jocko's

PASO ROBLES
Bistro Laurent

PISMO BEACH
Giuseppe's

SAN LUIS OBISPO
Apple Farm
Bon Temps Creole Café
Buona Tavola
Café Roma
Old Country Deli
Pete's Southside Café
San Luis Fish & Barbeque
SLO Brewing Company
SLO Maid Ice Cream Factory
Thai-Rrific

SANTA MARIA
Atari Ya
Chef Rick's Ultimately Fine Foods
Vintner's Bar & Grill

SANTA YNEZ
Trattoria Grappolo

SHELL BEACH
F. McLintock's

SOLVANG
Brothers
Café Angelica
Paula's Pancake House

TEMPLETON
McPhee's Grill

MOUNTAIN RESORTS

AGUA FRIA
Casual Elegance
El Papagayo's

BIG BEAR CITY
The Blue Ox Bar & Grill
Madlon's

BIG BEAR LAKE
The Blue Whale & Tail of the Whale
The Iron Squirrel
Maggio's Pizza
Stillwell's

BLUE JAY
The Royal Oak

CEDAR GLEN
Chef's Inn & Tavern

CRESTLINE
The Mulberry Tree

LAKE ARROWHEAD VILLAGE
Seasons

SNOW VALLEY
WR's Eatery at Snow Valley

TWIN PEAKS
Historic Antlers Inn

CATALINA ISLAND

AVALON
Antonio's Pizzeria
Armstrong's
Blue Parrot
Buffalo Springs Station

Café Prego
Catalina Cookie Company
Catalina Country Clubhouse
The Channel House
Ristorante Villa Portofino

TWO HARBORS
Doug's Harbor Reef

OUTLYING AREAS

CLAREMONT
El Tango
Tutti Mangia Italian Grill

SAUGUS
Le Chene

SIMI VALLEY
Dakota's

THOUSAND OAKS
2087-An American Bistro

UPLAND
Café Provençal

VALENCIA
Claim Jumper
Sisley Italian Kitchen

WESTLAKE VILLAGE
Bistrot by the Water
Fin's Seafood Grill
Galetto Caffe & Grill
Mandevilla
Ritrovo
Tuscany Il Ristorante

NORTHERN BAJA

ENSENADA
El Rey Sol
La Embotelladora Vieja
Punta Morro

ROSARITO BEACH
Carnitas La Flor de Michoacan
El Nido
Ortega's Buffet
Palmira
Puerto Nuevo

TIJUANA
Boccaccio's Nuevo Marianna
Cien Anos
Gypsys
Ortega's Buffet
The Ritz Pub-Café

LAS VEGAS

Antonio's
Bamboo Gardens
Bertonlini's
Buccaneer Bay Club
Buzio's
Carnival World Buffet
Chinois
Coyote Café Dining Room
Cozymel's
Drai's
Emeril's
Francesco's
Golden Nugget Buffet
Hard Rock Café
Isis
La Scala
Morton's of Chicago
Napa
P.F. Chang's
Palace Court
Piero's
Planet Hollywood
Ruth's Chris Steak House
Sfuzzi
Spago
Stage Deli
Terraza
Wolfgang Puck Café

GENERAL INDEX

A

B

D

E

M

T

U

V

W

X

Y

Z

LA RESTAURANTS

We wish to thank our generous sponsors for their invaluable contributions which made this book possible

- **Cambria Winery & Vineyard**
  www.cambriawine.com
- **De La Doucette**
- **Firestone Vineyards**
  www.firestonevineyard.com
- **Italcheese**
  www.italcheese.com
- **LACMA**
  www.lacma.org
- **Los Angeles Marriott Downtown**
  www.marriott.com
- **Meridian Vineyards**
  www.meridianvineyards.com
- **Omni Los Angeles Hotel and Center**
  800-843-6664
- **Perrier**
  www.perrier.com
- **Ramos-Pinto Port**
  (Maisons, Marques, & Domaines)
  www.winery.com
- **Regal Biltmore**
  www.thebiltmore.com
- **Roederer Champagne**
  www.winery.com/winery-bin/wine-inv?29+0
- **Santa Ynez Valley Wine Trail**
  800-563-3183
- **Sur La Table**
  www.surlatable.com
- **Vittel**
  www.nestle.com/brands/html/b8-4.html
- **Woltner Estates**
- **Zaca Mesa Winery**
- **Zone Vodka**